Mycroft's Blue Book Stock Guide

2014

Mycroft Psaras

ISBN: 0615900593
ISBN 13: 9780615900599

Library of Congress Control Number: 2013919892
Mycroft Mall LLC, Fonda, NY

Dedicated To

Charlie Munger and Warren Buffett

INTRODUCTION

On February 27, 1987 Warren Buffett released his 1986 Letter to Shareholders as part of the Berkshire Hathaway Annual Report for that year. That letter was probably one of his better-known pieces written as CEO of Berkshire Hathaway because it included a special section at the very end called:

Purchase-Price Accounting Adjustments and the "Cash Flow" Fallacy

Mr. Buffett provided, in essence, a tutorial on how both he and Charlie Munger select the important information in a company's financial statements. In doing so, he basically gave us their formula on how to successfully analyze companies. Here is that paragraph:

If we think through these questions, we can gain some insights about what may be called "owner earnings." These represent (a) reported earnings plus (b) depreciation, depletion, amortization, and certain other non-cash charges such as Company N's items (1) and (4) less (c) the average annual amount of capitalized expenditures for plant and equipment, etc. that the business requires to fully maintain its long-term competitive position and its unit volume. (If the business requires additional working capital to maintain its competitive position and unit volume, the increment also should be included in (c). However, businesses following the LIFO inventory method usually do not require additional working capital if unit volume does not change.)Our owner-earnings equation does not yield the deceptively precise figures provided by GAAP, since(c) must be a guess - and one sometimes very difficult to make. Despite this problem, we consider the owner earnings figure, not the GAAP figure, to be the relevant item for valuation purposes - both for investors in buying stocks and for managers in buying entire businesses. We agree with Keynes's observation: "I would rather be vaguely right than precisely wrong." (1) http://www.berkshirehathaway.com/letters/1986.html

This book is a 2014 stock guide for analyzing 2554 stocks, listed in alphabetical order. In designing this book, I have returned to the first principles of investing, as outlined by Buffett & Munger in the preceding paragraph. Moreover, I have included some additional ratios in an effort to help readers get a better understanding of what it takes to analyze a company correctly. Taken together, the database contained within this book was created to assist both the novice and professional investor alike. The calculations for all ratios used are presented herein, as I am a firm believer in the following Chinese Proverb:

"Give a man a fish and you feed him for a day. Teach a man to fish and you feed him for a lifetime." (2)
http://www.quotationspage.com/quotes/Chinese_Proverb/

I wrote this book because I am disturbed by the erratic behavior of the markets over the past two decades. I attribute this, in part, to the fact that many investors have little idea, interest, or both, in the true valuation of a company on Main Street, prior to purchasing a stock. Market roller coasters are caused, in part, by large numbers of investors buying at too high prices (overpaying; 1998-2000) or by selling at too low prices (2009). These extremes create tremendous buying opportunities for those who know what a company is really worth. This is one of the main reasons why Charlie Munger and Warren Buffett are billionaires.

Anyone with a brokerage account and an internet connection can go in and buy a stock and sell it one minute later. The markets are unique in this regard. In contrast, prior to buying real estate or a car, people usually exercise a great deal more caution and due diligence. For instance, you would never see a person go into a Toyota Dealership and pay $500,000 for a Toyota Prius, because each new car has a suggested sticker price. However, it has been my experience that most investors in the markets do little if any research before buying a stock. In the absence of determining an accurate valuation for a company, someone buying a little known stock may well pay the equivalent of $500,000 for a Toyota Prius, without ever knowing it.

I have coined this book **Mycroft's Blue Book Stock Guide (2014).** Readers should use this book as a consumer guide for stocks similar to a consumer report for a television or car.

I have designed this book so that it can be used often, as a reference guide, where the reader can derive an accurate, straightforward valuation of a company. The valuation of a company's stock is determined by comparing what it sells for in the stock market (its stock price, as assigned by Wall Street) to its "Main Street" valuation (as determined by analyzing its financials). This information should protect the investor from overpaying for a stock, or from selling a stock at the wrong price.

This book should not, however, be used exclusively as a one-shot answer on what stocks to buy and sell. It is a starting point in performing one's own due diligence. I fully expect that readers will read articles and research each company that they find to have an attractive valuation through this guide. By doing so, the reader should determine the quality of management, and decide whether a company is a good fit for their own personality and risk tolerance and whether the management is shareholder friendly or not. I will outline these steps in more detail elsewhere in this introduction.

I do not offer a get-rich-quick scheme here. Nevertheless most people do need to invest as part of their retirement plans through their 401k's or IRA's. Understanding this process is critical for a safe and comfortable retirement.

Thomas A. Edison is quoted as saying that "**Genius is one percent inspiration, ninety-nine percent perspiration.**" (3) Spoken statement (c. 1903); published in *Harper's Monthly* (September 1932).

What is Free Cash Flow?

Warren Buffett uses the term "Owner Earnings" in explaining his theory (Purchase-Price Accounting Adjustments and the "Cash Flow" Fallacy), but he also says the following:

"Our owner-earnings equation does not yield the deceptively precise figures provided by GAAP, since (c) must be a guess - and one sometimes very difficult to make. Despite this problem, we consider the owner earnings figure, not the GAAP figure, to be the relevant item for valuation purposes - both for investors in buying stocks and for managers in buying entire businesses. We agree with Keynes's observation:

> *"I would rather be vaguely right than precisely wrong."*

His formula for Owner Earnings, when deconstructed, is not intuitively obvious for the average investor. To understand it requires some practice and "thinking outside of the box" as Mr. Buffett does things a little differently than what you would find using GAAP (Generally Accepted Accounting Principles). The calculation can be summarized as follows:

cash flow – capital expenditures

Investopedia.com explains cash flow as the following:

1. In business as in personal finance, cash flows are essential to solvency. They can be presented as a record of something that has happened in the past, such as the sale of a particular product, or forecasted into the future, representing what a business or a person expects to take in and to spend. Cash flow is crucial to an entity's survival. Having ample cash on hand will ensure that creditors, employees and others can be paid on time. If a business or person does not have enough cash to support its operations, it is said to be insolvent, and a likely candidate for bankruptcy should the insolvency continue.

2. The statement of a business's cash flows is often used by analysts to gauge financial performance. Companies with ample cash on hand are able to invest the cash back into the business in order to generate more cash and profit. (3) http://www.investopedia.com/terms/c/cashflow.asp

Cash flow is calculated as net income + depreciation + amortization

Net income is simply the profit that the company makes.

Depreciation is an accounting term that is used to reduce the value of something you own over the life of the product. For example, a car you own will depreciate in value over a ten-year period and if the car was owned by a company, the company's accountant would depreciate its worth. So a new car purchased for $30,000 would be worth $5000, ten years later and thus depreciates $25,000 in value over that time.

Amortization is similar to depreciation except that it used for things like loans. You may be familiar with an "Amortization Schedule" that your mortgage company may have given you when you got your home loan. The schedule outlines how much you owe and tells you when your loan will be paid off or how much you owe during any particular month during the 360 months, for instance, on a 30-year loan.

So cash flow is essentially the amount of cash that a company has available to use to run its operations and to expand in the future.

Cash flow is so important that it gets its own statement in the three standard financial statements that every company reports. They are:

1) Income Statement
2) Balance Sheet
3) Cash Flow Statement

The Cash flow statement is separated into three parts:

1) Operating Activities
2) Investing Activities
3) Financing Activities

So the cash flow statement outlines how much cash flow is generated from operations and also reveals how that cash was invested and what financing options were used.

This is no different from what you do in your daily life as an individual. Your **operations** are your salary and other income. Your **investing** tells us where you put your profits and whether you used them for home improvements, for example. Finally, your **financing** activities indicates how much you charged on your credit cards or whether you took out a home or car loan.

When a company spends money to buy or improve a factory it is called capital spending or capital expenditures (cap ex). The main thrust of Mr. Buffett's analysis is that he finds that most investors make the serious mistake of only looking at cash flow alone when analyzing a company and do not include capital spending in their analysis. Allow me to illustrate this point by example.

If company A and company B, each had cash flows of $1000.00, they, in theory, would be equal, right?

That might seem so but Mr. Buffett wants investors to go one step further. He wants to know how much of that $1000 did each company use to run and improve their operations. That is where the key to the castle is hidden. That key is capital expenditures.

If company A uses $800 in capital expenditures and company B only uses $300 then;

Company A = $1000-$800 = $200 in free cash flow (FCF)

Company B = $1000-$300 = $700 in free cash flow (FCF)

The word "Free" in free cash flow signifies to the investor how much money is actually left in the till at the end of the day.

So right off of the bat you can clearly see that company B would be the better investment. But not so fast as this is where the stock market comes in and where things can get a little tricky if you are not careful.

Let us now say that each company, both A & B each have 100 shares of stock outstanding. Therefore each company has $10 a share in Cash Flow or $1000/100 shares.

But when you include the capital expenditures into the equation you have a different picture.

Company A = Free Cash Flow of $200/100 shares = $2 a share in free cash flow.

Company B = Free Cash Flow of $700/100 shares = $7 a share in free cash flow.

As you can see, company B is the real money maker on Main Street but may not be the better investment on Wall Street because of a thing called "**Valuation.**"

If both companies were trading at $100 a share in the stock market they would have a "price to free cash flow" of:

Company A = $100 stock market price/$2 a share free cash flow = 50 times the company's price to free cash flow.

Company B = $100 stock market price/$7 a share free cash flow = 14.28 times the company's price to free cash flow.

Therefore again Company B is much more attractive than company A.

But the stock market tends to value things kind of crazy at times and there may be moments when company A is a much better deal than B. Here is an example:

Stock market price for Company A = $20 = therefore $20 market price/$2 a share free cash flow = 10 times price to free cash flow

Stock market price for Company B = $350 = therefore $350 market price/$7 a share free cash flow = 50 times price to free cash flow

Due to the market way overvaluing Company B, Company A is 5 times cheaper than Company B.

The ultimate goal of every investor should be to find companies that have amazing free cash flow per share numbers and then buy the company's stock at a deeply discounted price.

The difficult part in Mr. Buffett's Owner Earnings calculation is that he has to factor in changes in working capital, which are not a one-step process, but require the following items to be factored in:

Increases/Decreases in the following:

1) Receivables
2) Inventories
3) Pre-Paid Expenses
4) Other Current Assets
5) Payables
6) Other Current Liabilities
7) Other Working Capital

And then factor in other Non-Cash Items like stock base compensation for example.

This obviously is way too complicated to figure out for the average investor as you really need to dive deep into a company's cash flow statement and rip it apart.

In my book I simplify the process by doing the following in figuring out my free cash flow results.

Free Cash Flow = Cash Flow from Operations – Capital Expenditures.

InvestingAnswers.com explains Cash Flow from Operations as the following:

Cash flow from operating activities is a section of the cash flow statement that provides information regarding the cash-generating abilities of a company's core activities.

Cash flow from operating activities is generally calculated according to the following formula:

Cash Flow from Operating Activities = Net income + Noncash Expenses + Changes in Working Capital

The noncash expenses are usually the depreciation and/or amortization expenses listed on the firm's income statement. Cash flows from operations primarily measures the cash-generating abilities of the company's core operations rather than from its ability to raise capital or purchase assets.

http://www.investinganswers.com/financial-dictionary/financial-statement-analysis/cash-flow-operating-activities-2784

Additional Ratios Included in the Database

Mycroft/Michaelis Ratio

One of the most legendary investors in modern times was George Michaelis. He was the portfolio manager for the closed end fund, Source Capital. His average annualized performance for the 15 years that he ran the fund was +18.4% and he beat the S&P 500 Index by 3 to 1 in relative side-by-side performance. Warren Buffett and Charlie Munger were so impressed with his performance that they bought a majority of the shares in his closed end fund.

Tragically, he was killed in a bicycle accident at the age of 59 and his loss was a great blow to the financial community. I first came across Mr. Michaelis when I read "The New Money Masters" by John Train. On page 281 of that book, Mr. Train included an excerpt from the December 31, 1985 Source Capital report that introduces what I call the Michaelis Ratio. This ratio allows us to determine an accurate future growth rate for any company. The ratio is as follows:

Yield = (Return on Equity X Payout Ratio)/ (Price to Book Value)

Growth = (Return on Equity X Reinvestment Rate)

Michaelis Ratio = Yield + Growth

Return on Equity = Net Income/ Shareholders Equity

Payout Ratio = Dividend per share/Earnings Per Share

Reinvestment Rate = 100% - Payout Ratio

I have been using the Michaelis ratio for years and over time, I have improved on it by replacing Return on Equity in the equation with my FROIC ratio (Free cash flow Return on Invested Capital).

FROIC = free cash flow/total capital

Free cash flow = cash flow from operations – capital expenditures

Total capital = long term debt + shareholders equity (found in the balance sheet)

By replacing Michaelis' Return on Equity with FROIC, I make it much harder for a company to achieve a higher total return or growth rate as I factor in the amount of debt as well as capital spending into the equation. Thus the result is more conservative. I have also made Yield equal to the dividend yield TTM (Trailing Twelve Months). It should also be noted that I use TTM in all the calculations found in this book.

Trailing Twelve Months Investopedia.com Definition

Trailing 12 months figures can be calculated by subtracting the previous year's results from the same quarter as the most recent quarter reported and adding the difference to the latest fiscal year end results.
(4) http://www.investopedia.com/terms/t/ttm.asp

The following is my variation on the Michaelis ratio and this variation I have named the **"Mycroft/Michaelis Growth Ratio."** The calculation is given below.

Yield = dividend per share/market price per share

Growth = (FROIC) X reinvestment rate

Mycroft/Michaelis growth = yield + growth

Essentially this formula gives me a growth rate, which I use to forecast the growth rate of each company's free cash flow per share for the following year. This is why I use TTM results and thus refer to my book as Mycroft's Blue Book Stock Guide (2014). Four of the data columns in the database contain the word, "estimate." Based on growth rates, I am forecasting out for the year 2014 in the database.   Thus the information contained in this book is relevant to the end of 2014.

Mycroft Free Cash Flow Per Share

The **Mycroft Free Cash Flow Per Share** estimate in the database is calculated as follows:

Mycroft Free Cash Flow Per Share = (free cash flow/diluted shares outstanding) x (100% + Mycroft/Michaelis growth ratio)

As for FROIC, I created this ratio because while Return on Invested Capital (ROIC) tells us how much profit is generated for every dollar invested, FROIC permits us to know how much free cash flow is generated for every dollar of invested capital.

CapFlow Ratio

Another original ratio you will find in the database is the **"CapFlow Ratio."** I created this ratio because I wanted to know what percentage of a company's cash flow was taken up by its capital expenditures. This is a qualitative ratio as it introduces into the equation, cost controls initiated by management and allows one to see just how smart management is. When taken over a multi-year time frame, one can deduce a lot about a company's managerial structure and management training program. I like to see CapFlows of 33% or less because when a company achieves such a great result, it means that at least 67% of the cash flow is free to be used to do things like buy back stock. I am a big fan of stock buy backs as it increases my percentage ownership stake (ever so small) in the company and shows that management is interested in pleasing its shareholders.

Price to Mycroft Free Cash Flow per share Ratio *(this is where the reader gets involved)*

Ninety-nine percent of my work is done through analysis of companies on "Main Street." I do this by ripping apart their financial statements and crunching the numbers. After I have obtained the final free cash flow per share result, I go to the stock market and see what Benjamin Graham's "Mr. Market" price will be for that day. Then I calculate the Price to Mycroft Free Cash Flow per share ratio as follows:

Price to Free Cash Flow = stock market price per share/Mycroft Free Cash Flow per share

This result is <u>not</u> provided to the reader in the database. Unlike everything else in the database, which changes only once a year, <u>Price to Mycroft Free Cash Flow per share</u> changes every time a stock price changes in the stock markets. In the database, I present the reader with the <u>Mycroft Free Cash Flow Per Share forward estimate</u> for all of 2014. This will be the denominator in your Price to Mycroft Free Cash Flow per share ratio. Now I ask that the reader obtain the current stock price (the numerator) from the Internet, Financial TV channel or from the financial section of your newspaper, and then calculate the "Price to Mycroft Free Cash Flow per share" for each company under consideration. This will be your current Price to Mycroft Free Cash Flow per share result. I consider a Price to Mycroft Free Cash Flow per share result of less than 15 to be good for purchase, and anything under 7.5 to be excellent.

The higher you go above 15, the more overvalued a company becomes. I use a Price to Mycroft Free Cash Flow per share result of 22.5 as my sell price, and 45 as my short price.

An appropriately priced stock should trade around a Price to Mycroft Free Cash Flow per share result of 15. This benchmark was determined by backtesting (see Appendix). Each page in the database contains brief instructions on how to use the database, located below the column headings. On the day of analysis, the reader should obtain the current market price for the stock in question, and compare it to the "ideal" prices listed in each category of buy, hold, sell, and short. This will give the reader a "real time" idea of where the Price to

Mycroft Free Cash Flow per share result will fall. Upon calculating the ratio, the reader will be able to determine if the stock is appropriately priced.

Buy (opinion) = A Price to Mycroft Free Cash Flow per share result of less than 7.5 is considered excellent (50% below the initial Hold level), and anything under 15 is attractive.

The result I give as my Buy opinion in the <u>database</u> uses a Price to Mycroft Free Cash Flow per share result of 7.5.

Hold (opinion) = 15 to 22.5 (I use 15 in the <u>database</u>).

Sell (opinion) = 22.5 or higher (50% above the initial Hold level). (I use 22.5 in the <u>database</u>).

Short (opinion) = 45 or greater. The Price to Mycroft Free Cash Flow per share result of 45 was determined by going back to the peak of the market (in the year 2000) and averaging the Price to Free Cash Flow per share results for the key players at that time. (I use 45 in the <u>database</u>).

<u>Concluding Remarks</u>

The best way to use the database is to identify companies trading near their **hold** column price and then to try and buy the stock at a discount to that price. The greater the discount, the better the bargain. That said, if you can find a company whose stock trades at or below its **buy** column price, then you should do some serious further analysis to try and determine **why** the stock is trading so cheaply. It may be due to some one-time gain or because Management is not communicating its message properly. Stocks that trade that low usually get there for a good reason, so before buying the stock, please find out what that reason is. Also when you see a company with a **"Negative Free Cash Flow "** result, it would be best, in my opinion, to walk away from it. The company is, in most cases, not being run well and is often not very shareholder friendly.

Lastly, please remember that this stock guide is just one tool of many in your toolbox and should not be used as a one-source answer to all your investing needs. Once you find a stock you like from the guide, please take the company and kick the tires for a while before buying it.

You will also notice that I haven't included any financial firms (banks, insurance companies, brokers, REITS, and credit firms) in this book as I have always found these extremely difficult to analyze. Similar to my idol, Phillip A. Fisher, ("Common Stocks and Uncommon Profits"), I prefer to avoid financial firms, as they tend to get really rocked when bad markets show up.

This was exemplified in the 2008-2009 bear market, when a number of financial firms fell as much as 90%.

Along with being the author of this book, I am also the portfolio manager and CEO of two Investment Advisory firms. Our newest firm, SIA Capital Management, has on its website an explanation of my investing strategy. You can view it at:
http://siacm.com/Investment_Strategy.html

Sincerely,

Mycroft Psaras

DISCLAIMER

Since we are not privy to each reader's specific investment objectives, financial situation, or particular needs, this stock guide should not be construed as being investment advice in any way but should be viewed as the opinion of the author on the valuation of each company analyzed. This analysis is based on the methodologies and data presented herein and was developed through actual real world investments in the stock market and by performing backtests. Databases, information, tools and articles published are solely for informational purposes and are not to be construed as a solicitation or an offer to buy or sell any securities or related financial instruments. References made to third parties are based on information obtained from sources believed to be reliable, but are not guaranteed to be accurate. Readers should not regard this stock guide as a substitute for the exercise of their own judgment. Any opinions expressed in this book are subject to change without notice and Mycroft Psaras or any affiliated companies or authors are not under any obligation to update or keep current the information contained herein.

Mycroft Psaras, associates or clients may have an interest in the securities or derivatives of any entities found in this stock guide. The Author or any affiliate company accepts no liability whatsoever for any loss or damage of any kind arising out of the use of all or any part of this stock guide. Our comments are an expression of opinion. While we believe our statements to be true, they always depend on the reliability of our own credible sources. The findings from this stock guide are merely a start to a means of further research to uncover a great business and investment. Mycroft Psaras or any affiliated company holds no responsibility for any investment whatsoever that is made by any reader.

NAME	TICKER	INDUSTRY	2014 BUY PRICE OPINION	2014 HOLD PRICE OPINION	2014 SELL PRICE OPINION	2014 SHORT PRICE OPINION	2014 MYCROFT FREE CASH FLOW PER SHARE ESTIMATE	2014 MYCROFT FREE CASH FLOW RETURN ON TOTAL CAPITAL ESTIMATE (FROIC) >15% = Great	2014 MYCROFT CAPFLOW ESTIMATE <33% = Great BUT NO NEGATIVE RESULTS	2014 MYCROFT MICHAELIS GROWTH RATE ESTIMATE >15% = Great	DIVIDEND YIELD
Step #1 = Look up the company's current stock market price on the day of analysis and compare it to our 2014 Buy, Hold, Sell & Short Price.												
Step #2 =Take the company's current market price; divide it by the "2014 Mycroft Free Cash Flow Per Share estimate." This gives the "Price to Free Cash Flow."												
All results below are based on the 2014 year end estimates using the "2014 Mycroft Michaelis Growth Rate" and are good until December 31, 2014.												
1-800 Flowers.com	FLWS	Retail	$3.15	$6.30	$9.45	$18.90	$0.42	13%	46%	13%	0.00%
3D Systems Corporation	DDD	Computers	$2.85	$5.70	$8.55	$17.10	$0.38	4%	16%	4%	0.00%
3M Co	MMM	Industrial	$51.45	$102.90	$154.35	$308.70	$6.86	18%	28%	12%	2.16%
8x8, Inc.	EGHT	Communication	$1.88	$3.75	$5.63	$11.25	$0.25	12%	25%	12%	0.00%
A Schulman	SHLM	Chemicals	$26.03	$52.05	$78.08	$156.15	$3.47	13%	23%	13%	2.84%
A V Homes	AVHI	Homebuilding	Negative Free Cash Flow	Negative Free Cash Flow	Negative Free Cash Flow	Negative Free Cash Flow	-$3.83	-20%	-5%	-20%	0.00%
A. T. Cross Company	ATX	Retail	$2.03	$4.05	$6.08	$12.15	$0.27	3%	64%	3%	0.00%
A.H. Belo Corporation	AHC	Publishing	$1.88	$3.75	$5.63	$11.25	$0.25	6%	65%	2%	4.10%
A.M. Castle.	CAS	Industrial	$19.35	$38.70	$58.05	$116.10	$2.58	9%	18%	9%	0.00%
A.O. Smith Corporation	AOS	Industrial	$9.30	$18.60	$27.90	$55.80	$1.24	11%	32%	7%	1.10%
AAON, Inc.	AAON	Building Supplies	$13.73	$27.45	$41.18	$82.35	$1.83	34%	13%	31%	0.52%

NAME	TICKER	INDUSTRY	2014 BUY PRICE OPINION	2014 HOLD PRICE OPINION	2014 SELL PRICE OPINION	2014 SHORT PRICE OPINION	2014 MYCROFT FREE CASH FLOW PER SHARE ESTIMATE	2014 MYCROFT FREE CASH FLOW RETURN ON TOTAL CAPITAL ESTIMATE (FROIC) >15% = Great	2014 MYCROFT CAPFLOW ESTIMATE <33% = Great BUT NO NEGATIVE RESULTS	2014 MYCROFT MICHAELIS GROWTH RATE ESTIMATE >15% = Great	DIVIDEND YIELD
Step #1 = Look up the company's current stock market price on the day of analysis and compare it to our 2014 Buy, Hold, Sell & Short Price.											
Step #2 = Take the company's current market price; divide it by the "2014 Mycroft Free Cash Flow Per Share estimate." This gives the "Price to Free Cash Flow."											
All results below are based on the 2014 year end estimates using the "2014 Mycroft Michaelis Growth Rate" and are good until December 31, 2014.											
AAR Corporation	AIR	Aerospace & Defense	$25.65	$51.30	$76.95	$153.90	$3.42	8%	23%	8%	1.12%
Aaron's, Inc.	AAN	Rentals	$6.38	$12.75	$19.13	$38.25	$0.85	5%	52%	4%	0.20%
Abaxis, Inc.	ABAX	Medical	$10.28	$20.55	$30.83	$61.65	$1.37	15%	16%	15%	0.00%
Abbott Laboratories	ABT	Medical	$25.65	$51.30	$76.95	$153.90	$3.42	14%	24%	13%	1.70%
AbbVie Inc	ABBV	Drugs	$35.03	$70.05	$105.08	$210.15	$4.67	30%	4%	21%	3.40%
Abercrombie & Fitch Company	ANF	Retail	$31.50	$63.00	$94.50	$189.00	$4.20	17%	44%	15%	2.30%
Abiomed, Inc.	ABMD	Medical	$4.13	$8.25	$12.38	$24.75	$0.55	13%	14%	13%	0.00%
ABM Industries	ABM	Business Services	$18.83	$37.65	$56.48	$112.95	$2.51	11%	17%	10%	2.34%
Abraxas Petroleum Corporation	AXAS	Oil & Gas	Negative Free Cash Flow	Negative Free Cash Flow	Negative Free Cash Flow	Negative Free Cash Flow	-$0.20	-10%	138%	-10%	0.00%
Acacia Research Coroporation	ACTG	Business Services	Negative Free Cash Flow	Negative Free Cash Flow	Negative Free Cash Flow	Negative Free Cash Flow	-$1.71	-14%	244%	-16%	2.30%
Acadia Healthcare Company, Inc.	ACHC	Health Care	Negative Free Cash Flow	Negative Free Cash Flow	Negative Free Cash Flow	Negative Free Cash Flow	-$0.82	-6%	181%	-6%	0.00%

NAME	TICKER	INDUSTRY	2014 BUY PRICE OPINION	2014 HOLD PRICE OPINION	2014 SELL PRICE OPINION	2014 SHORT PRICE OPINION	2014 MYCROFT FREE CASH FLOW PER SHARE ESTIMATE	2014 MYCROFT FREE CASH FLOW RETURN ON TOTAL CAPITAL ESTIMATE (FROIC) >15% = Great	2014 MYCROFT CAPFLOW ESTIMATE <33% = Great BUT NO NEGATIVE RESULTS	2014 MYCROFT MICHAELIS GROWTH RATE ESTIMATE >15% = Great	DIVIDEND YIELD
Step #1 = Look up the company's current stock market price on the day of analysis and compare it to our 2014 Buy, Hold, Sell & Short Price.											
Step #2 =Take the company's current market price; divide it by the "2014 Mycroft Free Cash Flow Per Share estimate." This gives the "Price to Free Cash Flow."											
All results below are based on the 2014 year end estimates using the "2014 Mycroft Michaelis Growth Rate" and are good until December 31, 2014.											
ACADIA Pharmaceuticals, Inc.	ACAD	Biotech	Negative Free Cash Flow	Negative Free Cash Flow	Negative Free Cash Flow	Negative Free Cash Flow	-$0.27	-13%	0%	-13%	0.00%
Accelerate Diagnostics Inc	AXDX	Computers	Negative Free Cash Flow	Negative Free Cash Flow	Negative Free Cash Flow	Negative Free Cash Flow	-$0.05	-7%	-8%	-7%	0.00%
Accelrys, Inc.	ACCL	Software	$2.18	$4.35	$6.53	$13.05	$0.29	6%	29%	6%	0.00%
Accenture PLC	ACN	Software	$53.78	$107.55	$161.33	$322.65	$7.17	63%	10%	44%	2.50%
ACCO Brands Corp	ACCO	Industrial	$12.23	$24.45	$36.68	$73.35	$1.63	9%	22%	9%	0.00%
Accretive Health Inc	AH	Software	$3.00	$6.00	$9.00	$18.00	$0.40	13%	33%	13%	0.00%
Accuray, Inc.	ARAY	Medical	Negative Free Cash Flow	Negative Free Cash Flow	Negative Free Cash Flow	Negative Free Cash Flow	-$1.09	-44%	-23%	-44%	0.00%
Accuride Corp	ACW	Truck Manufacturing	Negative Free Cash Flow	Negative Free Cash Flow	Negative Free Cash Flow	Negative Free Cash Flow	-$0.90	-12%	448%	-12%	0.00%
AcelRx Pharmaceuticals, Inc.	ACRX	Conglomerates	Negative Free Cash Flow	Negative Free Cash Flow	Negative Free Cash Flow	Negative Free Cash Flow	-$0.74	-174%	-1%	-174%	0.00%
Aceto Corporation	ACET	Chemicals	$6.08	$12.15	$18.23	$36.45	$0.81	9%	11%	8%	1.63%
Achillion Pharmaceuticals, Inc.	ACHN	Biotech	Negative Free Cash Flow	Negative Free Cash Flow	Negative Free Cash Flow	Negative Free Cash Flow	-$0.54	-29%	-1%	-29%	0.00%

NAME	TICKER	INDUSTRY	2014 BUY PRICE OPINION	2014 HOLD PRICE OPINION	2014 SELL PRICE OPINION	2014 SHORT PRICE OPINION	2014 MYCROFT FREE CASH FLOW PER SHARE ESTIMATE	2014 MYCROFT FREE CASH FLOW RETURN ON TOTAL CAPITAL ESTIMATE (FROIC) >15% = Great	2014 MYCROFT CAPFLOW ESTIMATE <33% = Great BUT NO NEGATIVE RESULTS	2014 MYCROFT MICHAELIS GROWTH RATE ESTIMATE >15% = Great	DIVIDEND YIELD
Step #1 = Look up the company's current stock market price on the day of analysis and compare it to our 2014 Buy, Hold, Sell & Short Price.											
Step #2 =Take the company's current market price; divide it by the "2014 Mycroft Free Cash Flow Per Share estimate." This gives the "Price to Free Cash Flow."											
All results below are based on the 2014 year end estimates using the "2014 Mycroft Michaelis Growth Rate" and are good until December 31, 2014.											
ACI Worldwide, Inc.	ACIW	Software	$8.33	$16.65	$24.98	$49.95	$1.11	5%	37%	5%	0.00%
Acme United Corporation	ACU	Consumer Goods	Negative Free Cash Flow	Negative Free Cash Flow	Negative Free Cash Flow	Negative Free Cash Flow	-$0.42	-2%	-359%	-2%	2.31%
Acorda Therapeutics	ACOR	Biotech	$5.25	$10.50	$15.75	$31.50	$0.70	7%	28%	7%	0.00%
Acorn Energy	ACFN	Engineering	Negative Free Cash Flow	Negative Free Cash Flow	Negative Free Cash Flow	Negative Free Cash Flow	-$1.38	-64%	-7%	-68%	2.80%
Actavis Inc	ACT	Drugs	$30.60	$61.20	$91.80	$183.60	$4.08	11%	25%	11%	0.00%
Active Network	ACTV	Software	$1.05	$2.10	$3.15	$6.30	$0.14	3%	84%	3%	0.00%
Active Power	ACPW	Industrial	Negative Free Cash Flow	Negative Free Cash Flow	Negative Free Cash Flow	Negative Free Cash Flow	-$0.05	-4%	1150%	-4%	0.00%
Activision Blizzard, Inc.	ATVI	Software	$10.80	$21.60	$32.40	$64.80	$1.44	12%	5%	11%	1.11%
Actuant Corp	ATU	Industrial	$16.35	$32.70	$49.05	$98.10	$2.18	10%	14%	10%	0.11%
Actuate Corporation	BIRT	Software	$2.25	$4.50	$6.75	$13.50	$0.30	10%	17%	10%	0.00%
Acuity Brands Inc	AYI	Computers	$17.33	$34.65	$51.98	$103.95	$2.31	7%	32%	6%	0.65%

NAME	TICKER	INDUSTRY	2014 BUY PRICE OPINION	2014 HOLD PRICE OPINION	2014 SELL PRICE OPINION	2014 SHORT PRICE OPINION	2014 MYCROFT FREE CASH FLOW PER SHARE ESTIMATE	2014 MYCROFT FREE CASH FLOW RETURN ON TOTAL CAPITAL ESTIMATE (FROIC) >15% = Great	2014 MYCROFT CAPFLOW ESTIMATE <33% = Great BUT NO NEGATIVE RESULTS	2014 MYCROFT MICHAELIS GROWTH RATE ESTIMATE >15% = Great	DIVIDEND YIELD
Step #1 = Look up the company's current stock market price on the day of analysis and compare it to our 2014 Buy, Hold, Sell & Short Price.											
Step #2 =Take the company's current market price; divide it by the "2014 Mycroft Free Cash Flow Per Share estimate." This gives the "Price to Free Cash Flow."											
All results below are based on the 2014 year end estimates using the "2014 Mycroft Michaelis Growth Rate" and are good until December 31, 2014.											
Acura Pharmaceuticals, Inc.	ACUR	Drugs	Negative Free Cash Flow	Negative Free Cash Flow	Negative Free Cash Flow	Negative Free Cash Flow	-$0.24	-54%	-1%	-54%	0.00%
Acxiom Corporation	ACXM	Software	$11.63	$23.25	$34.88	$69.75	$1.55	12%	39%	12%	0.00%
Adams Resources & Energy	AE	Oil & Gas	$2.18	$4.35	$6.53	$13.05	$0.29	1%	97%	0%	1.60%
AdCare Health Systems, Inc.	ADK	Health Care	Negative Free Cash Flow	Negative Free Cash Flow	Negative Free Cash Flow	Negative Free Cash Flow	-$0.40	-4%	601%	-4%	0.00%
Addus Homecare Corporation	ADUS	Health Care	$39.38	$78.75	$118.13	$236.25	$5.25	33%	2%	33%	0.00%
Adobe Systems	ADBE	Software	$18.90	$37.80	$56.70	$113.40	$2.52	16%	20%	16%	0.00%
ADT Corporation	ADT	Rentals	$45.60	$91.20	$136.80	$273.60	$6.08	23%	36%	22%	1.20%
Adtran, Inc.	ADTN	Communication	$9.83	$19.65	$29.48	$58.95	$1.31	11%	10%	9%	1.32%
Advance Auto Parts Inc	AAP	Retail	$41.85	$83.70	$125.55	$251.10	$5.58	18%	41%	17%	0.30%
Advanced Energy Industries	AEIS	Computers	$5.25	$10.50	$15.75	$31.50	$0.70	7%	27%	7%	0.00%
Advanced Emissions Solutions Inc	ADES	Industrial	$3.00	$6.00	$9.00	$18.00	$0.40	-72%	28%	-72%	0.00%

NAME	TICKER	INDUSTRY	2014 BUY PRICE OPINION	2014 HOLD PRICE OPINION	2014 SELL PRICE OPINION	2014 SHORT PRICE OPINION	2014 MYCROFT FREE CASH FLOW PER SHARE ESTIMATE	2014 MYCROFT FREE CASH FLOW RETURN ON TOTAL CAPITAL ESTIMATE (FROIC) >15% = Great	2014 MYCROFT CAPFLOW ESTIMATE <33% = Great BUT NO NEGATIVE RESULTS	2014 MYCROFT MICHAELIS GROWTH RATE ESTIMATE >15% = Great	DIVIDEND YIELD
Step #1 = Look up the company's current stock market price on the day of analysis and compare it to our 2014 Buy, Hold, Sell & Short Price.												
Step #2 =Take the company's current market price; divide it by the "2014 Mycroft Free Cash Flow Per Share estimate." This gives the "Price to Free Cash Flow."												
All results below are based on the 2014 year end estimates using the "2014 Mycroft Michaelis Growth Rate" and are good until December 31, 2014.												
Advanced Micro Devices Inc	AMD	Semiconductors	Negative Free Cash Flow	Negative Free Cash Flow	Negative Free Cash Flow	Negative Free Cash Flow	-$1.14	-228%	-14%	-228%	0.00%
Advent Software, Inc.	ADVS	Software	Negative Free Cash Flow	Negative Free Cash Flow	Negative Free Cash Flow	Negative Free Cash Flow	$1.72	-124%	7%	-124%	0.00%
Advisory Board Company	ABCO	Business Services	$9.15	$18.30	$27.45	$54.90	$1.22	13%	52%	13%	0.00%
AECOM Technology Corporation	ACM	Engineering	$36.00	$72.00	$108.00	$216.00	$4.80	14%	11%	14%	0.00%
Aegerion Pharmaceuticals, Inc.	AEGR	Biotech	Negative Free Cash Flow	Negative Free Cash Flow	Negative Free Cash Flow	Negative Free Cash Flow	-$2.01	-46%	-2%	-46%	0.00%
Aegion Corp	AEGN	Engineering	$6.75	$13.50	$20.25	$40.50	$0.90	4%	53%	4%	0.00%
AEP Industries	AEPI	Autos	$3.23	$6.45	$9.68	$19.35	$0.43	1%	96%	1%	0.00%
Aeroflex Holding Corp	ARX	Computers	$5.10	$10.20	$15.30	$30.60	$0.68	6%	28%	6%	0.00%
Aeropostale, Inc.	ARO	Retail	$1.35	$2.70	$4.05	$8.10	$0.18	3%	84%	3%	0.00%
AeroVironment, Inc.	AVAV	Aerospace & Defense	$4.88	$9.75	$14.63	$29.25	$0.65	5%	51%	5%	0.00%
AES Corp	AES	Utilities	$9.98	$19.95	$29.93	$59.85	$1.33	4%	68%	5%	1.20%

NAME	TICKER	INDUSTRY	2014 BUY PRICE OPINION	2014 HOLD PRICE OPINION	2014 SELL PRICE OPINION	2014 SHORT PRICE OPINION	2014 MYCROFT FREE CASH FLOW PER SHARE ESTIMATE	2014 MYCROFT FREE CASH FLOW RETURN ON TOTAL CAPITAL ESTIMATE (FROIC) >15% = Great	2014 MYCROFT CAPFLOW ESTIMATE <33% = Great BUT NO NEGATIVE RESULTS	2014 MYCROFT MICHAELIS GROWTH RATE ESTIMATE >15% = Great	DIVIDEND YIELD
Step #1 = Look up the company's current stock market price on the day of analysis and compare it to our 2014 Buy, Hold, Sell & Short Price.											
Step #2 =Take the company's current market price; divide it by the "2014 Mycroft Free Cash Flow Per Share estimate." This gives the "Price to Free Cash Flow."											
All results below are based on the 2014 year end estimates using the "2014 Mycroft Michaelis Growth Rate" and are good until December 31, 2014.											
Aetna Inc	AET	Health Care	$19.05	$38.10	$57.15	$114.30	$2.54	4%	29%	4%	1.20%
AFC Enterprises, Inc.	AFCE	Restaurants	Negative Free Cash Flow	Negative Free Cash Flow	Negative Free Cash Flow	Negative Free Cash Flow	-$0.07	-2%	104%	-2%	0.00%
Affymetrix, Inc.	AFFX	Medical	$2.78	$5.55	$8.33	$16.65	$0.37	6%	13%	6%	0.00%
AGCO Corp	AGCO	Agriculture	$47.48	$94.95	$142.43	$284.85	$6.33	11%	40%	11%	0.60%
Agenus, Inc.	AGEN	Biotech	Negative Free Cash Flow	Negative Free Cash Flow	Negative Free Cash Flow	Negative Free Cash Flow	-$0.57	-96%	-4%	-96%	0.00%
Agilent Technologies Inc	A	Medical	$26.85	$53.70	$80.55	$161.10	$3.58	16%	18%	14%	0.90%
Agilysys, Inc.	AGYS	Software	Negative Free Cash Flow	Negative Free Cash Flow	Negative Free Cash Flow	Negative Free Cash Flow	-$0.29	-6%	349%	-6%	0.00%
AGL Resources, Inc.	GAS	Utilities	$21.68	$43.35	$65.03	$130.05	$2.89	5%	70%	6%	4.20%
Air Lease Corp	AL	Rentals	Negative Free Cash Flow	Negative Free Cash Flow	Negative Free Cash Flow	Negative Free Cash Flow	-$14.16	-22%	358%	-22%	0.40%
Air Methods	AIRM	Health Care	$4.28	$8.55	$12.83	$25.65	$0.57	4%	83%	4%	0.00%
Air Products & Chemicals Inc	APD	Chemicals	$3.60	$7.20	$10.80	$21.60	$0.48	1%	94%	-2%	2.70%

NAME	TICKER	INDUSTRY	2014 BUY PRICE OPINION	2014 HOLD PRICE OPINION	2014 SELL PRICE OPINION	2014 SHORT PRICE OPINION	2014 MYCROFT FREE CASH FLOW PER SHARE ESTIMATE	2014 MYCROFT FREE CASH FLOW RETURN ON TOTAL CAPITAL ESTIMATE (FROIC) >15% = Great	2014 MYCROFT CAPFLOW ESTIMATE <33% = Great BUT NO NEGATIVE RESULTS	2014 MYCROFT MICHAELIS GROWTH RATE ESTIMATE >15% = Great	DIVIDEND YIELD
Step #1 = Look up the company's current stock market price on the day of analysis and compare it to our 2014 Buy, Hold, Sell & Short Price.											
Step #2 =Take the company's current market price; divide it by the "2014 Mycroft Free Cash Flow Per Share estimate." This gives the "Price to Free Cash Flow."											
All results below are based on the 2014 year end estimates using the "2014 Mycroft Michaelis Growth Rate" and are good until December 31, 2014.											
Air T, Inc.	AIRT	Transportation	$13.43	$26.85	$40.28	$80.55	$1.79	14%	8%	14%	2.70%
Air Transport Services Group, Inc.	ATSG	Transportation	Negative Free Cash Flow	Negative Free Cash Flow	Negative Free Cash Flow	Negative Free Cash Flow	-$1.00	-10%	169%	-10%	0.00%
Aircastle Ltd	AYR	Rentals	Negative Free Cash Flow	Negative Free Cash Flow	Negative Free Cash Flow	Negative Free Cash Flow	-$3.35	-15%	163%	-14%	3.70%
Airgas Inc	ARG	Chemicals	$26.55	$53.10	$79.65	$159.30	$3.54	7%	57%	5%	1.80%
AK Steel Holding Corporation	AKS	Steel	Negative Free Cash Flow	Negative Free Cash Flow	Negative Free Cash Flow	Negative Free Cash Flow	-$0.03	-1%	94%	-1%	0.00%
Akamai Technologies	AKAM	Software	$12.30	$24.60	$36.90	$73.80	$1.64	11%	49%	11%	0.00%
Akorn, Inc.	AKRX	Drugs	$2.33	$4.65	$6.98	$13.95	$0.31	8%	32%	8%	0.00%
Alamo Group Inc.	ALG	Agriculture	$17.18	$34.35	$51.53	$103.05	$2.29	7%	27%	7%	0.61%
Alaska Air Group, Inc.	ALK	Airlines	$45.08	$90.15	$135.23	$270.45	$6.01	15%	59%	14%	1.20%
Albany International Corporation	AIN	Homebuilding	$17.63	$35.25	$52.88	$105.75	$2.35	9%	43%	8%	1.81%
Albany Molecular Research, Inc.	AMRI	Biotech	$6.38	$12.75	$19.13	$38.25	$0.85	11%	31%	11%	0.00%

NAME	TICKER	INDUSTRY	2014 BUY PRICE OPINION	2014 HOLD PRICE OPINION	2014 SELL PRICE OPINION	2014 SHORT PRICE OPINION	2014 MYCROFT FREE CASH FLOW PER SHARE ESTIMATE	2014 MYCROFT FREE CASH FLOW RETURN ON TOTAL CAPITAL ESTIMATE (FROIC) >15% = Great	2014 MYCROFT CAPFLOW ESTIMATE <33% = Great BUT NO NEGATIVE RESULTS	2014 MYCROFT MICHAELIS GROWTH RATE ESTIMATE >15% = Great	DIVIDEND YIELD
Step #1 = Look up the company's current stock market price on the day of analysis and compare it to our 2014 Buy, Hold, Sell & Short Price.											
Step #2 =Take the company's current market price; divide it by the "2014 Mycroft Free Cash Flow Per Share estimate." This gives the "Price to Free Cash Flow."											
All results below are based on the 2014 year end estimates using the "2014 Mycroft Michaelis Growth Rate" and are good until December 31, 2014.											
Albemarle Corp	ALB	Chemicals	$22.58	$45.15	$67.73	$135.45	$3.01	11%	53%	9%	1.50%
Alcoa Inc	AA	Commodities	$3.00	$6.00	$9.00	$18.00	$0.40	2%	74%	3%	1.49%
Alere Inc	ALR	Medical	$4.13	$8.25	$12.38	$24.75	$0.55	1%	75%	1%	0.00%
Alexander & Baldwin Inc	ALEX	Real Estate	Negative Free Cash Flow	Negative Free Cash Flow	Negative Free Cash Flow	Negative Free Cash Flow	-$0.64	-3%	251%	-3%	0.00%
Alexion Pharmaceuticals, Inc.	ALXN	Biotech	$16.05	$32.10	$48.15	$96.30	$2.14	15%	7%	15%	0.00%
Alexza Pharmaceuticals, Inc.	ALXA	Drugs	$1.20	$2.40	$3.60	$7.20	$0.16	-47%	20%	-47%	0.00%
Alico, Inc.	ALCO	Consumer Goods	Negative Free Cash Flow	Negative Free Cash Flow	Negative Free Cash Flow	Negative Free Cash Flow	-$1.06	-5%	161%	-5%	1.20%
Align Technology	ALGN	Medical	$15.68	$31.35	$47.03	$94.05	$2.09	26%	14%	26%	0.00%
Alimera Sciences	ALIM	Drugs	Negative Free Cash Flow	Negative Free Cash Flow	Negative Free Cash Flow	Negative Free Cash Flow	-$0.96	-260%	-1%	-260%	0.00%
Alkermes PLC	ALKS	Biotech	$7.50	$15.00	$22.50	$45.00	$1.00	9%	13%	9%	0.00%
Allegheny Technologies Inc	ATI	Industrial	Negative Free Cash Flow	Negative Free Cash Flow	Negative Free Cash Flow	Negative Free Cash Flow	-$0.13	0%	103%	0%	2.30%

NAME	TICKER	INDUSTRY	2014 BUY PRICE OPINION	2014 HOLD PRICE OPINION	2014 SELL PRICE OPINION	2014 SHORT PRICE OPINION	2014 MYCROFT FREE CASH FLOW PER SHARE ESTIMATE	2014 MYCROFT FREE CASH FLOW RETURN ON TOTAL CAPITAL ESTIMATE (FROIC) >15% = Great	2014 MYCROFT CAPFLOW ESTIMATE <33% = Great BUT NO NEGATIVE RESULTS	2014 MYCROFT MICHAELIS GROWTH RATE ESTIMATE >15% = Great	DIVIDEND YIELD
Step #1 = Look up the company's current stock market price on the day of analysis and compare it to our 2014 Buy, Hold, Sell & Short Price.											
Step #2 =Take the company's current market price; divide it by the "2014 Mycroft Free Cash Flow Per Share estimate." This gives the "Price to Free Cash Flow."											
All results below are based on the 2014 year end estimates using the "2014 Mycroft Michaelis Growth Rate" and are good until December 31, 2014.											
Allegiant Travel Company, LLC.	ALGT	Airlines	$36.30	$72.60	$108.90	$217.80	$4.84	14%	60%	14%	0.00%
Allergan, Inc.	AGN	Drugs	$41.93	$83.85	$125.78	$251.55	$5.59	19%	11%	19%	0.20%
ALLETE, Inc.	ALE	Utilities	Negative Free Cash Flow	Negative Free Cash Flow	Negative Free Cash Flow	Negative Free Cash Flow	-$2.24	-4%	140%	-4%	4.00%
Alliance Data Systems Corporation	ADS	Business Services	$214.35	$428.70	$643.05	$1,286.10	$28.58	24%	10%	24%	0.00%
Alliance Fiber Optic Products, Inc.	AFOP	Semiconductors	$8.78	$17.55	$26.33	$52.65	$1.17	14%	22%	11%	0.61%
Alliance HealthCare Services Inc	AIQ	Medical	$43.65	$87.30	$130.95	$261.90	$5.82	13%	41%	13%	0.00%
Alliance One International Inc	AOI	Tobacco	Negative Free Cash Flow	Negative Free Cash Flow	Negative Free Cash Flow	Negative Free Cash Flow	-$1.08	-7%	-79%	-7%	0.00%
Alliant Energy Corporation	LNT	Utilities	$8.55	$17.10	$25.65	$51.30	$1.14	2%	87%	2%	3.80%
Alliant Techsystems Inc	ATK	Aerospace & Defense	$86.63	$173.25	$259.88	$519.75	$11.55	12%	24%	12%	1.07%
Allied Nevada Gold Corp	ANV	Commodities	Negative Free Cash Flow	Negative Free Cash Flow	Negative Free Cash Flow	Negative Free Cash Flow	-$4.02	-36%	-1634%	-36%	0.00%
Allison Transmission Holdings Inc	ALSN	Autos	$15.08	$30.15	$45.23	$90.45	$2.01	8%	20%	8%	1.90%

NAME	TICKER	INDUSTRY	2014 BUY PRICE OPINION	2014 HOLD PRICE OPINION	2014 SELL PRICE OPINION	2014 SHORT PRICE OPINION	2014 MYCROFT FREE CASH FLOW PER SHARE ESTIMATE	2014 MYCROFT FREE CASH FLOW RETURN ON TOTAL CAPITAL ESTIMATE (FROIC) >15% = Great	2014 MYCROFT CAPFLOW ESTIMATE <33% = Great BUT NO NEGATIVE RESULTS	2014 MYCROFT MICHAELIS GROWTH RATE ESTIMATE >15% = Great	DIVIDEND YIELD
Step #1 = Look up the company's current stock market price on the day of analysis and compare it to our 2014 Buy, Hold, Sell & Short Price.												
Step #2 =Take the company's current market price; divide it by the "2014 Mycroft Free Cash Flow Per Share estimate." This gives the "Price to Free Cash Flow."												
All results below are based on the 2014 year end estimates using the "2014 Mycroft Michaelis Growth Rate" and are good until December 31, 2014.												
Allscripts Healthcare Solutions Inc	MDRX	Medical	$0.75	$1.50	$2.25	$4.50	$0.10	1%	88%	1%	0.00%
Almost Family, Inc.	AFAM	Health Care	$10.28	$20.55	$30.83	$61.65	$1.37	6%	18%	6%	0.00%
Alnylam Pharmaceuticals, Inc.	ALNY	Biotech	Negative Free Cash Flow	Negative Free Cash Flow	Negative Free Cash Flow	Negative Free Cash Flow	-$1.54	-31%	-10%	-31%	0.00%
Alon USA Energy Inc	ALJ	Oil & Gas	$42.38	$84.75	$127.13	$254.25	$5.65	21%	23%	22%	2.40%
Alpha & Omega Semiconductor Ltd.	AOSL	Semiconductors	$3.15	$6.30	$9.45	$18.90	$0.42	4%	63%	4%	0.00%
Alpha Natural Resources Inc	ANR	Coal	$4.35	$8.70	$13.05	$26.10	$0.58	2%	72%	2%	0.00%
Alphatec Holdings	ATEC	Medical	Negative Free Cash Flow	Negative Free Cash Flow	Negative Free Cash Flow	Negative Free Cash Flow	-$0.07	-2%	161%	-2%	0.00%
Altair Nanotechnologies	ALTI	Computers	Negative Free Cash Flow	Negative Free Cash Flow	Negative Free Cash Flow	Negative Free Cash Flow	-$3.34	-126%	-175%	-126%	0.00%
Altera Corp.	ALTR	Semiconductors	$14.93	$29.85	$44.78	$89.55	$1.99	14%	9%	11%	1.60%
Alteva	ALTV	Communication	$2.18	$4.35	$6.53	$13.05	$0.29	22%	59%	-26%	12.80%
Altra Holdings, Inc.	AIMC	Industrial	$13.28	$26.55	$39.83	$79.65	$1.77	9%	36%	8%	1.50%

NAME	TICKER	INDUSTRY	2014 BUY PRICE OPINION	2014 HOLD PRICE OPINION	2014 SELL PRICE OPINION	2014 SHORT PRICE OPINION	2014 MYCROFT FREE CASH FLOW PER SHARE ESTIMATE	2014 MYCROFT FREE CASH FLOW RETURN ON TOTAL CAPITAL ESTIMATE (FROIC) >15% = Great	2014 MYCROFT CAPFLOW ESTIMATE <33% = Great BUT NO NEGATIVE RESULTS	2014 MYCROFT MICHAELIS GROWTH RATE ESTIMATE >15% = Great	DIVIDEND YIELD
Step #1 = Look up the company's current stock market price on the day of analysis and compare it to our 2014 Buy, Hold, Sell & Short Price.											
Step #2 =Take the company's current market price; divide it by the "2014 Mycroft Free Cash Flow Per Share estimate." This gives the "Price to Free Cash Flow."											
All results below are based on the 2014 year end estimates using the "2014 Mycroft Michaelis Growth Rate" and are good until December 31, 2014.											
Altria Group Inc.	MO	Tobacco	$18.08	$36.15	$54.23	$108.45	$2.41	27%	3%	9%	5.50%
AMAG Pharmaceuticals, Inc.	AMAG	Biotech	$2.55	$5.10	$7.65	$15.30	$0.34	4%	33%	4%	0.00%
Amazon.com Inc	AMZN	Retail	$4.50	$9.00	$13.50	$27.00	$0.60	3%	94%	3%	0.00%
Ambarella Inc	AMBA	Semiconductors	$3.30	$6.60	$9.90	$19.80	$0.44	9%	15%	9%	0.00%
AMC Networks Inc	AMCX	Communication	$28.43	$56.85	$85.28	$170.55	$3.79	15%	10%	15%	0.00%
AMCOL International Corporation	ACO	Commodities	$2.85	$5.70	$8.55	$17.10	$0.38	2%	87%	0%	2.40%
Amdocs Ltd.	DOX	Software	$24.68	$49.35	$74.03	$148.05	$3.29	14%	21%	13%	1.40%
Amedisys, Inc.	AMED	Health Care	$14.55	$29.10	$43.65	$87.30	$1.94	12%	46%	12%	0.00%
Amerco, Inc.	UHAL	Rentals	Negative Free Cash Flow	Negative Free Cash Flow	Negative Free Cash Flow	Negative Free Cash Flow	-$11.50	-17%	141%	-17%	0.00%
Ameren Corp	AEE	Utilities	$9.75	$19.50	$29.25	$58.50	$1.30	2%	82%	4%	4.60%
Ameresco, Inc.	AMRC	Industrial	Negative Free Cash Flow	Negative Free Cash Flow	Negative Free Cash Flow	Negative Free Cash Flow	-$0.75	-7%	217%	-7%	0.00%

NAME	TICKER	INDUSTRY	2014 BUY PRICE OPINION	2014 HOLD PRICE OPINION	2014 SELL PRICE OPINION	2014 SHORT PRICE OPINION	2014 MYCROFT FREE CASH FLOW PER SHARE ESTIMATE	2014 MYCROFT FREE CASH FLOW RETURN ON TOTAL CAPITAL ESTIMATE (FROIC) >15% = Great	2014 MYCROFT CAPFLOW ESTIMATE <33% = Great BUT NO NEGATIVE RESULTS	2014 MYCROFT MICHAELIS GROWTH RATE ESTIMATE >15% = Great	DIVIDEND YIELD

Step #1 = Look up the company's current stock market price on the day of analysis and compare it to our 2014 Buy, Hold, Sell & Short Price.

Step #2 = Take the company's current market price; divide it by the "2014 Mycroft Free Cash Flow Per Share estimate." This gives the "Price to Free Cash Flow."

All results below are based on the 2014 year end estimates using the "2014 Mycroft Michaelis Growth Rate" and are good until December 31, 2014.

NAME	TICKER	INDUSTRY	2014 BUY PRICE OPINION	2014 HOLD PRICE OPINION	2014 SELL PRICE OPINION	2014 SHORT PRICE OPINION	2014 MYCROFT FREE CASH FLOW PER SHARE ESTIMATE	FROIC	CAPFLOW	MICHAELIS	DIVIDEND YIELD
American Axle & Mfg Holdings, Inc.	AXL	Autos	Negative Free Cash Flow	Negative Free Cash Flow	Negative Free Cash Flow	Negative Free Cash Flow	-$5.40	-38%	-142%	-38%	0.00%
American Apparel	APP	Apparel & Furniture	Negative Free Cash Flow	Negative Free Cash Flow	Negative Free Cash Flow	Negative Free Cash Flow	-$0.11	-30%	172%	-30%	0.00%
American Electric Power	AEP	Utilities	$2.40	$4.80	$7.20	$14.40	$0.32	0%	96%	2%	4.50%
American Science & Engineering	ASEI	Industrial	$40.05	$80.10	$120.15	$240.30	$5.34	19%	8%	14%	3.30%
American Caresource Holdings, Inc.	ANCI	Health Care	Negative Free Cash Flow	Negative Free Cash Flow	Negative Free Cash Flow	Negative Free Cash Flow	-$0.48	-30%	-21%	-30%	0.00%
American Eagle Outfitters	AEO	Retail	$11.85	$23.70	$35.55	$71.10	$1.58	22%	40%	17%	3.60%
American Pacific Corporation	APFC	Chemicals	$33.68	$67.35	$101.03	$202.05	$4.49	16%	33%	16%	0.00%
American Public Education, Inc.	APEI	Education	$19.20	$38.40	$57.60	$115.20	$2.56	20%	42%	20%	0.00%
American Railcar Industries, Inc.	ARII	Transportation	Negative Free Cash Flow	Negative Free Cash Flow	Negative Free Cash Flow	Negative Free Cash Flow	-$3.01	-10%	156%	-10%	2.40%
American Shared Hospital Services	AMS	Health Care	$2.70	$5.40	$8.10	$16.20	$0.36	4%	79%	4%	0.00%
American Software, Inc. Class A	AMSWA	Software	$6.60	$13.20	$19.80	$39.60	$0.88	24%	15%	16%	4.60%

NAME	TICKER	INDUSTRY	2014 BUY PRICE OPINION	2014 HOLD PRICE OPINION	2014 SELL PRICE OPINION	2014 SHORT PRICE OPINION	2014 MYCROFT FREE CASH FLOW PER SHARE ESTIMATE	2014 MYCROFT FREE CASH FLOW RETURN ON TOTAL CAPITAL ESTIMATE (FROIC) >15% = Great	2014 MYCROFT CAPFLOW ESTIMATE <33% = Great BUT NO NEGATIVE RESULTS	2014 MYCROFT MICHAELIS GROWTH RATE ESTIMATE >15% = Great	DIVIDEND YIELD
Step #1 = Look up the company's current stock market price on the day of analysis and compare it to our 2014 Buy, Hold, Sell & Short Price.											
Step #2 =Take the company's current market price; divide it by the "2014 Mycroft Free Cash Flow Per Share estimate." This gives the "Price to Free Cash Flow."											
All results below are based on the 2014 year end estimates using the "2014 Mycroft Michaelis Growth Rate" and are good until December 31, 2014.											
American Spectrum Realty, Inc.	AQQ	Real Estate	$9.30	$18.60	$27.90	$55.80	$1.24	1%	2%	1%	0.00%
American States Water Co	AWR	Utilities	Negative Free Cash Flow	Negative Free Cash Flow	Negative Free Cash Flow	Negative Free Cash Flow	-$0.22	-1%	112%	-2%	3.00%
American Vanguard Corporation	AVD	Agriculture	$1.95	$3.90	$5.85	$11.70	$0.26	3%	69%	1%	0.70%
American Water Works Co Inc	AWK	Utilities	Negative Free Cash Flow	Negative Free Cash Flow	Negative Free Cash Flow	Negative Free Cash Flow	-$0.09	0%	102%	1%	2.80%
American Woodmark Corporation	AMWD	Apparel & Furniture	$12.30	$24.60	$36.90	$73.80	$1.64	12%	28%	12%	0.00%
America's Car-Mart, Inc.	CRMT	Autos	Negative Free Cash Flow	Negative Free Cash Flow	Negative Free Cash Flow	Negative Free Cash Flow	-$0.88	-3%	-507%	-3%	0.00%
Amerisource Bergen Corp	ABC	Medical	$47.25	$94.50	$141.75	$283.50	$6.30	30%	15%	26%	1.30%
Ametek, Inc.	AME	Computers	$20.40	$40.80	$61.20	$122.40	$2.72	15%	9%	14%	0.54%
Amgen Inc	AMGN	Biotech	$48.75	$97.50	$146.25	$292.50	$6.50	11%	13%	9%	1.70%
Amicus Therapeutics	FOLD	Biotech	Negative Free Cash Flow	Negative Free Cash Flow	Negative Free Cash Flow	Negative Free Cash Flow	-$0.80	-99%	-2%	-99%	0.00%
AmkorTechnology	AMKR	Semiconductors	Negative Free Cash Flow	Negative Free Cash Flow	Negative Free Cash Flow	Negative Free Cash Flow	-$0.35	-3%	117%	-3%	0.00%

NAME	TICKER	INDUSTRY	2014 BUY PRICE OPINION	2014 HOLD PRICE OPINION	2014 SELL PRICE OPINION	2014 SHORT PRICE OPINION	2014 MYCROFT FREE CASH FLOW PER SHARE ESTIMATE	2014 MYCROFT FREE CASH FLOW RETURN ON TOTAL CAPITAL ESTIMATE (FROIC) >15% = Great	2014 MYCROFT CAPFLOW ESTIMATE <33% = Great BUT NO NEGATIVE RESULTS	2014 MYCROFT MICHAELIS GROWTH RATE ESTIMATE >15% = Great	DIVIDEND YIELD
Step #1 = Look up the company's current stock market price on the day of analysis and compare it to our 2014 Buy, Hold, Sell & Short Price.											
Step #2 =Take the company's current market price; divide it by the "2014 Mycroft Free Cash Flow Per Share estimate." This gives the "Price to Free Cash Flow."											
All results below are based on the 2014 year end estimates using the "2014 Mycroft Michaelis Growth Rate" and are good until December 31, 2014.											
AMN Healthcare Services, Inc.	AHS	Services	$6.83	$13.65	$20.48	$40.95	$0.91	10%	19%	10%	0.00%
Ampco-Pittsburgh Corporation	AP	Industrial	$18.23	$36.45	$54.68	$109.35	$2.43	12%	32%	12%	4.10%
Amphenol Corp	APH	Computers	$32.63	$65.25	$97.88	$195.75	$4.35	15%	18%	13%	1.00%
Ampio Pharmaceuticals, Inc.	AMPE	Drugs	Negative Free Cash Flow	Negative Free Cash Flow	Negative Free Cash Flow	Negative Free Cash Flow	-$0.35	-71%	0%	-71%	0.00%
AMSC	AMSC	Industrial	Negative Free Cash Flow	Negative Free Cash Flow	Negative Free Cash Flow	Negative Free Cash Flow	-$0.71	-32%	-3%	-32%	0.00%
Amsurg Corporation	AMSG	Health Care	$80.33	$160.65	$240.98	$481.95	$10.71	25%	9%	25%	0.00%
Amtech Systems, Inc.	ASYS	Semiconductors	Negative Free Cash Flow	Negative Free Cash Flow	Negative Free Cash Flow	Negative Free Cash Flow	-$0.33	-5%	-8%	-5%	0.00%
Anacor Pharmaceuticals, Inc.	ANAC	Biotech	Negative Free Cash Flow	Negative Free Cash Flow	Negative Free Cash Flow	Negative Free Cash Flow	-$1.24	-358%	-1%	-358%	0.00%
Anadarko Petroleum Corp	APC	Oil & Gas	$35.33	$70.65	$105.98	$211.95	$4.71	6%	76%	6%	0.77%
Anadigics, Inc.	ANAD	Semiconductors	Negative Free Cash Flow	Negative Free Cash Flow	Negative Free Cash Flow	Negative Free Cash Flow	-$0.65	-56%	-8%	-56%	0.00%
Analog Devices Inc	ADI	Computers	$19.80	$39.60	$59.40	$118.80	$2.64	14%	13%	9%	2.90%

NAME	TICKER	INDUSTRY	2014 BUY PRICE OPINION	2014 HOLD PRICE OPINION	2014 SELL PRICE OPINION	2014 SHORT PRICE OPINION	2014 MYCROFT FREE CASH FLOW PER SHARE ESTIMATE	2014 MYCROFT FREE CASH FLOW RETURN ON TOTAL CAPITAL ESTIMATE (FROIC) >15% = Great	2014 MYCROFT CAPFLOW ESTIMATE <33% = Great BUT NO NEGATIVE RESULTS	2014 MYCROFT MICHAELIS GROWTH RATE ESTIMATE >15% = Great	DIVIDEND YIELD
Step #1 = Look up the company's current stock market price on the day of analysis and compare it to our 2014 Buy, Hold, Sell & Short Price.												
Step #2 =Take the company's current market price; divide it by the "2014 Mycroft Free Cash Flow Per Share estimate." This gives the "Price to Free Cash Flow."												
All results below are based on the 2014 year end estimates using the "2014 Mycroft Michaelis Growth Rate" and are good until December 31, 2014.												
Analogic Corporation	ALOG	Computers	Negative Free Cash Flow	Negative Free Cash Flow	Negative Free Cash Flow	Negative Free Cash Flow	-$0.19	0%	109%	-1%	0.50%
Analysts International	ANLY	Software	$7.05	$14.10	$21.15	$42.30	$0.94	20%	0%	20%	0.00%
Anaren, Inc.	ANEN	Communication	$12.98	$25.95	$38.93	$77.85	$1.73	11%	21%	11%	0.00%
Andersons, Inc.	ANDE	Retail	$133.73	$267.45	$401.18	$802.35	$17.83	27%	35%	27%	0.90%
Angie's List Inc	ANGI	Internet	Negative Free Cash Flow	Negative Free Cash Flow	Negative Free Cash Flow	Negative Free Cash Flow	-$0.05	-96%	-47%	-96%	0.00%
AngioDynamics, Inc.	ANGO	Medical	$3.08	$6.15	$9.23	$18.45	$0.41	2%	48%	2%	0.00%
ANI Pharmaceuticals Inc	ANIP	Biotech	Negative Free Cash Flow	Negative Free Cash Flow	Negative Free Cash Flow	Negative Free Cash Flow	-$2.88	-77%	-2%	-77%	0.00%
Anika Therapeutics, Inc.	ANIK	Biotech	$9.98	$19.95	$29.93	$59.85	$1.33	13%	3%	13%	0.00%
Anixter International Inc	AXE	Computers	$39.90	$79.80	$119.70	$239.40	$5.32	8%	17%	8%	0.00%
Ann, Inc.	ANN	Retail	$11.40	$22.80	$34.20	$68.40	$1.52	15%	71%	15%	0.00%
Annie's Inc	BNNY	Consumer Goods	$4.28	$8.55	$12.83	$25.65	$0.57	12%	21%	12%	0.00%

NAME	TICKER	INDUSTRY	2014 BUY PRICE OPINION	2014 HOLD PRICE OPINION	2014 SELL PRICE OPINION	2014 SHORT PRICE OPINION	2014 MYCROFT FREE CASH FLOW PER SHARE ESTIMATE	2014 MYCROFT FREE CASH FLOW RETURN ON TOTAL CAPITAL ESTIMATE (FROIC) >15% = Great	2014 MYCROFT CAPFLOW ESTIMATE <33% = Great BUT NO NEGATIVE RESULTS	2014 MYCROFT MICHAELIS GROWTH RATE ESTIMATE >15% = Great	DIVIDEND YIELD

Step #1 = Look up the company's current stock market price on the day of analysis and compare it to our 2014 Buy, Hold, Sell & Short Price.

Step #2 =Take the company's current market price; divide it by the "2014 Mycroft Free Cash Flow Per Share estimate." This gives the "Price to Free Cash Flow."

All results below are based on the 2014 year end estimates using the "2014 Mycroft Michaelis Growth Rate" and are good until December 31, 2014.

NAME	TICKER	INDUSTRY	BUY	HOLD	SELL	SHORT	FCF/SHARE	FROIC	CAPFLOW	GROWTH	DIV YIELD
Ansys, Inc.	ANSS	Software	$28.43	$56.85	$85.28	$170.55	$3.79	15%	6%	15%	0.00%
Antares Pharma, Inc.	ATRS	Medical	Negative Free Cash Flow	Negative Free Cash Flow	Negative Free Cash Flow	Negative Free Cash Flow	-$0.14	-23%	-38%	-23%	0.00%
Anthera Pharmaceuticals, Inc.	ANTH	Drugs	Negative Free Cash Flow	Negative Free Cash Flow	Negative Free Cash Flow	Negative Free Cash Flow	-$2.56	-113%	0%	-113%	0.00%
AOL, Inc.	AOL	Internet	$26.25	$52.50	$78.75	$157.50	$3.50	11%	21%	11%	0.00%
Apache Corporation	APA	Oil & Gas	Negative Free Cash Flow	Negative Free Cash Flow	Negative Free Cash Flow	Negative Free Cash Flow	-$4.65	-4%	121%	-4%	0.92%
Apco Oil and Gas International Inc.	APAGF	Oil & Gas	$0.60	$1.20	$1.80	$3.60	$0.08	1%	96%	1%	0.00%
API Technologies Corp	ATNY	Semiconductors	Negative Free Cash Flow	Negative Free Cash Flow	Negative Free Cash Flow	Negative Free Cash Flow	-$0.05	-1%	-616%	-1%	0.00%
Apogee Enterprises	APOG	Building Supplies	$5.25	$10.50	$15.75	$31.50	$0.70	5%	58%	4%	1.20%
Apollo Group Inc Class A	APOL	Education	$35.40	$70.80	$106.20	$212.40	$4.72	33%	24%	33%	0.00%
Apple Inc	AAPL	Computers	$441.38	$882.75	$1,324.13	$2,648.25	$58.85	30%	19%	25%	2.50%
Applied Materials	AMAT	Semiconductors	$5.55	$11.10	$16.65	$33.30	$0.74	9%	18%	6%	2.30%

NAME	TICKER	INDUSTRY	2014 BUY PRICE OPINION	2014 HOLD PRICE OPINION	2014 SELL PRICE OPINION	2014 SHORT PRICE OPINION	2014 MYCROFT FREE CASH FLOW PER SHARE ESTIMATE	2014 MYCROFT FREE CASH FLOW RETURN ON TOTAL CAPITAL ESTIMATE (FROIC) >15% = Great	2014 MYCROFT CAPFLOW ESTIMATE <33% = Great BUT NO NEGATIVE RESULTS	2014 MYCROFT MICHAELIS GROWTH RATE ESTIMATE >15% = Great	DIVIDEND YIELD
Step #1 = Look up the company's current stock market price on the day of analysis and compare it to our 2014 Buy, Hold, Sell & Short Price.											
Step #2 =Take the company's current market price; divide it by the "2014 Mycroft Free Cash Flow Per Share estimate." This gives the "Price to Free Cash Flow."											
All results below are based on the 2014 year end estimates using the "2014 Mycroft Michaelis Growth Rate" and are good until December 31, 2014.											
Applied Industrial Technologies	AIT	Industrial	$19.35	$38.70	$58.05	$116.10	$2.58	13%	11%	10%	1.83%
Applied Micro Circuits Corporation	AMCC	Semiconductors	Negative Free Cash Flow	Negative Free Cash Flow	Negative Free Cash Flow	Negative Free Cash Flow	-$0.47	-34%	-12%	-34%	0.00%
Approach Resources, Inc.	AREX	Oil & Gas	Negative Free Cash Flow	Negative Free Cash Flow	Negative Free Cash Flow	Negative Free Cash Flow	-$4.61	-23%	301%	-23%	0.00%
Apricus Biosciences	APRI	Drugs	Negative Free Cash Flow	Negative Free Cash Flow	Negative Free Cash Flow	Negative Free Cash Flow	-$0.46	-128%	-3%	-128%	0.00%
AptarGroup	ATR	Containers	$23.33	$46.65	$69.98	$139.95	$3.11	11%	44%	9%	1.70%
Aqua America	WTR	Utilities	$3.00	$6.00	$9.00	$18.00	$0.40	2%	82%	1%	2.50%
Arabian American Development Company	ARSD	Chemicals	$2.63	$5.25	$7.88	$15.75	$0.35	7%	50%	7%	0.00%
Arbitron Corporation	ARB	Advertising	$25.65	$51.30	$76.95	$153.90	$3.42	38%	24%	33%	0.84%
ARC Document Solutions Inc	ARC	Business Services	$3.75	$7.50	$11.25	$22.50	$0.50	18%	52%	18%	0.00%
ARCA Biopharma	ABIO	Biotech	Negative Free Cash Flow	Negative Free Cash Flow	Negative Free Cash Flow	Negative Free Cash Flow	-$0.27	-15%	0%	-15%	0.00%
Arch Coal Inc	ACI	Coal	Negative Free Cash Flow	Negative Free Cash Flow	Negative Free Cash Flow	Negative Free Cash Flow	-$0.41	-1%	130%	1%	3.00%

NAME	TICKER	INDUSTRY	2014 BUY PRICE OPINION	2014 HOLD PRICE OPINION	2014 SELL PRICE OPINION	2014 SHORT PRICE OPINION	2014 MYCROFT FREE CASH FLOW PER SHARE ESTIMATE	2014 MYCROFT FREE CASH FLOW RETURN ON TOTAL CAPITAL ESTIMATE (FROIC) >15% = Great	2014 MYCROFT CAPFLOW ESTIMATE <33% = Great BUT NO NEGATIVE RESULTS	2014 MYCROFT MICHAELIS GROWTH RATE ESTIMATE >15% = Great	DIVIDEND YIELD
Step #1 = Look up the company's current stock market price on the day of analysis and compare it to our 2014 Buy, Hold, Sell & Short Price.												
Step #2 = Take the company's current market price; divide it by the "2014 Mycroft Free Cash Flow Per Share estimate." This gives the "Price to Free Cash Flow."												
All results below are based on the 2014 year end estimates using the "2014 Mycroft Michaelis Growth Rate" and are good until December 31, 2014.												
Archer-Daniels Midland Company	ADM	Consumer Goods	$12.98	$25.95	$38.93	$77.85	$1.73	4%	53%	4%	2.10%
Arctic Cat, Inc.	ACAT	Autos	$27.30	$54.60	$81.90	$163.80	$3.64	22%	29%	20%	0.71%
Arden Group Inc Class A	ARDNA	Retail	$57.83	$115.65	$173.48	$346.95	$7.71	33%	33%	29%	0.80%
Arena Pharmaceuticals, Inc.	ARNA	Biotech	$0.45	$0.90	$1.35	$2.70	$0.06	9%	27%	9%	0.00%
Argan, Inc.	AGX	Engineering	Negative Free Cash Flow	Negative Free Cash Flow	Negative Free Cash Flow	Negative Free Cash Flow	-$1.83	-18%	-20%	-18%	0.00%
Ariad Pharmaceuticals	ARIA	Biotech	Negative Free Cash Flow	Negative Free Cash Flow	Negative Free Cash Flow	Negative Free Cash Flow	-$1.10	-66%	-2%	-66%	0.00%
Ark Restaurants Corp.	ARKR	Restaurants	$30.53	$61.05	$91.58	$183.15	$4.07	31%	23%	26%	4.70%
Arkansas Best Corporation	ABFS	Transportation	$20.25	$40.50	$60.75	$121.50	$2.70	10%	36%	10%	0.50%
Armstrong World Industries	AWI	Building Supplies	$2.48	$4.95	$7.43	$14.85	$0.33	1%	92%	1%	0.00%
Arotech Corporation	ARTX	Industrial	Negative Free Cash Flow	Negative Free Cash Flow	Negative Free Cash Flow	Negative Free Cash Flow	-$0.11	-4%	597%	-4%	0.00%
Arqule, Inc.	ARQL	Biotech	Negative Free Cash Flow	Negative Free Cash Flow	Negative Free Cash Flow	Negative Free Cash Flow	-$0.54	-48%	0%	-48%	0.00%

NAME	TICKER	INDUSTRY	2014 BUY PRICE OPINION	2014 HOLD PRICE OPINION	2014 SELL PRICE OPINION	2014 SHORT PRICE OPINION	2014 MYCROFT FREE CASH FLOW PER SHARE ESTIMATE	2014 MYCROFT FREE CASH FLOW RETURN ON TOTAL CAPITAL ESTIMATE (FROIC) >15% = Great	2014 MYCROFT CAPFLOW ESTIMATE <33% = Great BUT NO NEGATIVE RESULTS	2014 MYCROFT MICHAELIS GROWTH RATE ESTIMATE >15% = Great	DIVIDEND YIELD
Step #1 = Look up the company's current stock market price on the day of analysis and compare it to our 2014 Buy, Hold, Sell & Short Price.											
Step #2 =Take the company's current market price; divide it by the "2014 Mycroft Free Cash Flow Per Share estimate." This gives the "Price to Free Cash Flow."											
All results below are based on the 2014 year end estimates using the "2014 Mycroft Michaelis Growth Rate" and are good until December 31, 2014.											
Array BioPharma	ARRY	Biotech	Negative Free Cash Flow	Negative Free Cash Flow	Negative Free Cash Flow	Negative Free Cash Flow	-$0.78	-127%	-3%	-127%	0.00%
ARRIS Group Inc	ARRS	Communication	$21.83	$43.65	$65.48	$130.95	$2.91	22%	9%	22%	0.00%
Arrow Electronics	ARW	Computers	$32.18	$64.35	$96.53	$193.05	$4.29	7%	23%	7%	0.00%
Arrowhead Research Corporation	ARWR	Biotech	Negative Free Cash Flow	Negative Free Cash Flow	Negative Free Cash Flow	Negative Free Cash Flow	-$0.59	-52%	-2%	-52%	0.00%
Artesian Resource Corporation	ARTNA	Utilities	Negative Free Cash Flow	Negative Free Cash Flow	Negative Free Cash Flow	Negative Free Cash Flow	-$0.03	0%	101%	0%	3.70%
ArthroCare Corporation	ARTC	Medical	$21.98	$43.95	$65.93	$131.85	$2.93	19%	18%	19%	0.00%
Art's-Way Manufacturing Co., Inc.	ARTW	Agriculture	$9.38	$18.75	$28.13	$56.25	$1.25	17%	16%	16%	1.50%
Aruba Networks, Inc.	ARUN	Communication	$10.65	$21.30	$31.95	$63.90	$1.42	25%	13%	25%	0.00%
Asbury Automotive Group	ABG	Autos	Negative Free Cash Flow	Negative Free Cash Flow	Negative Free Cash Flow	Negative Free Cash Flow	-$2.14	-8%	404%	-8%	0.00%
Ascena Retail Group, Inc.	ASNA	Retail	$9.00	$18.00	$27.00	$54.00	$1.20	10%	56%	10%	0.00%
Ascent Capital Group Inc	ASCMA	Rentals	Negative Free Cash Flow	Negative Free Cash Flow	Negative Free Cash Flow	Negative Free Cash Flow	-$12.61	-12%	206%	-12%	0.00%

NAME	TICKER	INDUSTRY	2014 BUY PRICE OPINION	2014 HOLD PRICE OPINION	2014 SELL PRICE OPINION	2014 SHORT PRICE OPINION	2014 MYCROFT FREE CASH FLOW PER SHARE ESTIMATE	2014 MYCROFT FREE CASH FLOW RETURN ON TOTAL CAPITAL ESTIMATE (FROIC) >15% = Great	2014 MYCROFT CAPFLOW ESTIMATE <33% = Great BUT NO NEGATIVE RESULTS	2014 MYCROFT MICHAELIS GROWTH RATE ESTIMATE >15% = Great	DIVIDEND YIELD
Ashland Inc	ASH	Chemicals	$38.63	$77.25	$115.88	$231.75	$5.15	5%	46%	5%	1.60%
Aspen Technology	AZPN	Software	$26.70	$53.40	$80.10	$160.20	$3.56	137%	4%	137%	0.00%
Asta Funding	ASFI	Business Services	$2.48	$4.95	$7.43	$14.85	$0.33	2%	0%	4%	3.70%
Astec Industries	ASTE	Agriculture	Negative Free Cash Flow	Negative Free Cash Flow	Negative Free Cash Flow	Negative Free Cash Flow	-$0.50	-2%	161%	-3%	1.12%
Astex Pharmaceuticals	ASTX	Drugs	$0.83	$1.65	$2.48	$4.95	$0.11	4%	11%	4%	0.00%
Astro-Med, Inc.	ALOT	Computers	Negative Free Cash Flow	Negative Free Cash Flow	Negative Free Cash Flow	Negative Free Cash Flow	-$0.56	-7%	-28%	-7%	2.40%
Astronics Corporation	ATRO	Aerospace & Defense	$9.53	$19.05	$28.58	$57.15	$1.27	10%	49%	10%	0.00%
Asure Software	ASUR	Software	$1.95	$3.90	$5.85	$11.70	$0.26	15%	51%	15%	0.00%
AT&T Inc	T	Communication	$30.30	$60.60	$90.90	$181.80	$4.04	13%	52%	12%	5.30%
AthenaHealth	ATHN	Software	$3.15	$6.30	$9.45	$18.90	$0.42	4%	76%	4%	0.00%
AtlanticTele-Network	ATNI	Communication	$23.48	$46.95	$70.43	$140.85	$3.13	8%	68%	7%	2.00%

Step #1 = Look up the company's current stock market price on the day of analysis and compare it to our 2014 Buy, Hold, Sell & Short Price.

Step #2 =Take the company's current market price; divide it by the "2014 Mycroft Free Cash Flow Per Share estimate." This gives the "Price to Free Cash Flow."

All results below are based on the 2014 year end estimates using the "2014 Mycroft Michaelis Growth Rate" and are good until December 31, 2014.

NAME	TICKER	INDUSTRY	2014 BUY PRICE OPINION	2014 HOLD PRICE OPINION	2014 SELL PRICE OPINION	2014 SHORT PRICE OPINION	2014 MYCROFT FREE CASH FLOW PER SHARE ESTIMATE	2014 MYCROFT FREE CASH FLOW RETURN ON TOTAL CAPITAL ESTIMATE (FROIC) >15% = Great	2014 MYCROFT CAPFLOW ESTIMATE <33% = Great BUT NO NEGATIVE RESULTS	2014 MYCROFT MICHAELIS GROWTH RATE ESTIMATE >15% = Great	DIVIDEND YIELD
Step #1 = Look up the company's current stock market price on the day of analysis and compare it to our 2014 Buy, Hold, Sell & Short Price.											
Step #2 =Take the company's current market price; divide it by the "2014 Mycroft Free Cash Flow Per Share estimate." This gives the "Price to Free Cash Flow."											
All results below are based on the 2014 year end estimates using the "2014 Mycroft Michaelis Growth Rate" and are good until December 31, 2014.											
Atlas Air Worldwide Holdings Inc	AAWW	Transportation	Negative Free Cash Flow	Negative Free Cash Flow	Negative Free Cash Flow	Negative Free Cash Flow	-$17.17	-21%	244%	-21%	0.00%
Atmel Corporation	ATML	Semiconductors	$1.73	$3.45	$5.18	$10.35	$0.23	9%	31%	9%	0.00%
ATMI, Inc.	ATMI	Semiconductors	$5.63	$11.25	$16.88	$33.75	$0.75	5%	64%	5%	0.00%
Atmos Energy Corp	ATO	Utilities	Negative Free Cash Flow	Negative Free Cash Flow	Negative Free Cash Flow	Negative Free Cash Flow	-$2.65	-5%	142%	-5%	3.40%
AtriCure, Inc.	ATRC	Medical	Negative Free Cash Flow	Negative Free Cash Flow	Negative Free Cash Flow	Negative Free Cash Flow	-$0.30	-16%	-80%	-16%	0.00%
Atrion Corporation	ATRI	Medical	$119.78	$239.55	$359.33	$718.65	$15.97	19%	21%	17%	1.00%
Atwood Oceanics	ATW	Oil & Gas	Negative Free Cash Flow	Negative Free Cash Flow	Negative Free Cash Flow	Negative Free Cash Flow	-$6.58	-15%	224%	-15%	0.00%
Audience Inc	ADNC	Semiconductors	$4.28	$8.55	$12.83	$25.65	$0.57	7%	39%	7%	0.00%
Autobytel, Inc.	ABTL	Internet	$2.85	$5.70	$8.55	$17.10	$0.38	10%	19%	10%	0.00%
Autodesk, Inc.	ADSK	Software	$22.50	$45.00	$67.50	$135.00	$3.00	26%	12%	26%	0.00%
Automatic Data Processing	ADP	Business Services	$22.05	$44.10	$66.15	$132.30	$2.94	21%	18%	10%	2.40%

NAME	TICKER	INDUSTRY	2014 BUY PRICE OPINION	2014 HOLD PRICE OPINION	2014 SELL PRICE OPINION	2014 SHORT PRICE OPINION	2014 MYCROFT FREE CASH FLOW PER SHARE ESTIMATE	2014 MYCROFT FREE CASH FLOW RETURN ON TOTAL CAPITAL ESTIMATE (FROIC) >15% = Great	2014 MYCROFT CAPFLOW ESTIMATE <33% = Great BUT NO NEGATIVE RESULTS	2014 MYCROFT MICHAELIS GROWTH RATE ESTIMATE >15% = Great	DIVIDEND YIELD
Step #1 = Look up the company's current stock market price on the day of analysis and compare it to our 2014 Buy, Hold, Sell & Short Price.											
Step #2 =Take the company's current market price; divide it by the "2014 Mycroft Free Cash Flow Per Share estimate." This gives the "Price to Free Cash Flow."											
All results below are based on the 2014 year end estimates using the "2014 Mycroft Michaelis Growth Rate" and are good until December 31, 2014.											
AutoNation Inc	AN	Autos	$21.00	$42.00	$63.00	$126.00	$2.80	8%	34%	8%	0.00%
AutoZone Inc	AZO	Retail	$277.80	$555.60	$833.40	$1,666.80	$37.04	44%	31%	44%	0.00%
Auxilium Pharmaceuticals	AUXL	Drugs	Negative Free Cash Flow	Negative Free Cash Flow	Negative Free Cash Flow	Negative Free Cash Flow	-$0.85	-14%	-59%	-14%	0.00%
Avago Technologies	AVGO	Semiconductors	$15.83	$31.65	$47.48	$94.95	$2.11	18%	35%	12%	2.10%
Avalon Holdings	AWX	Waste Management	$3.23	$6.45	$9.68	$19.35	$0.43	4%	42%	4%	0.00%
AVANIR Pharmaceuticals	AVNR	Drugs	Negative Free Cash Flow	Negative Free Cash Flow	Negative Free Cash Flow	Negative Free Cash Flow	-$0.32	-94%	-1%	-94%	0.00%
AVEO Pharmaceuticals	AVEO	Biotech	Negative Free Cash Flow	Negative Free Cash Flow	Negative Free Cash Flow	Negative Free Cash Flow	-$2.12	-83%	-9%	-83%	0.00%
Avery Dennison	AVY	Industrial	$30.68	$61.35	$92.03	$184.05	$4.09	16%	32%	13%	2.70%
AVG Technologies NV	AVG	Software	$31.65	$63.30	$94.95	$189.90	$4.22	68%	11%	68%	0.00%
Aviat Networks, Inc.	AVNW	Communication	$0.90	$1.80	$2.70	$5.40	$0.12	4%	50%	4%	0.00%
Avid Technology	AVID	Software	$7.65	$15.30	$22.95	$45.90	$1.02	10%	21%	10%	0.00%

NAME	TICKER	INDUSTRY	2014 BUY PRICE OPINION	2014 HOLD PRICE OPINION	2014 SELL PRICE OPINION	2014 SHORT PRICE OPINION	2014 MYCROFT FREE CASH FLOW PER SHARE ESTIMATE	2014 MYCROFT FREE CASH FLOW RETURN ON TOTAL CAPITAL ESTIMATE (FROIC) >15% = Great	2014 MYCROFT CAPFLOW ESTIMATE <33% = Great BUT NO NEGATIVE RESULTS	2014 MYCROFT MICHAELIS GROWTH RATE ESTIMATE >15% = Great	DIVIDEND YIELD
Step #1 = Look up the company's current stock market price on the day of analysis and compare it to our 2014 Buy, Hold, Sell & Short Price.											
Step #2 =Take the company's current market price; divide it by the "2014 Mycroft Free Cash Flow Per Share estimate." This gives the "Price to Free Cash Flow."											
All results below are based on the 2014 year end estimates using the "2014 Mycroft Michaelis Growth Rate" and are good until December 31, 2014.											
Avis Budget Group	CAR	Rentals	Negative Free Cash Flow	Negative Free Cash Flow	Negative Free Cash Flow	Negative Free Cash Flow	-$88.25	-80%	567%	-80%	0.00%
Avista Corporation	AVA	Utilities	Negative Free Cash Flow	Negative Free Cash Flow	Negative Free Cash Flow	Negative Free Cash Flow	-$0.45	-1%	110%	1%	4.70%
Avnet Inc	AVT	Computers	$36.23	$72.45	$108.68	$217.35	$4.83	11%	14%	11%	1.40%
Avon Products	AVP	Consumer Goods	$6.83	$13.65	$20.48	$40.95	$0.91	10%	37%	8%	1.20%
AVX Corporation	AVX	Computers	$6.00	$12.00	$18.00	$36.00	$0.80	6%	23%	6%	2.59%
Aware, Inc.	AWRE	Communication	Negative Free Cash Flow	Negative Free Cash Flow	Negative Free Cash Flow	Negative Free Cash Flow	-$0.03	-1%	-31%	-1%	0.00%
Axcelis Technologies	ACLS	Semiconductors	Negative Free Cash Flow	Negative Free Cash Flow	Negative Free Cash Flow	Negative Free Cash Flow	-$0.09	-5%	-6%	-5%	0.00%
Axiall Corp	AXLL	Chemicals	$12.98	$25.95	$38.93	$77.85	$1.73	4%	45%	4%	0.76%
AXT, Inc.	AXTI	Semiconductors	$0.38	$0.75	$1.13	$2.25	$0.05	1%	79%	1%	0.00%
AZZ, Inc.	AZZ	Industrial	$27.98	$55.95	$83.93	$167.85	$3.73	15%	28%	14%	1.38%
B&G Foods Inc	BGS	Consumer Goods	$13.58	$27.15	$40.73	$81.45	$1.81	9%	10%	6%	3.60%

NAME	TICKER	INDUSTRY	2014 BUY PRICE OPINION	2014 HOLD PRICE OPINION	2014 SELL PRICE OPINION	2014 SHORT PRICE OPINION	2014 MYCROFT FREE CASH FLOW PER SHARE ESTIMATE	2014 MYCROFT FREE CASH FLOW RETURN ON TOTAL CAPITAL ESTIMATE (FROIC) >15% = Great	2014 MYCROFT CAPFLOW ESTIMATE <33% = Great BUT NO NEGATIVE RESULTS	2014 MYCROFT MICHAELIS GROWTH RATE ESTIMATE >15% = Great	DIVIDEND YIELD
Step #1 = Look up the company's current stock market price on the day of analysis and compare it to our 2014 Buy, Hold, Sell & Short Price.											
Step #2 =Take the company's current market price; divide it by the "2014 Mycroft Free Cash Flow Per Share estimate." This gives the "Price to Free Cash Flow."											
All results below are based on the 2014 year end estimates using the "2014 Mycroft Michaelis Growth Rate" and are good until December 31, 2014.											
B/E Aerospace	BEAV	Aerospace & Defense	$16.58	$33.15	$49.73	$99.45	$2.21	5%	39%	5%	0.00%
Babcock & Wilcox	BWC	Industrial	$15.08	$30.15	$45.23	$90.45	$2.01	20%	30%	17%	0.90%
Badger Meter	BMI	Computers	$14.10	$28.20	$42.30	$84.60	$1.88	14%	32%	10%	1.60%
Baker Hughes Inc.	BHI	Oil & Gas	$4.80	$9.60	$14.40	$28.80	$0.64	1%	90%	1%	1.19%
Balchem Corporation	BCPC	Chemicals	$8.25	$16.50	$24.75	$49.50	$1.10	10%	35%	8%	0.44%
Ball Corporation	BLL	Containers	$19.80	$39.60	$59.40	$118.80	$2.64	9%	51%	8%	1.15%
Ballantyne Strong Inc	BTN	Travel & Leisure	$5.03	$10.05	$15.08	$30.15	$0.67	12%	23%	12%	0.00%
Bally Technologies	BYI	Travel & Leisure	$47.48	$94.95	$142.43	$284.85	$6.33	31%	8%	31%	0.00%
Bankrate Inc	RATE	Internet	$4.58	$9.15	$13.73	$27.45	$0.61	6%	19%	6%	0.00%
Barnes & Noble, Inc.	BKS	Retail	Negative Free Cash Flow	Negative Free Cash Flow	Negative Free Cash Flow	Negative Free Cash Flow	-$1.11	-7%	166%	-7%	0.00%
Barnes Group	B	Industrial	$19.65	$39.30	$58.95	$117.90	$2.62	9%	25%	9%	1.20%

NAME	TICKER	INDUSTRY	2014 BUY PRICE OPINION	2014 HOLD PRICE OPINION	2014 SELL PRICE OPINION	2014 SHORT PRICE OPINION	2014 MYCROFT FREE CASH FLOW PER SHARE ESTIMATE	2014 MYCROFT FREE CASH FLOW RETURN ON TOTAL CAPITAL ESTIMATE (FROIC) >15% = Great	2014 MYCROFT CAPFLOW ESTIMATE <33% = Great BUT NO NEGATIVE RESULTS	2014 MYCROFT MICHAELIS GROWTH RATE ESTIMATE >15% = Great	DIVIDEND YIELD
Step #1 = Look up the company's current stock market price on the day of analysis and compare it to our 2014 Buy, Hold, Sell & Short Price.											
Step #2 = Take the company's current market price; divide it by the "2014 Mycroft Free Cash Flow Per Share estimate." This gives the "Price to Free Cash Flow."											
All results below are based on the 2014 year end estimates using the "2014 Mycroft Michaelis Growth Rate" and are good until December 31, 2014.											
Barnwell Industries Inc	BRN	Oil & Gas	$5.25	$10.50	$15.75	$31.50	$0.70	15%	0%	15%	0.00%
Barrett Business Services, Inc.	BBSI	Services	$82.65	$165.30	$247.95	$495.90	$11.02	78%	9%	73%	0.80%
Basic Energy Services, Inc.	BAS	Oil & Gas	$5.70	$11.40	$17.10	$34.20	$0.76	3%	84%	3%	0.00%
Bassett Furniture Industries	BSET	Apparel & Furniture	Negative Free Cash Flow	Negative Free Cash Flow	Negative Free Cash Flow	Negative Free Cash Flow	-$0.67	-4%	392%	-5%	1.70%
Baxano Surgical Inc	BAXS	Medical	Negative Free Cash Flow	Negative Free Cash Flow	Negative Free Cash Flow	Negative Free Cash Flow	-$0.62	-63%	-5%	-63%	0.00%
Baxter International Inc.	BAX	Medical	$23.33	$46.65	$69.98	$139.95	$3.11	21%	46%	9%	3.00%
Bazaarvoice Inc	BV	Software	Negative Free Cash Flow	Negative Free Cash Flow	Negative Free Cash Flow	Negative Free Cash Flow	-$0.55	-18%	-40%	-18%	0.00%
Beacon Roofing Supply, Inc.	BECN	Industrial	$12.68	$25.35	$38.03	$76.05	$1.69	8%	23%	8%	0.00%
Beam Inc	BEAM	Beverages	$8.78	$17.55	$26.33	$52.65	$1.17	3%	43%	2%	1.30%
Beazer Homes USA, Inc.	BZH	Homebuilding	Negative Free Cash Flow	Negative Free Cash Flow	Negative Free Cash Flow	Negative Free Cash Flow	-$4.84	-7%	-8%	-7%	0.00%
bebe stores, Inc.	BEBE	Retail	Negative Free Cash Flow	Negative Free Cash Flow	Negative Free Cash Flow	Negative Free Cash Flow	-$0.61	-17%	-1528%	-18%	1.60%

NAME	TICKER	INDUSTRY	2014 BUY PRICE OPINION	2014 HOLD PRICE OPINION	2014 SELL PRICE OPINION	2014 SHORT PRICE OPINION	2014 MYCROFT FREE CASH FLOW PER SHARE ESTIMATE	2014 MYCROFT FREE CASH FLOW RETURN ON TOTAL CAPITAL ESTIMATE (FROIC) >15% = Great	2014 MYCROFT CAPFLOW ESTIMATE <33% = Great BUT NO NEGATIVE RESULTS	2014 MYCROFT MICHAELIS GROWTH RATE ESTIMATE >15% = Great	DIVIDEND YIELD
Step #1 = Look up the company's current stock market price on the day of analysis and compare it to our 2014 Buy, Hold, Sell & Short Price.											
Step #2 =Take the company's current market price; divide it by the "2014 Mycroft Free Cash Flow Per Share estimate." This gives the "Price to Free Cash Flow."											
All results below are based on the 2014 year end estimates using the "2014 Mycroft Michaelis Growth Rate" and are good until December 31, 2014.											
Becton Dickinson & Co	BDX	Medical	$34.28	$68.55	$102.83	$205.65	$4.57	10%	41%	7%	2.00%
Bed Bath & Beyond, Inc.	BBBY	Retail	$35.18	$70.35	$105.53	$211.05	$4.69	21%	29%	21%	0.00%
Bel Fuse, Inc. Class B	BELFB	Computers	$1.35	$2.70	$4.05	$8.10	$0.18	1%	74%	1%	1.60%
Belden, Inc.	BDC	Computers	$9.38	$18.75	$28.13	$56.25	$1.25	4%	43%	4%	0.30%
Belo Corporation	BLC	Entertainment	$9.15	$18.30	$27.45	$54.90	$1.22	11%	16%	10%	2.30%
Bemis Co Inc	BMS	Containers	$19.43	$38.85	$58.28	$116.55	$2.59	8%	35%	7%	2.70%
Benchmark Electronics	BHE	Computers	$24.00	$48.00	$72.00	$144.00	$3.20	13%	21%	13%	0.00%
Berry Petroleum Co	BRY	Oil & Gas	Negative Free Cash Flow	Negative Free Cash Flow	Negative Free Cash Flow	Negative Free Cash Flow	-$4.40	-9%	149%	-9%	0.70%
Berry Plastics Group Inc	BERY	Autos	$17.63	$35.25	$52.88	$105.75	$2.35	6%	49%	6%	0.00%
Best Buy Co Inc	BBY	Retail	$13.50	$27.00	$40.50	$81.00	$1.80	12%	56%	9%	1.80%
Big 5 Sporting Goods Corporation	BGFV	Retail	$10.50	$21.00	$31.50	$63.00	$1.40	11%	35%	10%	2.50%

NAME	TICKER	INDUSTRY	2014 BUY PRICE OPINION	2014 HOLD PRICE OPINION	2014 SELL PRICE OPINION	2014 SHORT PRICE OPINION	2014 MYCROFT FREE CASH FLOW PER SHARE ESTIMATE	2014 MYCROFT FREE CASH FLOW RETURN ON TOTAL CAPITAL ESTIMATE (FROIC) >15% = Great	2014 MYCROFT CAPFLOW ESTIMATE <33% = Great BUT NO NEGATIVE RESULTS	2014 MYCROFT MICHAELIS GROWTH RATE ESTIMATE >15% = Great	DIVIDEND YIELD
Step #1 = Look up the company's current stock market price on the day of analysis and compare it to our 2014 Buy, Hold, Sell & Short Price.											
Step #2 =Take the company's current market price; divide it by the "2014 Mycroft Free Cash Flow Per Share estimate." This gives the "Price to Free Cash Flow."											
All results below are based on the 2014 year end estimates using the "2014 Mycroft Michaelis Growth Rate" and are good until December 31, 2014.											
Big Lots, Inc.	BIG	Retail	$11.93	$23.85	$35.78	$71.55	$1.59	8%	60%	8%	0.00%
Biglari Holdings, Inc.	BH	Restaurants	$211.28	$422.55	$633.83	$1,267.65	$28.17	7%	24%	7%	0.00%
Bill Barrett Corporation	BBG	Oil & Gas	Negative Free Cash Flow	Negative Free Cash Flow	Negative Free Cash Flow	Negative Free Cash Flow	-$7.95	-17%	217%	-17%	0.00%
Biocryst Pharmaceuticals	BCRX	Biotech	Negative Free Cash Flow	Negative Free Cash Flow	Negative Free Cash Flow	Negative Free Cash Flow	-$0.55	-157%	0%	-157%	0.00%
Biodel, Inc.	BIOD	Biotech	Negative Free Cash Flow	Negative Free Cash Flow	Negative Free Cash Flow	Negative Free Cash Flow	-$1.04	-62%	0%	-62%	0.00%
BioDelivery Sciences International, Inc.	BDSI	Biotech	Negative Free Cash Flow	Negative Free Cash Flow	Negative Free Cash Flow	Negative Free Cash Flow	-$1.22	-172%	0%	-172%	0.00%
BioFuel Energy Corporation	BIOF	Chemicals	$2.63	$5.25	$7.88	$15.75	$0.35	1%	38%	1%	0.00%
Biogen Idec Inc	BIIB	Biotech	Negative Free Cash Flow	Negative Free Cash Flow	Negative Free Cash Flow	Negative Free Cash Flow	-$6.86	-19%	188%	-19%	0.00%
Biolase Inc	BIOL	Medical	Negative Free Cash Flow	Negative Free Cash Flow	Negative Free Cash Flow	Negative Free Cash Flow	-$0.12	-51%	-20%	-51%	0.00%
Biomarin Pharmaceutical, Inc.	BMRN	Biotech	Negative Free Cash Flow	Negative Free Cash Flow	Negative Free Cash Flow	Negative Free Cash Flow	-$0.46	-4%	-405%	-4%	0.00%
Bio-Rad Laboratories Inc.	BIO	Computers	$19.58	$39.15	$58.73	$117.45	$2.61	3%	65%	3%	0.00%

NAME	TICKER	INDUSTRY	2014 BUY PRICE OPINION	2014 HOLD PRICE OPINION	2014 SELL PRICE OPINION	2014 SHORT PRICE OPINION	2014 MYCROFT FREE CASH FLOW PER SHARE ESTIMATE	2014 MYCROFT FREE CASH FLOW RETURN ON TOTAL CAPITAL ESTIMATE (FROIC) >15% = Great	2014 MYCROFT CAPFLOW ESTIMATE <33% = Great BUT NO NEGATIVE RESULTS	2014 MYCROFT MICHAELIS GROWTH RATE ESTIMATE >15% = Great	DIVIDEND YIELD

Step #1 = Look up the company's current stock market price on the day of analysis and compare it to our 2014 Buy, Hold, Sell & Short Price.

Step #2 =Take the company's current market price; divide it by the "2014 Mycroft Free Cash Flow Per Share estimate." This gives the "Price to Free Cash Flow."

All results below are based on the 2014 year end estimates using the "2014 Mycroft Michaelis Growth Rate" and are good until December 31, 2014.

NAME	TICKER	INDUSTRY	BUY	HOLD	SELL	SHORT	FCF/SHARE	FROIC	CAPFLOW	MICHAELIS	DIV YIELD
Bio-Reference Labs, Inc.	BRLI	Medical	$3.30	$6.60	$9.90	$19.80	$0.44	4%	66%	4%	0.00%
BioScrip, Inc.	BIOS	Drugs	Negative Free Cash Flow	Negative Free Cash Flow	Negative Free Cash Flow	Negative Free Cash Flow	-$0.52	-6%	-109%	-6%	0.00%
BioSpecifics Technologies Corporation	BSTC	Biotech	$5.70	$11.40	$17.10	$34.20	$0.76	20%	0%	20%	0.00%
BioTime, Inc.	BTX	Biotech	Negative Free Cash Flow	Negative Free Cash Flow	Negative Free Cash Flow	Negative Free Cash Flow	-$0.44	-122%	-4%	-122%	0.00%
BJ's Restaurants, Inc.	BJRI	Restaurants	Negative Free Cash Flow	Negative Free Cash Flow	Negative Free Cash Flow	Negative Free Cash Flow	-$0.43	-3%	112%	-3%	0.00%
Black Box Corporation	BBOX	Communication	$33.08	$66.15	$99.23	$198.45	$4.41	9%	9%	10%	1.20%
Black Diamond, Inc.	BDE	Travel & Leisure	Negative Free Cash Flow	Negative Free Cash Flow	Negative Free Cash Flow	Negative Free Cash Flow	-$0.24	-3%	-408%	-3%	0.00%
Black Hills Corporation	BKH	Utilities	Negative Free Cash Flow	Negative Free Cash Flow	Negative Free Cash Flow	Negative Free Cash Flow	-$0.22	0%	103%	0%	3.10%
Blackbaud, Inc.	BLKB	Software	$14.70	$29.40	$44.10	$88.20	$1.96	30%	23%	22%	1.20%
Blackstone Mortgage Trust,	BXMT	Real Estate	Negative Free Cash Flow	Negative Free Cash Flow	Negative Free Cash Flow	Negative Free Cash Flow	-$22.05	-51%	0%	-51%	0.00%
Bloomin Brands	BLMN	Restaurants	$11.85	$23.70	$35.55	$71.10	$1.58	9%	52%	9%	0.00%

NAME	TICKER	INDUSTRY	2014 BUY PRICE OPINION	2014 HOLD PRICE OPINION	2014 SELL PRICE OPINION	2014 SHORT PRICE OPINION	2014 MYCROFT FREE CASH FLOW PER SHARE ESTIMATE	2014 MYCROFT FREE CASH FLOW RETURN ON TOTAL CAPITAL ESTIMATE (FROIC) >15% = Great	2014 MYCROFT CAPFLOW ESTIMATE <33% = Great BUT NO NEGATIVE RESULTS	2014 MYCROFT MICHAELIS GROWTH RATE ESTIMATE >15% = Great	DIVIDEND YIELD
Step #1 = Look up the company's current stock market price on the day of analysis and compare it to our 2014 Buy, Hold, Sell & Short Price.										
Step #2 =Take the company's current market price; divide it by the "2014 Mycroft Free Cash Flow Per Share estimate." This gives the "Price to Free Cash Flow."										
All results below are based on the 2014 year end estimates using the "2014 Mycroft Michaelis Growth Rate" and are good until December 31, 2014.										
Blount International	BLT	Industrial	Negative Free Cash Flow	Negative Free Cash Flow	Negative Free Cash Flow	Negative Free Cash Flow	-$0.03	0%	103%	0%	0.00%
Blucora Inc	BCOR	Internet	$12.38	$24.75	$37.13	$74.25	$1.65	11%	8%	11%	0.00%
Blue Nile, Inc.	NILE	Retail	$33.23	$66.45	$99.68	$199.35	$4.43	141%	12%	141%	0.00%
Bluelinx Holdings, Inc.	BXC	Industrial	Negative Free Cash Flow	Negative Free Cash Flow	Negative Free Cash Flow	Negative Free Cash Flow	-$1.16	-28%	-4%	-28%	0.00%
Blyth, Inc.	BTH	Consumer Goods	$15.23	$30.45	$45.68	$91.35	$2.03	19%	42%	19%	1.50%
BMC Software	BMC	Software	$48.15	$96.30	$144.45	$288.90	$6.42	38%	19%	38%	0.00%
Bob Evans Farms	BOBE	Restaurants	$3.98	$7.95	$11.93	$23.85	$0.53	2%	92%	-1%	2.20%
Body Central	BODY	Retail	Negative Free Cash Flow	Negative Free Cash Flow	Negative Free Cash Flow	Negative Free Cash Flow	-$0.21	-4%	123%	-4%	0.00%
Boeing	BA	Aerospace & Defense	$110.18	$220.35	$330.53	$661.05	$14.69	48%	19%	41%	1.70%
Boingo Wireless	WIFI	Software	$0.15	$0.30	$0.45	$0.90	$0.02	1%	96%	1%	0.00%
Boise Cascade	BCC	Forest Products	Negative Free Cash Flow	Negative Free Cash Flow	Negative Free Cash Flow	Negative Free Cash Flow	-$0.02	0%	103%	0%	0.00%

NAME	TICKER	INDUSTRY	2014 BUY PRICE OPINION	2014 HOLD PRICE OPINION	2014 SELL PRICE OPINION	2014 SHORT PRICE OPINION	2014 MYCROFT FREE CASH FLOW PER SHARE ESTIMATE	2014 MYCROFT FREE CASH FLOW RETURN ON TOTAL CAPITAL ESTIMATE (FROIC) >15% = Great	2014 MYCROFT CAPFLOW ESTIMATE <33% = Great BUT NO NEGATIVE RESULTS	2014 MYCROFT MICHAELIS GROWTH RATE ESTIMATE >15% = Great	DIVIDEND YIELD

Step #1 = Look up the company's current stock market price on the day of analysis and compare it to our 2014 Buy, Hold, Sell & Short Price.

Step #2 =Take the company's current market price; divide it by the "2014 Mycroft Free Cash Flow Per Share estimate." This gives the "Price to Free Cash Flow."

All results below are based on the 2014 year end estimates using the "2014 Mycroft Michaelis Growth Rate" and are good until December 31, 2014.

NAME	TICKER	INDUSTRY	BUY	HOLD	SELL	SHORT	FCF/SHARE	FROIC	CAPFLOW	MICHAELIS	DIV YIELD
Boise Inc	BZ	Forest Products	$7.43	$14.85	$22.28	$44.55	$0.99	6%	62%	6%	0.00%
Bolt Technology Corporation	BOLT	Oil & Gas	$7.88	$15.75	$23.63	$47.25	$1.05	12%	8%	9%	2.03%
Bonanza Creek Energy Inc	BCEI	Oil & Gas	Negative Free Cash Flow	Negative Free Cash Flow	Negative Free Cash Flow	Negative Free Cash Flow	-$4.76	-29%	202%	-29%	0.00%
Bon-Ton Stores	BONT	Retail	$17.03	$34.05	$51.08	$102.15	$2.27	5%	62%	6%	1.90%
Books-A-Million, Inc.	BAMM	Retail	Negative Free Cash Flow	Negative Free Cash Flow	Negative Free Cash Flow	Negative Free Cash Flow	-$0.40	-5%	153%	-5%	0.00%
Booz Allen Hamilton Holding Corp	BAH	Business Services	$30.53	$61.05	$91.58	$183.15	$4.07	36%	7%	33%	2.10%
BorgWarner Inc	BWA	Autos	$32.55	$65.10	$97.65	$195.30	$4.34	11%	48%	9%	1.00%
Boston Beer Company, Inc. Class A	SAM	Beverages	$6.23	$12.45	$18.68	$37.35	$0.83	4%	89%	4%	0.00%
Boston Scientific, Inc.	BSX	Medical	$6.00	$12.00	$18.00	$36.00	$0.80	9%	18%	9%	0.00%
Bottomline Technologies	EPAY	Software	$9.23	$18.45	$27.68	$55.35	$1.23	12%	0%	12%	0.00%
Boulder Brands	BDBD	Consumer Goods	$0.60	$1.20	$1.80	$3.60	$0.08	1%	82%	1%	0.00%

46

NAME	TICKER	INDUSTRY	2014 BUY PRICE OPINION	2014 HOLD PRICE OPINION	2014 SELL PRICE OPINION	2014 SHORT PRICE OPINION	2014 MYCROFT FREE CASH FLOW PER SHARE ESTIMATE	2014 MYCROFT FREE CASH FLOW RETURN ON TOTAL CAPITAL ESTIMATE (FROIC) >15% = Great	2014 MYCROFT CAPFLOW ESTIMATE <33% = Great BUT NO NEGATIVE RESULTS	2014 MYCROFT MICHAELIS GROWTH RATE ESTIMATE >15% = Great	DIVIDEND YIELD
Step #1 = Look up the company's current stock market price on the day of analysis and compare it to our 2014 Buy, Hold, Sell & Short Price.											
Step #2 =Take the company's current market price; divide it by the "2014 Mycroft Free Cash Flow Per Share estimate." This gives the "Price to Free Cash Flow."											
All results below are based on the 2014 year end estimates using the "2014 Mycroft Michaelis Growth Rate" and are good until December 31, 2014.											
Bovie Medical Corporation	BVX	Medical	Negative Free Cash Flow	Negative Free Cash Flow	Negative Free Cash Flow	Negative Free Cash Flow	-$0.13	-11%	-49%	-11%	0.00%
Boyd Gaming Corporation	BYD	Travel & Leisure	$5.93	$11.85	$17.78	$35.55	$0.79	2%	58%	2%	0.00%
BPZ Resources	BPZ	Oil & Gas	Negative Free Cash Flow	Negative Free Cash Flow	Negative Free Cash Flow	Negative Free Cash Flow	-$0.67	-51%	-147%	-51%	0.00%
Brady Corporation	BRC	Rentals	$15.23	$30.45	$45.68	$91.35	$2.03	8%	27%	7%	2.60%
Bravo Brio Restaurant Group, Inc.	BBRG	Restaurants	$5.93	$11.85	$17.78	$35.55	$0.79	11%	70%	11%	0.00%
Breeze-Eastern Corporation	BZC	Aerospace & Defense	$2.03	$4.05	$6.08	$12.15	$0.27	6%	43%	6%	0.00%
Bridgepoint Education, Inc.	BPI	Education	$12.15	$24.30	$36.45	$72.90	$1.62	14%	22%	14%	0.00%
Bridgford Foods Corporation	BRID	Consumer Goods	Negative Free Cash Flow	Negative Free Cash Flow	Negative Free Cash Flow	Negative Free Cash Flow	-$0.39	-17%	1083%	-17%	0.00%
Briggs & Stratton Corporation	BGG	Industrial	$20.48	$40.95	$61.43	$122.85	$2.73	13%	28%	13%	2.40%
Bright Horizons Family Solutions	BFAM	Services	$4.05	$8.10	$12.15	$24.30	$0.54	4%	71%	4%	0.00%
Brightcove Inc	BCOV	Software	$0.00	$0.00	$0.00	$0.00	$0.00	0%	96%	0%	0.00%

NAME	TICKER	INDUSTRY	2014 BUY PRICE OPINION	2014 HOLD PRICE OPINION	2014 SELL PRICE OPINION	2014 SHORT PRICE OPINION	2014 MYCROFT FREE CASH FLOW PER SHARE ESTIMATE	2014 MYCROFT FREE CASH FLOW RETURN ON TOTAL CAPITAL ESTIMATE (FROIC) >15% = Great	2014 MYCROFT CAPFLOW ESTIMATE <33% = Great BUT NO NEGATIVE RESULTS	2014 MYCROFT MICHAELIS GROWTH RATE ESTIMATE >15% = Great	DIVIDEND YIELD
Step #1 = Look up the company's current stock market price on the day of analysis and compare it to our 2014 Buy, Hold, Sell & Short Price.											
Step #2 =Take the company's current market price; divide it by the "2014 Mycroft Free Cash Flow Per Share estimate." This gives the "Price to Free Cash Flow."											
All results below are based on the 2014 year end estimates using the "2014 Mycroft Michaelis Growth Rate" and are good until December 31, 2014.											
Brinker International, Inc.	EAT	Restaurants	$20.85	$41.70	$62.55	$125.10	$2.78	22%	45%	15%	2.40%
Brink's Company	BCO	Rentals	$11.40	$22.80	$34.20	$68.40	$1.52	8%	74%	8%	1.50%
Bristol-Myers Squibb Company	BMY	Drugs	$33.15	$66.30	$99.45	$198.90	$4.42	31%	8%	22%	2.90%
Bristow Group	BRS	Transportation	Negative Free Cash Flow	Negative Free Cash Flow	Negative Free Cash Flow	Negative Free Cash Flow	-$11.46	-18%	268%	-18%	1.40%
Broadcom Corporation	BRCM	Semiconductors	$26.03	$52.05	$78.08	$156.15	$3.47	19%	12%	18%	1.70%
Broadridge Financial Solutions	BR	Business Services	$15.53	$31.05	$46.58	$93.15	$2.07	16%	19%	12%	2.60%
BroadSoft, Inc.	BSFT	Software	$7.80	$15.60	$23.40	$46.80	$1.04	10%	13%	10%	0.00%
BroadVision, Inc.	BVSN	Software	Negative Free Cash Flow	Negative Free Cash Flow	Negative Free Cash Flow	Negative Free Cash Flow	-$0.80	-8%	-2%	-8%	0.00%
Broadwind Energy	BWEN	Industrial	$3.83	$7.65	$11.48	$22.95	$0.51	7%	48%	7%	0.00%
Brocade Communications Systems Inc	BRCD	Computers	$8.40	$16.80	$25.20	$50.40	$1.12	15%	12%	15%	0.00%
Brookdale Senior Living, Inc.	BKD	Health Care	$5.63	$11.25	$16.88	$33.75	$0.75	3%	71%	3%	0.00%

NAME	TICKER	INDUSTRY	2014 BUY PRICE OPINION	2014 HOLD PRICE OPINION	2014 SELL PRICE OPINION	2014 SHORT PRICE OPINION	2014 MYCROFT FREE CASH FLOW PER SHARE ESTIMATE	2014 MYCROFT FREE CASH FLOW RETURN ON TOTAL CAPITAL ESTIMATE (FROIC) >15% = Great	2014 MYCROFT CAPFLOW ESTIMATE <33% = Great BUT NO NEGATIVE RESULTS	2014 MYCROFT MICHAELIS GROWTH RATE ESTIMATE >15% = Great	DIVIDEND YIELD
Step #1 = Look up the company's current stock market price on the day of analysis and compare it to our 2014 Buy, Hold, Sell & Short Price.											
Step #2 =Take the company's current market price; divide it by the "2014 Mycroft Free Cash Flow Per Share estimate." This gives the "Price to Free Cash Flow."											
All results below are based on the 2014 year end estimates using the "2014 Mycroft Michaelis Growth Rate" and are good until December 31, 2014.											
Brooks Automation, Inc.	BRKS	Semiconductors	$3.30	$6.60	$9.90	$19.80	$0.44	5%	15%	4%	3.50%
Brown Shoe Company, Inc.	BWS	Apparel & Furniture	$15.38	$30.75	$46.13	$92.25	$2.05	13%	45%	12%	1.20%
Brown-Forman Corporation	BF.B	Beverages	$17.10	$34.20	$51.30	$102.60	$2.28	20%	19%	12%	1.60%
Bruker Corporation	BRKR	Computers	Negative Free Cash Flow	Negative Free Cash Flow	Negative Free Cash Flow	Negative Free Cash Flow	-$0.04	-1%	111%	-1%	0.00%
Brunswick Corporation	BC	Travel & Leisure	$4.95	$9.90	$14.85	$29.70	$0.66	6%	71%	6%	0.10%
BSD Medical Corporation	BSDM	Medical	Negative Free Cash Flow	Negative Free Cash Flow	Negative Free Cash Flow	Negative Free Cash Flow	-$0.19	-46%	0%	-46%	0.00%
Bsquare Corporation	BSQR	Software	$0.53	$1.05	$1.58	$3.15	$0.07	3%	26%	3%	0.00%
Buckle, Inc.	BKE	Retail	$38.10	$76.20	$114.30	$228.60	$5.08	54%	16%	43%	1.50%
Buffalo Wild Wings, Inc.	BWLD	Restaurants	$2.10	$4.20	$6.30	$12.60	$0.28	1%	97%	1%	0.00%
Build-A-Bear Workshop, Inc.	BBW	Retail	$2.03	$4.05	$6.08	$12.15	$0.27	6%	80%	6%	0.00%
Builders FirstSource, Inc.	BLDR	Retail	Negative Free Cash Flow	Negative Free Cash Flow	Negative Free Cash Flow	Negative Free Cash Flow	-$1.34	-43%	-10%	-43%	0.00%

NAME	TICKER	INDUSTRY	2014 BUY PRICE OPINION	2014 HOLD PRICE OPINION	2014 SELL PRICE OPINION	2014 SHORT PRICE OPINION	2014 MYCROFT FREE CASH FLOW PER SHARE ESTIMATE	2014 MYCROFT FREE CASH FLOW RETURN ON TOTAL CAPITAL ESTIMATE (FROIC) >15% = Great	2014 MYCROFT CAPFLOW ESTIMATE <33% = Great BUT NO NEGATIVE RESULTS	2014 MYCROFT MICHAELIS GROWTH RATE ESTIMATE >15% = Great	DIVIDEND YIELD
Step #1 = Look up the company's current stock market price on the day of analysis and compare it to our 2014 Buy, Hold, Sell & Short Price.											
Step #2 =Take the company's current market price; divide it by the "2014 Mycroft Free Cash Flow Per Share estimate." This gives the "Price to Free Cash Flow."											
All results below are based on the 2014 year end estimates using the "2014 Mycroft Michaelis Growth Rate" and are good until December 31, 2014.											
Bunge Ltd	BG	Consumer Goods	$31.65	$63.30	$94.95	$189.90	$4.22	4%	63%	5%	1.50%
Burger King Worldwide Inc	BKW	Restaurants	$5.70	$11.40	$17.10	$34.20	$0.76	6%	20%	5%	1.20%
C&J Energy Services Inc	CJES	Oil & Gas	$11.25	$22.50	$33.75	$67.50	$1.50	11%	71%	11%	0.00%
C.R. Bard, Inc.	BCR	Medical	$64.35	$128.70	$193.05	$386.10	$8.58	23%	13%	21%	0.71%
CA, Inc.	CA	Software	$19.13	$38.25	$57.38	$114.75	$2.55	15%	16%	12%	3.40%
Cabela's, Inc.	CAB	Retail	$9.30	$18.60	$27.90	$55.80	$1.24	5%	76%	5%	0.00%
Cablevision Systems Corp Class A	CVC	Communication	Negative Free Cash Flow	Negative Free Cash Flow	Negative Free Cash Flow	Negative Free Cash Flow	-$0.02	0%	101%	0%	3.50%
Cabot Corporation	CBT	Chemicals	$8.85	$17.70	$26.55	$53.10	$1.18	3%	80%	3%	1.80%
Cabot Microelectronics Corporation	CCMP	Semiconductors	$21.83	$43.65	$65.48	$130.95	$2.91	13%	21%	13%	0.00%
Cabot Oil & Gas Corporation	COG	Oil & Gas	Negative Free Cash Flow	Negative Free Cash Flow	Negative Free Cash Flow	Negative Free Cash Flow	-$0.45	-6%	122%	-6%	0.10%
Cache, Inc.	CACH	Retail	Negative Free Cash Flow	Negative Free Cash Flow	Negative Free Cash Flow	Negative Free Cash Flow	-$0.95	-71%	-60%	-71%	0.00%

NAME	TICKER	INDUSTRY	2014 BUY PRICE OPINION	2014 HOLD PRICE OPINION	2014 SELL PRICE OPINION	2014 SHORT PRICE OPINION	2014 MYCROFT FREE CASH FLOW PER SHARE ESTIMATE	2014 MYCROFT FREE CASH FLOW RETURN ON TOTAL CAPITAL ESTIMATE (FROIC) >15% = Great	2014 MYCROFT CAPFLOW ESTIMATE <33% = Great BUT NO NEGATIVE RESULTS	2014 MYCROFT MICHAELIS GROWTH RATE ESTIMATE >15% = Great	DIVIDEND YIELD
Step #1 = Look up the company's current stock market price on the day of analysis and compare it to our 2014 Buy, Hold, Sell & Short Price.											
Step #2 =Take the company's current market price; divide it by the "2014 Mycroft Free Cash Flow Per Share estimate." This gives the "Price to Free Cash Flow."											
All results below are based on the 2014 year end estimates using the "2014 Mycroft Michaelis Growth Rate" and are good until December 31, 2014.											
CACI International, Inc.	CACI	Software	$85.58	$171.15	$256.73	$513.45	$11.41	13%	6%	13%	0.00%
Cadence Design Systems, Inc.	CDNS	Software	$9.83	$19.65	$29.48	$58.95	$1.31	25%	12%	25%	0.00%
Cadence Pharmaceuticals, Inc.	CADX	Biotech	Negative Free Cash Flow	Negative Free Cash Flow	Negative Free Cash Flow	Negative Free Cash Flow	-$0.58	-80%	-1%	-80%	0.00%
Cadiz, Inc.	CDZI	Utilities	Negative Free Cash Flow	Negative Free Cash Flow	Negative Free Cash Flow	Negative Free Cash Flow	-$1.19	-68%	-16%	-68%	0.00%
Caesars Entertainment Corp	CZR	Travel & Leisure	Negative Free Cash Flow	Negative Free Cash Flow	Negative Free Cash Flow	Negative Free Cash Flow	-$5.84	-4%	-624%	-4%	0.00%
CAI International	CAP	Rentals	Negative Free Cash Flow	Negative Free Cash Flow	Negative Free Cash Flow	Negative Free Cash Flow	-$20.32	-46%	491%	-46%	0.00%
Cal Dive International	DVR	Oil & Gas	Negative Free Cash Flow	Negative Free Cash Flow	Negative Free Cash Flow	Negative Free Cash Flow	-$0.54	-13%	-54%	-13%	0.00%
CalAmp Corporation	CAMP	Communication	$4.28	$8.55	$12.83	$25.65	$0.57	14%	9%	14%	0.00%
Calavo Growers, Inc.	CVGW	Consumer Goods	$6.68	$13.35	$20.03	$40.05	$0.89	10%	34%	5%	2.20%
Calgon Carbon Corporation	CCC	Industrial	$3.68	$7.35	$11.03	$22.05	$0.49	7%	62%	7%	0.00%
California Water Service Group	CWT	Utilities	$0.75	$1.50	$2.25	$4.50	$0.10	0%	97%	1%	3.20%

NAME	TICKER	INDUSTRY	2014 BUY PRICE OPINION	2014 HOLD PRICE OPINION	2014 SELL PRICE OPINION	2014 SHORT PRICE OPINION	2014 MYCROFT FREE CASH FLOW PER SHARE ESTIMATE	2014 MYCROFT FREE CASH FLOW RETURN ON TOTAL CAPITAL ESTIMATE (FROIC) >15% = Great	2014 MYCROFT CAPFLOW ESTIMATE <33% = Great BUT NO NEGATIVE RESULTS	2014 MYCROFT MICHAELIS GROWTH RATE ESTIMATE >15% = Great	DIVIDEND YIELD
Step #1 = Look up the company's current stock market price on the day of analysis and compare it to our 2014 Buy, Hold, Sell & Short Price.										
Step #2 =Take the company's current market price; divide it by the "2014 Mycroft Free Cash Flow Per Share estimate." This gives the "Price to Free Cash Flow."										
All results below are based on the 2014 year end estimates using the "2014 Mycroft Michaelis Growth Rate" and are good until December 31, 2014.										
Calix, Inc.	CALX	Communication	$4.20	$8.40	$12.60	$25.20	$0.56	9%	22%	9%	0.00%
Callaway Golf Company	ELY	Travel & Leisure	Negative Free Cash Flow	Negative Free Cash Flow	Negative Free Cash Flow	Negative Free Cash Flow	-$0.21	-4%	-225%	-4%	0.60%
Callidus Software	CALD	Software	$0.08	$0.15	$0.23	$0.45	$0.01	1%	94%	1%	0.00%
Callon Petroleum	CPE	Oil & Gas	Negative Free Cash Flow	Negative Free Cash Flow	Negative Free Cash Flow	Negative Free Cash Flow	-$1.86	-19%	270%	-19%	0.00%
Cal-Maine Foods	CALM	Consumer Goods	$9.90	$19.80	$29.70	$59.40	$1.32	5%	46%	2%	0.60%
Calpine Corp	CPN	Utilities	Negative Free Cash Flow	Negative Free Cash Flow	Negative Free Cash Flow	Negative Free Cash Flow	-$0.21	-1%	118%	-1%	0.00%
Cambrex Corporation	CBM	Biotech	Negative Free Cash Flow	Negative Free Cash Flow	Negative Free Cash Flow	Negative Free Cash Flow	-$0.41	-5%	141%	-5%	0.00%
Cameron International Corporation	CAM	Oil & Gas	$9.53	$19.05	$28.58	$57.15	$1.27	3%	59%	3%	0.00%
Campbell Soup	CPB	Consumer Goods	$21.90	$43.80	$65.70	$131.40	$2.92	24%	31%	16%	3.10%
Cantel Medical Corporation	CMN	Medical	$9.45	$18.90	$28.35	$56.70	$1.26	12%	11%	11%	0.20%
Capella Education Company	CPLA	Education	$37.95	$75.90	$113.85	$227.70	$5.06	28%	31%	28%	0.00%

NAME	TICKER	INDUSTRY	2014 BUY PRICE OPINION	2014 HOLD PRICE OPINION	2014 SELL PRICE OPINION	2014 SHORT PRICE OPINION	2014 MYCROFT FREE CASH FLOW PER SHARE ESTIMATE	2014 MYCROFT FREE CASH FLOW RETURN ON TOTAL CAPITAL ESTIMATE (FROIC) >15% = Great	2014 MYCROFT CAPFLOW ESTIMATE <33% = Great BUT NO NEGATIVE RESULTS	2014 MYCROFT MICHAELIS GROWTH RATE ESTIMATE >15% = Great	DIVIDEND YIELD
Step #1 = Look up the company's current stock market price on the day of analysis and compare it to our 2014 Buy, Hold, Sell & Short Price.											
Step #2 =Take the company's current market price; divide it by the "2014 Mycroft Free Cash Flow Per Share estimate." This gives the "Price to Free Cash Flow."											
All results below are based on the 2014 year end estimates using the "2014 Mycroft Michaelis Growth Rate" and are good until December 31, 2014.											
Capital Senior Living Corporation	CSU	Health Care	$8.25	$16.50	$24.75	$49.50	$1.10	7%	28%	7%	0.00%
Capstone Turbine Corporation	CPST	Computers	Negative Free Cash Flow	Negative Free Cash Flow	Negative Free Cash Flow	Negative Free Cash Flow	-$0.09	-76%	-5%	-76%	0.00%
Carbo Ceramics	CRR	Oil & Gas	$25.58	$51.15	$76.73	$153.45	$3.41	10%	44%	8%	1.20%
Carbonite Inc	CARB	Business Services	$2.03	$4.05	$6.08	$12.15	$0.27	56%	70%	56%	0.00%
Cardica, Inc.	CRDC	Medical	Negative Free Cash Flow	Negative Free Cash Flow	Negative Free Cash Flow	Negative Free Cash Flow	-$0.32	-94%	-15%	-94%	0.00%
Cardinal Health	CAH	Medical	$39.15	$78.30	$117.45	$234.90	$5.22	18%	11%	16%	2.20%
CardioNet, Inc.	BEAT	Health Care	$0.90	$1.80	$2.70	$5.40	$0.12	4%	69%	4%	0.00%
Cardiovascular Systems, Inc.	CSII	Medical	Negative Free Cash Flow	Negative Free Cash Flow	Negative Free Cash Flow	Negative Free Cash Flow	-$0.57	-17%	-13%	-17%	0.00%
Cardtronics, Inc.	CATM	Business Services	$18.15	$36.30	$54.45	$108.90	$2.42	16%	42%	16%	0.00%
Career Education Corporation	CECO	Education	Negative Free Cash Flow	Negative Free Cash Flow	Negative Free Cash Flow	Negative Free Cash Flow	-$1.91	-23%	-28%	-23%	0.00%
CareFusion	CFN	Medical	$19.20	$38.40	$57.60	$115.20	$2.56	8%	17%	8%	0.00%

NAME	TICKER	INDUSTRY	2014 BUY PRICE OPINION	2014 HOLD PRICE OPINION	2014 SELL PRICE OPINION	2014 SHORT PRICE OPINION	2014 MYCROFT FREE CASH FLOW PER SHARE ESTIMATE	2014 MYCROFT FREE CASH FLOW RETURN ON TOTAL CAPITAL ESTIMATE (FROIC) >15% = Great	2014 MYCROFT CAPFLOW ESTIMATE <33% = Great BUT NO NEGATIVE RESULTS	2014 MYCROFT MICHAELIS GROWTH RATE ESTIMATE >15% = Great	DIVIDEND YIELD
Step #1 = Look up the company's current stock market price on the day of analysis and compare it to our 2014 Buy, Hold, Sell & Short Price.											
Step #2 =Take the company's current market price; divide it by the "2014 Mycroft Free Cash Flow Per Share estimate." This gives the "Price to Free Cash Flow."											
All results below are based on the 2014 year end estimates using the "2014 Mycroft Michaelis Growth Rate" and are good until December 31, 2014.											
Carlisle Companies, Inc.	CSL	Autos	$42.83	$85.65	$128.48	$256.95	$5.71	14%	29%	13%	1.30%
CarMax, Inc.	KMX	Autos	Negative Free Cash Flow	Negative Free Cash Flow	Negative Free Cash Flow	Negative Free Cash Flow	-$4.34	-13%	-31%	-13%	0.00%
Carmike Cinemas	CKEC	Entertainment	$6.90	$13.80	$20.70	$41.40	$0.92	6%	66%	6%	0.00%
Carnival Corporation	CCL	Travel & Leisure	$12.75	$25.50	$38.25	$76.50	$1.70	4%	58%	4%	3.10%
Carpenter Technology Corporation	CRS	Industrial	Negative Free Cash Flow	Negative Free Cash Flow	Negative Free Cash Flow	Negative Free Cash Flow	-$2.30	-8%	157%	-9%	1.27%
Carriage Services	CSV	Services	$10.80	$21.60	$32.40	$64.80	$1.44	6%	32%	6%	0.50%
Carrizo Oil & Gas	CRZO	Oil & Gas	Negative Free Cash Flow	Negative Free Cash Flow	Negative Free Cash Flow	Negative Free Cash Flow	-$9.90	-27%	226%	-27%	0.00%
Carrols Restaurant Group	TAST	Restaurants	Negative Free Cash Flow	Negative Free Cash Flow	Negative Free Cash Flow	Negative Free Cash Flow	-$1.90	-19%	1937%	-19%	0.00%
Carter's, Inc.	CRI	Apparel & Furniture	$14.03	$28.05	$42.08	$84.15	$1.87	9%	60%	6%	0.87%
Cascade Microtech, Inc.	CSCD	Semiconductors	$5.10	$10.20	$15.30	$30.60	$0.68	13%	19%	13%	0.00%
Casella Waste Systems, Inc.	CWST	Waste Management	$0.38	$0.75	$1.13	$2.25	$0.05	16%	97%	16%	0.00%

NAME	TICKER	INDUSTRY	2014 BUY PRICE OPINION	2014 HOLD PRICE OPINION	2014 SELL PRICE OPINION	2014 SHORT PRICE OPINION	2014 MYCROFT FREE CASH FLOW PER SHARE ESTIMATE	2014 MYCROFT FREE CASH FLOW RETURN ON TOTAL CAPITAL ESTIMATE (FROIC) >15% = Great	2014 MYCROFT CAPFLOW ESTIMATE <33% = Great BUT NO NEGATIVE RESULTS	2014 MYCROFT MICHAELIS GROWTH RATE ESTIMATE >15% = Great	DIVIDEND YIELD
Step #1 = Look up the company's current stock market price on the day of analysis and compare it to our 2014 Buy, Hold, Sell & Short Price.											
Step #2 =Take the company's current market price; divide it by the "2014 Mycroft Free Cash Flow Per Share estimate." This gives the "Price to Free Cash Flow."											
All results below are based on the 2014 year end estimates using the "2014 Mycroft Michaelis Growth Rate" and are good until December 31, 2014.											
Casey's General Stores, Inc.	CASY	Retail	$2.33	$4.65	$6.98	$13.95	$0.31	1%	96%	0%	1.00%
Cass Information Systems, Inc.	CASS	Business Services	$12.08	$24.15	$36.23	$72.45	$1.61	10%	21%	7%	1.40%
Catalyst Pharmaceutical Partners, Inc.	CPRX	Drugs	Negative Free Cash Flow	Negative Free Cash Flow	Negative Free Cash Flow	Negative Free Cash Flow	-$0.15	-69%	-1%	-69%	0.00%
Catamaran Corp	CTRX	Health Care	$11.55	$23.10	$34.65	$69.30	$1.54	6%	25%	6%	0.00%
Caterpillar Inc	CAT	Agriculture	$35.25	$70.50	$105.75	$211.50	$4.70	6%	63%	6%	2.77%
Cato Corporation Class A	CATO	Retail	$14.33	$28.65	$42.98	$85.95	$1.91	13%	42%	12%	0.74%
Cavco Industries, Inc.	CVCO	Homebuilding	$24.45	$48.90	$73.35	$146.70	$3.26	10%	3%	10%	0.00%
Cavium Inc	CAVM	Semiconductors	$3.68	$7.35	$11.03	$22.05	$0.49	9%	41%	9%	0.00%
Cbeyond Inc	CBEY	Communication	$4.80	$9.60	$14.40	$28.80	$0.64	10%	77%	10%	0.00%
CBIZ, Inc.	CBZ	Business Services	$5.63	$11.25	$16.88	$33.75	$0.75	6%	15%	6%	0.00%
CBRE Group Inc	CBG	Real Estate	$10.65	$21.30	$31.95	$63.90	$1.42	10%	26%	10%	0.00%

NAME	TICKER	INDUSTRY	2014 BUY PRICE OPINION	2014 HOLD PRICE OPINION	2014 SELL PRICE OPINION	2014 SHORT PRICE OPINION	2014 MYCROFT FREE CASH FLOW PER SHARE ESTIMATE	2014 MYCROFT FREE CASH FLOW RETURN ON TOTAL CAPITAL ESTIMATE (FROIC) >15% = Great	2014 MYCROFT CAPFLOW ESTIMATE <33% = Great BUT NO NEGATIVE RESULTS	2014 MYCROFT MICHAELIS GROWTH RATE ESTIMATE >15% = Great	DIVIDEND YIELD

Step #1 = Look up the company's current stock market price on the day of analysis and compare it to our 2014 Buy, Hold, Sell & Short Price.

Step #2 =Take the company's current market price; divide it by the "2014 Mycroft Free Cash Flow Per Share estimate." This gives the "Price to Free Cash Flow."

All results below are based on the 2014 year end estimates using the "2014 Mycroft Michaelis Growth Rate" and are good until December 31, 2014.

NAME	TICKER	INDUSTRY	BUY	HOLD	SELL	SHORT	FCF/SHARE	FROIC	CAPFLOW	GROWTH	DIV YIELD
CBS Corporation Class B	CBS	Entertainment	$18.08	$36.15	$54.23	$108.45	$2.41	9%	16%	8%	0.89%
CCA Industries, Inc.	CAW	Consumer Goods	Negative Free Cash Flow	Negative Free Cash Flow	Negative Free Cash Flow	Negative Free Cash Flow	-$0.27	-8%	-248%	-9%	8.10%
CDI Corporation	CDI	Services	$11.33	$22.65	$33.98	$67.95	$1.51	10%	19%	10%	3.54%
CEC Entertainment, Inc.	CEC	Restaurants	$32.85	$65.70	$98.55	$197.10	$4.38	13%	54%	12%	2.27%
CECO Environmental	CECE	Industrial	$7.88	$15.75	$23.63	$47.25	$1.05	19%	2%	17%	1.52%
Celadon Group, Inc.	CGI	Transportation	Negative Free Cash Flow	Negative Free Cash Flow	Negative Free Cash Flow	Negative Free Cash Flow	-$4.84	-51%	228%	-51%	0.42%
Celanese Corporation	CE	Chemicals	$17.40	$34.80	$52.20	$104.40	$2.32	7%	50%	6%	1.45%
Celgene Corporation	CELG	Biotech	$47.18	$94.35	$141.53	$283.05	$6.29	30%	8%	30%	0.00%
Cell Therapeutics, Inc.	CTIC	Biotech	Negative Free Cash Flow	Negative Free Cash Flow	Negative Free Cash Flow	Negative Free Cash Flow	-$0.38	-779%	-5%	-779%	0.00%
Celldex Therapeutics, Inc.	CLDX	Biotech	Negative Free Cash Flow	Negative Free Cash Flow	Negative Free Cash Flow	Negative Free Cash Flow	-$0.75	-33%	-2%	-33%	0.00%
Celsion Corporation	CLSN	Biotech	Negative Free Cash Flow	Negative Free Cash Flow	Negative Free Cash Flow	Negative Free Cash Flow	-$0.25	-41%	-2%	-41%	0.00%

NAME	TICKER	INDUSTRY	2014 BUY PRICE OPINION	2014 HOLD PRICE OPINION	2014 SELL PRICE OPINION	2014 SHORT PRICE OPINION	2014 MYCROFT FREE CASH FLOW PER SHARE ESTIMATE	2014 MYCROFT FREE CASH FLOW RETURN ON TOTAL CAPITAL ESTIMATE (FROIC) >15% = Great	2014 MYCROFT CAPFLOW ESTIMATE <33% = Great BUT NO NEGATIVE RESULTS	2014 MYCROFT MICHAELIS GROWTH RATE ESTIMATE >15% = Great	DIVIDEND YIELD
Step #1 = Look up the company's current stock market price on the day of analysis and compare it to our 2014 Buy, Hold, Sell & Short Price.											
Step #2 =Take the company's current market price; divide it by the "2014 Mycroft Free Cash Flow Per Share estimate." This gives the "Price to Free Cash Flow."											
All results below are based on the 2014 year end estimates using the "2014 Mycroft Michaelis Growth Rate" and are good until December 31, 2014.											
Cempra Inc	CEMP	Biotech	Negative Free Cash Flow	Negative Free Cash Flow	Negative Free Cash Flow	Negative Free Cash Flow	-$0.56	-17%	0%	-17%	0.00%
Centene Corporation	CNC	Health Care	$52.13	$104.25	$156.38	$312.75	$6.95	21%	15%	21%	0.00%
CenterPoint Energy Inc	CNP	Utilities	$8.18	$16.35	$24.53	$49.05	$1.09	4%	74%	4%	3.59%
Central European Media Enterprises	CETV	Entertainment	Negative Free Cash Flow	Negative Free Cash Flow	Negative Free Cash Flow	Negative Free Cash Flow	-$0.43	-3%	-172%	-3%	0.00%
Central Garden & Pet Company	CENTA	Consumer Goods	Negative Free Cash Flow	Negative Free Cash Flow	Negative Free Cash Flow	Negative Free Cash Flow	-$1.48	-8%	-80%	-8%	0.00%
Century Aluminum Company	CENX	Commodities	$3.90	$7.80	$11.70	$23.40	$0.52	4%	28%	4%	0.00%
Century Casinos, Inc.	CNTY	Travel & Leisure	$2.10	$4.20	$6.30	$12.60	$0.28	5%	35%	5%	0.00%
CenturyLink Inc	CTL	Communication	$43.05	$86.10	$129.15	$258.30	$5.74	8%	49%	11%	6.90%
Cenveo Inc	CVO	Business Services	$2.93	$5.85	$8.78	$17.55	$0.39	3%	51%	3%	0.00%
Cepheid	CPHD	Medical	Negative Free Cash Flow	Negative Free Cash Flow	Negative Free Cash Flow	Negative Free Cash Flow	-$0.25	-6%	195%	-6%	0.00%
Cerner Corporation	CERN	Software	$7.95	$15.90	$23.85	$47.70	$1.06	11%	56%	11%	0.00%

NAME	TICKER	INDUSTRY	2014 BUY PRICE OPINION	2014 HOLD PRICE OPINION	2014 SELL PRICE OPINION	2014 SHORT PRICE OPINION	2014 MYCROFT FREE CASH FLOW PER SHARE ESTIMATE	2014 MYCROFT FREE CASH FLOW RETURN ON TOTAL CAPITAL ESTIMATE (FROIC) >15% = Great	2014 MYCROFT CAPFLOW ESTIMATE <33% = Great BUT NO NEGATIVE RESULTS	2014 MYCROFT MICHAELIS GROWTH RATE ESTIMATE >15% = Great	DIVIDEND YIELD
Step #1 = Look up the company's current stock market price on the day of analysis and compare it to our 2014 Buy, Hold, Sell & Short Price.											
Step #2 =Take the company's current market price; divide it by the "2014 Mycroft Free Cash Flow Per Share estimate." This gives the "Price to Free Cash Flow."											
All results below are based on the 2014 year end estimates using the "2014 Mycroft Michaelis Growth Rate" and are good until December 31, 2014.											
Cerus Corporation	CERS	Biotech	Negative Free Cash Flow	Negative Free Cash Flow	Negative Free Cash Flow	Negative Free Cash Flow	-$0.27	-32%	-1%	-32%	0.00%
CEVA, Inc.	CEVA	Semiconductors	$3.23	$6.45	$9.68	$19.35	$0.43	5%	11%	5%	0.00%
CF Industries Holdings Inc	CF	Agriculture	$171.98	$343.95	$515.93	$1,031.85	$22.93	17%	41%	17%	0.81%
CH Robinson Worldwide, Inc.	CHRW	Transportation	$18.90	$37.80	$56.70	$113.40	$2.52	24%	12%	11%	2.36%
ChannelAdvisor	ECOM	Software	Negative Free Cash Flow	Negative Free Cash Flow	Negative Free Cash Flow	Negative Free Cash Flow	-$0.11	-2%	-1105%	-2%	0.00%
Charles & Colvard	CTHR	Retail	Negative Free Cash Flow	Negative Free Cash Flow	Negative Free Cash Flow	Negative Free Cash Flow	-$0.09	-3%	-85%	-3%	0.00%
Charles River Laboratories International	CRL	Medical	$31.35	$62.70	$94.05	$188.10	$4.18	25%	20%	25%	0.00%
Chart Industries, Inc.	GTLS	Industrial	$12.15	$24.30	$36.45	$72.90	$1.62	5%	55%	5%	0.00%
Charter Communications	CHTR	Communication	$15.68	$31.35	$47.03	$94.05	$2.09	2%	89%	2%	0.00%
Chase Corporation	CCF	Industrial	$15.08	$30.15	$45.23	$90.45	$2.01	15%	19%	13%	1.34%
Checkpoint Systems	CKP	Rentals	$12.53	$25.05	$37.58	$75.15	$1.67	13%	11%	13%	0.00%

NAME	TICKER	INDUSTRY	2014 BUY PRICE OPINION	2014 HOLD PRICE OPINION	2014 SELL PRICE OPINION	2014 SHORT PRICE OPINION	2014 MYCROFT FREE CASH FLOW PER SHARE ESTIMATE	2014 MYCROFT FREE CASH FLOW RETURN ON TOTAL CAPITAL ESTIMATE (FROIC) >15% = Great	2014 MYCROFT CAPFLOW ESTIMATE <33% = Great BUT NO NEGATIVE RESULTS	2014 MYCROFT MICHAELIS GROWTH RATE ESTIMATE >15% = Great	DIVIDEND YIELD
Step #1 = Look up the company's current stock market price on the day of analysis and compare it to our 2014 Buy, Hold, Sell & Short Price.										
Step #2 =Take the company's current market price; divide it by the "2014 Mycroft Free Cash Flow Per Share estimate." This gives the "Price to Free Cash Flow."										
All results below are based on the 2014 year end estimates using the "2014 Mycroft Michaelis Growth Rate" and are good until December 31, 2014.										
Cheesecake Factory, Inc.	CAKE	Restaurants	$19.13	$38.25	$57.38	$114.75	$2.55	19%	43%	15%	1.31%
Chefs Warehouse Holdings LLC	CHEF	Retail	$6.98	$13.95	$20.93	$41.85	$0.93	15%	21%	15%	0.00%
Chelsea Therapeutics International, Ltd.	CHTP	Biotech	Negative Free Cash Flow	Negative Free Cash Flow	Negative Free Cash Flow	Negative Free Cash Flow	-$0.28	-96%	0%	-96%	0.00%
Chemed Corporation	CHE	Health Care	$63.68	$127.35	$191.03	$382.05	$8.49	20%	18%	19%	1.21%
Chemocentryx Inc	CCXI	Biotech	Negative Free Cash Flow	Negative Free Cash Flow	Negative Free Cash Flow	Negative Free Cash Flow	-$0.84	-22%	-1%	-22%	0.00%
Chemtura Corporation	CHMT	Chemicals	Negative Free Cash Flow	Negative Free Cash Flow	Negative Free Cash Flow	Negative Free Cash Flow	-$0.19	-1%	112%	-1%	0.00%
Cheniere Energy Inc	LNG	Oil & Gas	Negative Free Cash Flow	Negative Free Cash Flow	Negative Free Cash Flow	Negative Free Cash Flow	-$9.97	-93%	-6766%	-93%	0.00%
Cherokee Inc.	CHKE	Retail	Negative Free Cash Flow	Negative Free Cash Flow	Negative Free Cash Flow	Negative Free Cash Flow	-$1.19	-69%	212%	-89%	3.32%
Chesapeake Energy Corp	CHK	Oil & Gas	Negative Free Cash Flow	Negative Free Cash Flow	Negative Free Cash Flow	Negative Free Cash Flow	-$8.15	-22%	267%	-22%	1.33%
Chesapeake Utilities Corp	CPK	Utilities	Negative Free Cash Flow	Negative Free Cash Flow	Negative Free Cash Flow	Negative Free Cash Flow	-$2.11	-5%	134%	-6%	2.98%
Chevron Corp	CVX	Oil & Gas	$0.00	$0.00	$0.00	$0.00	$0.00	0%	100%	-2%	3.25%

NAME	TICKER	INDUSTRY	2014 BUY PRICE OPINION	2014 HOLD PRICE OPINION	2014 SELL PRICE OPINION	2014 SHORT PRICE OPINION	2014 MYCROFT FREE CASH FLOW PER SHARE ESTIMATE	2014 MYCROFT FREE CASH FLOW RETURN ON TOTAL CAPITAL ESTIMATE (FROIC) >15% = Great	2014 MYCROFT CAPFLOW ESTIMATE <33% = Great BUT NO NEGATIVE RESULTS	2014 MYCROFT MICHAELIS GROWTH RATE ESTIMATE >15% = Great	DIVIDEND YIELD
Step #1 = Look up the company's current stock market price on the day of analysis and compare it to our 2014 Buy, Hold, Sell & Short Price.											
Step #2 =Take the company's current market price; divide it by the "2014 Mycroft Free Cash Flow Per Share estimate." This gives the "Price to Free Cash Flow."											
All results below are based on the 2014 year end estimates using the "2014 Mycroft Michaelis Growth Rate" and are good until December 31, 2014.											
Chicago Bridge & Iron Company	CBI	Engineering	Negative Free Cash Flow	Negative Free Cash Flow	Negative Free Cash Flow	Negative Free Cash Flow	-$2.41	-13%	-104%	-14%	0.32%
Chicago Rivet & Machine Co.	CVR	Industrial	$6.00	$12.00	$18.00	$36.00	$0.80	3%	76%	3%	2.13%
Chico's FAS, Inc.	CHS	Retail	$6.60	$13.20	$19.80	$39.60	$0.88	12%	55%	10%	1.35%
Children's Place Retail Stores, Inc.	PLCE	Retail	$50.70	$101.40	$152.10	$304.20	$6.76	22%	41%	22%	0.00%
Chimerix Inc	CMRX	Biotech	Negative Free Cash Flow	Negative Free Cash Flow	Negative Free Cash Flow	Negative Free Cash Flow	-$0.24	-5%	-3%	-5%	0.00%
Chindex International, Inc.	CHDX	Medical	Negative Free Cash Flow	Negative Free Cash Flow	Negative Free Cash Flow	Negative Free Cash Flow	-$1.11	-11%	271%	-11%	0.00%
Chipotle Mexican Grill, Inc.	CMG	Restaurants	$99.53	$199.05	$298.58	$597.15	$13.27	24%	36%	24%	0.00%
Chiquita Brands International	CQB	Consumer Goods	$3.60	$7.20	$10.80	$21.60	$0.48	2%	70%	2%	0.00%
Choice Hotels International, Inc.	CHH	Travel & Leisure	$30.98	$61.95	$92.93	$185.85	$4.13	106%	10%	74%	1.83%
Christopher & Banks Corporation	CBK	Retail	$1.58	$3.15	$4.73	$9.45	$0.21	9%	30%	9%	0.00%
Church & Dwight Company, Inc.	CHD	Consumer Goods	$27.15	$54.30	$81.45	$162.90	$3.62	18%	11%	14%	1.90%

NAME	TICKER	INDUSTRY	2014 BUY PRICE OPINION	2014 HOLD PRICE OPINION	2014 SELL PRICE OPINION	2014 SHORT PRICE OPINION	2014 MYCROFT FREE CASH FLOW PER SHARE ESTIMATE	2014 MYCROFT FREE CASH FLOW RETURN ON TOTAL CAPITAL ESTIMATE (FROIC) >15% = Great	2014 MYCROFT CAPFLOW ESTIMATE <33% = Great BUT NO NEGATIVE RESULTS	2014 MYCROFT MICHAELIS GROWTH RATE ESTIMATE >15% = Great	DIVIDEND YIELD
Step #1 = Look up the company's current stock market price on the day of analysis and compare it to our 2014 Buy, Hold, Sell & Short Price.											
Step #2 =Take the company's current market price; divide it by the "2014 Mycroft Free Cash Flow Per Share estimate." This gives the "Price to Free Cash Flow."											
All results below are based on the 2014 year end estimates using the "2014 Mycroft Michaelis Growth Rate" and are good until December 31, 2014.											
Churchill Downs Inc.	CHDN	Travel & Leisure	$44.55	$89.10	$133.65	$267.30	$5.94	12%	36%	12%	0.86%
Chuy's Holdings Inc	CHUY	Restaurants	Negative Free Cash Flow	Negative Free Cash Flow	Negative Free Cash Flow	Negative Free Cash Flow	-$0.04	0%	103%	0%	0.00%
ChyronHego Corp	CHYR	Software	Negative Free Cash Flow	Negative Free Cash Flow	Negative Free Cash Flow	Negative Free Cash Flow	-$0.04	-6%	-522%	-6%	0.00%
CIBER, Inc.	CBR	Software	$0.75	$1.50	$2.25	$4.50	$0.10	2%	20%	2%	0.00%
Ciena Corporation	CIEN	Communication	Negative Free Cash Flow	Negative Free Cash Flow	Negative Free Cash Flow	Negative Free Cash Flow	-$0.20	-2%	163%	-2%	0.00%
Cigna Corp	CI	Health Care	$0.00	$0.00	$0.00	$0.00	$0.00	0%	100%	0%	0.05%
Cimarex Energy Company	XEC	Oil & Gas	Negative Free Cash Flow	Negative Free Cash Flow	Negative Free Cash Flow	Negative Free Cash Flow	-$6.44	-13%	147%	-13%	0.63%
Cincinnati Bell Inc	CBB	Communication	Negative Free Cash Flow	Negative Free Cash Flow	Negative Free Cash Flow	Negative Free Cash Flow	-$0.82	-8%	197%	-8%	0.00%
Cinedigm Digital Cinema Corp.	CIDM	Business Services	$5.55	$11.10	$16.65	$33.30	$0.74	15%	21%	15%	0.00%
Cinemark Holdings Inc	CNK	Travel & Leisure	$7.80	$15.60	$23.40	$46.80	$1.04	4%	65%	3%	3.27%
Cintas Corporation	CTAS	Business Services	$24.00	$48.00	$72.00	$144.00	$3.20	11%	36%	10%	1.29%

NAME	TICKER	INDUSTRY	2014 BUY PRICE OPINION	2014 HOLD PRICE OPINION	2014 SELL PRICE OPINION	2014 SHORT PRICE OPINION	2014 MYCROFT FREE CASH FLOW PER SHARE ESTIMATE	2014 MYCROFT FREE CASH FLOW RETURN ON TOTAL CAPITAL ESTIMATE (FROIC) >15% = Great	2014 MYCROFT CAPFLOW ESTIMATE <33% = Great BUT NO NEGATIVE RESULTS	2014 MYCROFT MICHAELIS GROWTH RATE ESTIMATE >15% = Great	DIVIDEND YIELD
Step #1 = Look up the company's current stock market price on the day of analysis and compare it to our 2014 Buy, Hold, Sell & Short Price.											
Step #2 =Take the company's current market price; divide it by the "2014 Mycroft Free Cash Flow Per Share estimate." This gives the "Price to Free Cash Flow."											
All results below are based on the 2014 year end estimates using the "2014 Mycroft Michaelis Growth Rate" and are good until December 31, 2014.											
Circor International, Inc.	CIR	Industrial	$25.88	$51.75	$77.63	$155.25	$3.45	11%	23%	10%	0.25%
Cirrus Logic, Inc.	CRUS	Semiconductors	$24.45	$48.90	$73.35	$146.70	$3.26	28%	19%	28%	0.00%
Cisco Systems Inc	CSCO	Communication	$17.18	$34.35	$51.53	$103.05	$2.29	15%	9%	13%	2.82%
Citi Trends, Inc.	CTRN	Retail	$7.88	$15.75	$23.63	$47.25	$1.05	8%	39%	8%	0.00%
Citrix Systems, Inc.	CTXS	Software	$34.43	$68.85	$103.28	$206.55	$4.59	22%	18%	22%	0.00%
Clarcor Inc.	CLC	Industrial	$18.38	$36.75	$55.13	$110.25	$2.45	12%	24%	10%	0.96%
Clayton Williams Energy Inc.	CWEI	Oil & Gas	Negative Free Cash Flow	Negative Free Cash Flow	Negative Free Cash Flow	Negative Free Cash Flow	-$14.00	-16%	197%	-16%	0.00%
Clean Diesel Technologies, Inc.	CDTI	Industrial	Negative Free Cash Flow	Negative Free Cash Flow	Negative Free Cash Flow	Negative Free Cash Flow	-$0.21	-27%	-13%	-27%	0.00%
Clean Energy Fuels Corporation	CLNE	Oil & Gas	Negative Free Cash Flow	Negative Free Cash Flow	Negative Free Cash Flow	Negative Free Cash Flow	-$1.86	-30%	-1846%	-30%	0.00%
Clean Harbors, Inc.	CLH	Waste Management	$3.15	$6.30	$9.45	$18.90	$0.42	1%	91%	1%	0.00%
Clear Channel Outdoor Holdings	CCO	Advertising	$1.65	$3.30	$4.95	$9.90	$0.22	2%	74%	2%	0.00%

NAME	TICKER	INDUSTRY	2014 BUY PRICE OPINION	2014 HOLD PRICE OPINION	2014 SELL PRICE OPINION	2014 SHORT PRICE OPINION	2014 MYCROFT FREE CASH FLOW PER SHARE ESTIMATE	2014 MYCROFT FREE CASH FLOW RETURN ON TOTAL CAPITAL ESTIMATE (FROIC) >15% = Great	2014 MYCROFT CAPFLOW ESTIMATE <33% = Great BUT NO NEGATIVE RESULTS	2014 MYCROFT MICHAELIS GROWTH RATE ESTIMATE >15% = Great	DIVIDEND YIELD
Step #1 = Look up the company's current stock market price on the day of analysis and compare it to our 2014 Buy, Hold, Sell & Short Price.											
Step #2 =Take the company's current market price; divide it by the "2014 Mycroft Free Cash Flow Per Share estimate." This gives the "Price to Free Cash Flow."											
All results below are based on the 2014 year end estimates using the "2014 Mycroft Michaelis Growth Rate" and are good until December 31, 2014.											
Clearfield, Inc.	CLFD	Communication	$2.48	$4.95	$7.43	$14.85	$0.33	10%	21%	10%	0.00%
ClearOne Inc	CLRO	Communication	$38.85	$77.70	$116.55	$233.10	$5.18	47%	3%	47%	0.00%
Clearwater Paper Corp	CLW	Forest Products	Negative Free Cash Flow	Negative Free Cash Flow	Negative Free Cash Flow	Negative Free Cash Flow	-$0.09	0%	101%	0%	0.00%
Cleco Corporation	CNL	Utilities	$8.55	$17.10	$25.65	$51.30	$1.14	2%	77%	3%	3.24%
Cliffs Natural Resources Inc.	CLF	Commodities	Negative Free Cash Flow	Negative Free Cash Flow	Negative Free Cash Flow	Negative Free Cash Flow	-$1.00	-2%	119%	0%	2.52%
Clorox Company	CLX	Consumer Goods	$38.63	$77.25	$115.88	$231.75	$5.15	34%	25%	16%	3.39%
Cloud Peak Energy Inc	CLD	Coal	$20.93	$41.85	$62.78	$125.55	$2.79	10%	27%	10%	0.00%
Clovis Oncology Inc	CLVS	Biotech	Negative Free Cash Flow	Negative Free Cash Flow	Negative Free Cash Flow	Negative Free Cash Flow	-$2.17	-18%	0%	-18%	0.00%
CMS Energy Corp	CMS	Utilities	$4.65	$9.30	$13.95	$27.90	$0.62	2%	88%	3%	3.90%
CNH Global NV	CNH	Agriculture	$6.38	$12.75	$19.13	$38.25	$0.85	1%	85%	1%	0.00%
Coach, Inc.	COH	Retail	$42.23	$84.45	$126.68	$253.35	$5.63	49%	17%	35%	2.51%

NAME	TICKER	INDUSTRY	2014 BUY PRICE OPINION	2014 HOLD PRICE OPINION	2014 SELL PRICE OPINION	2014 SHORT PRICE OPINION	2014 MYCROFT FREE CASH FLOW PER SHARE ESTIMATE	2014 MYCROFT FREE CASH FLOW RETURN ON TOTAL CAPITAL ESTIMATE (FROIC) >15% = Great	2014 MYCROFT CAPFLOW ESTIMATE <33% = Great BUT NO NEGATIVE RESULTS	2014 MYCROFT MICHAELIS GROWTH RATE ESTIMATE >15% = Great	DIVIDEND YIELD
Step #1 = Look up the company's current stock market price on the day of analysis and compare it to our 2014 Buy, Hold, Sell & Short Price.											
Step #2 =Take the company's current market price; divide it by the "2014 Mycroft Free Cash Flow Per Share estimate." This gives the "Price to Free Cash Flow."											
All results below are based on the 2014 year end estimates using the "2014 Mycroft Michaelis Growth Rate" and are good until December 31, 2014.											
Cobalt International Energy, Inc.	CIE	Oil & Gas	Negative Free Cash Flow	Negative Free Cash Flow	Negative Free Cash Flow	Negative Free Cash Flow	-$1.82	-30%	-150%	-30%	0.00%
Cobra Electronics Corporation	COBR	Computers	Negative Free Cash Flow	Negative Free Cash Flow	Negative Free Cash Flow	Negative Free Cash Flow	-$0.37	-7%	-170%	-7%	0.00%
Coca-Cola Bottling Company Consolidated	COKE	Beverages	$26.03	$52.05	$78.08	$156.15	$3.47	6%	67%	5%	1.56%
Coca-Cola Co	KO	Beverages	$14.55	$29.10	$43.65	$87.30	$1.94	16%	24%	9%	2.89%
Coca-Cola Enterprises Inc	CCE	Beverages	$15.83	$31.65	$47.48	$94.95	$2.11	11%	40%	8%	2.02%
Codexis, Inc.	CDXS	Biotech	Negative Free Cash Flow	Negative Free Cash Flow	Negative Free Cash Flow	Negative Free Cash Flow	-$0.53	-34%	-5%	-34%	0.00%
Coeur Mining Inc	CDE	Commodities	$7.43	$14.85	$22.28	$44.55	$0.99	4%	56%	4%	0.00%
Coffee Holding Company, Inc.	JVA	Consumer Goods	$8.63	$17.25	$25.88	$51.75	$1.15	25%	12%	23%	3.77%
Cogent Communications Group, Inc.	CCOI	Communication	$5.78	$11.55	$17.33	$34.65	$0.77	9%	59%	4%	1.80%
Cognex Corporation	CGNX	Computers	$17.63	$35.25	$52.88	$105.75	$2.35	15%	9%	12%	0.68%
Cognizant Technology Solutions	CTSH	Software	$25.13	$50.25	$75.38	$150.75	$3.35	16%	27%	16%	0.00%

NAME	TICKER	INDUSTRY	2014 BUY PRICE OPINION	2014 HOLD PRICE OPINION	2014 SELL PRICE OPINION	2014 SHORT PRICE OPINION	2014 MYCROFT FREE CASH FLOW PER SHARE ESTIMATE	2014 MYCROFT FREE CASH FLOW RETURN ON TOTAL CAPITAL ESTIMATE (FROIC) >15% = Great	2014 MYCROFT CAPFLOW ESTIMATE <33% = Great BUT NO NEGATIVE RESULTS	2014 MYCROFT MICHAELIS GROWTH RATE ESTIMATE >15% = Great	DIVIDEND YIELD
Step #1 = Look up the company's current stock market price on the day of analysis and compare it to our 2014 Buy, Hold, Sell & Short Price.											
Step #2 =Take the company's current market price; divide it by the "2014 Mycroft Free Cash Flow Per Share estimate." This gives the "Price to Free Cash Flow."											
All results below are based on the 2014 year end estimates using the "2014 Mycroft Michaelis Growth Rate" and are good until December 31, 2014.											
Coherent, Inc.	COHR	Computers	$22.50	$45.00	$67.50	$135.00	$3.00	9%	24%	9%	0.00%
Cohu, Inc.	COHU	Semiconductors	$1.43	$2.85	$4.28	$8.55	$0.19	2%	47%	2%	2.29%
Coldwater Creek	CWTR	Retail	Negative Free Cash Flow	Negative Free Cash Flow	Negative Free Cash Flow	Negative Free Cash Flow	-$1.82	-304%	-35%	-304%	0.00%
Coleman Cable, Inc.	CCIX	Industrial	$17.48	$34.95	$52.43	$104.85	$2.33	9%	28%	9%	0.83%
Colfax Corporation	CFX	Industrial	$15.75	$31.50	$47.25	$94.50	$2.10	5%	28%	5%	0.00%
Colgate-Palmolive Company	CL	Consumer Goods	$27.15	$54.30	$81.45	$162.90	$3.62	41%	19%	24%	2.32%
Collectors Universe, Inc.	CLCT	Business Services	$6.60	$13.20	$19.80	$39.60	$0.88	39%	12%	-6%	8.90%
Columbia Laboratories, Inc.	CBRX	Drugs	$7.35	$14.70	$22.05	$44.10	$0.98	24%	1%	24%	0.00%
Columbia Sportswear Company	COLM	Apparel & Furniture	$52.13	$104.25	$156.38	$312.75	$6.95	18%	23%	17%	1.49%
Columbus McKinnon Corporation	CMCO	Agriculture	$11.25	$22.50	$33.75	$67.50	$1.50	7%	38%	7%	0.00%
CombiMatrix Corporation	CBMX	Medical	Negative Free Cash Flow	Negative Free Cash Flow	Negative Free Cash Flow	Negative Free Cash Flow	-$1.21	-101%	-2%	-101%	0.00%

NAME	TICKER	INDUSTRY	2014 BUY PRICE OPINION	2014 HOLD PRICE OPINION	2014 SELL PRICE OPINION	2014 SHORT PRICE OPINION	2014 MYCROFT FREE CASH FLOW PER SHARE ESTIMATE	2014 MYCROFT FREE CASH FLOW RETURN ON TOTAL CAPITAL ESTIMATE (FROIC) >15% = Great	2014 MYCROFT CAPFLOW ESTIMATE <33% = Great BUT NO NEGATIVE RESULTS	2014 MYCROFT MICHAELIS GROWTH RATE ESTIMATE >15% = Great	DIVIDEND YIELD
Step #1 = Look up the company's current stock market price on the day of analysis and compare it to our 2014 Buy, Hold, Sell & Short Price.										
Step #2 =Take the company's current market price; divide it by the "2014 Mycroft Free Cash Flow Per Share estimate." This gives the "Price to Free Cash Flow."										
All results below are based on the 2014 year end estimates using the "2014 Mycroft Michaelis Growth Rate" and are good until December 31, 2014.										
Comcast Corp Class A	CMCSA	Communication	$23.70	$47.40	$71.10	$142.20	$3.16	9%	48%	8%	1.82%
Comfort Systems USA, Inc.	FIX	Engineering	$5.93	$11.85	$17.78	$35.55	$0.79	9%	31%	8%	1.38%
Command Security Corporation	MOC	Rentals	Negative Free Cash Flow	Negative Free Cash Flow	Negative Free Cash Flow	Negative Free Cash Flow	-$0.49	-26%	-13%	-26%	0.00%
Commercial Metals Company	CMC	Steel	Negative Free Cash Flow	Negative Free Cash Flow	Negative Free Cash Flow	Negative Free Cash Flow	-$0.13	-1%	120%	0%	2.97%
Commercial Vehicle Group, Inc.	CVGI	Autos	$0.60	$1.20	$1.80	$3.60	$0.08	1%	89%	1%	0.00%
Communications Systems, Inc.	JCS	Communication	Negative Free Cash Flow	Negative Free Cash Flow	Negative Free Cash Flow	Negative Free Cash Flow	-$0.81	-7%	-64%	-8%	6.10%
Community Health Systems Inc	CYH	Health Care	$35.18	$70.35	$105.53	$211.05	$4.69	4%	61%	4%	0.00%
CommVault Systems, Inc.	CVLT	Software	$23.10	$46.20	$69.30	$138.60	$3.08	29%	6%	29%	0.00%
Compass Minerals International, Inc.	CMP	Commodities	$21.08	$42.15	$63.23	$126.45	$2.81	9%	58%	5%	2.89%
Computer Programs and Systems, Inc.	CPSI	Software	$15.30	$30.60	$45.90	$91.80	$2.04	35%	20%	3%	3.50%
Computer Sciences Corporation	CSC	Software	$26.10	$52.20	$78.30	$156.60	$3.48	10%	58%	9%	1.57%

NAME	TICKER	INDUSTRY	2014 BUY PRICE OPINION	2014 HOLD PRICE OPINION	2014 SELL PRICE OPINION	2014 SHORT PRICE OPINION	2014 MYCROFT FREE CASH FLOW PER SHARE ESTIMATE	2014 MYCROFT FREE CASH FLOW RETURN ON TOTAL CAPITAL ESTIMATE (FROIC) >15% = Great	2014 MYCROFT CAPFLOW ESTIMATE <33% = Great BUT NO NEGATIVE RESULTS	2014 MYCROFT MICHAELIS GROWTH RATE ESTIMATE >15% = Great	DIVIDEND YIELD
Step #1 = Look up the company's current stock market price on the day of analysis and compare it to our 2014 Buy, Hold, Sell & Short Price.												
Step #2 = Take the company's current market price; divide it by the "2014 Mycroft Free Cash Flow Per Share estimate." This gives the "Price to Free Cash Flow."												
All results below are based on the 2014 year end estimates using the "2014 Mycroft Michaelis Growth Rate" and are good until December 31, 2014.												
Computer Task Group, Inc.	CTG	Software	$5.33	$10.65	$15.98	$31.95	$0.71	11%	20%	9%	1.12%
Compuware Corporation	CPWR	Software	$3.23	$6.45	$9.68	$19.35	$0.43	9%	37%	3%	4.60%
comScore, Inc.	SCOR	Business Services	$13.35	$26.70	$40.05	$80.10	$1.78	25%	12%	25%	0.00%
Comstock Holding Co. Inc	CHCI	Real Estate	Negative Free Cash Flow	Negative Free Cash Flow	Negative Free Cash Flow	Negative Free Cash Flow	-$0.58	-82%	0%	-82%	0.00%
Comstock Resources, Inc.	CRK	Oil & Gas	Negative Free Cash Flow	Negative Free Cash Flow	Negative Free Cash Flow	Negative Free Cash Flow	-$4.84	-10%	202%	-8%	3.33%
Comtech Tele Communications	CMTL	Communication	$22.95	$45.90	$68.85	$137.70	$3.06	8%	11%	9%	4.30%
ConAgra Foods, Inc.	CAG	Consumer Goods	$18.45	$36.90	$55.35	$110.70	$2.46	12%	33%	10%	3.17%
Concho Resources, Inc.	CXO	Oil & Gas	Negative Free Cash Flow	Negative Free Cash Flow	Negative Free Cash Flow	Negative Free Cash Flow	-$14.82	-25%	240%	-25%	0.00%
Concur Technologies, Inc.	CNQR	Software	$5.55	$11.10	$16.65	$33.30	$0.74	4%	55%	4%	0.00%
Concurrent Computer Corporation	CCUR	Computers	$5.03	$10.05	$15.08	$30.15	$0.67	23%	21%	11%	7.10%
Conmed Corporation	CNMD	Medical	$19.88	$39.75	$59.63	$119.25	$2.65	9%	21%	9%	1.79%

NAME	TICKER	INDUSTRY	2014 BUY PRICE OPINION	2014 HOLD PRICE OPINION	2014 SELL PRICE OPINION	2014 SHORT PRICE OPINION	2014 MYCROFT FREE CASH FLOW PER SHARE ESTIMATE	2014 MYCROFT FREE CASH FLOW RETURN ON TOTAL CAPITAL ESTIMATE (FROIC) >15% = Great	2014 MYCROFT CAPFLOW ESTIMATE <33% = Great BUT NO NEGATIVE RESULTS	2014 MYCROFT MICHAELIS GROWTH RATE ESTIMATE >15% = Great	DIVIDEND YIELD
Step #1 = Look up the company's current stock market price on the day of analysis and compare it to our 2014 Buy, Hold, Sell & Short Price.											
Step #2 =Take the company's current market price; divide it by the "2014 Mycroft Free Cash Flow Per Share estimate." This gives the "Price to Free Cash Flow."											
All results below are based on the 2014 year end estimates using the "2014 Mycroft Michaelis Growth Rate" and are good until December 31, 2014.											
Connecticut Water Service, Inc.	CTWS	Utilities	$2.10	$4.20	$6.30	$12.60	$0.28	1%	90%	1%	3.17%
Conn's, Inc.	CONN	Retail	Negative Free Cash Flow	Negative Free Cash Flow	Negative Free Cash Flow	Negative Free Cash Flow	-$3.48	-16%	-48%	-16%	0.00%
ConocoPhillips	COP	Oil & Gas	$12.75	$25.50	$38.25	$76.50	$1.70	3%	87%	2%	3.90%
Consol Energy Inc	CNX	Coal	Negative Free Cash Flow	Negative Free Cash Flow	Negative Free Cash Flow	Negative Free Cash Flow	-$3.78	-12%	215%	-12%	1.45%
Consolidated Communications, Inc.	CNSL	Communication	$5.63	$11.25	$16.88	$33.75	$0.75	2%	79%	6%	8.80%
Consolidated Edison, Inc.	ED	Utilities	$2.25	$4.50	$6.75	$13.50	$0.30	0%	96%	2%	4.50%
Consolidated Graphics, Inc.	CGX	Business Services	$59.25	$118.50	$177.75	$355.50	$7.90	16%	31%	16%	0.00%
Consolidated Water Company, Ltd.	CWCO	Utilities	$3.75	$7.50	$11.25	$22.50	$0.50	5%	41%	4%	2.21%
Consolidated-Tomoka Land	CTO	Real Estate	Negative Free Cash Flow	Negative Free Cash Flow	Negative Free Cash Flow	Negative Free Cash Flow	-$7.41	-32%	1359%	-32%	0.16%
Constant Contact, Inc.	CTCT	Advertising	$4.80	$9.60	$14.40	$28.80	$0.64	9%	54%	9%	0.00%
Constellation Brands Inc.	STZ	Beverages	$16.88	$33.75	$50.63	$101.25	$2.25	6%	14%	6%	0.00%

NAME	TICKER	INDUSTRY	2014 BUY PRICE OPINION	2014 HOLD PRICE OPINION	2014 SELL PRICE OPINION	2014 SHORT PRICE OPINION	2014 MYCROFT FREE CASH FLOW PER SHARE ESTIMATE	2014 MYCROFT FREE CASH FLOW RETURN ON TOTAL CAPITAL ESTIMATE (FROIC) >15% = Great	2014 MYCROFT CAPFLOW ESTIMATE <33% = Great BUT NO NEGATIVE RESULTS	2014 MYCROFT MICHAELIS GROWTH RATE ESTIMATE >15% = Great	DIVIDEND YIELD
Step #1 = Look up the company's current stock market price on the day of analysis and compare it to our 2014 Buy, Hold, Sell & Short Price.											
Step #2 = Take the company's current market price; divide it by the "2014 Mycroft Free Cash Flow Per Share estimate." This gives the "Price to Free Cash Flow."											
All results below are based on the 2014 year end estimates using the "2014 Mycroft Michaelis Growth Rate" and are good until December 31, 2014.											
Contango Oil & Gas Company	MCF	Oil & Gas	$7.80	$15.60	$23.40	$46.80	$1.04	4%	84%	4%	0.00%
Continental Resources Inc	CLR	Oil & Gas	Negative Free Cash Flow	Negative Free Cash Flow	Negative Free Cash Flow	Negative Free Cash Flow	-$11.19	-35%	203%	-35%	0.00%
Convergys Corporation	CVG	Business Services	$3.68	$7.35	$11.03	$22.05	$0.49	4%	63%	3%	1.30%
Con-way Inc	CNW	Transportation	$0.30	$0.60	$0.90	$1.80	$0.04	0%	99%	0%	0.91%
Cooper Companies	COO	Medical	$40.13	$80.25	$120.38	$240.75	$5.35	8%	36%	8%	0.04%
Cooper Tire & Rubber Company	CTB	Autos	$9.68	$19.35	$29.03	$58.05	$1.29	7%	74%	6%	1.28%
Copa Holdings SA	CPA	Airlines	$28.95	$57.90	$86.85	$173.70	$3.86	6%	69%	3%	2.12%
Copart, Inc.	CPRT	Autos	$4.95	$9.90	$14.85	$29.70	$0.66	10%	65%	10%	0.00%
Corcept Therapeutics, Inc.	CORT	Biotech	Negative Free Cash Flow	Negative Free Cash Flow	Negative Free Cash Flow	Negative Free Cash Flow	-$0.39	-96%	0%	-96%	0.00%
Core Molding Technologies, Inc.	CMT	Autos	$13.05	$26.10	$39.15	$78.30	$1.74	16%	43%	16%	0.00%
CoreLogic, Inc.	CLGX	Business Services	$21.08	$42.15	$63.23	$126.45	$2.81	12%	29%	12%	0.00%

NAME	TICKER	INDUSTRY	2014 BUY PRICE OPINION	2014 HOLD PRICE OPINION	2014 SELL PRICE OPINION	2014 SHORT PRICE OPINION	2014 MYCROFT FREE CASH FLOW PER SHARE ESTIMATE	2014 MYCROFT FREE CASH FLOW RETURN ON TOTAL CAPITAL ESTIMATE (FROIC) >15% = Great	2014 MYCROFT CAPFLOW ESTIMATE <33% = Great BUT NO NEGATIVE RESULTS	2014 MYCROFT MICHAELIS GROWTH RATE ESTIMATE >15% = Great	DIVIDEND YIELD
Step #1 = Look up the company's current stock market price on the day of analysis and compare it to our 2014 Buy, Hold, Sell & Short Price.
Step #2 =Take the company's current market price; divide it by the "2014 Mycroft Free Cash Flow Per Share estimate." This gives the "Price to Free Cash Flow."
All results below are based on the 2014 year end estimates using the "2014 Mycroft Michaelis Growth Rate" and are good until December 31, 2014.
Core-Mark Holding Company, Inc.	CORE	Retail	$33.38	$66.75	$100.13	$200.25	$4.45	10%	32%	9%	1.15%
Corinthian Colleges, Inc.	COCO	Education	Negative Free Cash Flow	Negative Free Cash Flow	Negative Free Cash Flow	Negative Free Cash Flow	-$0.03	0%	106%	0%	0.00%
Cornerstone OnDemand, Inc.	CSOD	Software	$0.15	$0.30	$0.45	$0.90	$0.02	2%	89%	2%	0.00%
Cornerstone Therapeutics, Inc.	CRTX	Biotech	$6.15	$12.30	$18.45	$36.90	$0.82	8%	37%	8%	0.00%
Corning Inc	GLW	Computers	$8.25	$16.50	$24.75	$49.50	$1.10	6%	48%	6%	2.69%
Coronado Biosciences Inc	CNDO	Biotech	Negative Free Cash Flow	Negative Free Cash Flow	Negative Free Cash Flow	Negative Free Cash Flow	-$0.80	-55%	0%	-55%	0.00%
Corporate Executive Board Company	CEB	Business Services	$34.50	$69.00	$103.50	$207.00	$4.60	104%	22%	71%	1.31%
Corrections Corporation of America	CXW	Business Services	$18.98	$37.95	$56.93	$113.85	$2.53	10%	19%	7%	5.50%
Cosi, Inc.	COSI	Restaurants	Negative Free Cash Flow	Negative Free Cash Flow	Negative Free Cash Flow	Negative Free Cash Flow	-$0.35	-68%	-39%	-68%	0.00%
CoStar Group, Inc.	CSGP	Real Estate	$22.43	$44.85	$67.28	$134.55	$2.99	8%	18%	8%	0.00%
Costco Wholesale Corporation	COST	Retail	$31.13	$62.25	$93.38	$186.75	$4.15	14%	54%	10%	1.06%

NAME	TICKER	INDUSTRY	2014 BUY PRICE OPINION	2014 HOLD PRICE OPINION	2014 SELL PRICE OPINION	2014 SHORT PRICE OPINION	2014 MYCROFT FREE CASH FLOW PER SHARE ESTIMATE	2014 MYCROFT FREE CASH FLOW RETURN ON TOTAL CAPITAL ESTIMATE (FROIC) >15% = Great	2014 MYCROFT CAPFLOW ESTIMATE <33% = Great BUT NO NEGATIVE RESULTS	2014 MYCROFT MICHAELIS GROWTH RATE ESTIMATE >15% = Great	DIVIDEND YIELD
Step #1 = Look up the company's current stock market price on the day of analysis and compare it to our 2014 Buy, Hold, Sell & Short Price.											
Step #2 =Take the company's current market price; divide it by the "2014 Mycroft Free Cash Flow Per Share estimate." This gives the "Price to Free Cash Flow."											
All results below are based on the 2014 year end estimates using the "2014 Mycroft Michaelis Growth Rate" and are good until December 31, 2014.											
Courier Corporation	CRRC	Publishing	$12.90	$25.80	$38.70	$77.40	$1.72	11%	53%	10%	5.20%
Covance, Inc.	CVD	Medical	$3.38	$6.75	$10.13	$20.25	$0.45	2%	86%	2%	0.00%
Covanta Holding Corporation	CVA	Waste Management	$8.33	$16.65	$24.98	$49.95	$1.11	5%	53%	5%	3.04%
Covenant Transportation Group, Inc.	CVTI	Transportation	Negative Free Cash Flow	Negative Free Cash Flow	Negative Free Cash Flow	Negative Free Cash Flow	-$2.19	-17%	176%	-17%	0.00%
Covidien PLC	COV	Medical	$28.80	$57.60	$86.40	$172.80	$3.84	11%	26%	10%	1.69%
CPI Aerostructures Inc.	CVU	Aerospace & Defense	Negative Free Cash Flow	Negative Free Cash Flow	Negative Free Cash Flow	Negative Free Cash Flow	-$2.27	-22%	-4%	-22%	0.00%
CRA International, Inc.	CRAI	Business Services	Negative Free Cash Flow	Negative Free Cash Flow	Negative Free Cash Flow	Negative Free Cash Flow	-$1.13	-5%	-39%	-5%	0.00%
Cracker Barrel Old Country Store, Inc.	CBRL	Restaurants	$38.93	$77.85	$116.78	$233.55	$5.19	12%	38%	7%	2.98%
Craft Brew Alliance Inc	BREW	Beverages	Negative Free Cash Flow	Negative Free Cash Flow	Negative Free Cash Flow	Negative Free Cash Flow	-$0.08	-1%	117%	-1%	0.00%
Crane Company	CR	Industrial	$29.03	$58.05	$87.08	$174.15	$3.87	14%	12%	11%	1.97%
Crawford & Company Class B	CRD.B	Business Services	$14.63	$29.25	$43.88	$87.75	$1.95	46%	28%	43%	1.80%

NAME	TICKER	INDUSTRY	2014 BUY PRICE OPINION	2014 HOLD PRICE OPINION	2014 SELL PRICE OPINION	2014 SHORT PRICE OPINION	2014 MYCROFT FREE CASH FLOW PER SHARE ESTIMATE	2014 MYCROFT FREE CASH FLOW RETURN ON TOTAL CAPITAL ESTIMATE (FROIC) >15% = Great	2014 MYCROFT CAPFLOW ESTIMATE <33% = Great BUT NO NEGATIVE RESULTS	2014 MYCROFT MICHAELIS GROWTH RATE ESTIMATE >15% = Great	DIVIDEND YIELD
Step #1 = Look up the company's current stock market price on the day of analysis and compare it to our 2014 Buy, Hold, Sell & Short Price.											
Step #2 =Take the company's current market price; divide it by the "2014 Mycroft Free Cash Flow Per Share estimate." This gives the "Price to Free Cash Flow."											
All results below are based on the 2014 year end estimates using the "2014 Mycroft Michaelis Growth Rate" and are good until December 31, 2014.											
Cray, Inc.	CRAY	Computers	$11.40	$22.80	$34.20	$68.40	$1.52	16%	20%	16%	0.00%
Cree, Inc.	CREE	Semiconductors	$12.45	$24.90	$37.35	$74.70	$1.66	7%	34%	7%	0.00%
Crexendo Inc	EXE	Software	Negative Free Cash Flow	Negative Free Cash Flow	Negative Free Cash Flow	Negative Free Cash Flow	-$0.35	-39%	-6%	-39%	0.00%
Crimson Exploration, Inc.	CXPO	Oil & Gas	Negative Free Cash Flow	Negative Free Cash Flow	Negative Free Cash Flow	Negative Free Cash Flow	-$0.02	0%	101%	0%	0.00%
Crimson Wine Group Ltd	CWGL	Beverages	$0.60	$1.20	$1.80	$3.60	$0.08	1%	76%	1%	0.00%
Crocs, Inc.	CROX	Apparel & Furniture	$3.90	$7.80	$11.70	$23.40	$0.52	7%	61%	7%	0.00%
Cross Country Healthcare, Inc.	CCRN	Services	$2.48	$4.95	$7.43	$14.85	$0.33	4%	9%	4%	0.00%
Crosstex Energy, Inc.	XTXI	Oil & Gas	Negative Free Cash Flow	Negative Free Cash Flow	Negative Free Cash Flow	Negative Free Cash Flow	-$6.75	-35%	390%	-35%	2.39%
Crown Castle International Corp	CCI	Communication	$12.60	$25.20	$37.80	$75.60	$1.68	4%	53%	4%	0.00%
Crown Crafts, Inc.	CRWS	Apparel & Furniture	$6.60	$13.20	$19.80	$39.60	$0.88	22%	12%	17%	4.30%
Crown Holdings Inc	CCK	Containers	$15.90	$31.80	$47.70	$95.40	$2.12	8%	53%	8%	0.00%

NAME	TICKER	INDUSTRY	2014 BUY PRICE OPINION	2014 HOLD PRICE OPINION	2014 SELL PRICE OPINION	2014 SHORT PRICE OPINION	2014 MYCROFT FREE CASH FLOW PER SHARE ESTIMATE	2014 MYCROFT FREE CASH FLOW RETURN ON TOTAL CAPITAL ESTIMATE (FROIC) >15% = Great	2014 MYCROFT CAPFLOW ESTIMATE <33% = Great BUT NO NEGATIVE RESULTS	2014 MYCROFT MICHAELIS GROWTH RATE ESTIMATE >15% = Great	DIVIDEND YIELD
Step #1 = Look up the company's current stock market price on the day of analysis and compare it to our 2014 Buy, Hold, Sell & Short Price.											
Step #2 =Take the company's current market price; divide it by the "2014 Mycroft Free Cash Flow Per Share estimate." This gives the "Price to Free Cash Flow."											
All results below are based on the 2014 year end estimates using the "2014 Mycroft Michaelis Growth Rate" and are good until December 31, 2014.											
Crown Media Holdings, Inc. Class A	CRWN	Communication	$0.90	$1.80	$2.70	$5.40	$0.12	5%	4%	5%	0.00%
Cryo-Cell International, Inc.	CCEL	Health Care	$0.83	$1.65	$2.48	$4.95	$0.11	-24%	15%	-24%	0.00%
Cryolife	CRY	Medical	$4.28	$8.55	$12.83	$25.65	$0.57	11%	21%	10%	1.71%
CSG Systems International, Inc.	CSGS	Software	$18.08	$36.15	$54.23	$108.45	$2.41	12%	30%	11%	2.49%
CSP, Inc.	CSPI	Software	$9.00	$18.00	$27.00	$54.00	$1.20	16%	19%	15%	5.70%
CSS Industries, Inc.	CSS	Retail	$29.63	$59.25	$88.88	$177.75	$3.95	13%	13%	14%	2.51%
CSX Corp	CSX	Transportation	$7.95	$15.90	$23.85	$47.70	$1.06	6%	68%	5%	2.30%
CTS Corporation	CTS	Computers	$5.93	$11.85	$17.78	$35.55	$0.79	7%	37%	7%	0.93%
Cubic Corporation	CUB	Aerospace & Defense	Negative Free Cash Flow	Negative Free Cash Flow	Negative Free Cash Flow	Negative Free Cash Flow	-$1.12	-4%	-32%	-5%	0.45%
Cubist Pharmaceuticals, Inc.	CBST	Biotech	$20.55	$41.10	$61.65	$123.30	$2.74	11%	9%	11%	0.00%
CUI Global, Inc.	CUI	Computers	Negative Free Cash Flow	Negative Free Cash Flow	Negative Free Cash Flow	Negative Free Cash Flow	-$0.06	-2%	-180%	-2%	0.00%

NAME	TICKER	INDUSTRY	2014 BUY PRICE OPINION	2014 HOLD PRICE OPINION	2014 SELL PRICE OPINION	2014 SHORT PRICE OPINION	2014 MYCROFT FREE CASH FLOW PER SHARE ESTIMATE	2014 MYCROFT FREE CASH FLOW RETURN ON TOTAL CAPITAL ESTIMATE (FROIC) >15% = Great	2014 MYCROFT CAPFLOW ESTIMATE <33% = Great BUT NO NEGATIVE RESULTS	2014 MYCROFT MICHAELIS GROWTH RATE ESTIMATE >15% = Great	DIVIDEND YIELD
Step #1 = Look up the company's current stock market price on the day of analysis and compare it to our 2014 Buy, Hold, Sell & Short Price.											
Step #2 =Take the company's current market price; divide it by the "2014 Mycroft Free Cash Flow Per Share estimate." This gives the "Price to Free Cash Flow."											
All results below are based on the 2014 year end estimates using the "2014 Mycroft Michaelis Growth Rate" and are good until December 31, 2014.											
Culp, Inc.	CFI	Homebuilding	$12.38	$24.75	$37.13	$74.25	$1.65	17%	20%	16%	0.84%
Cumberland Pharmaceuticals, Inc.	CPIX	Drugs	$0.83	$1.65	$2.48	$4.95	$0.11	2%	66%	2%	0.00%
Cummins Inc	CMI	Industrial	$60.23	$120.45	$180.68	$361.35	$8.03	18%	37%	14%	1.90%
Cumulus Media, Inc. Class A	CMLS	Entertainment	$7.58	$15.15	$22.73	$45.45	$1.01	6%	5%	6%	0.00%
Curis, Inc.	CRIS	Biotech	Negative Free Cash Flow	Negative Free Cash Flow	Negative Free Cash Flow	Negative Free Cash Flow	-$0.27	-67%	-1%	-67%	0.00%
Curtiss-Wright Corporation	CW	Aerospace & Defense	$20.40	$40.80	$61.20	$122.40	$2.72	6%	38%	6%	0.87%
Cutera, Inc.	CUTR	Medical	$2.03	$4.05	$6.08	$12.15	$0.27	4%	19%	4%	0.00%
CVD Equipment Corporation	CVV	Industrial	Negative Free Cash Flow	Negative Free Cash Flow	Negative Free Cash Flow	Negative Free Cash Flow	-$1.08	-17%	-561%	-17%	0.00%
CVR Energy, Inc.	CVI	Oil & Gas	$49.95	$99.90	$149.85	$299.70	$6.66	36%	32%	24%	7.80%
CVS Caremark Corp	CVS	Retail	$20.55	$41.10	$61.65	$123.30	$2.74	7%	39%	6%	1.52%
Cyan Inc	CYNI	Communication	Negative Free Cash Flow	Negative Free Cash Flow	Negative Free Cash Flow	Negative Free Cash Flow	-$0.51	-23%	-45%	-23%	0.00%

NAME	TICKER	INDUSTRY	2014 BUY PRICE OPINION	2014 HOLD PRICE OPINION	2014 SELL PRICE OPINION	2014 SHORT PRICE OPINION	2014 MYCROFT FREE CASH FLOW PER SHARE ESTIMATE	2014 MYCROFT FREE CASH FLOW RETURN ON TOTAL CAPITAL ESTIMATE (FROIC) >15% = Great	2014 MYCROFT CAPFLOW ESTIMATE <33% = Great BUT NO NEGATIVE RESULTS	2014 MYCROFT MICHAELIS GROWTH RATE ESTIMATE >15% = Great	DIVIDEND YIELD
Step #1 = Look up the company's current stock market price on the day of analysis and compare it to our 2014 Buy, Hold, Sell & Short Price.												
Step #2 =Take the company's current market price; divide it by the "2014 Mycroft Free Cash Flow Per Share estimate." This gives the "Price to Free Cash Flow."												
All results below are based on the 2014 year end estimates using the "2014 Mycroft Michaelis Growth Rate" and are good until December 31, 2014.												
Cyanotech Corporation	CYAN	Biotech	Negative Free Cash Flow	Negative Free Cash Flow	Negative Free Cash Flow	Negative Free Cash Flow	-$0.65	-17%	355%	-17%	0.00%
Cyberonics, Inc.	CYBX	Medical	$19.13	$38.25	$57.38	$114.75	$2.55	24%	24%	24%	0.00%
Cyclacel Pharmaceuticals, Inc.	CYCC	Biotech	Negative Free Cash Flow	Negative Free Cash Flow	Negative Free Cash Flow	Negative Free Cash Flow	-$0.87	-50%	-1%	-50%	0.00%
Cynosure, Inc.	CYNO	Medical	Negative Free Cash Flow	Negative Free Cash Flow	Negative Free Cash Flow	Negative Free Cash Flow	-$0.31	-2%	-117%	-2%	0.00%
Cypress Semiconductor Corporation	CY	Semiconductors	$4.58	$9.15	$13.73	$27.45	$0.61	26%	27%	10%	3.75%
Cytec Industries	CYT	Chemicals	Negative Free Cash Flow	Negative Free Cash Flow	Negative Free Cash Flow	Negative Free Cash Flow	-$1.16	-2%	123%	-2%	0.64%
Cytokinetics Inc	CYTK	Biotech	Negative Free Cash Flow	Negative Free Cash Flow	Negative Free Cash Flow	Negative Free Cash Flow	-$0.75	-42%	-2%	-42%	0.00%
Cytori Therapeutics, Inc.	CYTX	Biotech	Negative Free Cash Flow	Negative Free Cash Flow	Negative Free Cash Flow	Negative Free Cash Flow	-$0.54	-182%	-2%	-182%	0.00%
CytRx Corporation	CYTR	Biotech	Negative Free Cash Flow	Negative Free Cash Flow	Negative Free Cash Flow	Negative Free Cash Flow	-$0.67	-99%	0%	-99%	0.00%
Daegis Inc	DAEG	Software	$2.18	$4.35	$6.53	$13.05	$0.29	17%	7%	17%	0.00%
Daily Journal Corporation	DJCO	Publishing	$16.35	$32.70	$49.05	$98.10	$2.18	3%	9%	3%	0.00%

NAME	TICKER	INDUSTRY	2014 BUY PRICE OPINION	2014 HOLD PRICE OPINION	2014 SELL PRICE OPINION	2014 SHORT PRICE OPINION	2014 MYCROFT FREE CASH FLOW PER SHARE ESTIMATE	2014 MYCROFT FREE CASH FLOW RETURN ON TOTAL CAPITAL ESTIMATE (FROIC) >15% = Great	2014 MYCROFT CAPFLOW ESTIMATE <33% = Great BUT NO NEGATIVE RESULTS	2014 MYCROFT MICHAELIS GROWTH RATE ESTIMATE >15% = Great	DIVIDEND YIELD
Step #1 = Look up the company's current stock market price on the day of analysis and compare it to our 2014 Buy, Hold, Sell & Short Price.											
Step #2 =Take the company's current market price; divide it by the "2014 Mycroft Free Cash Flow Per Share estimate." This gives the "Price to Free Cash Flow."											
All results below are based on the 2014 year end estimates using the "2014 Mycroft Michaelis Growth Rate" and are good until December 31, 2014.											
Daktronics, Inc.	DAKT	Computers	$3.23	$6.45	$9.68	$19.35	$0.43	9%	41%	4%	3.28%
Dana Holding Corp	DAN	Autos	$12.68	$25.35	$38.03	$76.05	$1.69	14%	31%	13%	0.89%
Danaher Corporation	DHR	Industrial	$33.68	$67.35	$101.03	$202.05	$4.49	11%	15%	11%	0.15%
Darden Restaurants Inc	DRI	Restaurants	$15.75	$31.50	$47.25	$94.50	$2.10	8%	72%	4%	4.70%
Darling International, Inc.	DAR	Waste Management	$8.25	$16.50	$24.75	$49.50	$1.10	9%	50%	9%	0.00%
Data I/O Corporation	DAIO	Computers	Negative Free Cash Flow	Negative Free Cash Flow	Negative Free Cash Flow	Negative Free Cash Flow	-$0.09	-5%	-109%	-5%	0.00%
Datalink Corporation	DTLK	Computers	$4.43	$8.85	$13.28	$26.55	$0.59	12%	20%	12%	0.00%
Dataram Corporation	DRAM	Computers	Negative Free Cash Flow	Negative Free Cash Flow	Negative Free Cash Flow	Negative Free Cash Flow	-$2.21	-130%	0%	-130%	0.00%
Datawatch Corporation	DWCH	Software	$4.43	$8.85	$13.28	$26.55	$0.59	24%	12%	24%	0.00%
DaVita HealthCare Partners Inc	DVA	Health Care	$26.48	$52.95	$79.43	$158.85	$3.53	8%	45%	8%	0.00%
Dawson Geophysical Company	DWSN	Oil & Gas	$82.43	$164.85	$247.28	$494.55	$10.99	31%	0%	31%	0.00%

NAME	TICKER	INDUSTRY	2014 BUY PRICE OPINION	2014 HOLD PRICE OPINION	2014 SELL PRICE OPINION	2014 SHORT PRICE OPINION	2014 MYCROFT FREE CASH FLOW PER SHARE ESTIMATE	2014 MYCROFT FREE CASH FLOW RETURN ON TOTAL CAPITAL ESTIMATE (FROIC) >15% = Great	2014 MYCROFT CAPFLOW ESTIMATE <33% = Great BUT NO NEGATIVE RESULTS	2014 MYCROFT MICHAELIS GROWTH RATE ESTIMATE >15% = Great	DIVIDEND YIELD
Step #1 = Look up the company's current stock market price on the day of analysis and compare it to our 2014 Buy, Hold, Sell & Short Price.											
Step #2 =Take the company's current market price; divide it by the "2014 Mycroft Free Cash Flow Per Share estimate." This gives the "Price to Free Cash Flow."											
All results below are based on the 2014 year end estimates using the "2014 Mycroft Michaelis Growth Rate" and are good until December 31, 2014.											
Daxor Corporation	DXR	Medical	Negative Free Cash Flow	Negative Free Cash Flow	Negative Free Cash Flow	Negative Free Cash Flow	-$1.61	-18%	-2%	-17%	5.80%
Dealertrack Technologies Inc	TRAK	Internet	$3.90	$7.80	$11.70	$23.40	$0.52	3%	66%	3%	0.00%
Dean Foods Company	DF	Consumer Goods	Negative Free Cash Flow	Negative Free Cash Flow	Negative Free Cash Flow	Negative Free Cash Flow	-$3.60	-8%	-224%	-8%	0.00%
Deckers Outdoor Corporation	DECK	Apparel & Furniture	$15.60	$31.20	$46.80	$93.60	$2.08	9%	52%	9%	0.00%
Deere & Co	DE	Agriculture	$9.15	$18.30	$27.45	$54.90	$1.22	2%	84%	1%	2.42%
Del Frisco's Restaurant Group Inc	DFRG	Restaurants	Negative Free Cash Flow	Negative Free Cash Flow	Negative Free Cash Flow	Negative Free Cash Flow	-$0.04	0%	103%	0%	0.00%
Delek US Holdings, Inc.	DK	Oil & Gas	$26.18	$52.35	$78.53	$157.05	$3.49	18%	45%	17%	2.55%
dELiA*s, Inc.	DLIA	Retail	Negative Free Cash Flow	Negative Free Cash Flow	Negative Free Cash Flow	Negative Free Cash Flow	-$0.44	-45%	-32%	-45%	0.00%
Dell Inc	DELL	Computers	$20.03	$40.05	$60.08	$120.15	$2.67	23%	13%	22%	2.31%
Delphi Automotive PLC	DLPH	Autos	$20.70	$41.40	$62.10	$124.20	$2.76	17%	46%	13%	1.18%
Delta Air Lines Inc	DAL	Airlines	$1.20	$2.40	$3.60	$7.20	$0.16	-108%	60%	-89%	1.06%

NAME	TICKER	INDUSTRY	2014 BUY PRICE OPINION	2014 HOLD PRICE OPINION	2014 SELL PRICE OPINION	2014 SHORT PRICE OPINION	2014 MYCROFT FREE CASH FLOW PER SHARE ESTIMATE	2014 MYCROFT FREE CASH FLOW RETURN ON TOTAL CAPITAL ESTIMATE (FROIC) >15% = Great	2014 MYCROFT CAPFLOW ESTIMATE <33% = Great BUT NO NEGATIVE RESULTS	2014 MYCROFT MICHAELIS GROWTH RATE ESTIMATE >15% = Great	DIVIDEND YIELD
Step #1 = Look up the company's current stock market price on the day of analysis and compare it to our 2014 Buy, Hold, Sell & Short Price.											
Step #2 =Take the company's current market price; divide it by the "2014 Mycroft Free Cash Flow Per Share estimate." This gives the "Price to Free Cash Flow."											
All results below are based on the 2014 year end estimates using the "2014 Mycroft Michaelis Growth Rate" and are good until December 31, 2014.											
Delta Apparel, Inc.	DLA	Apparel & Furniture	$25.50	$51.00	$76.50	$153.00	$3.40	10%	25%	10%	0.00%
Delta Natural Gas Company	DGAS	Utilities	$7.35	$14.70	$22.05	$44.10	$0.98	5%	53%	5%	4.01%
Deltic Timber Corporation	DEL	Forest Products	Negative Free Cash Flow	Negative Free Cash Flow	Negative Free Cash Flow	Negative Free Cash Flow	-$0.21	-1%	108%	-2%	0.66%
Deluxe Corporation	DLX	Business Services	$36.83	$73.65	$110.48	$220.95	$4.91	19%	14%	17%	2.46%
Demand Media, Inc.	DMD	Internet	$5.10	$10.20	$15.30	$30.60	$0.68	11%	44%	11%	0.00%
Demandware Inc	DWRE	Software	$0.15	$0.30	$0.45	$0.90	$0.02	1%	89%	1%	0.00%
Denbury Resources Inc	DNR	Oil & Gas	Negative Free Cash Flow	Negative Free Cash Flow	Negative Free Cash Flow	Negative Free Cash Flow	-$0.09	0%	102%	0%	0.00%
Dendreon Corp	DNDN	Biotech	Negative Free Cash Flow	Negative Free Cash Flow	Negative Free Cash Flow	Negative Free Cash Flow	-$1.69	-59%	-5%	-59%	0.00%
Denny's Corporation	DENN	Restaurants	$4.43	$8.85	$13.28	$26.55	$0.59	23%	31%	23%	0.00%
DENTSPLY International, Inc.	XRAY	Medical	$16.95	$33.90	$50.85	$101.70	$2.26	8%	25%	8%	0.56%
DepoMed, Inc.	DEPO	Drugs	$1.28	$2.55	$3.83	$7.65	$0.17	11%	68%	11%	0.00%

NAME	TICKER	INDUSTRY	2014 BUY PRICE OPINION	2014 HOLD PRICE OPINION	2014 SELL PRICE OPINION	2014 SHORT PRICE OPINION	2014 MYCROFT FREE CASH FLOW PER SHARE ESTIMATE	2014 MYCROFT FREE CASH FLOW RETURN ON TOTAL CAPITAL ESTIMATE (FROIC) >15% = Great	2014 MYCROFT CAPFLOW ESTIMATE <33% = Great BUT NO NEGATIVE RESULTS	2014 MYCROFT MICHAELIS GROWTH RATE ESTIMATE >15% = Great	DIVIDEND YIELD
Step #1 = Look up the company's current stock market price on the day of analysis and compare it to our 2014 Buy, Hold, Sell & Short Price.											
Step #2 =Take the company's current market price; divide it by the "2014 Mycroft Free Cash Flow Per Share estimate." This gives the "Price to Free Cash Flow."											
All results below are based on the 2014 year end estimates using the "2014 Mycroft Michaelis Growth Rate" and are good until December 31, 2014.											
Derma Sciences, Inc.	DSCI	Medical	Negative Free Cash Flow	Negative Free Cash Flow	Negative Free Cash Flow	Negative Free Cash Flow	-$0.96	-19%	-23%	-19%	0.00%
Destination Maternity Corp	DEST	Retail	$16.13	$32.25	$48.38	$96.75	$2.15	21%	34%	15%	2.56%
Destination XL Group Inc	DXLG	Retail	Negative Free Cash Flow	Negative Free Cash Flow	Negative Free Cash Flow	Negative Free Cash Flow	-$0.34	-11%	169%	-11%	0.00%
Devon Energy Corp	DVN	Oil & Gas	Negative Free Cash Flow	Negative Free Cash Flow	Negative Free Cash Flow	Negative Free Cash Flow	-$6.47	-9%	154%	-9%	1.50%
DeVry, Inc.	DV	Education	$19.65	$39.30	$58.95	$117.90	$2.62	11%	43%	10%	1.08%
DexCom, Inc.	DXCM	Medical	Negative Free Cash Flow	Negative Free Cash Flow	Negative Free Cash Flow	Negative Free Cash Flow	-$0.39	-39%	-38%	-39%	0.00%
Diamond Foods, Inc.	DMND	Consumer Goods	$3.45	$6.90	$10.35	$20.70	$0.46	1%	52%	1%	0.00%
Diamond Offshore Drilling, Inc.	DO	Oil & Gas	$20.33	$40.65	$60.98	$121.95	$2.71	6%	71%	5%	0.77%
Diamondback Energy Inc	FANG	Oil & Gas	Negative Free Cash Flow	Negative Free Cash Flow	Negative Free Cash Flow	Negative Free Cash Flow	-$2.17	-14%	230%	-14%	0.00%
Dice Holdings Incorporated	DHX	Services	$7.20	$14.40	$21.60	$43.20	$0.96	22%	16%	22%	0.00%
Dick's Sporting Goods, Inc.	DKS	Retail	$10.05	$20.10	$30.15	$60.30	$1.34	9%	58%	7%	0.99%

NAME	TICKER	INDUSTRY	2014 BUY PRICE OPINION	2014 HOLD PRICE OPINION	2014 SELL PRICE OPINION	2014 SHORT PRICE OPINION	2014 MYCROFT FREE CASH FLOW PER SHARE ESTIMATE	2014 MYCROFT FREE CASH FLOW RETURN ON TOTAL CAPITAL ESTIMATE (FROIC) >15% = Great	2014 MYCROFT CAPFLOW ESTIMATE <33% = Great BUT NO NEGATIVE RESULTS	2014 MYCROFT MICHAELIS GROWTH RATE ESTIMATE >15% = Great	DIVIDEND YIELD
Step #1 = Look up the company's current stock market price on the day of analysis and compare it to our 2014 Buy, Hold, Sell & Short Price.											
Step #2 =Take the company's current market price; divide it by the "2014 Mycroft Free Cash Flow Per Share estimate." This gives the "Price to Free Cash Flow."											
All results below are based on the 2014 year end estimates using the "2014 Mycroft Michaelis Growth Rate" and are good until December 31, 2014.											
Diebold Incorporated	DBD	Software	$4.43	$8.85	$13.28	$26.55	$0.59	4%	57%	0%	3.90%
Digi International	DGII	Communication	$3.30	$6.60	$9.90	$19.80	$0.44	4%	24%	4%	0.00%
Digimarc Corporation	DMRC	Software	$8.63	$17.25	$25.88	$51.75	$1.15	14%	18%	10%	2.19%
Digirad Corporation	DRAD	Medical	Negative Free Cash Flow	Negative Free Cash Flow	Negative Free Cash Flow	Negative Free Cash Flow	-$0.14	-8%	-70%	-8%	0.00%
Digital Ally, Inc.	DGLY	Computers	Negative Free Cash Flow	Negative Free Cash Flow	Negative Free Cash Flow	Negative Free Cash Flow	-$0.11	-3%	177%	-3%	0.00%
Digital Generation Inc	DGIT	Business Services	$20.85	$41.70	$62.55	$125.10	$2.78	10%	27%	10%	0.00%
Digital River, Inc.	DRIV	Software	Negative Free Cash Flow	Negative Free Cash Flow	Negative Free Cash Flow	Negative Free Cash Flow	-$0.07	0%	109%	0%	0.00%
DigitalGlobe Inc	DGI	Aerospace & Defense	Negative Free Cash Flow	Negative Free Cash Flow	Negative Free Cash Flow	Negative Free Cash Flow	-$1.52	-6%	176%	-6%	0.00%
Dillards, Inc.	DDS	Retail	$76.95	$153.90	$230.85	$461.70	$10.26	15%	18%	14%	0.30%
DineEquity Inc	DIN	Restaurants	$25.73	$51.45	$77.18	$154.35	$3.43	4%	13%	5%	4.50%
Diodes Inc.	DIOD	Semiconductors	$6.30	$12.60	$18.90	$37.80	$0.84	5%	61%	5%	0.00%

NAME	TICKER	INDUSTRY	2014 BUY PRICE OPINION	2014 HOLD PRICE OPINION	2014 SELL PRICE OPINION	2014 SHORT PRICE OPINION	2014 MYCROFT FREE CASH FLOW PER SHARE ESTIMATE	2014 MYCROFT FREE CASH FLOW RETURN ON TOTAL CAPITAL ESTIMATE (FROIC) >15% = Great	2014 MYCROFT CAPFLOW ESTIMATE <33% = Great BUT NO NEGATIVE RESULTS	2014 MYCROFT MICHAELIS GROWTH RATE ESTIMATE >15% = Great	DIVIDEND YIELD

Step #1 = Look up the company's current stock market price on the day of analysis and compare it to our 2014 Buy, Hold, Sell & Short Price.

Step #2 =Take the company's current market price; divide it by the "2014 Mycroft Free Cash Flow Per Share estimate." This gives the "Price to Free Cash Flow."

All results below are based on the 2014 year end estimates using the "2014 Mycroft Michaelis Growth Rate" and are good until December 31, 2014.

NAME	TICKER	INDUSTRY	2014 BUY PRICE OPINION	2014 HOLD PRICE OPINION	2014 SELL PRICE OPINION	2014 SHORT PRICE OPINION	2014 MYCROFT FREE CASH FLOW PER SHARE ESTIMATE	FROIC	CAPFLOW	GROWTH RATE	DIVIDEND YIELD
Directv	DTV	Communication	$34.73	$69.45	$104.18	$208.35	$4.63	21%	63%	21%	0.00%
Discovery Communications Inc Class A	DISCA	Entertainment	$36.23	$72.45	$108.68	$217.35	$4.83	9%	9%	9%	0.00%
Discovery Laboratories, Inc.	DSCO	Biotech	Negative Free Cash Flow	Negative Free Cash Flow	Negative Free Cash Flow	Negative Free Cash Flow	-$0.73	-235%	-1%	-235%	0.00%
DISH Network Corp	DISH	Communication	$38.18	$76.35	$114.53	$229.05	$5.09	215%	61%	215%	0.00%
Diversicare Healthcare Services Inc	DVCR	Health Care	Negative Free Cash Flow	Negative Free Cash Flow	Negative Free Cash Flow	Negative Free Cash Flow	-$0.77	-33%	646%	-38%	4.20%
Dixie Group, Inc.	DXYN	Homebuilding	Negative Free Cash Flow	Negative Free Cash Flow	Negative Free Cash Flow	Negative Free Cash Flow	-$0.74	-7%	-262%	-7%	0.00%
Document Security Systems, Inc.	DSS	Business Services	Negative Free Cash Flow	Negative Free Cash Flow	Negative Free Cash Flow	Negative Free Cash Flow	-$0.06	-32%	-10%	-32%	0.00%
Dolby Laboratories, Inc.	DLB	Entertainment	$11.78	$23.55	$35.33	$70.65	$1.57	10%	49%	10%	0.00%
Dole Food Co Inc	DOLE	Consumer Goods	Negative Free Cash Flow	Negative Free Cash Flow	Negative Free Cash Flow	Negative Free Cash Flow	-$2.57	-10%	-113%	-10%	0.00%
Dollar General Corporation	DG	Retail	$16.73	$33.45	$50.18	$100.35	$2.23	8%	46%	8%	0.00%
Dollar Tree Stores, Inc.	DLTR	Retail	$12.68	$25.35	$38.03	$76.05	$1.69	16%	53%	16%	0.00%

NAME	TICKER	INDUSTRY	2014 BUY PRICE OPINION	2014 HOLD PRICE OPINION	2014 SELL PRICE OPINION	2014 SHORT PRICE OPINION	2014 MYCROFT FREE CASH FLOW PER SHARE ESTIMATE	2014 MYCROFT FREE CASH FLOW RETURN ON TOTAL CAPITAL ESTIMATE (FROIC) >15% = Great	2014 MYCROFT CAPFLOW ESTIMATE <33% = Great BUT NO NEGATIVE RESULTS	2014 MYCROFT MICHAELIS GROWTH RATE ESTIMATE >15% = Great	DIVIDEND YIELD
Step #1 = Look up the company's current stock market price on the day of analysis and compare it to our 2014 Buy, Hold, Sell & Short Price.											
Step #2 =Take the company's current market price; divide it by the "2014 Mycroft Free Cash Flow Per Share estimate." This gives the "Price to Free Cash Flow."											
All results below are based on the 2014 year end estimates using the "2014 Mycroft Michaelis Growth Rate" and are good until December 31, 2014.											
Dominion Resources Inc	D	Utilities	Negative Free Cash Flow	Negative Free Cash Flow	Negative Free Cash Flow	Negative Free Cash Flow	-$1.04	-2%	117%	-3%	3.85%
Domino's Pizza, Inc.	DPZ	Restaurants	$30.83	$61.65	$92.48	$184.95	$4.11	69%	18%	50%	1.24%
Domtar Corp	UFS	Forest Products	$71.33	$142.65	$213.98	$427.95	$9.51	8%	47%	9%	3.32%
Donaldson Company, Inc.	DCI	Industrial	$11.63	$23.25	$34.88	$69.75	$1.55	16%	30%	11%	1.38%
Dorman Products, Inc.	DORM	Autos	$6.90	$13.80	$20.70	$41.40	$0.92	8%	34%	8%	0.00%
Dot Hill Systems Corporation	HILL	Computers	Negative Free Cash Flow	Negative Free Cash Flow	Negative Free Cash Flow	Negative Free Cash Flow	-$0.04	-6%	152%	-6%	0.00%
Double Eagle Petroleum Company	DBLE	Oil & Gas	Negative Free Cash Flow	Negative Free Cash Flow	Negative Free Cash Flow	Negative Free Cash Flow	-$0.16	-2%	110%	-2%	0.00%
Douglas Dynamics, Inc.	PLOW	Autos	$6.75	$13.50	$20.25	$40.50	$0.90	7%	9%	6%	5.70%
Dover Corporation	DOV	Industrial	$49.73	$99.45	$149.18	$298.35	$6.63	14%	20%	12%	1.68%
Dover Downs Gaming & Entertainment, Inc.	DDE	Travel & Leisure	$2.25	$4.50	$6.75	$13.50	$0.30	5%	16%	9%	5.80%
Dover Motorsports, Inc.	DVD	Travel & Leisure	$2.25	$4.50	$6.75	$13.50	$0.30	12%	4%	12%	0.00%

NAME	TICKER	INDUSTRY	2014 BUY PRICE OPINION	2014 HOLD PRICE OPINION	2014 SELL PRICE OPINION	2014 SHORT PRICE OPINION	2014 MYCROFT FREE CASH FLOW PER SHARE ESTIMATE	2014 MYCROFT FREE CASH FLOW RETURN ON TOTAL CAPITAL ESTIMATE (FROIC) >15% = Great	2014 MYCROFT CAPFLOW ESTIMATE <33% = Great BUT NO NEGATIVE RESULTS	2014 MYCROFT MICHAELIS GROWTH RATE ESTIMATE >15% = Great	DIVIDEND YIELD
Step #1 = Look up the company's current stock market price on the day of analysis and compare it to our 2014 Buy, Hold, Sell & Short Price.											
Step #2 =Take the company's current market price; divide it by the "2014 Mycroft Free Cash Flow Per Share estimate." This gives the "Price to Free Cash Flow."											
All results below are based on the 2014 year end estimates using the "2014 Mycroft Michaelis Growth Rate" and are good until December 31, 2014.											
Dow Chemical Co	DOW	Chemicals	$24.38	$48.75	$73.13	$146.25	$3.25	10%	36%	9%	3.21%
DR Horton Inc	DHI	Homebuilding	Negative Free Cash Flow	Negative Free Cash Flow	Negative Free Cash Flow	Negative Free Cash Flow	-$4.06	-32%	-4%	-33%	0.79%
Dr Pepper Snapple Group, Inc.	DPS	Beverages	$24.60	$49.20	$73.80	$147.60	$3.28	14%	22%	10%	3.41%
Dreamworks Animation SKG, Inc.	DWA	Entertainment	Negative Free Cash Flow	Negative Free Cash Flow	Negative Free Cash Flow	Negative Free Cash Flow	-$0.11	-1%	124%	-1%	0.00%
Dresser-Rand Group, Inc.	DRC	Oil & Gas	Negative Free Cash Flow	Negative Free Cash Flow	Negative Free Cash Flow	Negative Free Cash Flow	-$0.36	-1%	146%	-1%	0.00%
Drew Industries, Inc.	DW	Autos	$7.13	$14.25	$21.38	$42.75	$0.95	6%	64%	6%	0.00%
Dril-Quip, Inc.	DRQ	Oil & Gas	$12.53	$25.05	$37.58	$75.15	$1.67	6%	42%	6%	0.00%
DSP Group	DSPG	Semiconductors	$2.70	$5.40	$8.10	$16.20	$0.36	5%	14%	5%	0.00%
DST Systems, Inc.	DST	Business Services	$48.53	$97.05	$145.58	$291.15	$6.47	12%	28%	11%	1.63%
DSW Inc	DSW	Retail	$32.55	$65.10	$97.65	$195.30	$4.34	18%	44%	15%	1.18%
DTE Energy Holding Company	DTE	Utilities	$19.05	$38.10	$57.15	$114.30	$2.54	3%	81%	4%	4.00%

NAME	TICKER	INDUSTRY	2014 BUY PRICE OPINION	2014 HOLD PRICE OPINION	2014 SELL PRICE OPINION	2014 SHORT PRICE OPINION	2014 MYCROFT FREE CASH FLOW PER SHARE ESTIMATE	2014 MYCROFT FREE CASH FLOW RETURN ON TOTAL CAPITAL ESTIMATE (FROIC) >15% = Great	2014 MYCROFT CAPFLOW ESTIMATE <33% = Great BUT NO NEGATIVE RESULTS	2014 MYCROFT MICHAELIS GROWTH RATE ESTIMATE >15% = Great	DIVIDEND YIELD
Step #1 = Look up the company's current stock market price on the day of analysis and compare it to our 2014 Buy, Hold, Sell & Short Price.											
Step #2 =Take the company's current market price; divide it by the "2014 Mycroft Free Cash Flow Per Share estimate." This gives the "Price to Free Cash Flow."											
All results below are based on the 2014 year end estimates using the "2014 Mycroft Michaelis Growth Rate" and are good until December 31, 2014.											
DTS, Inc.	DTSI	Software	$1.13	$2.25	$3.38	$6.75	$0.15	2%	64%	2%	0.00%
Ducommun Inc	DCO	Aerospace & Defense	$27.08	$54.15	$81.23	$162.45	$3.61	6%	25%	6%	0.00%
Duke Energy Corporation	DUK	Utilities	$1.28	$2.55	$3.83	$7.65	$0.17	0%	98%	1%	4.70%
Dun & Bradstreet Corporation	DNB	Business Services	$34.65	$69.30	$103.95	$207.90	$4.62	-49%	19%	-36%	1.54%
Dunkin Brands Group Inc	DNKN	Restaurants	$8.18	$16.35	$24.53	$49.05	$1.09	6%	18%	3%	1.75%
Durata Therapeutics Inc	DRTX	Biotech	Negative Free Cash Flow	Negative Free Cash Flow	Negative Free Cash Flow	Negative Free Cash Flow	-$2.74	-113%	0%	-113%	0.00%
Durect Corporation	DRRX	Drugs	Negative Free Cash Flow	Negative Free Cash Flow	Negative Free Cash Flow	Negative Free Cash Flow	-$0.14	-49%	-2%	-49%	0.00%
DXP Enterprises, Inc.	DXPE	Industrial	$34.05	$68.10	$102.15	$204.30	$4.54	14%	13%	14%	0.00%
Dyax Corporation	DYAX	Biotech	Negative Free Cash Flow	Negative Free Cash Flow	Negative Free Cash Flow	Negative Free Cash Flow	-$0.21	-59%	-3%	-59%	0.00%
Dycom Industries Inc	DY	Engineering	$6.45	$12.90	$19.35	$38.70	$0.86	5%	69%	5%	0.00%
Dynamic Materials Corporation	BOOM	Industrial	$4.28	$8.55	$12.83	$25.65	$0.57	4%	72%	3%	0.69%

NAME	TICKER	INDUSTRY	2014 BUY PRICE OPINION	2014 HOLD PRICE OPINION	2014 SELL PRICE OPINION	2014 SHORT PRICE OPINION	2014 MYCROFT FREE CASH FLOW PER SHARE ESTIMATE	2014 MYCROFT FREE CASH FLOW RETURN ON TOTAL CAPITAL ESTIMATE (FROIC) >15% = Great	2014 MYCROFT CAPFLOW ESTIMATE <33% = Great BUT NO NEGATIVE RESULTS	2014 MYCROFT MICHAELIS GROWTH RATE ESTIMATE >15% = Great	DIVIDEND YIELD
Step #1 = Look up the company's current stock market price on the day of analysis and compare it to our 2014 Buy, Hold, Sell & Short Price.											
Step #2 =Take the company's current market price; divide it by the "2014 Mycroft Free Cash Flow Per Share estimate." This gives the "Price to Free Cash Flow."											
All results below are based on the 2014 year end estimates using the "2014 Mycroft Michaelis Growth Rate" and are good until December 31, 2014.											
Dynamics Research Corporation	DRCO	Software	$16.43	$32.85	$49.28	$98.55	$2.19	11%	7%	11%	0.00%
Dynavax Technologies Corporation	DVAX	Biotech	Negative Free Cash Flow	Negative Free Cash Flow	Negative Free Cash Flow	Negative Free Cash Flow	-$0.31	-67%	-4%	-67%	0.00%
Dynegy Inc	DYN	Utilities	Negative Free Cash Flow	Negative Free Cash Flow	Negative Free Cash Flow	Negative Free Cash Flow	-$1.95	-9%	-268%	-9%	0.00%
E.I. du Pont de Nemours & Company	DD	Chemicals	$12.00	$24.00	$36.00	$72.00	$1.60	11%	56%	1%	3.10%
E.W. Scripps Company	SSP	Publishing	$10.58	$21.15	$31.73	$63.45	$1.41	10%	33%	10%	0.00%
E2open Inc	EOPN	Software	Negative Free Cash Flow	Negative Free Cash Flow	Negative Free Cash Flow	Negative Free Cash Flow	-$0.15	-25%	-15%	-25%	0.00%
Eagle Bulk Shipping, Inc.	EGLE	Transportation	$3.45	$6.90	$10.35	$20.70	$0.46	0%	2%	0%	0.00%
Eagle Materials, Inc.	EXP	Building Supplies	$8.63	$17.25	$25.88	$51.75	$1.15	6%	56%	4%	0.58%
Earthlink, Inc.	ELNK	Communication	Negative Free Cash Flow	Negative Free Cash Flow	Negative Free Cash Flow	Negative Free Cash Flow	-$0.22	-5%	116%	-5%	4.10%
Eastern Co	EML	Industrial	$10.88	$21.75	$32.63	$65.25	$1.45	10%	36%	10%	2.58%
Eastman Chemical Company	EMN	Chemicals	$36.00	$72.00	$108.00	$216.00	$4.80	10%	41%	9%	1.54%

NAME	TICKER	INDUSTRY	2014 BUY PRICE OPINION	2014 HOLD PRICE OPINION	2014 SELL PRICE OPINION	2014 SHORT PRICE OPINION	2014 MYCROFT FREE CASH FLOW PER SHARE ESTIMATE	2014 MYCROFT FREE CASH FLOW RETURN ON TOTAL CAPITAL ESTIMATE (FROIC) >15% = Great	2014 MYCROFT CAPFLOW ESTIMATE <33% = Great BUT NO NEGATIVE RESULTS	2014 MYCROFT MICHAELIS GROWTH RATE ESTIMATE >15% = Great	DIVIDEND YIELD
Step #1 = Look up the company's current stock market price on the day of analysis and compare it to our 2014 Buy, Hold, Sell & Short Price.											
Step #2 =Take the company's current market price; divide it by the "2014 Mycroft Free Cash Flow Per Share estimate." This gives the "Price to Free Cash Flow."											
All results below are based on the 2014 year end estimates using the "2014 Mycroft Michaelis Growth Rate" and are good until December 31, 2014.											
Eaton Corporation PLC	ETN	Computers	$23.18	$46.35	$69.53	$139.05	$3.09	7%	31%	6%	2.47%
eBay Inc	EBAY	Retail	$20.93	$41.85	$62.78	$125.55	$2.79	14%	29%	14%	0.00%
Ebix, Inc.	EBIX	Software	$13.80	$27.60	$41.40	$82.80	$1.84	15%	2%	15%	2.80%
Echo Global Logistics, Inc.	ECHO	Transportation	$6.90	$13.80	$20.70	$41.40	$0.92	12%	32%	12%	0.00%
EchoStar Corp	SATS	Communication	$1.80	$3.60	$5.40	$10.80	$0.24	1%	96%	1%	0.00%
Ecolab, Inc.	ECL	Chemicals	$19.88	$39.75	$59.63	$119.25	$2.65	7%	45%	5%	0.96%
Ecology and Environment, Inc.	EEI	Waste Management	$20.55	$41.10	$61.65	$123.30	$2.74	20%	23%	20%	4.00%
Edgen Group Inc Class A	EDG	Industrial	$7.65	$15.30	$22.95	$45.90	$1.02	21%	7%	21%	0.00%
Edgewater Technology, Inc.	EDGW	Software	$4.05	$8.10	$12.15	$24.30	$0.54	15%	12%	15%	0.00%
Edison International	EIX	Utilities	Negative Free Cash Flow	Negative Free Cash Flow	Negative Free Cash Flow	Negative Free Cash Flow	-$1.09	-2%	112%	-1%	2.96%
Education Management Corporation	EDMC	Education	$6.90	$13.80	$20.70	$41.40	$0.92	6%	44%	6%	0.00%

NAME	TICKER	INDUSTRY	2014 BUY PRICE OPINION	2014 HOLD PRICE OPINION	2014 SELL PRICE OPINION	2014 SHORT PRICE OPINION	2014 MYCROFT FREE CASH FLOW PER SHARE ESTIMATE	2014 MYCROFT FREE CASH FLOW RETURN ON TOTAL CAPITAL ESTIMATE (FROIC) >15% = Great	2014 MYCROFT CAPFLOW ESTIMATE <33% = Great BUT NO NEGATIVE RESULTS	2014 MYCROFT MICHAELIS GROWTH RATE ESTIMATE >15% = Great	DIVIDEND YIELD
Step #1 = Look up the company's current stock market price on the day of analysis and compare it to our 2014 Buy, Hold, Sell & Short Price.											
Step #2 =Take the company's current market price; divide it by the "2014 Mycroft Free Cash Flow Per Share estimate." This gives the "Price to Free Cash Flow."											
All results below are based on the 2014 year end estimates using the "2014 Mycroft Michaelis Growth Rate" and are good until December 31, 2014.											
Educational Development Corporation	EDUC	Publishing	$1.20	$2.40	$3.60	$7.20	$0.16	2%	3%	8%	11.60%
Edwards Lifesciences Corporation	EW	Medical	$26.93	$53.85	$80.78	$161.55	$3.59	19%	28%	19%	0.00%
EGain Corp	EGAN	Software	$3.23	$6.45	$9.68	$19.35	$0.43	61%	19%	61%	0.00%
Einstein Noah Restaurant Group	BAGL	Restaurants	$8.03	$16.05	$24.08	$48.15	$1.07	18%	58%	12%	3.03%
El Paso Electric Company	EE	Utilities	Negative Free Cash Flow	Negative Free Cash Flow	Negative Free Cash Flow	Negative Free Cash Flow	-$0.67	-2%	112%	-1%	3.20%
Electro Rent Corporation	ELRC	Rentals	$1.13	$2.25	$3.38	$6.75	$0.15	2%	95%	-2%	4.60%
Electro Scientific Industries	ESIO	Semiconductors	Negative Free Cash Flow	Negative Free Cash Flow	Negative Free Cash Flow	Negative Free Cash Flow	-$0.31	-4%	-218%	-5%	2.62%
Electronic Arts, Inc.	EA	Software	$5.63	$11.25	$16.88	$33.75	$0.75	7%	33%	7%	0.00%
Electronics for Imaging Inc	EFII	Computers	$8.10	$16.20	$24.30	$48.60	$1.08	7%	39%	7%	0.00%
Eli Lilly and Company	LLY	Drugs	$31.73	$63.45	$95.18	$190.35	$4.23	20%	19%	13%	3.71%
Elizabeth Arden, Inc.	RDEN	Consumer Goods	$5.63	$11.25	$16.88	$33.75	$0.75	3%	65%	3%	0.00%

NAME	TICKER	INDUSTRY	2014 BUY PRICE OPINION	2014 HOLD PRICE OPINION	2014 SELL PRICE OPINION	2014 SHORT PRICE OPINION	2014 MYCROFT FREE CASH FLOW PER SHARE ESTIMATE	2014 MYCROFT FREE CASH FLOW RETURN ON TOTAL CAPITAL ESTIMATE (FROIC) >15% = Great	2014 MYCROFT CAPFLOW ESTIMATE <33% = Great BUT NO NEGATIVE RESULTS	2014 MYCROFT MICHAELIS GROWTH RATE ESTIMATE >15% = Great	DIVIDEND YIELD
Step #1 = Look up the company's current stock market price on the day of analysis and compare it to our 2014 Buy, Hold, Sell & Short Price.											
Step #2 =Take the company's current market price; divide it by the "2014 Mycroft Free Cash Flow Per Share estimate." This gives the "Price to Free Cash Flow."											
All results below are based on the 2014 year end estimates using the "2014 Mycroft Michaelis Growth Rate" and are good until December 31, 2014.											
Ellie Mae Inc	ELLI	Software	$10.13	$20.25	$30.38	$60.75	$1.35	17%	20%	17%	0.00%
eMagin Corporation	EMAN	Semiconductors	$0.90	$1.80	$2.70	$5.40	$0.12	7%	42%	7%	0.00%
EMC Corporation	EMC	Computers	$21.23	$42.45	$63.68	$127.35	$2.83	22%	22%	20%	1.48%
EMCOR Group, Inc.	EME	Engineering	$12.98	$25.95	$38.93	$77.85	$1.73	7%	24%	7%	0.61%
Emcore Corporation	EMKR	Semiconductors	Negative Free Cash Flow	Negative Free Cash Flow	Negative Free Cash Flow	Negative Free Cash Flow	-$1.23	-36%	-39%	-36%	0.00%
Emerald Oil Inc	EOX	Oil & Gas	Negative Free Cash Flow	Negative Free Cash Flow	Negative Free Cash Flow	Negative Free Cash Flow	-$1.30	-29%	2101%	-29%	0.00%
Emergent BioSolutions, Inc.	EBS	Biotech	Negative Free Cash Flow	Negative Free Cash Flow	Negative Free Cash Flow	Negative Free Cash Flow	-$0.04	0%	104%	0%	0.00%
Emeritus Corporation	ESC	Health Care	$7.50	$15.00	$22.50	$45.00	$1.00	3%	55%	3%	0.00%
Emerson Electric Co.	EMR	Computers	$34.13	$68.25	$102.38	$204.75	$4.55	20%	18%	15%	2.58%
Emmis Communications Corp	EMMS	Entertainment	$0.98	$1.95	$2.93	$5.85	$0.13	2%	41%	2%	0.00%
Empire District Electric	EDE	Utilities	$1.43	$2.85	$4.28	$8.55	$0.19	1%	95%	2%	4.70%

NAME	TICKER	INDUSTRY	2014 BUY PRICE OPINION	2014 HOLD PRICE OPINION	2014 SELL PRICE OPINION	2014 SHORT PRICE OPINION	2014 MYCROFT FREE CASH FLOW PER SHARE ESTIMATE	2014 MYCROFT FREE CASH FLOW RETURN ON TOTAL CAPITAL ESTIMATE (FROIC) >15% = Great	2014 MYCROFT CAPFLOW ESTIMATE <33% = Great BUT NO NEGATIVE RESULTS	2014 MYCROFT MICHAELIS GROWTH RATE ESTIMATE >15% = Great	DIVIDEND YIELD
Step #1 = Look up the company's current stock market price on the day of analysis and compare it to our 2014 Buy, Hold, Sell & Short Price.											
Step #2 =Take the company's current market price; divide it by the "2014 Mycroft Free Cash Flow Per Share estimate." This gives the "Price to Free Cash Flow."											
All results below are based on the 2014 year end estimates using the "2014 Mycroft Michaelis Growth Rate" and are good until December 31, 2014.											
Empire Resorts, Inc.	NYNY	Travel & Leisure	Negative Free Cash Flow	Negative Free Cash Flow	Negative Free Cash Flow	Negative Free Cash Flow	-$0.27	-37%	-1016%	-37%	0.00%
Emulex Corporation	ELX	Computers	Negative Free Cash Flow	Negative Free Cash Flow	Negative Free Cash Flow	Negative Free Cash Flow	-$0.06	-1%	148%	-1%	0.00%
Enanta Pharmaceuticals Inc	ENTA	Biotech	$5.03	$10.05	$15.08	$30.15	$0.67	10%	5%	10%	0.00%
Encore Wire Corporation	WIRE	Computers	Negative Free Cash Flow	Negative Free Cash Flow	Negative Free Cash Flow	Negative Free Cash Flow	-$2.19	-10%	1726%	-11%	0.20%
Endeavour International Corp	END	Oil & Gas	Negative Free Cash Flow	Negative Free Cash Flow	Negative Free Cash Flow	Negative Free Cash Flow	-$2.11	-11%	172%	-11%	0.00%
Endo Health Solutions Inc	ENDP	Drugs	$42.68	$85.35	$128.03	$256.05	$5.69	13%	15%	13%	0.00%
Endocyte, Inc.	ECYT	Biotech	Negative Free Cash Flow	Negative Free Cash Flow	Negative Free Cash Flow	Negative Free Cash Flow	-$1.13	-45%	-4%	-45%	0.00%
Endologix, Inc.	ELGX	Medical	Negative Free Cash Flow	Negative Free Cash Flow	Negative Free Cash Flow	Negative Free Cash Flow	-$0.18	-11%	-32%	-11%	0.00%
Energen Corp	EGN	Oil & Gas	Negative Free Cash Flow	Negative Free Cash Flow	Negative Free Cash Flow	Negative Free Cash Flow	-$5.91	-11%	150%	-11%	0.83%
Energizer Holdings, Inc.	ENR	Consumer Goods	$90.83	$181.65	$272.48	$544.95	$12.11	15%	12%	14%	2.10%
Energy Recovery, Inc.	ERII	Industrial	Negative Free Cash Flow	Negative Free Cash Flow	Negative Free Cash Flow	Negative Free Cash Flow	-$0.14	-9%	-43%	-9%	0.00%

NAME	TICKER	INDUSTRY	2014 BUY PRICE OPINION	2014 HOLD PRICE OPINION	2014 SELL PRICE OPINION	2014 SHORT PRICE OPINION	2014 MYCROFT FREE CASH FLOW PER SHARE ESTIMATE	2014 MYCROFT FREE CASH FLOW RETURN ON TOTAL CAPITAL ESTIMATE (FROIC) >15% = Great	2014 MYCROFT CAPFLOW ESTIMATE <33% = Great BUT NO NEGATIVE RESULTS	2014 MYCROFT MICHAELIS GROWTH RATE ESTIMATE >15% = Great	DIVIDEND YIELD
Step #1 = Look up the company's current stock market price on the day of analysis and compare it to our 2014 Buy, Hold, Sell & Short Price.											
Step #2 =Take the company's current market price; divide it by the "2014 Mycroft Free Cash Flow Per Share estimate." This gives the "Price to Free Cash Flow."											
All results below are based on the 2014 year end estimates using the "2014 Mycroft Michaelis Growth Rate" and are good until December 31, 2014.											
Energy XXI (Bermuda) Ltd	EXXI	Oil & Gas	Negative Free Cash Flow	Negative Free Cash Flow	Negative Free Cash Flow	Negative Free Cash Flow	-$2.35	-7%	128%	-7%	1.74%
EnerNOC, Inc.	ENOC	Business Services	$1.28	$2.55	$3.83	$7.65	$0.17	3%	87%	3%	0.00%
EnerSys, Inc.	ENS	Computers	$37.05	$74.10	$111.15	$222.30	$4.94	17%	20%	16%	0.91%
Engility Holdings Inc	EGL	Engineering	$19.88	$39.75	$59.63	$119.25	$2.65	10%	6%	10%	0.00%
ENGlobal Corporation	ENG	Engineering	$3.15	$6.30	$9.45	$18.90	$0.42	33%	6%	33%	0.00%
Ennis, Inc.	EBF	Industrial	$17.10	$34.20	$51.30	$102.60	$2.28	12%	5%	12%	3.83%
Enphase Energy Inc	ENPH	Semiconductors	Negative Free Cash Flow	Negative Free Cash Flow	Negative Free Cash Flow	Negative Free Cash Flow	-$0.70	-57%	-41%	-57%	0.00%
Enpro Industries, Inc.	NPO	Industrial	$27.08	$54.15	$81.23	$162.45	$3.61	7%	40%	7%	0.00%
Ensign Group, Inc.	ENSG	Health Care	$17.70	$35.40	$53.10	$106.20	$2.36	9%	43%	9%	0.65%
Entegris, Inc.	ENTG	Semiconductors	$3.53	$7.05	$10.58	$21.15	$0.47	8%	47%	8%	0.00%
Entercom Communications Corporation	ETM	Entertainment	$14.03	$28.05	$42.08	$84.15	$1.87	8%	8%	8%	0.00%

NAME	TICKER	INDUSTRY	2014 BUY PRICE OPINION	2014 HOLD PRICE OPINION	2014 SELL PRICE OPINION	2014 SHORT PRICE OPINION	2014 MYCROFT FREE CASH FLOW PER SHARE ESTIMATE	2014 MYCROFT FREE CASH FLOW RETURN ON TOTAL CAPITAL ESTIMATE (FROIC) >15% = Great	2014 MYCROFT CAPFLOW ESTIMATE <33% = Great BUT NO NEGATIVE RESULTS	2014 MYCROFT MICHAELIS GROWTH RATE ESTIMATE >15% = Great	DIVIDEND YIELD
Step #1 = Look up the company's current stock market price on the day of analysis and compare it to our 2014 Buy, Hold, Sell & Short Price.												
Step #2 =Take the company's current market price; divide it by the "2014 Mycroft Free Cash Flow Per Share estimate." This gives the "Price to Free Cash Flow."												
All results below are based on the 2014 year end estimates using the "2014 Mycroft Michaelis Growth Rate" and are good until December 31, 2014.												
Entergy Corp	ETR	Utilities	Negative Free Cash Flow	Negative Free Cash Flow	Negative Free Cash Flow	Negative Free Cash Flow	-$4.38	-4%	127%	-1%	5.20%
EnteroMedics, Inc.	ETRM	Medical	Negative Free Cash Flow	Negative Free Cash Flow	Negative Free Cash Flow	Negative Free Cash Flow	-$0.37	-90%	0%	-90%	0.00%
Entravision Communications Corporation	EVC	Entertainment	$3.30	$6.60	$9.90	$19.80	$0.44	10%	23%	10%	0.00%
EntreMed, Inc.	ENMD	Biotech	Negative Free Cash Flow	Negative Free Cash Flow	Negative Free Cash Flow	Negative Free Cash Flow	-$0.11	-18%	0%	-18%	0.00%
Entropic Communications, Inc.	ENTR	Semiconductors	$3.30	$6.60	$9.90	$19.80	$0.44	12%	26%	12%	0.00%
Envestnet, Inc.	ENV	Business Services	$5.93	$11.85	$17.78	$35.55	$0.79	17%	22%	17%	0.00%
Enzo Biochem, Inc.	ENZ	Medical	Negative Free Cash Flow	Negative Free Cash Flow	Negative Free Cash Flow	Negative Free Cash Flow	-$0.23	-26%	-14%	-26%	0.00%
EOG Resources	EOG	Oil & Gas	Negative Free Cash Flow	Negative Free Cash Flow	Negative Free Cash Flow	Negative Free Cash Flow	-$2.74	-4%	112%	-4%	0.46%
eOn Communications Corporation	EONC	Communication	Negative Free Cash Flow	Negative Free Cash Flow	Negative Free Cash Flow	Negative Free Cash Flow	-$0.19	-7%	-107%	-7%	0.00%
EPAM Systems Inc	EPAM	Software	$2.70	$5.40	$8.10	$16.20	$0.36	5%	64%	5%	0.00%
Epiq Systems, Inc.	EPIQ	Software	Negative Free Cash Flow	Negative Free Cash Flow	Negative Free Cash Flow	Negative Free Cash Flow	-$0.18	-2%	133%	-3%	2.84%

NAME	TICKER	INDUSTRY	2014 BUY PRICE OPINION	2014 HOLD PRICE OPINION	2014 SELL PRICE OPINION	2014 SHORT PRICE OPINION	2014 MYCROFT FREE CASH FLOW PER SHARE ESTIMATE	2014 MYCROFT FREE CASH FLOW RETURN ON TOTAL CAPITAL ESTIMATE (FROIC) >15% = Great	2014 MYCROFT CAPFLOW ESTIMATE <33% = Great BUT NO NEGATIVE RESULTS	2014 MYCROFT MICHAELIS GROWTH RATE ESTIMATE >15% = Great	DIVIDEND YIELD
Step #1 = Look up the company's current stock market price on the day of analysis and compare it to our 2014 Buy, Hold, Sell & Short Price.											
Step #2 =Take the company's current market price; divide it by the "2014 Mycroft Free Cash Flow Per Share estimate." This gives the "Price to Free Cash Flow."											
All results below are based on the 2014 year end estimates using the "2014 Mycroft Michaelis Growth Rate" and are good until December 31, 2014.											
Epizyme Inc	EPZM	Biotech	Negative Free Cash Flow	Negative Free Cash Flow	Negative Free Cash Flow	Negative Free Cash Flow	-$1.54	-46%	-3%	-46%	0.00%
EPL Oil & Gas Inc	EPL	Oil & Gas	Negative Free Cash Flow	Negative Free Cash Flow	Negative Free Cash Flow	Negative Free Cash Flow	-$12.88	-59%	269%	-59%	0.00%
Eplus, Inc.	PLUS	Software	$28.65	$57.30	$85.95	$171.90	$3.82	10%	38%	10%	0.00%
EQT Corp	EQT	Oil & Gas	Negative Free Cash Flow	Negative Free Cash Flow	Negative Free Cash Flow	Negative Free Cash Flow	-$3.53	-8%	152%	-9%	0.14%
Equifax, Inc.	EFX	Business Services	$30.45	$60.90	$91.35	$182.70	$4.06	14%	13%	12%	1.48%
Equinix, Inc.	EQIX	Internet	Negative Free Cash Flow	Negative Free Cash Flow	Negative Free Cash Flow	Negative Free Cash Flow	-$2.09	-2%	119%	-2%	0.00%
Era Group Inc	ERA	Transportation	$3.83	$7.65	$11.48	$22.95	$0.51	2%	85%	2%	0.00%
Erickson Air-Crane Inc	EAC	Aerospace & Defense	Negative Free Cash Flow	Negative Free Cash Flow	Negative Free Cash Flow	Negative Free Cash Flow	-$1.12	-38%	-297%	-38%	0.00%
Escalade, Inc.	ESCA	Travel & Leisure	$2.63	$5.25	$7.88	$15.75	$0.35	5%	31%	4%	4.10%
ESCO Technologies, Inc.	ESE	Computers	Negative Free Cash Flow	Negative Free Cash Flow	Negative Free Cash Flow	Negative Free Cash Flow	-$0.05	0%	104%	0%	0.99%
Esperion Therapeutics Inc	ESPR	Biotech	Negative Free Cash Flow	Negative Free Cash Flow	Negative Free Cash Flow	Negative Free Cash Flow	-$0.72	25%	0%	25%	0.00%

NAME	TICKER	INDUSTRY	2014 BUY PRICE OPINION	2014 HOLD PRICE OPINION	2014 SELL PRICE OPINION	2014 SHORT PRICE OPINION	2014 MYCROFT FREE CASH FLOW PER SHARE ESTIMATE	2014 MYCROFT FREE CASH FLOW RETURN ON TOTAL CAPITAL ESTIMATE (FROIC) >15% = Great	2014 MYCROFT CAPFLOW ESTIMATE <33% = Great BUT NO NEGATIVE RESULTS	2014 MYCROFT MICHAELIS GROWTH RATE ESTIMATE >15% = Great	DIVIDEND YIELD
Step #1 = Look up the company's current stock market price on the day of analysis and compare it to our 2014 Buy, Hold, Sell & Short Price.											
Step #2 =Take the company's current market price; divide it by the "2014 Mycroft Free Cash Flow Per Share estimate." This gives the "Price to Free Cash Flow."											
All results below are based on the 2014 year end estimates using the "2014 Mycroft Michaelis Growth Rate" and are good until December 31, 2014.											
Espey Manufacturing & Electronics	ESP	Computers	$11.78	$23.55	$35.33	$70.65	$1.57	12%	7%	7%	3.52%
Estee Lauder Cos Inc Class A	EL	Consumer Goods	$16.65	$33.30	$49.95	$99.90	$2.22	18%	38%	12%	1.03%
Esterline Technologies	ESL	Aerospace & Defense	$49.05	$98.10	$147.15	$294.30	$6.54	7%	20%	7%	0.00%
Ethan Allen Interiors, Inc.	ETH	Apparel & Furniture	$11.85	$23.70	$35.55	$71.10	$1.58	9%	31%	8%	1.45%
Euronet Worldwide, Inc.	EEFT	Business Services	$23.18	$46.35	$69.53	$139.05	$3.09	19%	24%	19%	0.00%
Evertec Inc	EVTC	Software	Negative Free Cash Flow	Negative Free Cash Flow	Negative Free Cash Flow	Negative Free Cash Flow	-$0.05	0%	116%	-2%	1.69%
Evolution Petroleum Corporation	EPM	Oil & Gas	$0.98	$1.95	$2.93	$5.85	$0.13	6%	72%	6%	0.00%
Evolving Systems, Inc.	EVOL	Software	$3.75	$7.50	$11.25	$22.50	$0.50	18%	3%	7%	3.80%
Exa Corp	EXA	Software	Negative Free Cash Flow	Negative Free Cash Flow	Negative Free Cash Flow	Negative Free Cash Flow	-$0.03	-1%	208%	-1%	0.00%
Exact Sciences Corporation	EXAS	Biotech	Negative Free Cash Flow	Negative Free Cash Flow	Negative Free Cash Flow	Negative Free Cash Flow	-$0.63	-29%	-4%	-29%	0.00%
Exactech, Inc.	EXAC	Medical	Negative Free Cash Flow	Negative Free Cash Flow	Negative Free Cash Flow	Negative Free Cash Flow	-$0.34	-2%	128%	-2%	0.00%

NAME	TICKER	INDUSTRY	2014 BUY PRICE OPINION	2014 HOLD PRICE OPINION	2014 SELL PRICE OPINION	2014 SHORT PRICE OPINION	2014 MYCROFT FREE CASH FLOW PER SHARE ESTIMATE	2014 MYCROFT FREE CASH FLOW RETURN ON TOTAL CAPITAL ESTIMATE (FROIC) >15% = Great	2014 MYCROFT CAPFLOW ESTIMATE <33% = Great BUT NO NEGATIVE RESULTS	2014 MYCROFT MICHAELIS GROWTH RATE ESTIMATE >15% = Great	DIVIDEND YIELD
Step #1 = Look up the company's current stock market price on the day of analysis and compare it to our 2014 Buy, Hold, Sell & Short Price.											
Step #2 =Take the company's current market price; divide it by the "2014 Mycroft Free Cash Flow Per Share estimate." This gives the "Price to Free Cash Flow."											
All results below are based on the 2014 year end estimates using the "2014 Mycroft Michaelis Growth Rate" and are good until December 31, 2014.											
ExamWorks Group, Inc.	EXAM	Business Services	$4.35	$8.70	$13.05	$26.10	$0.58	4%	24%	4%	0.00%
Exar Corporation	EXAR	Semiconductors	$1.50	$3.00	$4.50	$9.00	$0.20	4%	12%	4%	0.00%
EXCO Resources, Inc.	XCO	Oil & Gas	$0.38	$0.75	$1.13	$2.25	$0.05	1%	97%	1%	2.86%
Exelis Inc	XLS	Aerospace & Defense	$21.00	$42.00	$63.00	$126.00	$2.80	23%	19%	21%	2.65%
Exelixis, Inc.	EXEL	Biotech	Negative Free Cash Flow	Negative Free Cash Flow	Negative Free Cash Flow	Negative Free Cash Flow	-$0.93	-47%	-2%	-47%	0.00%
Exelon Corp	EXC	Utilities	$2.03	$4.05	$6.08	$12.15	$0.27	1%	96%	2%	4.20%
ExlService Holdings, Inc.	EXLS	Business Services	$14.85	$29.70	$44.55	$89.10	$1.98	16%	22%	16%	0.00%
ExOne Co	XONE	Industrial	Negative Free Cash Flow	Negative Free Cash Flow	Negative Free Cash Flow	Negative Free Cash Flow	-$0.84	-13%	-19%	-13%	0.00%
Expedia, Inc.	EXPE	Travel & Leisure	$49.95	$99.90	$149.85	$299.70	$6.66	22%	27%	20%	1.16%
Expeditors International of Washington, Inc.	EXPD	Transportation	$13.35	$26.70	$40.05	$80.10	$1.78	16%	13%	11%	1.35%
Exponent, Inc.	EXPO	Business Services	$25.43	$50.85	$76.28	$152.55	$3.39	17%	15%	15%	0.88%

NAME	TICKER	INDUSTRY	2014 BUY PRICE OPINION	2014 HOLD PRICE OPINION	2014 SELL PRICE OPINION	2014 SHORT PRICE OPINION	2014 MYCROFT FREE CASH FLOW PER SHARE ESTIMATE	2014 MYCROFT FREE CASH FLOW RETURN ON TOTAL CAPITAL ESTIMATE (FROIC) >15% = Great	2014 MYCROFT CAPFLOW ESTIMATE <33% = Great BUT NO NEGATIVE RESULTS	2014 MYCROFT MICHAELIS GROWTH RATE ESTIMATE >15% = Great	DIVIDEND YIELD
Step #1 = Look up the company's current stock market price on the day of analysis and compare it to our 2014 Buy, Hold, Sell & Short Price.											
Step #2 =Take the company's current market price; divide it by the "2014 Mycroft Free Cash Flow Per Share estimate." This gives the "Price to Free Cash Flow."											
All results below are based on the 2014 year end estimates using the "2014 Mycroft Michaelis Growth Rate" and are good until December 31, 2014.											
Express Scripts	ESRX	Health Care	$40.65	$81.30	$121.95	$243.90	$5.42	10%	7%	10%	0.00%
Express, Inc.	EXPR	Retail	$14.33	$28.65	$42.98	$85.95	$1.91	21%	43%	21%	0.00%
Exterran Holdings, Inc.	EXH	Oil & Gas	$0.15	$0.30	$0.45	$0.90	$0.02	0%	100%	0%	0.00%
Extreme Networks, Inc.	EXTR	Communication	$1.65	$3.30	$4.95	$9.90	$0.22	10%	41%	10%	0.00%
Exxon Mobil Corporation	XOM	Oil & Gas	$24.38	$48.75	$73.13	$146.25	$3.25	8%	71%	4%	2.87%
EZCorp, Inc.	EZPW	Retail	$14.10	$28.20	$42.30	$84.60	$1.88	8%	33%	8%	0.00%
F5 Networks, Inc.	FFIV	Software	$58.88	$117.75	$176.63	$353.25	$7.85	31%	7%	31%	0.00%
FAB Universal Corp	FU	Software	$13.73	$27.45	$41.18	$82.35	$1.83	22%	2%	22%	0.00%
Fabrinet	FN	Computers	$9.08	$18.15	$27.23	$54.45	$1.21	11%	22%	11%	0.00%
Facebook Inc Class A	FB	Internet	$7.20	$14.40	$21.60	$43.20	$0.96	16%	32%	16%	0.00%
FactSet Research Systems, Inc.	FDS	Business Services	$51.98	$103.95	$155.93	$311.85	$6.93	38%	8%	30%	1.25%

NAME	TICKER	INDUSTRY	2014 BUY PRICE OPINION	2014 HOLD PRICE OPINION	2014 SELL PRICE OPINION	2014 SHORT PRICE OPINION	2014 MYCROFT FREE CASH FLOW PER SHARE ESTIMATE	2014 MYCROFT FREE CASH FLOW RETURN ON TOTAL CAPITAL ESTIMATE (FROIC) >15% = Great	2014 MYCROFT CAPFLOW ESTIMATE <33% = Great BUT NO NEGATIVE RESULTS	2014 MYCROFT MICHAELIS GROWTH RATE ESTIMATE >15% = Great	DIVIDEND YIELD
Step #1 = Look up the company's current stock market price on the day of analysis and compare it to our 2014 Buy, Hold, Sell & Short Price.											
Step #2 =Take the company's current market price; divide it by the "2014 Mycroft Free Cash Flow Per Share estimate." This gives the "Price to Free Cash Flow."											
All results below are based on the 2014 year end estimates using the "2014 Mycroft Michaelis Growth Rate" and are good until December 31, 2014.											
Fair Isaac Corp	FICO	Software	$22.65	$45.30	$67.95	$135.90	$3.02	10%	21%	9%	0.15%
Fairchild Semiconductor International Inc	FCS	Semiconductors	$2.10	$4.20	$6.30	$12.60	$0.28	2%	76%	2%	0.00%
FairPoint Communications, Inc.	FRP	Communication	$12.60	$25.20	$37.80	$75.60	$1.68	7%	78%	7%	0.00%
Fairway Group Holdings Corp Class A	FWM	Retail	Negative Free Cash Flow	Negative Free Cash Flow	Negative Free Cash Flow	Negative Free Cash Flow	-$0.04	-23%	-241%	-23%	0.00%
Family Dollar Stores, Inc.	FDO	Retail	Negative Free Cash Flow	Negative Free Cash Flow	Negative Free Cash Flow	Negative Free Cash Flow	-$3.22	-18%	184%	-23%	1.43%
Famous Dave's of America, Inc.	DAVE	Restaurants	$10.58	$21.15	$31.73	$63.45	$1.41	17%	37%	17%	0.00%
Farmer Bros. Co.	FARM	Consumer Goods	$3.98	$7.95	$11.93	$23.85	$0.53	12%	68%	12%	0.00%
Faro Technologies, Inc.	FARO	Computers	$17.40	$34.80	$52.20	$104.40	$2.32	12%	10%	12%	0.00%
Fastenal Company	FAST	Industrial	$6.00	$12.00	$18.00	$36.00	$0.80	14%	43%	-1%	1.99%
Federal Signal Corp	FSS	Autos	$1.58	$3.15	$4.73	$9.45	$0.21	5%	57%	5%	0.00%
Federal-Mogul Corp	FDML	Autos	Negative Free Cash Flow	Negative Free Cash Flow	Negative Free Cash Flow	Negative Free Cash Flow	-$1.87	-8%	500%	-8%	0.00%

NAME	TICKER	INDUSTRY	2014 BUY PRICE OPINION	2014 HOLD PRICE OPINION	2014 SELL PRICE OPINION	2014 SHORT PRICE OPINION	2014 MYCROFT FREE CASH FLOW PER SHARE ESTIMATE	2014 MYCROFT FREE CASH FLOW RETURN ON TOTAL CAPITAL ESTIMATE (FROIC) >15% = Great	2014 MYCROFT CAPFLOW ESTIMATE <33% = Great BUT NO NEGATIVE RESULTS	2014 MYCROFT MICHAELIS GROWTH RATE ESTIMATE >15% = Great	DIVIDEND YIELD
Step #1 = Look up the company's current stock market price on the day of analysis and compare it to our 2014 Buy, Hold, Sell & Short Price.										
Step #2 =Take the company's current market price; divide it by the "2014 Mycroft Free Cash Flow Per Share estimate." This gives the "Price to Free Cash Flow."										
All results below are based on the 2014 year end estimates using the "2014 Mycroft Michaelis Growth Rate" and are good until December 31, 2014.										
FedEx Corporation	FDX	Transportation	$33.08	$66.15	$99.23	$198.45	$4.41	7%	72%	6%	0.54%
FEI Company	FEIC	Computers	$22.65	$45.30	$67.95	$135.90	$3.02	12%	32%	10%	0.57%
Female Health Company	FHCO	Consumer Goods	$4.35	$8.70	$13.05	$26.10	$0.58	51%	4%	22%	3.09%
Ferro Corp	FOE	Chemicals	Negative Free Cash Flow	Negative Free Cash Flow	Negative Free Cash Flow	Negative Free Cash Flow	-$0.34	-6%	394%	-6%	0.00%
Fibrocell Science Inc	FCSC	Drugs	Negative Free Cash Flow	Negative Free Cash Flow	Negative Free Cash Flow	Negative Free Cash Flow	-$0.79	-80%	-1%	-80%	0.00%
Fidelity National Information Services, Inc.	FIS	Software	$17.63	$35.25	$52.88	$105.75	$2.35	6%	31%	5%	1.92%
FieldPoint Petroleum Corporation	FPP	Oil & Gas	$2.25	$4.50	$6.75	$13.50	$0.30	11%	65%	11%	0.00%
Fiesta Restaurant Group Inc	FRGI	Restaurants	Negative Free Cash Flow	Negative Free Cash Flow	Negative Free Cash Flow	Negative Free Cash Flow	-$0.56	-6%	132%	-6%	0.00%
Fifth & Pacific Companies Inc	FNP	Apparel & Furniture	Negative Free Cash Flow	Negative Free Cash Flow	Negative Free Cash Flow	Negative Free Cash Flow	-$0.91	-46%	-826%	-46%	0.00%
Finisar Corporation	FNSR	Communication	$4.58	$9.15	$13.73	$27.45	$0.61	6%	65%	6%	0.00%
Finish Line Inc	FINL	Retail	$0.98	$1.95	$2.93	$5.85	$0.13	1%	92%	0%	1.26%

NAME	TICKER	INDUSTRY	2014 BUY PRICE OPINION	2014 HOLD PRICE OPINION	2014 SELL PRICE OPINION	2014 SHORT PRICE OPINION	2014 MYCROFT FREE CASH FLOW PER SHARE ESTIMATE	2014 MYCROFT FREE CASH FLOW RETURN ON TOTAL CAPITAL ESTIMATE (FROIC) >15% = Great	2014 MYCROFT CAPFLOW ESTIMATE <33% = Great BUT NO NEGATIVE RESULTS	2014 MYCROFT MICHAELIS GROWTH RATE ESTIMATE >15% = Great	DIVIDEND YIELD
Step #1 = Look up the company's current stock market price on the day of analysis and compare it to our 2014 Buy, Hold, Sell & Short Price.											
Step #2 =Take the company's current market price; divide it by the "2014 Mycroft Free Cash Flow Per Share estimate." This gives the "Price to Free Cash Flow."											
All results below are based on the 2014 year end estimates using the "2014 Mycroft Michaelis Growth Rate" and are good until December 31, 2014.											
First Solar, Inc.	FSLR	Semiconductors	$32.03	$64.05	$96.08	$192.15	$4.27	8%	40%	8%	0.00%
FirstEnergy Corp	FE	Utilities	Negative Free Cash Flow	Negative Free Cash Flow	Negative Free Cash Flow	Negative Free Cash Flow	-$1.02	-3%	116%	-5%	6.00%
Fiserv, Inc.	FISV	Business Services	$40.95	$81.90	$122.85	$245.70	$5.46	10%	24%	10%	0.00%
Five Below Inc	FIVE	Retail	$2.55	$5.10	$7.65	$15.30	$0.34	15%	62%	15%	0.00%
Five Star Quality Care, Inc.	FVE	Health Care	Negative Free Cash Flow	Negative Free Cash Flow	Negative Free Cash Flow	Negative Free Cash Flow	-$0.53	-7%	184%	-7%	0.00%
Fleetcor Technologies, Inc.	FLT	Business Services	$25.20	$50.40	$75.60	$151.20	$3.36	18%	8%	18%	0.00%
FleetMatics Group PLC	FLTX	Software	$0.45	$0.90	$1.35	$2.70	$0.06	1%	94%	1%	0.00%
Flexsteel Industries, Inc.	FLXS	Apparel & Furniture	Negative Free Cash Flow	Negative Free Cash Flow	Negative Free Cash Flow	Negative Free Cash Flow	-$0.05	0%	105%	0%	2.66%
FLIR Systems, Inc.	FLIR	Aerospace & Defense	$18.30	$36.60	$54.90	$109.80	$2.44	17%	15%	15%	1.11%
Flotek Industries, Inc.	FTK	Chemicals	$2.93	$5.85	$8.78	$17.55	$0.39	8%	52%	8%	0.00%
Flow International Corporation	FLOW	Industrial	$0.23	$0.45	$0.68	$1.35	$0.03	1%	84%	1%	0.00%

NAME	TICKER	INDUSTRY	2014 BUY PRICE OPINION	2014 HOLD PRICE OPINION	2014 SELL PRICE OPINION	2014 SHORT PRICE OPINION	2014 MYCROFT FREE CASH FLOW PER SHARE ESTIMATE	2014 MYCROFT FREE CASH FLOW RETURN ON TOTAL CAPITAL ESTIMATE (FROIC) >15% = Great	2014 MYCROFT CAPFLOW ESTIMATE <33% = Great BUT NO NEGATIVE RESULTS	2014 MYCROFT MICHAELIS GROWTH RATE ESTIMATE >15% = Great	DIVIDEND YIELD
Step #1 = Look up the company's current stock market price on the day of analysis and compare it to our 2014 Buy, Hold, Sell & Short Price.											
Step #2 =Take the company's current market price; divide it by the "2014 Mycroft Free Cash Flow Per Share estimate." This gives the "Price to Free Cash Flow."											
All results below are based on the 2014 year end estimates using the "2014 Mycroft Michaelis Growth Rate" and are good until December 31, 2014.											
Flowers Foods, Inc.	FLO	Consumer Goods	$7.05	$14.10	$21.15	$42.30	$0.94	13%	32%	8%	2.18%
Flowserve Corporation	FLS	Industrial	$16.73	$33.45	$50.18	$100.35	$2.23	13%	33%	11%	0.91%
Fluidigm Corporation	FLDM	Computers	Negative Free Cash Flow	Negative Free Cash Flow	Negative Free Cash Flow	Negative Free Cash Flow	-$0.53	-14%	-31%	-14%	0.00%
Fluor Corporation	FLR	Engineering	$27.30	$54.60	$81.90	$163.80	$3.64	13%	32%	11%	0.96%
FMC Corporation	FMC	Chemicals	$6.98	$13.95	$20.93	$41.85	$0.93	5%	64%	3%	0.78%
FMC Technologies, Inc.	FTI	Oil & Gas	$4.95	$9.90	$14.85	$29.70	$0.66	5%	71%	5%	0.00%
Fonar Corporation	FONR	Medical	$18.38	$36.75	$55.13	$110.25	$2.45	89%	13%	89%	0.00%
Foot Locker Inc	FL	Apparel & Furniture	$19.95	$39.90	$59.85	$119.70	$2.66	14%	33%	12%	2.40%
Ford Motor Co	F	Autos	$6.08	$12.15	$18.23	$36.45	$0.81	3%	67%	4%	2.28%
Forest City Enterprises Inc Class A	FCE.A	Real Estate	Negative Free Cash Flow	Negative Free Cash Flow	Negative Free Cash Flow	Negative Free Cash Flow	-$1.75	-4%	232%	-4%	0.00%
Forest Laboratories, Inc.	FRX	Drugs	Negative Free Cash Flow	Negative Free Cash Flow	Negative Free Cash Flow	Negative Free Cash Flow	-$0.68	-3%	1209%	-3%	0.00%

NAME	TICKER	INDUSTRY	2014 BUY PRICE OPINION	2014 HOLD PRICE OPINION	2014 SELL PRICE OPINION	2014 SHORT PRICE OPINION	2014 MYCROFT FREE CASH FLOW PER SHARE ESTIMATE	2014 MYCROFT FREE CASH FLOW RETURN ON TOTAL CAPITAL ESTIMATE (FROIC) >15% = Great	2014 MYCROFT CAPFLOW ESTIMATE <33% = Great BUT NO NEGATIVE RESULTS	2014 MYCROFT MICHAELIS GROWTH RATE ESTIMATE >15% = Great	DIVIDEND YIELD
Step #1 = Look up the company's current stock market price on the day of analysis and compare it to our 2014 Buy, Hold, Sell & Short Price.											
Step #2 =Take the company's current market price; divide it by the "2014 Mycroft Free Cash Flow Per Share estimate." This gives the "Price to Free Cash Flow."											
All results below are based on the 2014 year end estimates using the "2014 Mycroft Michaelis Growth Rate" and are good until December 31, 2014.											
Forest Oil Corp	FST	Oil & Gas	Negative Free Cash Flow	Negative Free Cash Flow	Negative Free Cash Flow	Negative Free Cash Flow	-$1.92	-12%	175%	-12%	0.00%
Forestar Group, Inc.	FOR	Real Estate	Negative Free Cash Flow	Negative Free Cash Flow	Negative Free Cash Flow	Negative Free Cash Flow	-$1.05	-5%	286%	-5%	0.00%
FormFactor, Inc.	FORM	Semiconductors	Negative Free Cash Flow	Negative Free Cash Flow	Negative Free Cash Flow	Negative Free Cash Flow	-$0.48	-8%	-54%	-8%	0.00%
Forrester Research, Inc.	FORR	Business Services	$21.00	$42.00	$63.00	$126.00	$2.80	22%	6%	18%	1.82%
Fortinet, Inc.	FTNT	Software	$8.40	$16.80	$25.20	$50.40	$1.12	25%	13%	25%	0.00%
Fortune Brands Home & Security Inc	FBHS	Apparel & Furniture	$9.45	$18.90	$28.35	$56.70	$1.26	7%	28%	6%	0.98%
Forum Energy Technologies Inc	FET	Oil & Gas	$13.13	$26.25	$39.38	$78.75	$1.75	9%	27%	9%	0.00%
Forward Air Corporation	FWRD	Transportation	$13.80	$27.60	$41.40	$82.80	$1.84	13%	38%	11%	1.03%
Forward Industries, Inc.	FORD	Computers	Negative Free Cash Flow	Negative Free Cash Flow	Negative Free Cash Flow	Negative Free Cash Flow	-$0.19	-16%	-4%	-16%	0.00%
Fossil Group Inc	FOSL	Apparel & Furniture	$57.00	$114.00	$171.00	$342.00	$7.60	27%	29%	27%	0.00%
Francescas Holdings Corp	FRAN	Retail	$7.73	$15.45	$23.18	$46.35	$1.03	32%	38%	32%	0.00%

NAME	TICKER	INDUSTRY	2014 BUY PRICE OPINION	2014 HOLD PRICE OPINION	2014 SELL PRICE OPINION	2014 SHORT PRICE OPINION	2014 MYCROFT FREE CASH FLOW PER SHARE ESTIMATE	2014 MYCROFT FREE CASH FLOW RETURN ON TOTAL CAPITAL ESTIMATE (FROIC) >15% = Great	2014 MYCROFT CAPFLOW ESTIMATE <33% = Great BUT NO NEGATIVE RESULTS	2014 MYCROFT MICHAELIS GROWTH RATE ESTIMATE >15% = Great	DIVIDEND YIELD
Step #1 = Look up the company's current stock market price on the day of analysis and compare it to our 2014 Buy, Hold, Sell & Short Price.											
Step #2 =Take the company's current market price; divide it by the "2014 Mycroft Free Cash Flow Per Share estimate." This gives the "Price to Free Cash Flow."											
All results below are based on the 2014 year end estimates using the "2014 Mycroft Michaelis Growth Rate" and are good until December 31, 2014.											
Franklin Covey Company	FC	Education	$5.48	$10.95	$16.43	$32.85	$0.73	9%	30%	9%	0.00%
Franklin Electric Co.	FELE	Industrial	$2.93	$5.85	$8.78	$17.55	$0.39	3%	78%	1%	0.81%
Fred's, Inc.	FRED	Retail	$3.75	$7.50	$11.25	$22.50	$0.50	4%	72%	3%	1.50%
Freeport-McMoRan Copper & Gold	FCX	Commodities	Negative Free Cash Flow	Negative Free Cash Flow	Negative Free Cash Flow	Negative Free Cash Flow	-$0.26	-1%	107%	-3%	3.70%
Freescale Semiconductor Ltd	FSL	Semiconductors	$1.28	$2.55	$3.83	$7.65	$0.17	2%	82%	2%	0.00%
FreightCar America, Inc.	RAIL	Transportation	Negative Free Cash Flow	Negative Free Cash Flow	Negative Free Cash Flow	Negative Free Cash Flow	-$3.32	-19%	-111%	-20%	1.29%
Frequency Electronics	FEIM	Communication	$0.53	$1.05	$1.58	$3.15	$0.07	1%	80%	1%	0.00%
Fresh Del Monte Produce, Inc.	FDP	Consumer Goods	$0.15	$0.30	$0.45	$0.90	$0.02	0%	99%	0%	1.67%
Fresh Market, Inc.	TFM	Retail	$2.93	$5.85	$8.78	$17.55	$0.39	6%	84%	6%	0.00%
Friedman Industries	FRD	Steel	$13.35	$26.70	$40.05	$80.10	$1.78	16%	4%	16%	3.10%
Frisch's Restaurants, Inc.	FRS	Restaurants	$15.23	$30.45	$45.68	$91.35	$2.03	9%	51%	9%	3.22%

NAME	TICKER	INDUSTRY	2014 BUY PRICE OPINION	2014 HOLD PRICE OPINION	2014 SELL PRICE OPINION	2014 SHORT PRICE OPINION	2014 MYCROFT FREE CASH FLOW PER SHARE ESTIMATE	2014 MYCROFT FREE CASH FLOW RETURN ON TOTAL CAPITAL ESTIMATE (FROIC) >15% = Great	2014 MYCROFT CAPFLOW ESTIMATE <33% = Great BUT NO NEGATIVE RESULTS	2014 MYCROFT MICHAELIS GROWTH RATE ESTIMATE >15% = Great	DIVIDEND YIELD
Step #1 = Look up the company's current stock market price on the day of analysis and compare it to our 2014 Buy, Hold, Sell & Short Price.											
Step #2 =Take the company's current market price; divide it by the "2014 Mycroft Free Cash Flow Per Share estimate." This gives the "Price to Free Cash Flow."											
All results below are based on the 2014 year end estimates using the "2014 Mycroft Michaelis Growth Rate" and are good until December 31, 2014.											
Frontier Communications Corp Class B	FTR	Communication	$6.30	$12.60	$18.90	$37.80	$0.84	6%	49%	12%	9.30%
Frontline Ltd	FRO	Transportation	$1.13	$2.25	$3.38	$6.75	$0.15	2%	56%	2%	0.00%
FTI Consulting, Inc.	FCN	Business Services	$36.08	$72.15	$108.23	$216.45	$4.81	16%	14%	16%	0.00%
Fuel Systems Solutions, Inc.	FSYS	Autos	$1.80	$3.60	$5.40	$10.80	$0.24	1%	69%	1%	0.00%
Full House Resorts, Inc.	FLL	Travel & Leisure	$0.30	$0.60	$0.90	$1.80	$0.04	1%	83%	1%	0.00%
Furiex Pharmaceuticals, Inc.	FURX	Business Services	Negative Free Cash Flow	Negative Free Cash Flow	Negative Free Cash Flow	Negative Free Cash Flow	-$2.19	-63%	0%	-63%	0.00%
Furmanite Corporation	FRM	Engineering	$0.90	$1.80	$2.70	$5.40	$0.12	3%	75%	3%	0.00%
Fusion-io Inc	FIO	Computers	$1.95	$3.90	$5.85	$11.70	$0.26	5%	37%	5%	0.00%
FutureFuel Corp	FF	Chemicals	$7.65	$15.30	$22.95	$45.90	$1.02	13%	21%	9%	2.59%
FX Energy, Inc.	FXEN	Oil & Gas	Negative Free Cash Flow	Negative Free Cash Flow	Negative Free Cash Flow	Negative Free Cash Flow	-$0.41	-26%	-1375%	-26%	0.00%
G & K Services, Inc. Class A	GK	Business Services	$32.10	$64.20	$96.30	$192.60	$4.28	11%	32%	10%	1.97%

NAME	TICKER	INDUSTRY	2014 BUY PRICE OPINION	2014 HOLD PRICE OPINION	2014 SELL PRICE OPINION	2014 SHORT PRICE OPINION	2014 MYCROFT FREE CASH FLOW PER SHARE ESTIMATE	2014 MYCROFT FREE CASH FLOW RETURN ON TOTAL CAPITAL ESTIMATE (FROIC) >15% = Great	2014 MYCROFT CAPFLOW ESTIMATE <33% = Great BUT NO NEGATIVE RESULTS	2014 MYCROFT MICHAELIS GROWTH RATE ESTIMATE >15% = Great	DIVIDEND YIELD
Step #1 = Look up the company's current stock market price on the day of analysis and compare it to our 2014 Buy, Hold, Sell & Short Price.											
Step #2 =Take the company's current market price; divide it by the "2014 Mycroft Free Cash Flow Per Share estimate." This gives the "Price to Free Cash Flow."											
All results below are based on the 2014 year end estimates using the "2014 Mycroft Michaelis Growth Rate" and are good until December 31, 2014.											
G. Willi-Food International, Ltd.	WILC	Retail	Negative Free Cash Flow	Negative Free Cash Flow	Negative Free Cash Flow	Negative Free Cash Flow	-$0.05	-1%	150%	-1%	0.00%
Gaiam, Inc.	GAIA	Retail	Negative Free Cash Flow	Negative Free Cash Flow	Negative Free Cash Flow	Negative Free Cash Flow	-$0.28	-5%	-119%	-5%	0.00%
Galena Biopharma Inc	GALE	Biotech	Negative Free Cash Flow	Negative Free Cash Flow	Negative Free Cash Flow	Negative Free Cash Flow	-$0.26	-144%	0%	-144%	0.00%
GameStop Corp Class A	GME	Retail	$22.65	$45.30	$67.95	$135.90	$3.02	14%	31%	11%	2.19%
Gaming Partners International Corporation	GPIC	Travel & Leisure	Negative Free Cash Flow	Negative Free Cash Flow	Negative Free Cash Flow	Negative Free Cash Flow	-$0.32	-5%	-291%	-5%	0.00%
Gannett Co Inc	GCI	Publishing	$20.63	$41.25	$61.88	$123.75	$2.75	14%	15%	12%	3.15%
Gap, Inc.	GPS	Retail	$21.60	$43.20	$64.80	$129.60	$2.88	23%	37%	17%	1.93%
Garmin, Ltd.	GRMN	Computers	$23.25	$46.50	$69.75	$139.50	$3.10	16%	9%	10%	3.80%
Gartner, Inc.	IT	Software	$35.85	$71.70	$107.55	$215.10	$4.78	60%	14%	60%	0.00%
Gas Natural, Inc.	EGAS	Utilities	Negative Free Cash Flow	Negative Free Cash Flow	Negative Free Cash Flow	Negative Free Cash Flow	-$0.55	-5%	142%	-5%	5.30%
GasLog Ltd	GLOG	Transportation	Negative Free Cash Flow	Negative Free Cash Flow	Negative Free Cash Flow	Negative Free Cash Flow	-$8.31	-60%	1372%	-60%	2.94%

NAME	TICKER	INDUSTRY	2014 BUY PRICE OPINION	2014 HOLD PRICE OPINION	2014 SELL PRICE OPINION	2014 SHORT PRICE OPINION	2014 MYCROFT FREE CASH FLOW PER SHARE ESTIMATE	2014 MYCROFT FREE CASH FLOW RETURN ON TOTAL CAPITAL ESTIMATE (FROIC) >15% = Great	2014 MYCROFT CAPFLOW ESTIMATE <33% = Great BUT NO NEGATIVE RESULTS	2014 MYCROFT MICHAELIS GROWTH RATE ESTIMATE >15% = Great	DIVIDEND YIELD
Step #1 = Look up the company's current stock market price on the day of analysis and compare it to our 2014 Buy, Hold, Sell & Short Price.											
Step #2 =Take the company's current market price; divide it by the "2014 Mycroft Free Cash Flow Per Share estimate." This gives the "Price to Free Cash Flow."											
All results below are based on the 2014 year end estimates using the "2014 Mycroft Michaelis Growth Rate" and are good until December 31, 2014.											
Gastar Exploration Ltd.	GST	Oil & Gas	Negative Free Cash Flow	Negative Free Cash Flow	Negative Free Cash Flow	Negative Free Cash Flow	-$2.11	-95%	287%	-95%	0.00%
GATX Corp	GMT	Rentals	Negative Free Cash Flow	Negative Free Cash Flow	Negative Free Cash Flow	Negative Free Cash Flow	-$7.69	-8%	192%	-6%	2.60%
Geeknet, Inc.	GKNT	Internet	$0.08	$0.15	$0.23	$0.45	$0.01	0%	22%	0%	0.00%
Gencor Industries, Inc.	GENC	Agriculture	Negative Free Cash Flow	Negative Free Cash Flow	Negative Free Cash Flow	Negative Free Cash Flow	-$0.24	-2%	-114%	-2%	0.00%
GenCorp Inc.	GY	Aerospace & Defense	$0.98	$1.95	$2.93	$5.85	$0.13	-7%	86%	-7%	0.00%
Generac Holdings, Inc.	GNRC	Industrial	$29.55	$59.10	$88.65	$177.30	$3.94	21%	11%	21%	0.00%
General Cable Corporation	BGC	Computers	$6.75	$13.50	$20.25	$40.50	$0.90	2%	70%	3%	2.29%
General Communication Class A	GNCMA	Communication	Negative Free Cash Flow	Negative Free Cash Flow	Negative Free Cash Flow	Negative Free Cash Flow	-$0.07	0%	102%	0%	0.00%
General Dynamics	GD	Aerospace & Defense	$50.85	$101.70	$152.55	$305.10	$6.78	14%	17%	12%	2.58%
General Electric Co	GE	Industrial	$10.80	$21.60	$32.40	$64.80	$1.44	4%	52%	5%	3.18%
General Mills, Inc.	GIS	Consumer Goods	$30.83	$61.65	$92.48	$184.95	$4.11	19%	21%	14%	3.12%

NAME	TICKER	INDUSTRY	2014 BUY PRICE OPINION	2014 HOLD PRICE OPINION	2014 SELL PRICE OPINION	2014 SHORT PRICE OPINION	2014 MYCROFT FREE CASH FLOW PER SHARE ESTIMATE	2014 MYCROFT FREE CASH FLOW RETURN ON TOTAL CAPITAL ESTIMATE (FROIC) >15% = Great	2014 MYCROFT CAPFLOW ESTIMATE <33% = Great BUT NO NEGATIVE RESULTS	2014 MYCROFT MICHAELIS GROWTH RATE ESTIMATE >15% = Great	DIVIDEND YIELD
Step #1 = Look up the company's current stock market price on the day of analysis and compare it to our 2014 Buy, Hold, Sell & Short Price.											
Step #2 =Take the company's current market price; divide it by the "2014 Mycroft Free Cash Flow Per Share estimate." This gives the "Price to Free Cash Flow."											
All results below are based on the 2014 year end estimates using the "2014 Mycroft Michaelis Growth Rate" and are good until December 31, 2014.											
General Moly, Inc.	GMO	Commodities	Negative Free Cash Flow	Negative Free Cash Flow	Negative Free Cash Flow	Negative Free Cash Flow	-$0.67	-46%	-210%	-46%	0.00%
General Motors Co	GM	Autos	$1.88	$3.75	$5.63	$11.25	$0.25	1%	95%	1%	0.00%
Genesco, Inc.	GCO	Retail	$21.45	$42.90	$64.35	$128.70	$2.86	7%	54%	7%	0.00%
Genesee & Wyoming, Inc. Class A	GWR	Transportation	Negative Free Cash Flow	Negative Free Cash Flow	Negative Free Cash Flow	Negative Free Cash Flow	-$0.10	0%	102%	0%	0.00%
Genie Energy Ltd Class B	GNE	Oil & Gas	Negative Free Cash Flow	Negative Free Cash Flow	Negative Free Cash Flow	Negative Free Cash Flow	-$0.07	-2%	-19%	-2%	0.00%
GenMark Diagnostics, Inc.	GNMK	Medical	Negative Free Cash Flow	Negative Free Cash Flow	Negative Free Cash Flow	Negative Free Cash Flow	-$0.79	-55%	-24%	-55%	0.00%
Genomic Health, Inc.	GHDX	Medical	$3.00	$6.00	$9.00	$18.00	$0.40	8%	49%	8%	0.00%
Genpact Ltd.	G	Business Services	$8.40	$16.80	$25.20	$50.40	$1.12	17%	24%	17%	0.00%
Gentex Corporation	GNTX	Autos	$15.60	$31.20	$46.80	$93.60	$2.08	21%	22%	17%	2.26%
Gentherm Inc	THRM	Autos	$2.25	$4.50	$6.75	$13.50	$0.30	4%	79%	4%	0.00%
Gentiva Health Services, Inc.	GTIV	Health Care	$19.28	$38.55	$57.83	$115.65	$2.57	8%	14%	8%	0.00%

NAME	TICKER	INDUSTRY	2014 BUY PRICE OPINION	2014 HOLD PRICE OPINION	2014 SELL PRICE OPINION	2014 SHORT PRICE OPINION	2014 MYCROFT FREE CASH FLOW PER SHARE ESTIMATE	2014 MYCROFT FREE CASH FLOW RETURN ON TOTAL CAPITAL ESTIMATE (FROIC) >15% = Great	2014 MYCROFT CAPFLOW ESTIMATE <33% = Great BUT NO NEGATIVE RESULTS	2014 MYCROFT MICHAELIS GROWTH RATE ESTIMATE >15% = Great	DIVIDEND YIELD
Step #1 = Look up the company's current stock market price on the day of analysis and compare it to our 2014 Buy, Hold, Sell & Short Price.											
Step #2 =Take the company's current market price; divide it by the "2014 Mycroft Free Cash Flow Per Share estimate." This gives the "Price to Free Cash Flow."											
All results below are based on the 2014 year end estimates using the "2014 Mycroft Michaelis Growth Rate" and are good until December 31, 2014.											
Genuine Parts Company	GPC	Autos	$48.30	$96.60	$144.90	$289.80	$6.44	24%	11%	17%	2.66%
Geo Group, Inc.	GEO	Rentals	$12.08	$24.15	$36.23	$72.45	$1.61	4%	54%	5%	6.10%
Geospace Technologies Corp	GEOS	Computers	Negative Free Cash Flow	Negative Free Cash Flow	Negative Free Cash Flow	Negative Free Cash Flow	-$7.20	-34%	-93%	-34%	0.00%
Geron Corporation	GERN	Biotech	Negative Free Cash Flow	Negative Free Cash Flow	Negative Free Cash Flow	Negative Free Cash Flow	-$0.38	-72%	-1%	-72%	0.00%
Gevo, Inc.	GEVO	Chemicals	Negative Free Cash Flow	Negative Free Cash Flow	Negative Free Cash Flow	Negative Free Cash Flow	-$1.78	-84%	-33%	-84%	0.00%
Gibraltar Industries Inc	ROCK	Steel	$11.93	$23.85	$35.78	$71.55	$1.59	7%	20%	7%	0.00%
Giga-tronics, Inc.	GIGA	Computers	Negative Free Cash Flow	Negative Free Cash Flow	Negative Free Cash Flow	Negative Free Cash Flow	-$0.04	-70%	-13%	-70%	0.00%
GigOptix, Inc.	GIG	Semiconductors	Negative Free Cash Flow	Negative Free Cash Flow	Negative Free Cash Flow	Negative Free Cash Flow	-$0.14	-12%	-82%	-12%	0.00%
G-III Apparel Group, Ltd.	GIII	Apparel & Furniture	$14.10	$28.20	$42.30	$84.60	$1.88	8%	33%	8%	0.00%
Gilead Sciences Inc	GILD	Biotech	$14.93	$29.85	$44.78	$89.55	$1.99	15%	14%	15%	0.00%
Global Brass & Copper Holdings Inc	BRSS	Industrial	$4.43	$8.85	$13.28	$26.55	$0.59	3%	64%	3%	0.00%

NAME	TICKER	INDUSTRY	2014 BUY PRICE OPINION	2014 HOLD PRICE OPINION	2014 SELL PRICE OPINION	2014 SHORT PRICE OPINION	2014 MYCROFT FREE CASH FLOW PER SHARE ESTIMATE	2014 MYCROFT FREE CASH FLOW RETURN ON TOTAL CAPITAL ESTIMATE (FROIC) >15% = Great	2014 MYCROFT CAPFLOW ESTIMATE <33% = Great BUT NO NEGATIVE RESULTS	2014 MYCROFT MICHAELIS GROWTH RATE ESTIMATE >15% = Great	DIVIDEND YIELD
Step #1 = Look up the company's current stock market price on the day of analysis and compare it to our 2014 Buy, Hold, Sell & Short Price.											
Step #2 =Take the company's current market price; divide it by the "2014 Mycroft Free Cash Flow Per Share estimate." This gives the "Price to Free Cash Flow."											
All results below are based on the 2014 year end estimates using the "2014 Mycroft Michaelis Growth Rate" and are good until December 31, 2014.											
Global Cash Access Holdings Inc	GCA	Business Services	$7.50	$15.00	$22.50	$45.00	$1.00	17%	22%	17%	0.00%
Global Eagle Entertainment Inc	ENT	Conglomerates	Negative Free Cash Flow	Negative Free Cash Flow	Negative Free Cash Flow	Negative Free Cash Flow	-$0.56	-16%	0%	-16%	0.00%
Global Payments, Inc.	GPN	Business Services	$15.45	$30.90	$46.35	$92.70	$2.06	10%	41%	10%	0.16%
Global Power Equipment Group, Inc.	GLPW	Industrial	$6.45	$12.90	$19.35	$38.70	$0.86	5%	30%	5%	1.91%
Global Sources, Ltd.	GSOL	Business Services	$7.73	$15.45	$23.18	$46.35	$1.03	18%	3%	18%	0.00%
Globe Specialty Metals, Inc.	GSM	Commodities	$2.93	$5.85	$8.78	$17.55	$0.39	5%	61%	3%	1.99%
Globecomm Systems, Inc.	GCOM	Communication	$5.93	$11.85	$17.78	$35.55	$0.79	7%	45%	7%	0.00%
Globus Medical Inc Class A	GMED	Medical	$3.83	$7.65	$11.48	$22.95	$0.51	10%	37%	10%	0.00%
Glu Mobile, Inc.	GLUU	Software	Negative Free Cash Flow	Negative Free Cash Flow	Negative Free Cash Flow	Negative Free Cash Flow	-$0.16	-29%	-17%	-29%	0.00%
GNC Holdings Inc	GNC	Retail	$18.45	$36.90	$55.35	$110.70	$2.46	12%	17%	10%	1.12%
Gogo Inc	GOGO	Communication	Negative Free Cash Flow	Negative Free Cash Flow	Negative Free Cash Flow	Negative Free Cash Flow	-$1.27	-24%	1541%	-24%	0.00%

NAME	TICKER	INDUSTRY	2014 BUY PRICE OPINION	2014 HOLD PRICE OPINION	2014 SELL PRICE OPINION	2014 SHORT PRICE OPINION	2014 MYCROFT FREE CASH FLOW PER SHARE ESTIMATE	2014 MYCROFT FREE CASH FLOW RETURN ON TOTAL CAPITAL ESTIMATE (FROIC) >15% = Great	2014 MYCROFT CAPFLOW ESTIMATE <33% = Great BUT NO NEGATIVE RESULTS	2014 MYCROFT MICHAELIS GROWTH RATE ESTIMATE >15% = Great	DIVIDEND YIELD
Step #1 = Look up the company's current stock market price on the day of analysis and compare it to our 2014 Buy, Hold, Sell & Short Price.											
Step #2 =Take the company's current market price; divide it by the "2014 Mycroft Free Cash Flow Per Share estimate." This gives the "Price to Free Cash Flow."											
All results below are based on the 2014 year end estimates using the "2014 Mycroft Michaelis Growth Rate" and are good until December 31, 2014.											
Golar LNG, Ltd.	GLNG	Transportation	Negative Free Cash Flow	Negative Free Cash Flow	Negative Free Cash Flow	Negative Free Cash Flow	-$3.46	-10%	239%	-10%	4.70%
Gold Resource Corp	GORO	Commodities	$2.55	$5.10	$7.65	$15.30	$0.34	21%	33%	3%	6.50%
Golden Enterprises, Inc.	GLDC	Consumer Goods	$0.30	$0.60	$0.90	$1.80	$0.04	2%	90%	0%	3.50%
Golden Minerals Co	AUMN	Commodities	Negative Free Cash Flow	Negative Free Cash Flow	Negative Free Cash Flow	Negative Free Cash Flow	-$0.85	-59%	-20%	-59%	0.00%
Goldfield Corp	GV	Engineering	Negative Free Cash Flow	Negative Free Cash Flow	Negative Free Cash Flow	Negative Free Cash Flow	-$0.01	-1%	102%	-1%	0.00%
Goodrich Petroleum Corp	GDP	Oil & Gas	Negative Free Cash Flow	Negative Free Cash Flow	Negative Free Cash Flow	Negative Free Cash Flow	-$2.76	-14%	179%	-14%	0.00%
Goodyear Tire & Rubber Co	GT	Autos	Negative Free Cash Flow	Negative Free Cash Flow	Negative Free Cash Flow	Negative Free Cash Flow	-$0.13	-14%	110%	-14%	0.00%
Google, Inc.	GOOG	Internet	$318.83	$637.65	$956.48	$1,912.95	$42.51	15%	28%	15%	0.00%
Gordman's Stores, Inc.	GMAN	Retail	Negative Free Cash Flow	Negative Free Cash Flow	Negative Free Cash Flow	Negative Free Cash Flow	-$0.96	-17%	157%	-17%	0.00%
Gorman-Rupp Company	GRC	Industrial	$13.05	$26.10	$39.15	$78.30	$1.74	13%	21%	11%	1.04%
GP Strategies Corporation	GPX	Education	$10.28	$20.55	$30.83	$61.65	$1.37	13%	12%	13%	0.00%

NAME	TICKER	INDUSTRY	2014 BUY PRICE OPINION	2014 HOLD PRICE OPINION	2014 SELL PRICE OPINION	2014 SHORT PRICE OPINION	2014 MYCROFT FREE CASH FLOW PER SHARE ESTIMATE	2014 MYCROFT FREE CASH FLOW RETURN ON TOTAL CAPITAL ESTIMATE (FROIC) >15% = Great	2014 MYCROFT CAPFLOW ESTIMATE <33% = Great BUT NO NEGATIVE RESULTS	2014 MYCROFT MICHAELIS GROWTH RATE ESTIMATE >15% = Great	DIVIDEND YIELD
Step #1 = Look up the company's current stock market price on the day of analysis and compare it to our 2014 Buy, Hold, Sell & Short Price.											
Step #2 =Take the company's current market price; divide it by the "2014 Mycroft Free Cash Flow Per Share estimate." This gives the "Price to Free Cash Flow."											
All results below are based on the 2014 year end estimates using the "2014 Mycroft Michaelis Growth Rate" and are good until December 31, 2014.											
Graco Incorporated	GGG	Industrial	$28.88	$57.75	$86.63	$173.25	$3.85	17%	8%	14%	1.37%
GrafTech International Ltd	GTI	Industrial	$2.25	$4.50	$6.75	$13.50	$0.30	2%	72%	2%	0.00%
Graham Corporation	GHM	Industrial	$5.85	$11.70	$17.55	$35.10	$0.78	8%	18%	7%	0.33%
Grand Canyon Education, Inc.	LOPE	Education	$1.58	$3.15	$4.73	$9.45	$0.21	3%	91%	3%	0.00%
Granite City Food & Brewery Ltd.	GCFB	Restaurants	Negative Free Cash Flow	Negative Free Cash Flow	Negative Free Cash Flow	Negative Free Cash Flow	-$1.07	-42%	329%	-42%	0.00%
Granite Construction Inc.	GVA	Engineering	$7.50	$15.00	$22.50	$45.00	$1.00	4%	50%	3%	1.76%
Graphic Packaging Holding Co	GPK	Containers	$5.33	$10.65	$15.98	$31.95	$0.71	8%	47%	8%	0.00%
Gray Television, Inc.	GTN	Entertainment	$5.85	$11.70	$17.55	$35.10	$0.78	4%	38%	4%	0.00%
Great Lakes Dredge & Dock Corporation	GLDD	Engineering	Negative Free Cash Flow	Negative Free Cash Flow	Negative Free Cash Flow	Negative Free Cash Flow	-$1.24	-15%	-1145%	-15%	0.00%
Great Plains Energy Inc	GXP	Utilities	Negative Free Cash Flow	Negative Free Cash Flow	Negative Free Cash Flow	Negative Free Cash Flow	-$0.08	0%	102%	2%	4.00%
Greatbatch, Inc.	GB	Medical	$1.35	$2.70	$4.05	$8.10	$0.18	1%	87%	1%	0.00%

NAME	TICKER	INDUSTRY	2014 BUY PRICE OPINION	2014 HOLD PRICE OPINION	2014 SELL PRICE OPINION	2014 SHORT PRICE OPINION	2014 MYCROFT FREE CASH FLOW PER SHARE ESTIMATE	2014 MYCROFT FREE CASH FLOW RETURN ON TOTAL CAPITAL ESTIMATE (FROIC) >15% = Great	2014 MYCROFT CAPFLOW ESTIMATE <33% = Great BUT NO NEGATIVE RESULTS	2014 MYCROFT MICHAELIS GROWTH RATE ESTIMATE >15% = Great	DIVIDEND YIELD
Step #1 = Look up the company's current stock market price on the day of analysis and compare it to our 2014 Buy, Hold, Sell & Short Price.											
Step #2 =Take the company's current market price; divide it by the "2014 Mycroft Free Cash Flow Per Share estimate." This gives the "Price to Free Cash Flow."											
All results below are based on the 2014 year end estimates using the "2014 Mycroft Michaelis Growth Rate" and are good until December 31, 2014.											
Green Dot Corp	GDOT	Business Services	$23.55	$47.10	$70.65	$141.30	$3.14	25%	31%	25%	0.00%
Green Mountain Coffee Roasters, Inc.	GMCR	Consumer Goods	$27.53	$55.05	$82.58	$165.15	$3.67	16%	38%	16%	0.00%
Green Plains Renewable Energy, Inc.	GPRE	Chemicals	$22.28	$44.55	$66.83	$133.65	$2.97	8%	17%	9%	0.94%
Greenbrier Companies, Inc.	GBX	Transportation	Negative Free Cash Flow	Negative Free Cash Flow	Negative Free Cash Flow	Negative Free Cash Flow	-$0.51	-2%	117%	-2%	0.00%
GreenHunter Resources Inc	GRH	Industrial	Negative Free Cash Flow	Negative Free Cash Flow	Negative Free Cash Flow	Negative Free Cash Flow	-$0.69	-85%	-135%	-85%	0.00%
Greenway Medical Technologies Inc	GWAY	Software	Negative Free Cash Flow	Negative Free Cash Flow	Negative Free Cash Flow	Negative Free Cash Flow	-$0.62	-18%	488%	-18%	0.00%
Greif, Inc.	GEF	Containers	$22.28	$44.55	$66.83	$133.65	$2.97	6%	48%	5%	3.18%
Griffin Land & Nurseries, Inc.	GRIF	Agriculture	Negative Free Cash Flow	Negative Free Cash Flow	Negative Free Cash Flow	Negative Free Cash Flow	-$4.16	-13%	-2546%	-13%	0.65%
Griffon Corporation	GFF	Building Supplies	$0.45	$0.90	$1.35	$2.70	$0.06	0%	94%	1%	0.85%
Group 1 Automotive Inc	GPI	Autos	Negative Free Cash Flow	Negative Free Cash Flow	Negative Free Cash Flow	Negative Free Cash Flow	-$1.62	-3%	169%	-3%	0.83%
Groupon Inc	GRPN	Internet	$0.90	$1.80	$2.70	$5.40	$0.12	9%	54%	9%	0.00%

NAME	TICKER	INDUSTRY	2014 BUY PRICE OPINION	2014 HOLD PRICE OPINION	2014 SELL PRICE OPINION	2014 SHORT PRICE OPINION	2014 MYCROFT FREE CASH FLOW PER SHARE ESTIMATE	2014 MYCROFT FREE CASH FLOW RETURN ON TOTAL CAPITAL ESTIMATE (FROIC) >15% = Great	2014 MYCROFT CAPFLOW ESTIMATE <33% = Great BUT NO NEGATIVE RESULTS	2014 MYCROFT MICHAELIS GROWTH RATE ESTIMATE >15% = Great	DIVIDEND YIELD
Step #1 = Look up the company's current stock market price on the day of analysis and compare it to our 2014 Buy, Hold, Sell & Short Price.											
Step #2 =Take the company's current market price; divide it by the "2014 Mycroft Free Cash Flow Per Share estimate." This gives the "Price to Free Cash Flow."											
All results below are based on the 2014 year end estimates using the "2014 Mycroft Michaelis Growth Rate" and are good until December 31, 2014.											
GSE Holding Inc	GSE	Autos	$5.63	$11.25	$16.88	$33.75	$0.75	6%	62%	6%	0.00%
GSE Systems	GVP	Software	$3.38	$6.75	$10.13	$20.25	$0.45	21%	28%	21%	0.00%
GSI Group, Inc.	GSIG	Computers	$5.55	$11.10	$16.65	$33.30	$0.74	9%	15%	9%	0.00%
GSI Technology, Inc.	GSIT	Semiconductors	$5.18	$10.35	$15.53	$31.05	$0.69	13%	1%	13%	0.00%
GT Advanced Technologies Inc	GTAT	Semiconductors	Negative Free Cash Flow	Negative Free Cash Flow	Negative Free Cash Flow	Negative Free Cash Flow	-$1.37	-43%	-44%	-43%	0.00%
Guess? Inc	GES	Retail	$24.68	$49.35	$74.03	$148.05	$3.29	22%	28%	18%	2.60%
Guidance Software, Inc.	GUID	Software	$0.15	$0.30	$0.45	$0.90	$0.02	2%	95%	2%	0.00%
Guidewire Software Inc	GWRE	Software	$2.33	$4.65	$6.98	$13.95	$0.31	8%	39%	8%	0.00%
Gulf Island Fabrication, Inc.	GIFI	Industrial	$2.48	$4.95	$7.43	$14.85	$0.33	2%	85%	1%	1.66%
GulfMark Offshore, Inc.	GLF	Oil & Gas	Negative Free Cash Flow	Negative Free Cash Flow	Negative Free Cash Flow	Negative Free Cash Flow	-$5.58	-11%	313%	-11%	2.01%
Gulfport Energy Corporation	GPOR	Oil & Gas	Negative Free Cash Flow	Negative Free Cash Flow	Negative Free Cash Flow	Negative Free Cash Flow	-$11.12	-53%	598%	-53%	0.00%

NAME	TICKER	INDUSTRY	2014 BUY PRICE OPINION	2014 HOLD PRICE OPINION	2014 SELL PRICE OPINION	2014 SHORT PRICE OPINION	2014 MYCROFT FREE CASH FLOW PER SHARE ESTIMATE	2014 MYCROFT FREE CASH FLOW RETURN ON TOTAL CAPITAL ESTIMATE (FROIC) >15% = Great	2014 MYCROFT CAPFLOW ESTIMATE <33% = Great BUT NO NEGATIVE RESULTS	2014 MYCROFT MICHAELIS GROWTH RATE ESTIMATE >15% = Great	DIVIDEND YIELD
Step #1 = Look up the company's current stock market price on the day of analysis and compare it to our 2014 Buy, Hold, Sell & Short Price.											
Step #2 =Take the company's current market price; divide it by the "2014 Mycroft Free Cash Flow Per Share estimate." This gives the "Price to Free Cash Flow."											
All results below are based on the 2014 year end estimates using the "2014 Mycroft Michaelis Growth Rate" and are good until December 31, 2014.											
H&E Equipment Services, Inc.	HEES	Industrial	Negative Free Cash Flow	Negative Free Cash Flow	Negative Free Cash Flow	Negative Free Cash Flow	-$7.04	-79%	581%	-79%	0.00%
H&R Block Inc	HRB	Services	$13.28	$26.55	$39.83	$79.65	$1.77	28%	24%	16%	2.94%
H.B. Fuller Company	FUL	Chemicals	$6.60	$13.20	$19.80	$39.60	$0.88	3%	62%	3%	1.00%
Hackett Group, Inc.	HCKT	Business Services	$4.65	$9.30	$13.95	$27.90	$0.62	17%	12%	15%	1.54%
Haemonetics Corporation	HAE	Medical	$4.73	$9.45	$14.18	$28.35	$0.63	4%	68%	4%	0.00%
Hain Celestial Group, Inc.	HAIN	Retail	$7.80	$15.60	$23.40	$46.80	$1.04	3%	60%	3%	0.00%
Halcon Resources	HK	Oil & Gas	Negative Free Cash Flow	Negative Free Cash Flow	Negative Free Cash Flow	Negative Free Cash Flow	-$3.77	-56%	539%	-56%	0.00%
Halliburton Company	HAL	Oil & Gas	$5.70	$11.40	$17.10	$34.20	$0.76	3%	83%	2%	0.99%
Halozyme Therapeutics, Inc.	HALO	Biotech	Negative Free Cash Flow	Negative Free Cash Flow	Negative Free Cash Flow	Negative Free Cash Flow	-$0.49	-487%	-2%	-487%	0.00%
Handy & Harman Ltd.	HNH	Steel	$15.00	$30.00	$45.00	$90.00	$2.00	12%	46%	12%	0.00%
Hanesbrands Inc	HBI	Apparel & Furniture	$45.98	$91.95	$137.93	$275.85	$6.13	19%	7%	18%	1.27%

NAME	TICKER	INDUSTRY	2014 BUY PRICE OPINION	2014 HOLD PRICE OPINION	2014 SELL PRICE OPINION	2014 SHORT PRICE OPINION	2014 MYCROFT FREE CASH FLOW PER SHARE ESTIMATE	2014 MYCROFT FREE CASH FLOW RETURN ON TOTAL CAPITAL ESTIMATE (FROIC) >15% = Great	2014 MYCROFT CAPFLOW ESTIMATE <33% = Great BUT NO NEGATIVE RESULTS	2014 MYCROFT MICHAELIS GROWTH RATE ESTIMATE >15% = Great	DIVIDEND YIELD
Step #1 = Look up the company's current stock market price on the day of analysis and compare it to our 2014 Buy, Hold, Sell & Short Price.											
Step #2 =Take the company's current market price; divide it by the "2014 Mycroft Free Cash Flow Per Share estimate." This gives the "Price to Free Cash Flow."											
All results below are based on the 2014 year end estimates using the "2014 Mycroft Michaelis Growth Rate" and are good until December 31, 2014.											
Hanger Inc	HGR	Health Care	$10.58	$21.15	$31.73	$63.45	$1.41	5%	43%	5%	0.00%
Hansen Medical, Inc.	HNSN	Medical	Negative Free Cash Flow	Negative Free Cash Flow	Negative Free Cash Flow	Negative Free Cash Flow	-$0.64	-146%	-2%	-146%	0.00%
Harbinger Group, Inc.	HRG	Conglomerates	$25.58	$51.15	$76.73	$153.45	$3.41	13%	15%	13%	0.00%
Hardinge, Inc.	HDNG	Industrial	$15.30	$30.60	$45.90	$91.80	$2.04	13%	16%	13%	0.54%
Harley-Davidson Inc	HOG	Autos	$26.03	$52.05	$78.08	$156.15	$3.47	11%	22%	9%	1.32%
Harman International Industries, Inc.	HAR	Computers	Negative Free Cash Flow	Negative Free Cash Flow	Negative Free Cash Flow	Negative Free Cash Flow	-$0.87	-4%	241%	-7%	1.82%
Harmonic, Inc.	HLIT	Communication	$3.83	$7.65	$11.48	$22.95	$0.51	10%	24%	10%	0.00%
Harris Corporation	HRS	Communication	$53.55	$107.10	$160.65	$321.30	$7.14	19%	21%	17%	2.89%
Harris Interactive, Inc.	HPOL	Business Services	$1.13	$2.25	$3.38	$6.75	$0.15	41%	20%	41%	0.00%
Harris Teeter Supermarkets Inc	HTSI	Retail	$8.78	$17.55	$26.33	$52.65	$1.17	5%	79%	4%	1.22%
Harsco Corporation	HSC	Building Supplies	Negative Free Cash Flow	Negative Free Cash Flow	Negative Free Cash Flow	Negative Free Cash Flow	-$0.72	-3%	126%	-4%	3.21%

NAME	TICKER	INDUSTRY	2014 BUY PRICE OPINION	2014 HOLD PRICE OPINION	2014 SELL PRICE OPINION	2014 SHORT PRICE OPINION	2014 MYCROFT FREE CASH FLOW PER SHARE ESTIMATE	2014 MYCROFT FREE CASH FLOW RETURN ON TOTAL CAPITAL ESTIMATE (FROIC) >15% = Great	2014 MYCROFT CAPFLOW ESTIMATE <33% = Great BUT NO NEGATIVE RESULTS	2014 MYCROFT MICHAELIS GROWTH RATE ESTIMATE >15% = Great	DIVIDEND YIELD
Step #1 = Look up the company's current stock market price on the day of analysis and compare it to our 2014 Buy, Hold, Sell & Short Price.											
Step #2 =Take the company's current market price; divide it by the "2014 Mycroft Free Cash Flow Per Share estimate." This gives the "Price to Free Cash Flow."											
All results below are based on the 2014 year end estimates using the "2014 Mycroft Michaelis Growth Rate" and are good until December 31, 2014.											
Harte-Hanks, Inc.	HHS	Advertising	$8.70	$17.40	$26.10	$52.20	$1.16	14%	22%	14%	4.02%
Harvard Bioscience, Inc.	HBIO	Medical	$0.90	$1.80	$2.70	$5.40	$0.12	3%	33%	3%	0.00%
Hasbro, Inc.	HAS	Travel & Leisure	$34.13	$68.25	$102.38	$204.75	$4.55	18%	18%	14%	3.39%
Haverty Furniture Companies, Inc.	HVT	Retail	$7.95	$15.90	$23.85	$47.70	$1.06	8%	50%	7%	1.38%
Hawaiian Electric Industries Inc	HE	Utilities	$2.33	$4.65	$6.98	$13.95	$0.31	1%	92%	2%	5.00%
Hawaiian Holdings, Inc.	HA	Airlines	Negative Free Cash Flow	Negative Free Cash Flow	Negative Free Cash Flow	Negative Free Cash Flow	-$0.37	-2%	107%	-2%	0.00%
Hawaiian Telcom Holdco, Inc.	HCOM	Communication	Negative Free Cash Flow	Negative Free Cash Flow	Negative Free Cash Flow	Negative Free Cash Flow	-$0.34	-1%	104%	-1%	0.00%
Hawkins, Inc.	HWKN	Chemicals	Negative Free Cash Flow	Negative Free Cash Flow	Negative Free Cash Flow	Negative Free Cash Flow	-$0.35	-2%	116%	-5%	1.85%
Haynes International, Inc.	HAYN	Industrial	$1.58	$3.15	$4.73	$9.45	$0.21	1%	94%	-1%	1.94%
HCA Holdings Inc	HCA	Health Care	$27.38	$54.75	$82.13	$164.25	$3.65	9%	57%	9%	0.00%
Headwaters, Inc.	HW	Building Supplies	$1.65	$3.30	$4.95	$9.90	$0.22	3%	67%	3%	0.00%

NAME	TICKER	INDUSTRY	2014 BUY PRICE OPINION	2014 HOLD PRICE OPINION	2014 SELL PRICE OPINION	2014 SHORT PRICE OPINION	2014 MYCROFT FREE CASH FLOW PER SHARE ESTIMATE	2014 MYCROFT FREE CASH FLOW RETURN ON TOTAL CAPITAL ESTIMATE (FROIC) >15% = Great	2014 MYCROFT CAPFLOW ESTIMATE <33% = Great BUT NO NEGATIVE RESULTS	2014 MYCROFT MICHAELIS GROWTH RATE ESTIMATE >15% = Great	DIVIDEND YIELD
Step #1 = Look up the company's current stock market price on the day of analysis and compare it to our 2014 Buy, Hold, Sell & Short Price.												
Step #2 =Take the company's current market price; divide it by the "2014 Mycroft Free Cash Flow Per Share estimate." This gives the "Price to Free Cash Flow."												
All results below are based on the 2014 year end estimates using the "2014 Mycroft Michaelis Growth Rate" and are good until December 31, 2014.												
Health Insurance Innovations Inc	HIIQ	Health Care	Negative Free Cash Flow	Negative Free Cash Flow	Negative Free Cash Flow	Negative Free Cash Flow	-$0.28	-18%	-5%	-18%	0.00%
Health Management Associates, Inc.	HMA	Health Care	$3.00	$6.00	$9.00	$18.00	$0.40	9%	78%	9%	0.00%
Health Net Inc	HNT	Health Care	Negative Free Cash Flow	Negative Free Cash Flow	Negative Free Cash Flow	Negative Free Cash Flow	-$3.63	-14%	-28%	-14%	0.00%
Healthcare Services Group	HCSG	Business Services	$4.73	$9.45	$14.18	$28.35	$0.63	18%	7%	1%	2.70%
Healthsouth Corp	HLS	Health Care	$24.60	$49.20	$73.80	$147.60	$3.28	20%	33%	17%	2.18%
HealthStream, Inc.	HSTM	Internet	$5.18	$10.35	$15.53	$31.05	$0.69	12%	32%	12%	0.00%
Healthways, Inc.	HWAY	Health Care	$6.30	$12.60	$18.90	$37.80	$0.84	5%	60%	5%	0.00%
Heartland Express, Inc.	HTLD	Transportation	Negative Free Cash Flow	Negative Free Cash Flow	Negative Free Cash Flow	Negative Free Cash Flow	-$0.25	-6%	119%	-8%	0.56%
Heartland Payment Systems, Inc.	HPY	Business Services	$30.98	$61.95	$92.93	$185.85	$4.13	39%	27%	36%	0.73%
Heartware International, Inc.	HTWR	Medical	Negative Free Cash Flow	Negative Free Cash Flow	Negative Free Cash Flow	Negative Free Cash Flow	-$3.47	-20%	-8%	-20%	0.00%
Hecla Mining Company	HL	Commodities	Negative Free Cash Flow	Negative Free Cash Flow	Negative Free Cash Flow	Negative Free Cash Flow	-$0.22	-6%	254%	-5%	0.31%

NAME	TICKER	INDUSTRY	2014 BUY PRICE OPINION	2014 HOLD PRICE OPINION	2014 SELL PRICE OPINION	2014 SHORT PRICE OPINION	2014 MYCROFT FREE CASH FLOW PER SHARE ESTIMATE	2014 MYCROFT FREE CASH FLOW RETURN ON TOTAL CAPITAL ESTIMATE (FROIC) >15% = Great	2014 MYCROFT CAPFLOW ESTIMATE <33% = Great BUT NO NEGATIVE RESULTS	2014 MYCROFT MICHAELIS GROWTH RATE ESTIMATE >15% = Great	DIVIDEND YIELD
Step #1 = Look up the company's current stock market price on the day of analysis and compare it to our 2014 Buy, Hold, Sell & Short Price.											
Step #2 =Take the company's current market price; divide it by the "2014 Mycroft Free Cash Flow Per Share estimate." This gives the "Price to Free Cash Flow."											
All results below are based on the 2014 year end estimates using the "2014 Mycroft Michaelis Growth Rate" and are good until December 31, 2014.											
Heico Corporation	HEI	Aerospace & Defense	$22.65	$45.30	$67.95	$135.90	$3.02	19%	11%	18%	0.22%
Heidrick & Struggles International, Inc.	HSII	Services	$17.63	$35.25	$52.88	$105.75	$2.35	15%	9%	15%	3.14%
Helen of Troy, Ltd.	HELE	Consumer Goods	$24.75	$49.50	$74.25	$148.50	$3.30	9%	23%	9%	0.00%
Helix Energy Solutions Group Inc	HLX	Oil & Gas	Negative Free Cash Flow	Negative Free Cash Flow	Negative Free Cash Flow	Negative Free Cash Flow	-$1.01	-4%	153%	-4%	0.00%
Helmerich & Payne, Inc.	HP	Oil & Gas	$15.00	$30.00	$45.00	$90.00	$2.00	5%	82%	3%	3.02%
Henry Schein, Inc.	HSIC	Medical	$46.28	$92.55	$138.83	$277.65	$6.17	15%	10%	15%	0.00%
Herbalife, Ltd.	HLF	Consumer Goods	$54.38	$108.75	$163.13	$326.25	$7.25	53%	21%	42%	1.77%
Hercules Offshore, Inc.	HERO	Oil & Gas	Negative Free Cash Flow	Negative Free Cash Flow	Negative Free Cash Flow	Negative Free Cash Flow	-$0.19	-2%	123%	-2%	0.00%
Heritage-Crystal Clean Inc	HCCI	Industrial	Negative Free Cash Flow	Negative Free Cash Flow	Negative Free Cash Flow	Negative Free Cash Flow	-$0.33	-4%	168%	-4%	0.00%
Herman Miller, Inc.	MLHR	Industrial	$12.30	$24.60	$36.90	$73.80	$1.64	15%	37%	12%	1.92%
Hershey	HSY	Consumer Goods	$33.30	$66.60	$99.90	$199.80	$4.44	32%	26%	18%	2.12%

NAME	TICKER	INDUSTRY	2014 BUY PRICE OPINION	2014 HOLD PRICE OPINION	2014 SELL PRICE OPINION	2014 SHORT PRICE OPINION	2014 MYCROFT FREE CASH FLOW PER SHARE ESTIMATE	2014 MYCROFT FREE CASH FLOW RETURN ON TOTAL CAPITAL ESTIMATE (FROIC) >15% = Great	2014 MYCROFT CAPFLOW ESTIMATE <33% = Great BUT NO NEGATIVE RESULTS	2014 MYCROFT MICHAELIS GROWTH RATE ESTIMATE >15% = Great	DIVIDEND YIELD
Step #1 = Look up the company's current stock market price on the day of analysis and compare it to our 2014 Buy, Hold, Sell & Short Price.											
Step #2 =Take the company's current market price; divide it by the "2014 Mycroft Free Cash Flow Per Share estimate." This gives the "Price to Free Cash Flow."											
All results below are based on the 2014 year end estimates using the "2014 Mycroft Michaelis Growth Rate" and are good until December 31, 2014.											
Hertz Global Holdings Inc	HTZ	Rentals	$58.80	$117.60	$176.40	$352.80	$7.84	18%	11%	18%	0.00%
Heska Corporation	HSKA	Medical	Negative Free Cash Flow	Negative Free Cash Flow	Negative Free Cash Flow	Negative Free Cash Flow	-$0.89	-11%	-49%	-10%	0.00%
Hess Corp	HES	Oil & Gas	Negative Free Cash Flow	Negative Free Cash Flow	Negative Free Cash Flow	Negative Free Cash Flow	-$4.32	-5%	127%	-5%	1.29%
Hewlett-Packard Co	HPQ	Computers	$45.53	$91.05	$136.58	$273.15	$6.07	20%	25%	20%	2.61%
Hexcel Corporation	HXL	Aerospace & Defense	$4.35	$8.70	$13.05	$26.10	$0.58	4%	79%	4%	0.00%
HFF, Inc.	HF	Real Estate	$12.90	$25.80	$38.70	$77.40	$1.72	34%	2%	34%	0.00%
HHGregg Incorporated	HGG	Retail	$15.00	$30.00	$45.00	$90.00	$2.00	16%	45%	16%	0.00%
Hibbett Sports Inc	HIBB	Retail	$12.83	$25.65	$38.48	$76.95	$1.71	14%	47%	14%	0.00%
Hickory Tech Corp	HTCO	Communication	Negative Free Cash Flow	Negative Free Cash Flow	Negative Free Cash Flow	Negative Free Cash Flow	-$0.47	-3%	120%	-2%	5.50%
Higher One Holdings, Inc.	ONE	Business Services	$7.73	$15.45	$23.18	$46.35	$1.03	43%	20%	43%	0.00%
Hillenbrand, Inc.	HI	Industrial	$6.60	$13.20	$19.80	$39.60	$0.88	7%	33%	3%	2.94%

NAME	TICKER	INDUSTRY	2014 BUY PRICE OPINION	2014 HOLD PRICE OPINION	2014 SELL PRICE OPINION	2014 SHORT PRICE OPINION	2014 MYCROFT FREE CASH FLOW PER SHARE ESTIMATE	2014 MYCROFT FREE CASH FLOW RETURN ON TOTAL CAPITAL ESTIMATE (FROIC) >15% = Great	2014 MYCROFT CAPFLOW ESTIMATE <33% = Great BUT NO NEGATIVE RESULTS	2014 MYCROFT MICHAELIS GROWTH RATE ESTIMATE >15% = Great	DIVIDEND YIELD
Step #1 = Look up the company's current stock market price on the day of analysis and compare it to our 2014 Buy, Hold, Sell & Short Price.											
Step #2 =Take the company's current market price; divide it by the "2014 Mycroft Free Cash Flow Per Share estimate." This gives the "Price to Free Cash Flow."											
All results below are based on the 2014 year end estimates using the "2014 Mycroft Michaelis Growth Rate" and are good until December 31, 2014.											
Hill-Rom Holdings, Inc.	HRC	Medical	$25.65	$51.30	$76.95	$153.90	$3.42	20%	30%	18%	1.56%
Hillshire Brands Co	HSH	Consumer Goods	$7.20	$14.40	$21.60	$43.20	$0.96	8%	55%	4%	2.22%
Hi-Tech Pharmacal Co., Inc.	HITK	Drugs	$20.18	$40.35	$60.53	$121.05	$2.69	13%	29%	13%	0.00%
Hittite Microwave Corporation	HITT	Semiconductors	$17.40	$34.80	$52.20	$104.40	$2.32	11%	14%	11%	0.00%
HKN, Inc.	HKNI	Oil & Gas	Negative Free Cash Flow	Negative Free Cash Flow	Negative Free Cash Flow	Negative Free Cash Flow	-$15.57	-11%	-260%	-11%	0.00%
HMS Holdings Corporation	HMSY	Business Services	$5.18	$10.35	$15.53	$31.05	$0.69	7%	31%	7%	0.00%
HNI Corporation	HNI	Industrial	$9.00	$18.00	$27.00	$54.00	$1.20	9%	59%	4%	2.78%
HollyFrontier Corp	HFC	Oil & Gas	$57.38	$114.75	$172.13	$344.25	$7.65	17%	22%	17%	2.80%
Hollywood Media Corporation	HOLL	Advertising	Negative Free Cash Flow	Negative Free Cash Flow	Negative Free Cash Flow	Negative Free Cash Flow	-$0.21	-20%	-2%	-20%	0.00%
Hologic Inc	HOLX	Medical	$12.08	$24.15	$36.23	$72.45	$1.61	9%	20%	9%	0.00%
Home Depot, Inc.	HD	Retail	$37.13	$74.25	$111.38	$222.75	$4.95	23%	18%	17%	2.08%

NAME	TICKER	INDUSTRY	2014 BUY PRICE OPINION	2014 HOLD PRICE OPINION	2014 SELL PRICE OPINION	2014 SHORT PRICE OPINION	2014 MYCROFT FREE CASH FLOW PER SHARE ESTIMATE	2014 MYCROFT FREE CASH FLOW RETURN ON TOTAL CAPITAL ESTIMATE (FROIC) >15% = Great	2014 MYCROFT CAPFLOW ESTIMATE <33% = Great BUT NO NEGATIVE RESULTS	2014 MYCROFT MICHAELIS GROWTH RATE ESTIMATE >15% = Great	DIVIDEND YIELD
Step #1 = Look up the company's current stock market price on the day of analysis and compare it to our 2014 Buy, Hold, Sell & Short Price.											
Step #2 =Take the company's current market price; divide it by the "2014 Mycroft Free Cash Flow Per Share estimate." This gives the "Price to Free Cash Flow."											
All results below are based on the 2014 year end estimates using the "2014 Mycroft Michaelis Growth Rate" and are good until December 31, 2014.											
HomeAway Inc	AWAY	Internet	$8.25	$16.50	$24.75	$49.50	$1.10	14%	18%	14%	0.00%
Honeywell International, Inc.	HON	Industrial	$32.48	$64.95	$97.43	$194.85	$4.33	15%	22%	11%	1.95%
Hooker Furniture Corporation	HOFT	Apparel & Furniture	Negative Free Cash Flow	Negative Free Cash Flow	Negative Free Cash Flow	Negative Free Cash Flow	-$1.22	-10%	-26%	-10%	2.86%
Horizon Pharma Inc	HZNP	Drugs	Negative Free Cash Flow	Negative Free Cash Flow	Negative Free Cash Flow	Negative Free Cash Flow	-$1.15	-63%	-1%	-63%	0.00%
Hormel Foods Corporation	HRL	Consumer Goods	$17.85	$35.70	$53.55	$107.10	$2.38	17%	16%	13%	1.60%
Hornbeck Offshore Services, Inc.	HOS	Oil & Gas	$34.58	$69.15	$103.73	$207.45	$4.61	7%	21%	7%	0.00%
Horsehead Holding Corporation	ZINC	Commodities	Negative Free Cash Flow	Negative Free Cash Flow	Negative Free Cash Flow	Negative Free Cash Flow	-$5.40	-51%	995%	-51%	0.00%
Hospira, Inc.	HSP	Drugs	Negative Free Cash Flow	Negative Free Cash Flow	Negative Free Cash Flow	Negative Free Cash Flow	-$0.04	0%	102%	0%	0.00%
Houston Wire & Cable Company	HWCC	Industrial	$9.30	$18.60	$27.90	$55.80	$1.24	12%	5%	10%	3.31%
Howard Hughes Corp	HHC	Real Estate	$12.08	$24.15	$36.23	$72.45	$1.61	2%	71%	2%	0.00%
HSN, Inc.	HSNI	Retail	$21.15	$42.30	$63.45	$126.90	$2.82	19%	27%	14%	1.28%

NAME	TICKER	INDUSTRY	2014 BUY PRICE OPINION	2014 HOLD PRICE OPINION	2014 SELL PRICE OPINION	2014 SHORT PRICE OPINION	2014 MYCROFT FREE CASH FLOW PER SHARE ESTIMATE	2014 MYCROFT FREE CASH FLOW RETURN ON TOTAL CAPITAL ESTIMATE (FROIC) >15% = Great	2014 MYCROFT CAPFLOW ESTIMATE <33% = Great BUT NO NEGATIVE RESULTS	2014 MYCROFT MICHAELIS GROWTH RATE ESTIMATE >15% = Great	DIVIDEND YIELD
Step #1 = Look up the company's current stock market price on the day of analysis and compare it to our 2014 Buy, Hold, Sell & Short Price.											
Step #2 =Take the company's current market price; divide it by the "2014 Mycroft Free Cash Flow Per Share estimate." This gives the "Price to Free Cash Flow."											
All results below are based on the 2014 year end estimates using the "2014 Mycroft Michaelis Growth Rate" and are good until December 31, 2014.											
Hub Group, Inc. Class A	HUBG	Transportation	$5.48	$10.95	$16.43	$32.85	$0.73	5%	74%	5%	0.00%
Hubbell, Inc. Class B	HUB.B	Computers	$41.55	$83.10	$124.65	$249.30	$5.54	13%	15%	10%	1.73%
Hudson Global Inc	HSON	Services	$0.45	$0.90	$1.35	$2.70	$0.06	2%	64%	2%	0.00%
Hudson Technology, Inc.	HDSN	Industrial	Negative Free Cash Flow	Negative Free Cash Flow	Negative Free Cash Flow	Negative Free Cash Flow	-$0.83	-48%	-6%	-48%	0.00%
Humana	HUM	Health Care	Negative Free Cash Flow	Negative Free Cash Flow	Negative Free Cash Flow	Negative Free Cash Flow	-$6.11	-9%	-76%	-9%	1.11%
Huntington Ingalls Industries Inc	HII	Aerospace & Defense	$1.95	$3.90	$5.85	$11.70	$0.26	0%	92%	0%	0.60%
Huntsman Corporation	HUN	Chemicals	Negative Free Cash Flow	Negative Free Cash Flow	Negative Free Cash Flow	Negative Free Cash Flow	-$0.02	0%	101%	0%	2.68%
Hurco Companies, Inc.	HURC	Computers	$16.20	$32.40	$48.60	$97.20	$2.16	9%	14%	9%	0.74%
Huron Consulting Group, Inc.	HURN	Business Services	$19.88	$39.75	$59.63	$119.25	$2.65	8%	28%	8%	0.00%
Hutchinson Technology	HTCH	Computers	Negative Free Cash Flow	Negative Free Cash Flow	Negative Free Cash Flow	Negative Free Cash Flow	-$0.57	-6%	384%	-6%	0.00%
Hyatt Hotels Corporation	H	Travel & Leisure	$9.60	$19.20	$28.80	$57.60	$1.28	3%	55%	3%	0.00%

NAME	TICKER	INDUSTRY	2014 BUY PRICE OPINION	2014 HOLD PRICE OPINION	2014 SELL PRICE OPINION	2014 SHORT PRICE OPINION	2014 MYCROFT FREE CASH FLOW PER SHARE ESTIMATE	2014 MYCROFT FREE CASH FLOW RETURN ON TOTAL CAPITAL ESTIMATE (FROIC) >15% = Great	2014 MYCROFT CAPFLOW ESTIMATE <33% = Great BUT NO NEGATIVE RESULTS	2014 MYCROFT MICHAELIS GROWTH RATE ESTIMATE >15% = Great	DIVIDEND YIELD
Step #1 = Look up the company's current stock market price on the day of analysis and compare it to our 2014 Buy, Hold, Sell & Short Price.												
Step #2 =Take the company's current market price; divide it by the "2014 Mycroft Free Cash Flow Per Share estimate." This gives the "Price to Free Cash Flow."												
All results below are based on the 2014 year end estimates using the "2014 Mycroft Michaelis Growth Rate" and are good until December 31, 2014.												
Hyperion Therapeutics Inc	HPTX	Biotech	Negative Free Cash Flow	Negative Free Cash Flow	Negative Free Cash Flow	Negative Free Cash Flow	-$1.27	-21%	-2%	-21%	0.00%
Hyster-Yale Materials Handling Inc	HY	Truck Manufacturing	$45.23	$90.45	$135.68	$271.35	$6.03	22%	27%	19%	1.12%
I.D. Systems, Inc.	IDSY	Communication	Negative Free Cash Flow	Negative Free Cash Flow	Negative Free Cash Flow	Negative Free Cash Flow	-$0.48	-15%	-6%	-15%	0.00%
IAC/InterActiveCorp	IACI	Internet	$30.53	$61.05	$91.58	$183.15	$4.07	17%	21%	14%	1.82%
icad, Inc.	ICAD	Software	Negative Free Cash Flow	Negative Free Cash Flow	Negative Free Cash Flow	Negative Free Cash Flow	-$0.12	-3%	-129%	-3%	0.00%
ICF International, Inc.	ICFI	Business Services	$32.70	$65.40	$98.10	$196.20	$4.36	13%	14%	13%	0.00%
Iconix Brand Group, Inc.	ICON	Apparel & Furniture	$29.85	$59.70	$89.55	$179.10	$3.98	13%	1%	13%	0.00%
ICU Medical, Inc.	ICUI	Medical	$20.55	$41.10	$61.65	$123.30	$2.74	9%	39%	9%	0.00%
Idacorp, Inc.	IDA	Utilities	$8.40	$16.80	$25.20	$50.40	$1.12	2%	80%	3%	3.24%
Idenix Pharmaceuticals, Inc.	IDIX	Biotech	Negative Free Cash Flow	Negative Free Cash Flow	Negative Free Cash Flow	Negative Free Cash Flow	-$0.69	-57%	-2%	-57%	0.00%
Idera Pharmaceuticals, Inc.	IDRA	Biotech	Negative Free Cash Flow	Negative Free Cash Flow	Negative Free Cash Flow	Negative Free Cash Flow	-$0.09	-122%	0%	-122%	0.00%

NAME	TICKER	INDUSTRY	2014 BUY PRICE OPINION	2014 HOLD PRICE OPINION	2014 SELL PRICE OPINION	2014 SHORT PRICE OPINION	2014 MYCROFT FREE CASH FLOW PER SHARE ESTIMATE	2014 MYCROFT FREE CASH FLOW RETURN ON TOTAL CAPITAL ESTIMATE (FROIC) >15% = Great	2014 MYCROFT CAPFLOW ESTIMATE <33% = Great BUT NO NEGATIVE RESULTS	2014 MYCROFT MICHAELIS GROWTH RATE ESTIMATE >15% = Great	DIVIDEND YIELD
Step #1 = Look up the company's current stock market price on the day of analysis and compare it to our 2014 Buy, Hold, Sell & Short Price.											
Step #2 =Take the company's current market price; divide it by the "2014 Mycroft Free Cash Flow Per Share estimate." This gives the "Price to Free Cash Flow."											
All results below are based on the 2014 year end estimates using the "2014 Mycroft Michaelis Growth Rate" and are good until December 31, 2014.											
Idex Corporation	IEX	Industrial	$34.80	$69.60	$104.40	$208.80	$4.64	15%	9%	13%	1.46%
Idexx Laboratories	IDXX	Medical	$30.83	$61.65	$92.48	$184.95	$4.11	30%	34%	30%	0.00%
IDT Corporation Class B	IDT	Communication	$24.53	$49.05	$73.58	$147.15	$3.27	41%	21%	35%	3.51%
IEC Electronics Corp.	IEC	Computers	$0.00	$0.00	$0.00	$0.00	$0.00	0%	99%	0%	0.00%
Igate Corporation	IGTE	Software	$11.93	$23.85	$35.78	$71.55	$1.59	8%	32%	8%	0.00%
IGI, Inc.	IG	Biotech	Negative Free Cash Flow	Negative Free Cash Flow	Negative Free Cash Flow	Negative Free Cash Flow	-$0.04	-38%	-7%	-38%	0.00%
Ignite Restaurant Group Inc	IRG	Restaurants	Negative Free Cash Flow	Negative Free Cash Flow	Negative Free Cash Flow	Negative Free Cash Flow	-$0.37	-4%	129%	-4%	0.00%
IHS, Inc. Class A	IHS	Business Services	$41.55	$83.10	$124.65	$249.30	$5.54	13%	19%	13%	0.00%
II-VI, Inc.	IIVI	Computers	$11.18	$22.35	$33.53	$67.05	$1.49	13%	23%	13%	0.00%
Ikanos Communications, Inc.	IKAN	Communication	Negative Free Cash Flow	Negative Free Cash Flow	Negative Free Cash Flow	Negative Free Cash Flow	-$0.21	-41%	-54%	-41%	0.00%
Illinois Tool Works Inc	ITW	Industrial	$34.65	$69.30	$103.95	$207.90	$4.62	14%	17%	10%	2.26%

NAME	TICKER	INDUSTRY	2014 BUY PRICE OPINION	2014 HOLD PRICE OPINION	2014 SELL PRICE OPINION	2014 SHORT PRICE OPINION	2014 MYCROFT FREE CASH FLOW PER SHARE ESTIMATE	2014 MYCROFT FREE CASH FLOW RETURN ON TOTAL CAPITAL ESTIMATE (FROIC) >15% = Great	2014 MYCROFT CAPFLOW ESTIMATE <33% = Great BUT NO NEGATIVE RESULTS	2014 MYCROFT MICHAELIS GROWTH RATE ESTIMATE >15% = Great	DIVIDEND YIELD
Step #1 = Look up the company's current stock market price on the day of analysis and compare it to our 2014 Buy, Hold, Sell & Short Price.												
Step #2 =Take the company's current market price; divide it by the "2014 Mycroft Free Cash Flow Per Share estimate." This gives the "Price to Free Cash Flow."												
All results below are based on the 2014 year end estimates using the "2014 Mycroft Michaelis Growth Rate" and are good until December 31, 2014.												
Illumina, Inc.	ILMN	Medical	$14.78	$29.55	$44.33	$88.65	$1.97	10%	27%	10%	0.00%
Image Sensing Systems, Inc.	ISNS	Software	Negative Free Cash Flow	Negative Free Cash Flow	Negative Free Cash Flow	Negative Free Cash Flow	-$0.08	-1%	174%	-1%	0.00%
Imation Corporation	IMN	Computers	Negative Free Cash Flow	Negative Free Cash Flow	Negative Free Cash Flow	Negative Free Cash Flow	-$0.64	-7%	-88%	-7%	0.00%
Immersion Corporation	IMMR	Computers	$2.78	$5.55	$8.33	$16.65	$0.37	16%	30%	16%	0.00%
ImmunoCellular Therapeutics Limited	IMUC	Biotech	Negative Free Cash Flow	Negative Free Cash Flow	Negative Free Cash Flow	Negative Free Cash Flow	-$0.18	-42%	0%	-42%	0.00%
Immunogen, Inc.	IMGN	Biotech	Negative Free Cash Flow	Negative Free Cash Flow	Negative Free Cash Flow	Negative Free Cash Flow	-$0.75	-53%	-6%	-53%	0.00%
Immunomedics, Inc.	IMMU	Biotech	Negative Free Cash Flow	Negative Free Cash Flow	Negative Free Cash Flow	Negative Free Cash Flow	-$0.08	-18%	-10%	-18%	0.00%
Impax Laboratories, Inc.	IPXL	Drugs	$32.33	$64.65	$96.98	$193.95	$4.31	28%	0%	28%	0.00%
Imperva Inc	IMPV	Software	$1.58	$3.15	$4.73	$9.45	$0.21	6%	43%	6%	0.00%
inContact, Inc.	SAAS	Software	Negative Free Cash Flow	Negative Free Cash Flow	Negative Free Cash Flow	Negative Free Cash Flow	-$0.08	-6%	176%	-6%	0.00%
Incyte Corp Ltd	INCY	Biotech	Negative Free Cash Flow	Negative Free Cash Flow	Negative Free Cash Flow	Negative Free Cash Flow	-$0.12	-7%	-17%	-7%	0.00%

NAME	TICKER	INDUSTRY	2014 BUY PRICE OPINION	2014 HOLD PRICE OPINION	2014 SELL PRICE OPINION	2014 SHORT PRICE OPINION	2014 MYCROFT FREE CASH FLOW PER SHARE ESTIMATE	2014 MYCROFT FREE CASH FLOW RETURN ON TOTAL CAPITAL ESTIMATE (FROIC) >15% = Great	2014 MYCROFT CAPFLOW ESTIMATE <33% = Great BUT NO NEGATIVE RESULTS	2014 MYCROFT MICHAELIS GROWTH RATE ESTIMATE >15% = Great	DIVIDEND YIELD
Step #1 = Look up the company's current stock market price on the day of analysis and compare it to our 2014 Buy, Hold, Sell & Short Price.											
Step #2 =Take the company's current market price; divide it by the "2014 Mycroft Free Cash Flow Per Share estimate." This gives the "Price to Free Cash Flow."											
All results below are based on the 2014 year end estimates using the "2014 Mycroft Michaelis Growth Rate" and are good until December 31, 2014.											
Infinera Corporation	INFN	Communication	Negative Free Cash Flow	Negative Free Cash Flow	Negative Free Cash Flow	Negative Free Cash Flow	-$0.33	-10%	-62%	-10%	0.00%
Infinity Pharmaceuticals, Inc.	INFI	Biotech	Negative Free Cash Flow	Negative Free Cash Flow	Negative Free Cash Flow	Negative Free Cash Flow	-$2.49	-40%	-2%	-40%	0.00%
Infoblox Inc	BLOX	Business Services	$3.38	$6.75	$10.13	$20.25	$0.45	12%	42%	12%	0.00%
Informatica Corporation	INFA	Software	$15.90	$31.80	$47.70	$95.40	$2.12	17%	6%	17%	0.00%
Information Services Group, Inc.	III	Business Services	$3.08	$6.15	$9.23	$18.45	$0.41	13%	12%	13%	0.00%
Ingersoll-Rand PLC	IR	Industrial	$28.58	$57.15	$85.73	$171.45	$3.81	10%	22%	9%	1.30%
Ingles Markets, Inc. Class A	IMKTA	Retail	$6.23	$12.45	$18.68	$37.35	$0.83	2%	86%	3%	2.45%
Ingram Micro, Inc.	IM	Computers	$10.50	$21.00	$31.50	$63.00	$1.40	5%	30%	5%	0.00%
Ingredion Inc	INGR	Consumer Goods	$21.15	$42.30	$63.45	$126.90	$2.82	5%	60%	5%	2.38%
InnerWorkings, Inc.	INWK	Advertising	$2.55	$5.10	$7.65	$15.30	$0.34	5%	44%	5%	0.00%
Innodata Inc	INOD	Software	$1.28	$2.55	$3.83	$7.65	$0.17	7%	57%	7%	0.00%

NAME	TICKER	INDUSTRY	2014 BUY PRICE OPINION	2014 HOLD PRICE OPINION	2014 SELL PRICE OPINION	2014 SHORT PRICE OPINION	2014 MYCROFT FREE CASH FLOW PER SHARE ESTIMATE	2014 MYCROFT FREE CASH FLOW RETURN ON TOTAL CAPITAL ESTIMATE (FROIC) >15% = Great	2014 MYCROFT CAPFLOW ESTIMATE <33% = Great BUT NO NEGATIVE RESULTS	2014 MYCROFT MICHAELIS GROWTH RATE ESTIMATE >15% = Great	DIVIDEND YIELD
Step #1 = Look up the company's current stock market price on the day of analysis and compare it to our 2014 Buy, Hold, Sell & Short Price.											
Step #2 =Take the company's current market price; divide it by the "2014 Mycroft Free Cash Flow Per Share estimate." This gives the "Price to Free Cash Flow."											
All results below are based on the 2014 year end estimates using the "2014 Mycroft Michaelis Growth Rate" and are good until December 31, 2014.											
Innophos Holdings, Inc.	IPHS	Chemicals	$11.70	$23.40	$35.10	$70.20	$1.56	6%	54%	3%	2.76%
Innospec, Inc.	IOSP	Chemicals	$17.78	$35.55	$53.33	$106.65	$2.37	13%	28%	13%	0.00%
Innovative Solutions and Support, Inc.	ISSC	Aerospace & Defense	Negative Free Cash Flow	Negative Free Cash Flow	Negative Free Cash Flow	Negative Free Cash Flow	-$0.05	-2%	-244%	-2%	0.00%
Inovio Pharmaceuticals, Inc.	INO	Biotech	Negative Free Cash Flow	Negative Free Cash Flow	Negative Free Cash Flow	Negative Free Cash Flow	-$0.11	-76%	0%	-76%	0.00%
Inphi Corp	IPHI	Semiconductors	Negative Free Cash Flow	Negative Free Cash Flow	Negative Free Cash Flow	Negative Free Cash Flow	-$0.28	-5%	245%	-5%	0.00%
Insight Enterprises, Inc.	NSIT	Software	$24.30	$48.60	$72.90	$145.80	$3.24	15%	17%	15%	0.00%
Insignia Systems Inc.	ISIG	Advertising	$1.95	$3.90	$5.85	$11.70	$0.26	12%	7%	12%	0.00%
Insmed, Inc.	INSM	Biotech	Negative Free Cash Flow	Negative Free Cash Flow	Negative Free Cash Flow	Negative Free Cash Flow	-$0.90	-31%	-2%	-31%	0.00%
Insperity, Inc.	NSP	Business Services	$19.50	$39.00	$58.50	$117.00	$2.60	23%	22%	18%	1.98%
Insteel Industries, Inc.	IIIN	Steel	$16.43	$32.85	$49.28	$98.55	$2.19	19%	23%	18%	0.75%
Insulet Corporation	PODD	Medical	Negative Free Cash Flow	Negative Free Cash Flow	Negative Free Cash Flow	Negative Free Cash Flow	-$0.28	-6%	-161%	-6%	0.00%

NAME	TICKER	INDUSTRY	2014 BUY PRICE OPINION	2014 HOLD PRICE OPINION	2014 SELL PRICE OPINION	2014 SHORT PRICE OPINION	2014 MYCROFT FREE CASH FLOW PER SHARE ESTIMATE	2014 MYCROFT FREE CASH FLOW RETURN ON TOTAL CAPITAL ESTIMATE (FROIC) >15% = Great	2014 MYCROFT CAPFLOW ESTIMATE <33% = Great BUT NO NEGATIVE RESULTS	2014 MYCROFT MICHAELIS GROWTH RATE ESTIMATE >15% = Great	DIVIDEND YIELD
Step #1 = Look up the company's current stock market price on the day of analysis and compare it to our 2014 Buy, Hold, Sell & Short Price.											
Step #2 =Take the company's current market price; divide it by the "2014 Mycroft Free Cash Flow Per Share estimate." This gives the "Price to Free Cash Flow."											
All results below are based on the 2014 year end estimates using the "2014 Mycroft Michaelis Growth Rate" and are good until December 31, 2014.											
Insys Therapeutics Inc	INSY	Biotech	Negative Free Cash Flow	Negative Free Cash Flow	Negative Free Cash Flow	Negative Free Cash Flow	-$0.41	-25%	-3%	-25%	0.00%
Integra LifeSciences Holdings, Inc.	IART	Medical	Negative Free Cash Flow	Negative Free Cash Flow	Negative Free Cash Flow	Negative Free Cash Flow	-$1.21	-3%	197%	-3%	0.00%
Integrated Device Technology	IDTI	Semiconductors	$1.28	$2.55	$3.83	$7.65	$0.17	4%	48%	4%	0.00%
Integrated Electrical Services, Inc.	IESC	Engineering	$0.60	$1.20	$1.80	$3.60	$0.08	2%	46%	2%	0.00%
Integrated Silicon Solution, Inc.	ISSI	Semiconductors	$4.88	$9.75	$14.63	$29.25	$0.65	6%	52%	6%	0.00%
Integrys Energy Group Inc	TEG	Utilities	Negative Free Cash Flow	Negative Free Cash Flow	Negative Free Cash Flow	Negative Free Cash Flow	-$0.76	-1%	110%	-1%	4.90%
Intel Corp	INTC	Semiconductors	$16.95	$33.90	$50.85	$101.70	$2.26	16%	51%	13%	3.90%
Inteliquent Inc	IQNT	Communication	$11.33	$22.65	$33.98	$67.95	$1.51	36%	34%	31%	2.85%
Intelsat SA	I	Communication	Negative Free Cash Flow	Negative Free Cash Flow	Negative Free Cash Flow	Negative Free Cash Flow	-$1.19	-1%	121%	-1%	0.00%
Inter Parfums, Inc.	IPAR	Consumer Goods	$5.93	$11.85	$17.78	$35.55	$0.79	6%	52%	4%	1.67%
Interactive Intelligence Group Inc	ININ	Software	$1.28	$2.55	$3.83	$7.65	$0.17	2%	87%	2%	0.00%

NAME	TICKER	INDUSTRY	2014 BUY PRICE OPINION	2014 HOLD PRICE OPINION	2014 SELL PRICE OPINION	2014 SHORT PRICE OPINION	2014 MYCROFT FREE CASH FLOW PER SHARE ESTIMATE	2014 MYCROFT FREE CASH FLOW RETURN ON TOTAL CAPITAL ESTIMATE (FROIC) >15% = Great	2014 MYCROFT CAPFLOW ESTIMATE <33% = Great BUT NO NEGATIVE RESULTS	2014 MYCROFT MICHAELIS GROWTH RATE ESTIMATE >15% = Great	DIVIDEND YIELD
Step #1 = Look up the company's current stock market price on the day of analysis and compare it to our 2014 Buy, Hold, Sell & Short Price.											
Step #2 =Take the company's current market price; divide it by the "2014 Mycroft Free Cash Flow Per Share estimate." This gives the "Price to Free Cash Flow."											
All results below are based on the 2014 year end estimates using the "2014 Mycroft Michaelis Growth Rate" and are good until December 31, 2014.											
Intercept Pharmaceuticals Inc	ICPT	Drugs	Negative Free Cash Flow	Negative Free Cash Flow	Negative Free Cash Flow	Negative Free Cash Flow	-$1.00	-17%	0%	-17%	0.00%
InterDigital Inc	IDCC	Communication	$109.58	$219.15	$328.73	$657.45	$14.61	55%	11%	54%	1.07%
Interface, Inc. Class A	TILE	Homebuilding	Negative Free Cash Flow	Negative Free Cash Flow	Negative Free Cash Flow	Negative Free Cash Flow	-$0.61	-7%	378%	-8%	0.63%
Intermec, Inc.	IN	Computers	$4.88	$9.75	$14.63	$29.25	$0.65	18%	23%	18%	0.00%
Intermolecular Inc	IMI	Semiconductors	Negative Free Cash Flow	Negative Free Cash Flow	Negative Free Cash Flow	Negative Free Cash Flow	-$0.04	-2%	116%	-2%	0.00%
InterMune, Inc.	ITMN	Biotech	Negative Free Cash Flow	Negative Free Cash Flow	Negative Free Cash Flow	Negative Free Cash Flow	-$2.46	-53%	-1%	-53%	0.00%
Internap Network Services	INAP	Software	Negative Free Cash Flow	Negative Free Cash Flow	Negative Free Cash Flow	Negative Free Cash Flow	-$0.46	-9%	175%	-9%	0.00%
International Business Machines Corp	IBM	Software	$125.63	$251.25	$376.88	$753.75	$16.75	34%	19%	26%	2.04%
International Flavors & Fragrances	IFF	Chemicals	$16.58	$33.15	$49.73	$99.45	$2.21	8%	43%	4%	1.94%
International Game Technology	IGT	Travel & Leisure	$9.75	$19.50	$29.25	$58.50	$1.30	10%	30%	9%	2.00%
International Paper Co.	IP	Forest Products	$32.40	$64.80	$97.20	$194.40	$4.32	9%	38%	9%	2.44%

NAME	TICKER	INDUSTRY	2014 BUY PRICE OPINION	2014 HOLD PRICE OPINION	2014 SELL PRICE OPINION	2014 SHORT PRICE OPINION	2014 MYCROFT FREE CASH FLOW PER SHARE ESTIMATE	2014 MYCROFT FREE CASH FLOW RETURN ON TOTAL CAPITAL ESTIMATE (FROIC) >15% = Great	2014 MYCROFT CAPFLOW ESTIMATE <33% = Great BUT NO NEGATIVE RESULTS	2014 MYCROFT MICHAELIS GROWTH RATE ESTIMATE >15% = Great	DIVIDEND YIELD
Step #1 = Look up the company's current stock market price on the day of analysis and compare it to our 2014 Buy, Hold, Sell & Short Price.											
Step #2 =Take the company's current market price; divide it by the "2014 Mycroft Free Cash Flow Per Share estimate." This gives the "Price to Free Cash Flow."											
All results below are based on the 2014 year end estimates using the "2014 Mycroft Michaelis Growth Rate" and are good until December 31, 2014.											
International Rectifier	IRF	Semiconductors	$7.50	$15.00	$22.50	$45.00	$1.00	6%	52%	6%	0.00%
International Shipholding Corporation	ISH	Transportation	$8.10	$16.20	$24.30	$48.60	$1.08	2%	62%	4%	3.84%
International Speedway Corporation	ISCA	Travel & Leisure	$12.90	$25.80	$38.70	$77.40	$1.72	5%	51%	5%	0.68%
Internet Patents Corp	PTNT	Business Services	Negative Free Cash Flow	Negative Free Cash Flow	Negative Free Cash Flow	Negative Free Cash Flow	-$0.26	-6%	0%	-6%	0.00%
Interphase Corp.	INPH	Computers	Negative Free Cash Flow	Negative Free Cash Flow	Negative Free Cash Flow	Negative Free Cash Flow	-$0.41	-27%	-3%	-27%	0.00%
Interpublic Group of Cos Inc	IPG	Advertising	Negative Free Cash Flow	Negative Free Cash Flow	Negative Free Cash Flow	Negative Free Cash Flow	-$0.11	-1%	148%	-4%	1.78%
Intersections, Inc.	INTX	Business Services	$16.80	$33.60	$50.40	$100.80	$2.24	31%	11%	26%	9.20%
Intersil Corporation	ISIL	Semiconductors	$4.13	$8.25	$12.38	$24.75	$0.55	6%	23%	5%	4.30%
Interval Leisure Group, Inc.	IILG	Travel & Leisure	$11.18	$22.35	$33.53	$67.05	$1.49	13%	16%	11%	1.94%
inTest Corporation	INTT	Semiconductors	$4.28	$8.55	$12.83	$25.65	$0.57	17%	7%	17%	0.00%
IntraLinks Holdings, Inc.	IL	Software	$1.73	$3.45	$5.18	$10.35	$0.23	3%	66%	3%	0.00%

NAME	TICKER	INDUSTRY	2014 BUY PRICE OPINION	2014 HOLD PRICE OPINION	2014 SELL PRICE OPINION	2014 SHORT PRICE OPINION	2014 MYCROFT FREE CASH FLOW PER SHARE ESTIMATE	2014 MYCROFT FREE CASH FLOW RETURN ON TOTAL CAPITAL ESTIMATE (FROIC) >15% = Great	2014 MYCROFT CAPFLOW ESTIMATE <33% = Great BUT NO NEGATIVE RESULTS	2014 MYCROFT MICHAELIS GROWTH RATE ESTIMATE >15% = Great	DIVIDEND YIELD
Step #1 = Look up the company's current stock market price on the day of analysis and compare it to our 2014 Buy, Hold, Sell & Short Price.											
Step #2 =Take the company's current market price; divide it by the "2014 Mycroft Free Cash Flow Per Share estimate." This gives the "Price to Free Cash Flow."											
All results below are based on the 2014 year end estimates using the "2014 Mycroft Michaelis Growth Rate" and are good until December 31, 2014.											
Intrepid Potash, Inc.	IPI	Agriculture	Negative Free Cash Flow	Negative Free Cash Flow	Negative Free Cash Flow	Negative Free Cash Flow	-$1.93	-16%	207%	-16%	0.00%
IntriCon Corporation	IIN	Industrial	$1.28	$2.55	$3.83	$7.65	$0.17	4%	49%	4%	0.00%
Intuit, Inc.	INTU	Software	$36.38	$72.75	$109.13	$218.25	$4.85	29%	16%	24%	1.15%
Intuitive Surgical, Inc.	ISRG	Medical	$172.43	$344.85	$517.28	$1,034.55	$22.99	20%	14%	20%	0.00%
Inuvo, Inc.	INUV	Advertising	$0.08	$0.15	$0.23	$0.45	$0.01	1%	93%	1%	0.00%
Invacare Corporation	IVC	Medical	$1.58	$3.15	$4.73	$9.45	$0.21	1%	73%	1%	0.31%
InvenSense Inc	INVN	Semiconductors	$3.45	$6.90	$10.35	$20.70	$0.46	13%	18%	13%	0.00%
Inventure Foods, Inc.	SNAK	Consumer Goods	$0.30	$0.60	$0.90	$1.80	$0.04	1%	89%	1%	0.00%
ION Geophysical Corporation	IO	Computers	$4.88	$9.75	$14.63	$29.25	$0.65	17%	17%	17%	0.00%
iPass, Inc.	IPAS	Communication	Negative Free Cash Flow	Negative Free Cash Flow	Negative Free Cash Flow	Negative Free Cash Flow	-$0.04	-7%	2218%	-7%	0.00%
IPC The Hospitalist Company, Inc.	IPCM	Health Care	$19.50	$39.00	$58.50	$117.00	$2.60	13%	8%	13%	0.00%

NAME	TICKER	INDUSTRY	2014 BUY PRICE OPINION	2014 HOLD PRICE OPINION	2014 SELL PRICE OPINION	2014 SHORT PRICE OPINION	2014 MYCROFT FREE CASH FLOW PER SHARE ESTIMATE	2014 MYCROFT FREE CASH FLOW RETURN ON TOTAL CAPITAL ESTIMATE (FROIC) >15% = Great	2014 MYCROFT CAPFLOW ESTIMATE <33% = Great BUT NO NEGATIVE RESULTS	2014 MYCROFT MICHAELIS GROWTH RATE ESTIMATE >15% = Great	DIVIDEND YIELD
Step #1 = Look up the company's current stock market price on the day of analysis and compare it to our 2014 Buy, Hold, Sell & Short Price.											
Step #2 =Take the company's current market price; divide it by the "2014 Mycroft Free Cash Flow Per Share estimate." This gives the "Price to Free Cash Flow."											
All results below are based on the 2014 year end estimates using the "2014 Mycroft Michaelis Growth Rate" and are good until December 31, 2014.											
IPG Photonics Corporation	IPGP	Semiconductors	$8.48	$16.95	$25.43	$50.85	$1.13	7%	55%	7%	0.00%
Iridium Communications, Inc.	IRDM	Communication	Negative Free Cash Flow	Negative Free Cash Flow	Negative Free Cash Flow	Negative Free Cash Flow	-$2.89	-24%	220%	-24%	0.00%
iRobot Corporation	IRBT	Consumer Goods	$11.78	$23.55	$35.33	$70.65	$1.57	13%	14%	13%	0.00%
Iron Mountain Inc	IRM	Business Services	$4.58	$9.15	$13.73	$27.45	$0.61	3%	74%	2%	4.10%
Ironwood Pharmaceuticals, Inc.	IRWD	Medical	Negative Free Cash Flow	Negative Free Cash Flow	Negative Free Cash Flow	Negative Free Cash Flow	-$1.39	-121%	-8%	-121%	0.00%
Isis Pharmaceuticals	ISIS	Biotech	$1.28	$2.55	$3.83	$7.65	$0.17	3%	19%	3%	0.00%
Isle of Capri Casinos, Inc.	ISLE	Travel & Leisure	Negative Free Cash Flow	Negative Free Cash Flow	Negative Free Cash Flow	Negative Free Cash Flow	-$1.47	-5%	167%	-5%	0.00%
Isramco Inc.	ISRL	Oil & Gas	Negative Free Cash Flow	Negative Free Cash Flow	Negative Free Cash Flow	Negative Free Cash Flow	-$0.34	-4%	106%	-4%	0.00%
ITC Holdings Corp	ITC	Utilities	Negative Free Cash Flow	Negative Free Cash Flow	Negative Free Cash Flow	Negative Free Cash Flow	-$7.83	-9%	208%	-9%	1.90%
Iteris, Inc.	ITI	Communication	$0.53	$1.05	$1.58	$3.15	$0.07	4%	34%	4%	0.00%
Itron Inc.	ITRI	Computers	$15.30	$30.60	$45.90	$91.80	$2.04	5%	42%	5%	0.00%

NAME	TICKER	INDUSTRY	2014 BUY PRICE OPINION	2014 HOLD PRICE OPINION	2014 SELL PRICE OPINION	2014 SHORT PRICE OPINION	2014 MYCROFT FREE CASH FLOW PER SHARE ESTIMATE	2014 MYCROFT FREE CASH FLOW RETURN ON TOTAL CAPITAL ESTIMATE (FROIC) >15% = Great	2014 MYCROFT CAPFLOW ESTIMATE <33% = Great BUT NO NEGATIVE RESULTS	2014 MYCROFT MICHAELIS GROWTH RATE ESTIMATE >15% = Great	DIVIDEND YIELD
Step #1 = Look up the company's current stock market price on the day of analysis and compare it to our 2014 Buy, Hold, Sell & Short Price.											
Step #2 =Take the company's current market price; divide it by the "2014 Mycroft Free Cash Flow Per Share estimate." This gives the "Price to Free Cash Flow."											
All results below are based on the 2014 year end estimates using the "2014 Mycroft Michaelis Growth Rate" and are good until December 31, 2014.											
ITT Corp	ITT	Industrial	$10.73	$21.45	$32.18	$64.35	$1.43	17%	44%	13%	1.13%
ITT Educational Services, Inc.	ESI	Education	$22.95	$45.90	$68.85	$137.70	$3.06	18%	14%	18%	0.00%
Ixia	XXIA	Internet	$7.05	$14.10	$21.15	$42.30	$0.94	9%	23%	9%	0.00%
IXYS Corporation	IXYS	Semiconductors	$3.00	$6.00	$9.00	$18.00	$0.40	4%	39%	4%	1.22%
J&J Snack Foods Corp.	JJSF	Consumer Goods	$22.13	$44.25	$66.38	$132.75	$2.95	10%	44%	9%	0.84%
J.B. Hunt Transport Services, Inc.	JBHT	Transportation	$7.88	$15.75	$23.63	$47.25	$1.05	8%	80%	4%	0.80%
J.C. Penney Co Inc	JCP	Retail	Negative Free Cash Flow	Negative Free Cash Flow	Negative Free Cash Flow	Negative Free Cash Flow	-$5.00	-19%	-496%	-19%	0.00%
J.M. Smucker Co.	SJM	Consumer Goods	$42.98	$85.95	$128.93	$257.85	$5.73	8%	26%	7%	2.15%
j2 Global Inc	JCOM	Software	$35.93	$71.85	$107.78	$215.55	$4.79	28%	7%	23%	1.94%
Jabil Circuit, Inc.	JBL	Computers	$27.53	$55.05	$82.58	$165.15	$3.67	27%	53%	25%	1.33%
Jack Henry & Associates, Inc	JKHY	Business Services	$21.15	$42.30	$63.45	$126.90	$2.82	18%	32%	14%	1.55%

NAME	TICKER	INDUSTRY	2014 BUY PRICE OPINION	2014 HOLD PRICE OPINION	2014 SELL PRICE OPINION	2014 SHORT PRICE OPINION	2014 MYCROFT FREE CASH FLOW PER SHARE ESTIMATE	2014 MYCROFT FREE CASH FLOW RETURN ON TOTAL CAPITAL ESTIMATE (FROIC) >15% = Great	2014 MYCROFT CAPFLOW ESTIMATE <33% = Great BUT NO NEGATIVE RESULTS	2014 MYCROFT MICHAELIS GROWTH RATE ESTIMATE >15% = Great	DIVIDEND YIELD
Step #1 = Look up the company's current stock market price on the day of analysis and compare it to our 2014 Buy, Hold, Sell & Short Price.											
Step #2 =Take the company's current market price; divide it by the "2014 Mycroft Free Cash Flow Per Share estimate." This gives the "Price to Free Cash Flow."											
All results below are based on the 2014 year end estimates using the "2014 Mycroft Michaelis Growth Rate" and are good until December 31, 2014.											
Jack In The Box, Inc.	JACK	Restaurants	$21.68	$43.35	$65.03	$130.05	$2.89	13%	43%	13%	0.00%
Jacobs Engineering Group	JEC	Engineering	$29.63	$59.25	$88.88	$177.75	$3.95	10%	21%	10%	0.00%
Jakks Pacific, Inc.	JAKK	Travel & Leisure	Negative Free Cash Flow	Negative Free Cash Flow	Negative Free Cash Flow	Negative Free Cash Flow	-$0.74	-7%	688%	-5%	6.00%
Jamba, Inc.	JMBA	Restaurants	$0.83	$1.65	$2.48	$4.95	$0.11	6%	86%	6%	0.00%
Jarden Corporation	JAH	Apparel & Furniture	$18.23	$36.45	$54.68	$109.35	$2.43	6%	41%	6%	0.00%
Jazz Pharmaceuticals PLC	JAZZ	Biotech	$30.08	$60.15	$90.23	$180.45	$4.01	13%	7%	13%	0.00%
JDS Uniphase Corp (CA)	JDSU	Communication	$4.28	$8.55	$12.83	$25.65	$0.57	11%	35%	11%	0.00%
JetBlue Airways Corporation	JBLU	Airlines	Negative Free Cash Flow	Negative Free Cash Flow	Negative Free Cash Flow	Negative Free Cash Flow	-$0.53	-8%	124%	-8%	0.00%
Jive Software Inc	JIVE	Software	Negative Free Cash Flow	Negative Free Cash Flow	Negative Free Cash Flow	Negative Free Cash Flow	-$0.05	-3%	159%	-3%	0.00%
Joe's Jeans Inc.	JOEZ	Apparel & Furniture	$0.98	$1.95	$2.93	$5.85	$0.13	12%	27%	12%	0.00%
John B. Sanfilippo & Son	JBSS	Consumer Goods	$21.83	$43.65	$65.48	$130.95	$2.91	11%	20%	11%	0.00%

NAME	TICKER	INDUSTRY	2014 BUY PRICE OPINION	2014 HOLD PRICE OPINION	2014 SELL PRICE OPINION	2014 SHORT PRICE OPINION	2014 MYCROFT FREE CASH FLOW PER SHARE ESTIMATE	2014 MYCROFT FREE CASH FLOW RETURN ON TOTAL CAPITAL ESTIMATE (FROIC) >15% = Great	2014 MYCROFT CAPFLOW ESTIMATE <33% = Great BUT NO NEGATIVE RESULTS	2014 MYCROFT MICHAELIS GROWTH RATE ESTIMATE >15% = Great	DIVIDEND YIELD
Step #1 = Look up the company's current stock market price on the day of analysis and compare it to our 2014 Buy, Hold, Sell & Short Price.												
Step #2 =Take the company's current market price; divide it by the "2014 Mycroft Free Cash Flow Per Share estimate." This gives the "Price to Free Cash Flow."												
All results below are based on the 2014 year end estimates using the "2014 Mycroft Michaelis Growth Rate" and are good until December 31, 2014.												
John Bean Technologies Corporation	JBT	Industrial	$11.70	$23.40	$35.10	$70.20	$1.56	14%	41%	12%	1.55%
John Wiley & Sons, Inc. Class A	JW.A	Publishing	$45.75	$91.50	$137.25	$274.50	$6.10	20%	16%	18%	2.20%
Johnson & Johnson	JNJ	Drugs	$36.30	$72.60	$108.90	$217.80	$4.84	15%	20%	9%	2.98%
Johnson Controls Inc	JCI	Autos	$11.63	$23.25	$34.88	$69.75	$1.55	6%	57%	5%	1.79%
Johnson Outdoors, Inc. Class A	JOUT	Travel & Leisure	$10.58	$21.15	$31.73	$63.45	$1.41	6%	52%	6%	0.00%
Jones Group Inc	JNY	Apparel & Furniture	Negative Free Cash Flow	Negative Free Cash Flow	Negative Free Cash Flow	Negative Free Cash Flow	-$0.97	-4%	-712%	-4%	1.32%
Jones Lang LaSalle, Inc.	JLL	Real Estate	$19.95	$39.90	$59.85	$119.70	$2.66	4%	45%	4%	0.50%
Jos A Bank Clothiers Inc	JOSB	Retail	$11.55	$23.10	$34.65	$69.30	$1.54	6%	47%	6%	0.00%
Journal Communications, Inc. Class A	JRN	Publishing	$11.63	$23.25	$34.88	$69.75	$1.55	26%	17%	26%	0.00%
Joy Global, Inc.	JOY	Agriculture	$35.40	$70.80	$106.20	$212.40	$4.72	10%	29%	10%	1.29%
Juniper Networks, Inc.	JNPR	Communication	$3.15	$6.30	$9.45	$18.90	$0.42	3%	66%	3%	0.00%

NAME	TICKER	INDUSTRY	2014 BUY PRICE OPINION	2014 HOLD PRICE OPINION	2014 SELL PRICE OPINION	2014 SHORT PRICE OPINION	2014 MYCROFT FREE CASH FLOW PER SHARE ESTIMATE	2014 MYCROFT FREE CASH FLOW RETURN ON TOTAL CAPITAL ESTIMATE (FROIC) >15% = Great	2014 MYCROFT CAPFLOW ESTIMATE <33% = Great BUT NO NEGATIVE RESULTS	2014 MYCROFT MICHAELIS GROWTH RATE ESTIMATE >15% = Great	DIVIDEND YIELD
K12, Inc.	LRN	Education	$9.00	$18.00	$27.00	$54.00	$1.20	8%	53%	8%	0.00%
Kadant, Inc.	KAI	Industrial	$28.50	$57.00	$85.50	$171.00	$3.80	14%	14%	14%	1.50%
Kaiser Aluminum Corporation	KALU	Commodities	$30.98	$61.95	$92.93	$185.85	$4.13	5%	42%	5%	1.69%
KaloBios Pharmaceuticals Inc	KBIO	Drugs	Negative Free Cash Flow	Negative Free Cash Flow	Negative Free Cash Flow	Negative Free Cash Flow	-$1.48	-67%	0%	-67%	0.00%
Kaman Corporation	KAMN	Aerospace & Defense	$8.40	$16.80	$25.20	$50.40	$1.12	4%	59%	4%	1.71%
Kansas City Southern, Inc.	KSU	Transportation	Negative Free Cash Flow	Negative Free Cash Flow	Negative Free Cash Flow	Negative Free Cash Flow	-$0.51	-1%	108%	-2%	0.77%
KapStone Paper And Packaging Corporation	KS	Forest Products	$13.58	$27.15	$40.73	$81.45	$1.81	9%	48%	9%	0.00%
KAR Auction Services, Inc.	KAR	Autos	$12.98	$25.95	$38.93	$77.85	$1.73	7%	34%	6%	2.66%
Kaydon Corporation	KDN	Industrial	$26.18	$52.35	$78.53	$157.05	$3.49	18%	13%	16%	2.25%
KB Home	KBH	Homebuilding	Negative Free Cash Flow	Negative Free Cash Flow	Negative Free Cash Flow	Negative Free Cash Flow	-$1.73	-7%	-1%	-7%	0.59%
KBR, Inc.	KBR	Engineering	$0.90	$1.80	$2.70	$5.40	$0.12	1%	82%	0%	1.02%

Step #1 = Look up the company's current stock market price on the day of analysis and compare it to our 2014 Buy, Hold, Sell & Short Price.

Step #2 =Take the company's current market price; divide it by the "2014 Mycroft Free Cash Flow Per Share estimate." This gives the "Price to Free Cash Flow."

All results below are based on the 2014 year end estimates using the "2014 Mycroft Michaelis Growth Rate" and are good until December 31, 2014.

NAME	TICKER	INDUSTRY	2014 BUY PRICE OPINION	2014 HOLD PRICE OPINION	2014 SELL PRICE OPINION	2014 SHORT PRICE OPINION	2014 MYCROFT FREE CASH FLOW PER SHARE ESTIMATE	2014 MYCROFT FREE CASH FLOW RETURN ON TOTAL CAPITAL ESTIMATE (FROIC) >15% = Great	2014 MYCROFT CAPFLOW ESTIMATE <33% = Great BUT NO NEGATIVE RESULTS	2014 MYCROFT MICHAELIS GROWTH RATE ESTIMATE >15% = Great	DIVIDEND YIELD
Step #1 = Look up the company's current stock market price on the day of analysis and compare it to our 2014 Buy, Hold, Sell & Short Price.											
Step #2 =Take the company's current market price; divide it by the "2014 Mycroft Free Cash Flow Per Share estimate." This gives the "Price to Free Cash Flow."											
All results below are based on the 2014 year end estimates using the "2014 Mycroft Michaelis Growth Rate" and are good until December 31, 2014.											
Kellogg Company	K	Consumer Goods	$26.33	$52.65	$78.98	$157.95	$3.51	14%	35%	9%	3.09%
Kelly Services, Inc. Class A	KELYA	Services	$4.13	$8.25	$12.38	$24.75	$0.55	3%	47%	3%	1.03%
Kemet Corporation	KEM	Computers	Negative Free Cash Flow	Negative Free Cash Flow	Negative Free Cash Flow	Negative Free Cash Flow	-$1.73	-13%	-166%	-13%	0.00%
Kennametal Inc.	KMT	Industrial	$21.30	$42.60	$63.90	$127.80	$2.84	11%	29%	10%	1.57%
Kennedy-Wilson Holdings, Inc.	KW	Real Estate	Negative Free Cash Flow	Negative Free Cash Flow	Negative Free Cash Flow	Negative Free Cash Flow	-$3.34	-27%	-587%	-28%	1.46%
Keryx Biopharmaceuticals, Inc.	KERX	Drugs	Negative Free Cash Flow	Negative Free Cash Flow	Negative Free Cash Flow	Negative Free Cash Flow	-$0.27	-30%	0%	-30%	0.00%
Key Energy Services, Inc.	KEG	Oil & Gas	$0.68	$1.35	$2.03	$4.05	$0.09	1%	94%	1%	0.00%
Key Tronic Corporation	KTCC	Computers	$22.80	$45.60	$68.40	$136.80	$3.04	24%	12%	24%	0.00%
KEYW Holding Corp	KEYW	Software	$1.35	$2.70	$4.05	$8.10	$0.18	2%	67%	2%	0.00%
Kforce, Inc.	KFRC	Services	$10.95	$21.90	$32.85	$65.70	$1.46	23%	15%	23%	0.00%
Kid Brands, Inc.	KID	Retail	$0.38	$0.75	$1.13	$2.25	$0.05	2%	66%	2%	0.00%

NAME	TICKER	INDUSTRY	2014 BUY PRICE OPINION	2014 HOLD PRICE OPINION	2014 SELL PRICE OPINION	2014 SHORT PRICE OPINION	2014 MYCROFT FREE CASH FLOW PER SHARE ESTIMATE	2014 MYCROFT FREE CASH FLOW RETURN ON TOTAL CAPITAL ESTIMATE (FROIC) >15% = Great	2014 MYCROFT CAPFLOW ESTIMATE <33% = Great BUT NO NEGATIVE RESULTS	2014 MYCROFT MICHAELIS GROWTH RATE ESTIMATE >15% = Great	DIVIDEND YIELD
Step #1 = Look up the company's current stock market price on the day of analysis and compare it to our 2014 Buy, Hold, Sell & Short Price.											
Step #2 =Take the company's current market price; divide it by the "2014 Mycroft Free Cash Flow Per Share estimate." This gives the "Price to Free Cash Flow."											
All results below are based on the 2014 year end estimates using the "2014 Mycroft Michaelis Growth Rate" and are good until December 31, 2014.											
Kimball International, Inc. Class B	KBALB	Computers	$7.50	$15.00	$22.50	$45.00	$1.00	9%	45%	9%	1.98%
Kimberly-Clark Corporation	KMB	Consumer Goods	$44.63	$89.25	$133.88	$267.75	$5.95	20%	35%	11%	3.45%
Kinder Morgan, Inc.	KMI	Oil & Gas	$7.05	$14.10	$21.15	$42.30	$0.94	2%	73%	3%	4.50%
Kindred Healthcare, Inc.	KND	Health Care	$22.80	$45.60	$68.40	$136.80	$3.04	5%	48%	8%	3.56%
KiOR Inc	KIOR	Oil & Gas	Negative Free Cash Flow	Negative Free Cash Flow	Negative Free Cash Flow	Negative Free Cash Flow	-$1.15	-55%	-24%	-55%	0.00%
Kirby Corp.	KEX	Transportation	$18.38	$36.75	$55.13	$110.25	$2.45	5%	71%	5%	0.00%
Kirkland's, Inc.	KIRK	Retail	$6.90	$13.80	$20.70	$41.40	$0.92	12%	68%	12%	0.00%
KLA-Tencor Corporation	KLAC	Semiconductors	$43.95	$87.90	$131.85	$263.70	$5.86	20%	8%	16%	3.02%
KMG Chemicals, Inc.	KMG	Chemicals	$4.58	$9.15	$13.73	$27.45	$0.61	5%	43%	4%	0.52%
Knight Transportation, Inc.	KNX	Transportation	$3.53	$7.05	$10.58	$21.15	$0.47	6%	77%	4%	1.43%
Knightsbridge Tankers, Ltd.	VLCCF	Transportation	Negative Free Cash Flow	Negative Free Cash Flow	Negative Free Cash Flow	Negative Free Cash Flow	-$2.82	-17%	560%	-14%	7.10%

NAME	TICKER	INDUSTRY	2014 BUY PRICE OPINION	2014 HOLD PRICE OPINION	2014 SELL PRICE OPINION	2014 SHORT PRICE OPINION	2014 MYCROFT FREE CASH FLOW PER SHARE ESTIMATE	2014 MYCROFT FREE CASH FLOW RETURN ON TOTAL CAPITAL ESTIMATE (FROIC) >15% = Great	2014 MYCROFT CAPFLOW ESTIMATE <33% = Great BUT NO NEGATIVE RESULTS	2014 MYCROFT MICHAELIS GROWTH RATE ESTIMATE >15% = Great	DIVIDEND YIELD
Step #1 = Look up the company's current stock market price on the day of analysis and compare it to our 2014 Buy, Hold, Sell & Short Price.											
Step #2 =Take the company's current market price; divide it by the "2014 Mycroft Free Cash Flow Per Share estimate." This gives the "Price to Free Cash Flow."											
All results below are based on the 2014 year end estimates using the "2014 Mycroft Michaelis Growth Rate" and are good until December 31, 2014.											
Knoll, Inc.	KNL	Industrial	$9.00	$18.00	$27.00	$54.00	$1.20	13%	35%	10%	3.05%
Kodiak Oil & Gas Corp.	KOG	Oil & Gas	Negative Free Cash Flow	Negative Free Cash Flow	Negative Free Cash Flow	Negative Free Cash Flow	-$3.60	-50%	344%	-50%	0.00%
Kohl's Corp	KSS	Retail	$30.23	$60.45	$90.68	$181.35	$4.03	10%	44%	9%	2.67%
Kona Grill, Inc.	KONA	Restaurants	$5.18	$10.35	$15.53	$31.05	$0.69	22%	33%	22%	0.00%
Kopin Corporation	KOPN	Semiconductors	Negative Free Cash Flow	Negative Free Cash Flow	Negative Free Cash Flow	Negative Free Cash Flow	-$0.14	-6%	-99%	-6%	0.00%
Koppers Holdings, Inc.	KOP	Chemicals	$23.63	$47.25	$70.88	$141.75	$3.15	13%	37%	11%	2.52%
Korn/Ferry International	KFY	Services	$8.78	$17.55	$26.33	$52.65	$1.17	8%	22%	8%	0.00%
Kosmos Energy Ltd	KOS	Oil & Gas	$2.78	$5.55	$8.33	$16.65	$0.37	6%	73%	6%	0.00%
Kraft Foods Group Inc	KRFT	Consumer Goods	$32.40	$64.80	$97.20	$194.40	$4.32	48%	19%	24%	3.77%
Kraton Performance Polymers Inc	KRA	Chemicals	Negative Free Cash Flow	Negative Free Cash Flow	Negative Free Cash Flow	Negative Free Cash Flow	-$0.26	-1%	112%	-1%	0.00%
Kratos Defense & Security Solutions, Inc.	KTOS	Rentals	$4.73	$9.45	$14.18	$28.35	$0.63	4%	34%	4%	0.00%

NAME	TICKER	INDUSTRY	2014 BUY PRICE OPINION	2014 HOLD PRICE OPINION	2014 SELL PRICE OPINION	2014 SHORT PRICE OPINION	2014 MYCROFT FREE CASH FLOW PER SHARE ESTIMATE	2014 MYCROFT FREE CASH FLOW RETURN ON TOTAL CAPITAL ESTIMATE (FROIC) >15% = Great	2014 MYCROFT CAPFLOW ESTIMATE <33% = Great BUT NO NEGATIVE RESULTS	2014 MYCROFT MICHAELIS GROWTH RATE ESTIMATE >15% = Great	DIVIDEND YIELD
Step #1 = Look up the company's current stock market price on the day of analysis and compare it to our 2014 Buy, Hold, Sell & Short Price.											
Step #2 =Take the company's current market price; divide it by the "2014 Mycroft Free Cash Flow Per Share estimate." This gives the "Price to Free Cash Flow."											
All results below are based on the 2014 year end estimates using the "2014 Mycroft Michaelis Growth Rate" and are good until December 31, 2014.											
Krispy Kreme Doughnuts, Inc.	KKD	Restaurants	$6.00	$12.00	$18.00	$36.00	$0.80	16%	29%	16%	0.00%
Kroger Co	KR	Retail	$17.18	$34.35	$51.53	$103.05	$2.29	22%	68%	17%	1.59%
Kronos Worldwide, Inc.	KRO	Chemicals	$3.45	$6.90	$10.35	$20.70	$0.46	4%	60%	3%	3.90%
KVH Industries, Inc.	KVHI	Communication	$9.15	$18.30	$27.45	$54.90	$1.22	14%	17%	14%	0.00%
KYTHERA Biopharmaceuticals Inc	KYTH	Drugs	Negative Free Cash Flow	Negative Free Cash Flow	Negative Free Cash Flow	Negative Free Cash Flow	-$2.70	-110%	0%	-110%	0.00%
L & L Energy, Inc.	LLEN	Commodities	Negative Free Cash Flow	Negative Free Cash Flow	Negative Free Cash Flow	Negative Free Cash Flow	-$0.21	-4%	111%	-4%	0.00%
L Brands Inc	LTD	Retail	$25.80	$51.60	$77.40	$154.80	$3.44	24%	43%	16%	2.06%
L.S. Starrett Company	SCX	Industrial	$15.00	$30.00	$45.00	$90.00	$2.00	8%	38%	10%	3.88%
L-3 Communications Holdings Inc	LLL	Aerospace & Defense	$97.65	$195.30	$292.95	$585.90	$13.02	11%	19%	11%	2.37%
Laboratory Corporation of America Holdings	LH	Medical	$56.10	$112.20	$168.30	$336.60	$7.48	13%	25%	13%	0.00%
Laclede Group, Inc.	LG	Utilities	$9.00	$18.00	$27.00	$54.00	$1.20	3%	77%	3%	3.89%

NAME	TICKER	INDUSTRY	2014 BUY PRICE OPINION	2014 HOLD PRICE OPINION	2014 SELL PRICE OPINION	2014 SHORT PRICE OPINION	2014 MYCROFT FREE CASH FLOW PER SHARE ESTIMATE	2014 MYCROFT FREE CASH FLOW RETURN ON TOTAL CAPITAL ESTIMATE (FROIC) >15% = Great	2014 MYCROFT CAPFLOW ESTIMATE <33% = Great BUT NO NEGATIVE RESULTS	2014 MYCROFT MICHAELIS GROWTH RATE ESTIMATE >15% = Great	DIVIDEND YIELD
Step #1 = Look up the company's current stock market price on the day of analysis and compare it to our 2014 Buy, Hold, Sell & Short Price.											
Step #2 =Take the company's current market price; divide it by the "2014 Mycroft Free Cash Flow Per Share estimate." This gives the "Price to Free Cash Flow."											
All results below are based on the 2014 year end estimates using the "2014 Mycroft Michaelis Growth Rate" and are good until December 31, 2014.											
Lakeland Industries, Inc.	LAKE	Medical	$1.50	$3.00	$4.50	$9.00	$0.20	3%	54%	3%	0.00%
Lakes Entertainment, Inc.	LACO	Travel & Leisure	Negative Free Cash Flow	Negative Free Cash Flow	Negative Free Cash Flow	Negative Free Cash Flow	-$0.40	-9%	225%	-9%	0.00%
Lam Research Corporation	LRCX	Semiconductors	$28.88	$57.75	$86.63	$173.25	$3.85	12%	22%	12%	0.00%
Lamar Advertising Co Class A	LAMR	Advertising	$24.83	$49.65	$74.48	$148.95	$3.31	10%	28%	10%	0.00%
Lancaster Colony Corporation	LANC	Consumer Goods	$33.90	$67.80	$101.70	$203.40	$4.52	21%	18%	15%	2.14%
Landauer, Inc.	LDR	Computers	$10.05	$20.10	$30.15	$60.30	$1.34	7%	41%	0%	4.50%
Landec Corporation	LNDC	Chemicals	$3.68	$7.35	$11.03	$22.05	$0.49	6%	42%	6%	0.00%
Landstar System, Inc.	LSTR	Transportation	$31.20	$62.40	$93.60	$187.20	$4.16	30%	4%	28%	0.42%
Lannett Company, Inc.	LCI	Drugs	$3.68	$7.35	$11.03	$22.05	$0.49	10%	35%	10%	0.00%
Lantronix, Inc.	LTRX	Communication	Negative Free Cash Flow	Negative Free Cash Flow	Negative Free Cash Flow	Negative Free Cash Flow	-$0.37	-27%	-19%	-27%	0.00%
Laredo Petroleum Holdings Inc	LPI	Oil & Gas	Negative Free Cash Flow	Negative Free Cash Flow	Negative Free Cash Flow	Negative Free Cash Flow	-$3.32	-24%	233%	-24%	0.00%

NAME	TICKER	INDUSTRY	2014 BUY PRICE OPINION	2014 HOLD PRICE OPINION	2014 SELL PRICE OPINION	2014 SHORT PRICE OPINION	2014 MYCROFT FREE CASH FLOW PER SHARE ESTIMATE	2014 MYCROFT FREE CASH FLOW RETURN ON TOTAL CAPITAL ESTIMATE (FROIC) >15% = Great	2014 MYCROFT CAPFLOW ESTIMATE <33% = Great BUT NO NEGATIVE RESULTS	2014 MYCROFT MICHAELIS GROWTH RATE ESTIMATE >15% = Great	DIVIDEND YIELD
Step #1 = Look up the company's current stock market price on the day of analysis and compare it to our 2014 Buy, Hold, Sell & Short Price.											
Step #2 =Take the company's current market price; divide it by the "2014 Mycroft Free Cash Flow Per Share estimate." This gives the "Price to Free Cash Flow."											
All results below are based on the 2014 year end estimates using the "2014 Mycroft Michaelis Growth Rate" and are good until December 31, 2014.											
Las Vegas Sands Corp	LVS	Travel & Leisure	$25.20	$50.40	$75.60	$151.20	$3.36	15%	31%	10%	2.22%
Lattice Semiconductor	LSCC	Semiconductors	$0.08	$0.15	$0.23	$0.45	$0.01	0%	95%	0%	0.00%
Lawson Products, Inc.	LAWS	Industrial	Negative Free Cash Flow	Negative Free Cash Flow	Negative Free Cash Flow	Negative Free Cash Flow	-$1.28	-16%	-71%	-16%	0.00%
Layne Christensen Company	LAYN	Engineering	Negative Free Cash Flow	Negative Free Cash Flow	Negative Free Cash Flow	Negative Free Cash Flow	-$1.56	-7%	240%	-7%	0.00%
La-Z-Boy, Inc.	LZB	Apparel & Furniture	$11.85	$23.70	$35.55	$71.10	$1.58	15%	25%	14%	0.70%
LB Foster Company Class A	FSTR	Industrial	$14.03	$28.05	$42.08	$84.15	$1.87	6%	23%	6%	0.27%
LCA-Vision, Inc.	LCAV	Health Care	Negative Free Cash Flow	Negative Free Cash Flow	Negative Free Cash Flow	Negative Free Cash Flow	-$0.49	-43%	-9%	-43%	0.00%
Leap Wireless International, Inc.	LEAP	Communication	Negative Free Cash Flow	Negative Free Cash Flow	Negative Free Cash Flow	Negative Free Cash Flow	-$1.02	-2%	155%	-2%	0.00%
Leapfrog Enterprises, Inc.	LF	Travel & Leisure	$6.68	$13.35	$20.03	$40.05	$0.89	16%	39%	16%	0.00%
Lear Corporation	LEA	Autos	$33.60	$67.20	$100.80	$201.60	$4.48	10%	60%	9%	0.95%
Learning Tree International, Inc.	LTRE	Education	Negative Free Cash Flow	Negative Free Cash Flow	Negative Free Cash Flow	Negative Free Cash Flow	-$0.93	-72%	-120%	-72%	0.00%

NAME	TICKER	INDUSTRY	2014 BUY PRICE OPINION	2014 HOLD PRICE OPINION	2014 SELL PRICE OPINION	2014 SHORT PRICE OPINION	2014 MYCROFT FREE CASH FLOW PER SHARE ESTIMATE	2014 MYCROFT FREE CASH FLOW RETURN ON TOTAL CAPITAL ESTIMATE (FROIC) >15% = Great	2014 MYCROFT CAPFLOW ESTIMATE <33% = Great BUT NO NEGATIVE RESULTS	2014 MYCROFT MICHAELIS GROWTH RATE ESTIMATE >15% = Great	DIVIDEND YIELD
Step #1 = Look up the company's current stock market price on the day of analysis and compare it to our 2014 Buy, Hold, Sell & Short Price.											
Step #2 =Take the company's current market price; divide it by the "2014 Mycroft Free Cash Flow Per Share estimate." This gives the "Price to Free Cash Flow."											
All results below are based on the 2014 year end estimates using the "2014 Mycroft Michaelis Growth Rate" and are good until December 31, 2014.											
Lee Enterprises Inc.	LEE	Publishing	$8.25	$16.50	$24.75	$49.50	$1.10	7%	16%	7%	0.00%
Leggett & Platt, Inc.	LEG	Apparel & Furniture	$20.78	$41.55	$62.33	$124.65	$2.77	16%	18%	12%	4.10%
LeMaitre Vascular, Inc.	LMAT	Medical	$0.53	$1.05	$1.58	$3.15	$0.07	2%	73%	0%	1.80%
Lender Processing Services, Inc.	LPS	Business Services	$6.08	$12.15	$18.23	$36.45	$0.81	4%	70%	3%	1.23%
Lennar Corporation	LEN	Homebuilding	Negative Free Cash Flow	Negative Free Cash Flow	Negative Free Cash Flow	Negative Free Cash Flow	-$3.74	-10%	12%	-10%	0.48%
Lennox International, Inc.	LII	Industrial	$13.73	$27.45	$41.18	$82.35	$1.83	9%	40%	5%	1.32%
Leucadia National Corporation	LUK	Consumer Goods	$10.58	$21.15	$31.73	$63.45	$1.41	4%	19%	4%	0.89%
Level 3 Communications Inc	LVLT	Communication	Negative Free Cash Flow	Negative Free Cash Flow	Negative Free Cash Flow	Negative Free Cash Flow	-$0.49	-1%	116%	-1%	0.00%
Lexicon Pharmaceuticals, Inc.	LXRX	Biotech	Negative Free Cash Flow	Negative Free Cash Flow	Negative Free Cash Flow	Negative Free Cash Flow	-$0.18	-39%	-2%	-39%	0.00%
Lexmark International, Inc.	LXK	Computers	$32.78	$65.55	$98.33	$196.65	$4.37	15%	40%	14%	3.51%
LHC Group, Inc.	LHCG	Health Care	$27.60	$55.20	$82.80	$165.60	$3.68	19%	14%	19%	0.00%

NAME	TICKER	INDUSTRY	2014 BUY PRICE OPINION	2014 HOLD PRICE OPINION	2014 SELL PRICE OPINION	2014 SHORT PRICE OPINION	2014 MYCROFT FREE CASH FLOW PER SHARE ESTIMATE	2014 MYCROFT FREE CASH FLOW RETURN ON TOTAL CAPITAL ESTIMATE (FROIC) >15% = Great	2014 MYCROFT CAPFLOW ESTIMATE <33% = Great BUT NO NEGATIVE RESULTS	2014 MYCROFT MICHAELIS GROWTH RATE ESTIMATE >15% = Great	DIVIDEND YIELD
Step #1 = Look up the company's current stock market price on the day of analysis and compare it to our 2014 Buy, Hold, Sell & Short Price.												
Step #2 =Take the company's current market price; divide it by the "2014 Mycroft Free Cash Flow Per Share estimate." This gives the "Price to Free Cash Flow."												
All results below are based on the 2014 year end estimates using the "2014 Mycroft Michaelis Growth Rate" and are good until December 31, 2014.												
Libbey Inc.	LBY	Consumer Goods	Negative Free Cash Flow	Negative Free Cash Flow	Negative Free Cash Flow	Negative Free Cash Flow	-$1.18	-5%	413%	-5%	0.00%
Liberty Global PLC Class A	LBTYA	Communication	$18.75	$37.50	$56.25	$112.50	$2.50	8%	67%	8%	0.00%
Liberty Interactive Corp Class A	LINTA	Entertainment	$12.75	$25.50	$38.25	$76.50	$1.70	7%	28%	7%	0.00%
Liberty Media Corporation Class A	LMCA	Entertainment	$44.55	$89.10	$133.65	$267.30	$5.94	5%	12%	5%	0.00%
Life Technologies Corp	LIFE	Medical	$30.15	$60.30	$90.45	$180.90	$4.02	9%	18%	9%	0.00%
Life Time Fitness, Inc.	LTM	Travel & Leisure	Negative Free Cash Flow	Negative Free Cash Flow	Negative Free Cash Flow	Negative Free Cash Flow	-$0.41	-1%	107%	-1%	0.00%
LifeLock Inc	LOCK	Software	$4.95	$9.90	$14.85	$29.70	$0.66	18%	15%	18%	0.00%
LifePoint Hospitals, Inc.	LPNT	Health Care	$27.53	$55.05	$82.58	$165.15	$3.67	4%	53%	4%	0.00%
Lifetime Brands, Inc.	LCUT	Apparel & Furniture	$25.88	$51.75	$77.63	$155.25	$3.45	15%	11%	15%	0.89%
Lifevantage Corporation	LFVN	Medical	$1.13	$2.25	$3.38	$6.75	$0.15	36%	29%	36%	0.00%
Ligand Pharmaceuticals, Inc.	LGND	Drugs	$2.48	$4.95	$7.43	$14.85	$0.33	9%	40%	9%	0.00%

NAME	TICKER	INDUSTRY	2014 BUY PRICE OPINION	2014 HOLD PRICE OPINION	2014 SELL PRICE OPINION	2014 SHORT PRICE OPINION	2014 MYCROFT FREE CASH FLOW PER SHARE ESTIMATE	2014 MYCROFT FREE CASH FLOW RETURN ON TOTAL CAPITAL ESTIMATE (FROIC) >15% = Great	2014 MYCROFT CAPFLOW ESTIMATE <33% = Great BUT NO NEGATIVE RESULTS	2014 MYCROFT MICHAELIS GROWTH RATE ESTIMATE >15% = Great	DIVIDEND YIELD
Step #1 = Look up the company's current stock market price on the day of analysis and compare it to our 2014 Buy, Hold, Sell & Short Price.											
Step #2 =Take the company's current market price; divide it by the "2014 Mycroft Free Cash Flow Per Share estimate." This gives the "Price to Free Cash Flow."											
All results below are based on the 2014 year end estimates using the "2014 Mycroft Michaelis Growth Rate" and are good until December 31, 2014.											
LightPath Technologies, Inc. Class A	LPTH	Semiconductors	Negative Free Cash Flow	Negative Free Cash Flow	Negative Free Cash Flow	Negative Free Cash Flow	-$0.04	-8%	196%	-8%	0.00%
Limelight Networks, Inc.	LLNW	Internet	$0.15	$0.30	$0.45	$0.90	$0.02	1%	89%	1%	0.00%
Limoneira Co	LMNR	Consumer Goods	Negative Free Cash Flow	Negative Free Cash Flow	Negative Free Cash Flow	Negative Free Cash Flow	-$0.24	-2%	148%	-2%	0.67%
Lincoln Educational Services Corporation	LINC	Education	Negative Free Cash Flow	Negative Free Cash Flow	Negative Free Cash Flow	Negative Free Cash Flow	-$0.34	-5%	-264%	-3%	6.20%
Lincoln Electric Holdings, Inc.	LECO	Industrial	$19.80	$39.60	$59.40	$118.80	$2.64	14%	23%	11%	1.19%
Lindsay Corp	LNN	Agriculture	$37.88	$75.75	$113.63	$227.25	$5.05	15%	16%	14%	0.64%
Linear Technology	LLTC	Semiconductors	$21.00	$42.00	$63.00	$126.00	$2.80	31%	3%	19%	2.61%
LinkedIn Corp	LNKD	Internet	$14.18	$28.35	$42.53	$85.05	$1.89	16%	53%	16%	0.00%
Lionbridge Technologies, Inc.	LIOX	Business Services	$0.83	$1.65	$2.48	$4.95	$0.11	7%	58%	7%	0.00%
Lions Gate Entertainment Corporation	LGF	Entertainment	$6.00	$12.00	$18.00	$36.00	$0.80	19%	4%	19%	0.00%
Liquidity Service, Inc.	LQDT	Retail	$3.83	$7.65	$11.48	$22.95	$0.51	5%	48%	5%	0.00%

NAME	TICKER	INDUSTRY	2014 BUY PRICE OPINION	2014 HOLD PRICE OPINION	2014 SELL PRICE OPINION	2014 SHORT PRICE OPINION	2014 MYCROFT FREE CASH FLOW PER SHARE ESTIMATE	2014 MYCROFT FREE CASH FLOW RETURN ON TOTAL CAPITAL ESTIMATE (FROIC) >15% = Great	2014 MYCROFT CAPFLOW ESTIMATE <33% = Great BUT NO NEGATIVE RESULTS	2014 MYCROFT MICHAELIS GROWTH RATE ESTIMATE >15% = Great	DIVIDEND YIELD
Step #1 = Look up the company's current stock market price on the day of analysis and compare it to our 2014 Buy, Hold, Sell & Short Price.											
Step #2 =Take the company's current market price; divide it by the "2014 Mycroft Free Cash Flow Per Share estimate." This gives the "Price to Free Cash Flow."											
All results below are based on the 2014 year end estimates using the "2014 Mycroft Michaelis Growth Rate" and are good until December 31, 2014.											
Lithia Motors, Inc. Class A	LAD	Autos	Negative Free Cash Flow	Negative Free Cash Flow	Negative Free Cash Flow	Negative Free Cash Flow	-$3.87	-14%	-178%	-15%	0.74%
Littelfuse Inc.	LFUS	Computers	$34.95	$69.90	$104.85	$209.70	$4.66	15%	25%	13%	1.11%
Live Nation Entertainment, Inc.	LYV	Entertainment	$12.30	$24.60	$36.90	$73.80	$1.64	10%	32%	10%	0.00%
LivePerson, Inc.	LPSN	Business Services	$0.23	$0.45	$0.68	$1.35	$0.03	1%	90%	1%	0.00%
LKQ Corporation	LKQ	Autos	$5.55	$11.10	$16.65	$33.30	$0.74	7%	29%	7%	0.00%
LMI Aerospace, Inc.	LMIA	Aerospace & Defense	Negative Free Cash Flow	Negative Free Cash Flow	Negative Free Cash Flow	Negative Free Cash Flow	-$3.35	-21%	-238%	-21%	0.00%
Local Corp	LOCM	Internet	Negative Free Cash Flow	Negative Free Cash Flow	Negative Free Cash Flow	Negative Free Cash Flow	-$0.50	-50%	-35%	-50%	0.00%
Lockheed Martin Corporation	LMT	Aerospace & Defense	$53.33	$106.65	$159.98	$319.95	$7.11	29%	31%	12%	3.68%
LogMeIn, Inc.	LOGM	Software	$4.73	$9.45	$14.18	$28.35	$0.63	8%	43%	8%	0.00%
LoJack Corporation	LOJN	Rentals	Negative Free Cash Flow	Negative Free Cash Flow	Negative Free Cash Flow	Negative Free Cash Flow	-$0.02	-1%	108%	-1%	0.00%
Loral Space & Communications, Inc.	LORL	Communication	Negative Free Cash Flow	Negative Free Cash Flow	Negative Free Cash Flow	Negative Free Cash Flow	-$3.37	-33%	0%	-33%	0.00%

NAME	TICKER	INDUSTRY	2014 BUY PRICE OPINION	2014 HOLD PRICE OPINION	2014 SELL PRICE OPINION	2014 SHORT PRICE OPINION	2014 MYCROFT FREE CASH FLOW PER SHARE ESTIMATE	2014 MYCROFT FREE CASH FLOW RETURN ON TOTAL CAPITAL ESTIMATE (FROIC) >15% = Great	2014 MYCROFT CAPFLOW ESTIMATE <33% = Great BUT NO NEGATIVE RESULTS	2014 MYCROFT MICHAELIS GROWTH RATE ESTIMATE >15% = Great	DIVIDEND YIELD
Step #1 = Look up the company's current stock market price on the day of analysis and compare it to our 2014 Buy, Hold, Sell & Short Price.												
Step #2 =Take the company's current market price; divide it by the "2014 Mycroft Free Cash Flow Per Share estimate." This gives the "Price to Free Cash Flow."												
All results below are based on the 2014 year end estimates using the "2014 Mycroft Michaelis Growth Rate" and are good until December 31, 2014.												
Lorillard, Inc.	LO	Tobacco	$38.40	$76.80	$115.20	$230.40	$5.12	161%	6%	57%	4.90%
Louisiana-Pacific Corp.	LPX	Building Supplies	$14.55	$29.10	$43.65	$87.30	$1.94	12%	17%	12%	0.00%
Lowe's Companies Inc.	LOW	Retail	$27.15	$54.30	$81.45	$162.90	$3.62	15%	22%	13%	1.53%
LRAD Corp	LRAD	Computers	$0.15	$0.30	$0.45	$0.90	$0.02	3%	24%	3%	0.00%
LSB Industries, Inc.	LXU	Chemicals	Negative Free Cash Flow	Negative Free Cash Flow	Negative Free Cash Flow	Negative Free Cash Flow	-$6.34	-33%	389%	-33%	0.00%
LSI Corporation	LSI	Semiconductors	$4.05	$8.10	$12.15	$24.30	$0.54	22%	28%	18%	1.50%
LSI Industries, Inc.	LYTS	Computers	$0.38	$0.75	$1.13	$2.25	$0.05	1%	86%	0%	3.27%
LTX-Credence Corporation	LTXC	Semiconductors	$0.75	$1.50	$2.25	$4.50	$0.10	2%	39%	2%	0.00%
Luby's, Inc.	LUB	Restaurants	Negative Free Cash Flow	Negative Free Cash Flow	Negative Free Cash Flow	Negative Free Cash Flow	-$0.06	-1%	106%	-1%	0.00%
Lucas Energy, Inc.	LEI	Oil & Gas	Negative Free Cash Flow	Negative Free Cash Flow	Negative Free Cash Flow	Negative Free Cash Flow	-$0.27	-27%	-3905%	-27%	0.00%
Lumber Liquidators Holdings Inc	LL	Retail	$18.00	$36.00	$54.00	$108.00	$2.40	20%	20%	20%	0.00%

NAME	TICKER	INDUSTRY	2014 BUY PRICE OPINION	2014 HOLD PRICE OPINION	2014 SELL PRICE OPINION	2014 SHORT PRICE OPINION	2014 MYCROFT FREE CASH FLOW PER SHARE ESTIMATE	2014 MYCROFT FREE CASH FLOW RETURN ON TOTAL CAPITAL ESTIMATE (FROIC) >15% = Great	2014 MYCROFT CAPFLOW ESTIMATE <33% = Great BUT NO NEGATIVE RESULTS	2014 MYCROFT MICHAELIS GROWTH RATE ESTIMATE >15% = Great	DIVIDEND YIELD
Step #1 = Look up the company's current stock market price on the day of analysis and compare it to our 2014 Buy, Hold, Sell & Short Price.											
Step #2 =Take the company's current market price; divide it by the "2014 Mycroft Free Cash Flow Per Share estimate." This gives the "Price to Free Cash Flow."											
All results below are based on the 2014 year end estimates using the "2014 Mycroft Michaelis Growth Rate" and are good until December 31, 2014.											
Luminex Corporation	LMNX	Medical	$1.50	$3.00	$4.50	$9.00	$0.20	3%	63%	3%	0.00%
Lumos Networks Corp	LMOS	Communication	$5.48	$10.95	$16.43	$32.85	$0.73	4%	79%	4%	3.42%
Lydall, Inc.	LDL	Conglomerates	$8.48	$16.95	$25.43	$50.85	$1.13	9%	39%	9%	0.00%
LyondellBasell Industries NV	LYB	Chemicals	$64.35	$128.70	$193.05	$386.10	$8.58	25%	25%	21%	2.82%
M.D.C. Holdings, Inc.	MDC	Homebuilding	Negative Free Cash Flow	Negative Free Cash Flow	Negative Free Cash Flow	Negative Free Cash Flow	-$4.93	-13%	-1%	-12%	3.42%
M/A-COM Technology Solutions Holdings Inc	MTSI	Semiconductors	$6.68	$13.35	$20.03	$40.05	$0.89	16%	20%	16%	0.00%
M/I Homes, Inc.	MHO	Homebuilding	Negative Free Cash Flow	Negative Free Cash Flow	Negative Free Cash Flow	Negative Free Cash Flow	-$1.79	-8%	-4%	-8%	0.00%
Mac-Gray Corporation	TUC	Services	$13.65	$27.30	$40.95	$81.90	$1.82	19%	60%	17%	2.44%
Macy's Inc	M	Retail	$32.03	$64.05	$96.08	$192.15	$4.27	12%	37%	11%	2.24%
Madison Square Garden Co	MSG	Entertainment	$3.38	$6.75	$10.13	$20.25	$0.45	2%	87%	2%	0.00%
Magellan Health Services, Inc.	MGLN	Health Care	$42.00	$84.00	$126.00	$252.00	$5.60	13%	31%	13%	0.00%

NAME	TICKER	INDUSTRY	2014 BUY PRICE OPINION	2014 HOLD PRICE OPINION	2014 SELL PRICE OPINION	2014 SHORT PRICE OPINION	2014 MYCROFT FREE CASH FLOW PER SHARE ESTIMATE	2014 MYCROFT FREE CASH FLOW RETURN ON TOTAL CAPITAL ESTIMATE (FROIC) >15% = Great	2014 MYCROFT CAPFLOW ESTIMATE <33% = Great BUT NO NEGATIVE RESULTS	2014 MYCROFT MICHAELIS GROWTH RATE ESTIMATE >15% = Great	DIVIDEND YIELD
Step #1 = Look up the company's current stock market price on the day of analysis and compare it to our 2014 Buy, Hold, Sell & Short Price.											
Step #2 =Take the company's current market price; divide it by the "2014 Mycroft Free Cash Flow Per Share estimate." This gives the "Price to Free Cash Flow."											
All results below are based on the 2014 year end estimates using the "2014 Mycroft Michaelis Growth Rate" and are good until December 31, 2014.											
Magellan Petroleum Corporation	MPET	Oil & Gas	Negative Free Cash Flow	Negative Free Cash Flow	Negative Free Cash Flow	Negative Free Cash Flow	-$0.49	-46%	-43%	-46%	0.00%
magicJack VocalTec Ltd	CALL	Communication	Negative Free Cash Flow	Negative Free Cash Flow	Negative Free Cash Flow	Negative Free Cash Flow	$2.29	-347%	10%	-347%	0.00%
Magnetek	MAG	Computers	Negative Free Cash Flow	Negative Free Cash Flow	Negative Free Cash Flow	Negative Free Cash Flow	-$0.78	10%	-22%	10%	0.00%
Magnum Hunter Resources Corportion	MHR	Oil & Gas	Negative Free Cash Flow	Negative Free Cash Flow	Negative Free Cash Flow	Negative Free Cash Flow	-$1.91	-38%	751%	-38%	0.00%
Maidenform Brands, Inc.	MFB	Apparel & Furniture	$1.65	$3.30	$4.95	$9.90	$0.22	2%	57%	2%	0.00%
MAKO Surgical Corporation	MAKO	Medical	Negative Free Cash Flow	Negative Free Cash Flow	Negative Free Cash Flow	Negative Free Cash Flow	-$0.41	-16%	-76%	-16%	0.00%
Management Network Group, Inc.	TMNG	Business Services	$1.20	$2.40	$3.60	$7.20	$0.16	5%	23%	5%	0.00%
Manhattan Associates, Inc.	MANH	Software	$37.65	$75.30	$112.95	$225.90	$5.02	41%	8%	41%	0.00%
Manitex International, Inc.	MNTX	Industrial	Negative Free Cash Flow	Negative Free Cash Flow	Negative Free Cash Flow	Negative Free Cash Flow	-$0.39	-5%	-51%	-5%	0.00%
Manitowoc Co Inc	MTW	Agriculture	$8.03	$16.05	$24.08	$48.15	$1.07	5%	38%	5%	0.39%
MannKind Corporation	MNKD	Biotech	Negative Free Cash Flow	Negative Free Cash Flow	Negative Free Cash Flow	Negative Free Cash Flow	-$0.41	-45%	-1%	-45%	0.00%

NAME	TICKER	INDUSTRY	2014 BUY PRICE OPINION	2014 HOLD PRICE OPINION	2014 SELL PRICE OPINION	2014 SHORT PRICE OPINION	2014 MYCROFT FREE CASH FLOW PER SHARE ESTIMATE	2014 MYCROFT FREE CASH FLOW RETURN ON TOTAL CAPITAL ESTIMATE (FROIC) >15% = Great	2014 MYCROFT CAPFLOW ESTIMATE <33% = Great BUT NO NEGATIVE RESULTS	2014 MYCROFT MICHAELIS GROWTH RATE ESTIMATE >15% = Great	DIVIDEND YIELD
Step #1 = Look up the company's current stock market price on the day of analysis and compare it to our 2014 Buy, Hold, Sell & Short Price.											
Step #2 =Take the company's current market price; divide it by the "2014 Mycroft Free Cash Flow Per Share estimate." This gives the "Price to Free Cash Flow."											
All results below are based on the 2014 year end estimates using the "2014 Mycroft Michaelis Growth Rate" and are good until December 31, 2014.											
ManpowerGroup	MAN	Services	$24.15	$48.30	$72.45	$144.90	$3.22	8%	21%	7%	1.25%
Mantech International Corp Class A	MANT	Software	$24.30	$48.60	$72.90	$145.80	$3.24	8%	11%	9%	2.95%
Marathon Oil Corp	MRO	Oil & Gas	Negative Free Cash Flow	Negative Free Cash Flow	Negative Free Cash Flow	Negative Free Cash Flow	-$1.08	-3%	116%	-3%	2.12%
Marathon Petroleum Corp	MPC	Oil & Gas	$133.58	$267.15	$400.73	$801.45	$17.81	29%	21%	28%	2.47%
Marchex, Inc. Class B	MCHX	Advertising	$1.65	$3.30	$4.95	$9.90	$0.22	6%	30%	4%	1.99%
Marcus Corporation	MCS	Travel & Leisure	$12.08	$24.15	$36.23	$72.45	$1.61	10%	37%	10%	2.61%
Marin Software Inc	MRIN	Software	Negative Free Cash Flow	Negative Free Cash Flow	Negative Free Cash Flow	Negative Free Cash Flow	-$0.91	-23%	-37%	-23%	0.00%
Marine Products Corporation	MPX	Autos	$1.58	$3.15	$4.73	$9.45	$0.21	10%	5%	5%	1.31%
MarineMax, Inc.	HZO	Retail	Negative Free Cash Flow	Negative Free Cash Flow	Negative Free Cash Flow	Negative Free Cash Flow	-$1.01	-11%	-62%	-11%	0.00%
Marketo Inc	MKTO	Software	Negative Free Cash Flow	Negative Free Cash Flow	Negative Free Cash Flow	Negative Free Cash Flow	-$0.69	-23%	-47%	-23%	0.00%
Marriott International, Inc. Class A	MAR	Travel & Leisure	$23.40	$46.80	$70.20	$140.40	$3.12	90%	50%	59%	1.63%

NAME	TICKER	INDUSTRY	2014 BUY PRICE OPINION	2014 HOLD PRICE OPINION	2014 SELL PRICE OPINION	2014 SHORT PRICE OPINION	2014 MYCROFT FREE CASH FLOW PER SHARE ESTIMATE	2014 MYCROFT FREE CASH FLOW RETURN ON TOTAL CAPITAL ESTIMATE (FROIC) >15% = Great	2014 MYCROFT CAPFLOW ESTIMATE <33% = Great BUT NO NEGATIVE RESULTS	2014 MYCROFT MICHAELIS GROWTH RATE ESTIMATE >15% = Great	DIVIDEND YIELD
Step #1 = Look up the company's current stock market price on the day of analysis and compare it to our 2014 Buy, Hold, Sell & Short Price.										
Step #2 =Take the company's current market price; divide it by the "2014 Mycroft Free Cash Flow Per Share estimate." This gives the "Price to Free Cash Flow."										
All results below are based on the 2014 year end estimates using the "2014 Mycroft Michaelis Growth Rate" and are good until December 31, 2014.										
Marriott Vacations Worldwide Corp	VAC	Travel & Leisure	$16.28	$32.55	$48.83	$97.65	$2.17	4%	19%	4%	0.00%
Marten Transport, Ltd.	MRTN	Transportation	Negative Free Cash Flow	Negative Free Cash Flow	Negative Free Cash Flow	Negative Free Cash Flow	-$1.02	-10%	136%	-10%	0.57%
Martin Marietta Materials	MLM	Building Supplies	$18.15	$36.30	$54.45	$108.90	$2.42	4%	55%	3%	1.61%
Marvell Technology Group, Ltd.	MRVL	Semiconductors	$6.53	$13.05	$19.58	$39.15	$0.87	9%	22%	8%	1.88%
Masco Corporation	MAS	Building Supplies	$4.80	$9.60	$14.40	$28.80	$0.64	5%	37%	4%	1.45%
Masimo Corporation	MASI	Medical	$9.98	$19.95	$29.93	$59.85	$1.33	21%	19%	21%	0.00%
MasTec, Inc.	MTZ	Engineering	$6.98	$13.95	$20.93	$41.85	$0.93	5%	64%	5%	0.00%
Matador Resources Co	MTDR	Oil & Gas	Negative Free Cash Flow	Negative Free Cash Flow	Negative Free Cash Flow	Negative Free Cash Flow	-$3.39	-42%	221%	-42%	0.00%
Material Sciences Corporation	MASC	Industrial	$0.23	$0.45	$0.68	$1.35	$0.03	0%	95%	0%	0.00%
Materion Corp	MTRN	Commodities	$8.55	$17.10	$25.65	$51.30	$1.14	5%	66%	4%	1.02%
Matrix Service Company	MTRX	Engineering	$11.10	$22.20	$33.30	$66.60	$1.48	14%	41%	14%	0.00%

NAME	TICKER	INDUSTRY	2014 BUY PRICE OPINION	2014 HOLD PRICE OPINION	2014 SELL PRICE OPINION	2014 SHORT PRICE OPINION	2014 MYCROFT FREE CASH FLOW PER SHARE ESTIMATE	2014 MYCROFT FREE CASH FLOW RETURN ON TOTAL CAPITAL ESTIMATE (FROIC) >15% = Great	2014 MYCROFT CAPFLOW ESTIMATE <33% = Great BUT NO NEGATIVE RESULTS	2014 MYCROFT MICHAELIS GROWTH RATE ESTIMATE >15% = Great	DIVIDEND YIELD
Step #1 = Look up the company's current stock market price on the day of analysis and compare it to our 2014 Buy, Hold, Sell & Short Price.											
Step #2 =Take the company's current market price; divide it by the "2014 Mycroft Free Cash Flow Per Share estimate." This gives the "Price to Free Cash Flow."											
All results below are based on the 2014 year end estimates using the "2014 Mycroft Michaelis Growth Rate" and are good until December 31, 2014.											
Matson Inc	MATX	Transportation	$16.58	$33.15	$49.73	$99.45	$2.21	13%	26%	11%	2.23%
Mattel, Inc.	MAT	Travel & Leisure	$20.03	$40.05	$60.08	$120.15	$2.67	20%	22%	12%	3.42%
Mattersight Corp	MATR	Software	Negative Free Cash Flow	Negative Free Cash Flow	Negative Free Cash Flow	Negative Free Cash Flow	-$0.49	-817%	-32%	-817%	0.00%
Matthews International Corporation	MATW	Services	$21.98	$43.95	$65.93	$131.85	$2.93	9%	26%	9%	1.05%
Mattress Firm Holding Corp	MFRM	Apparel & Furniture	$5.70	$11.40	$17.10	$34.20	$0.76	5%	73%	5%	0.00%
Mattson Technology	MTSN	Semiconductors	Negative Free Cash Flow	Negative Free Cash Flow	Negative Free Cash Flow	Negative Free Cash Flow	-$0.41	-78%	-6%	-78%	0.00%
Maxim Integrated Products Inc.	MXIM	Semiconductors	$18.30	$36.60	$54.90	$109.80	$2.44	24%	26%	16%	3.64%
Maximus, Inc.	MMS	Business Services	$8.85	$17.70	$26.55	$53.10	$1.18	15%	40%	13%	0.45%
MaxLinear, Inc.	MXL	Semiconductors	$2.03	$4.05	$6.08	$12.15	$0.27	10%	42%	10%	0.00%
Maxwell Technologies, Inc.	MXWL	Computers	$5.18	$10.35	$15.53	$31.05	$0.69	14%	43%	14%	0.00%
McClatchy Company	MNI	Publishing	$6.30	$12.60	$18.90	$37.80	$0.84	4%	37%	4%	0.00%

NAME	TICKER	INDUSTRY	2014 BUY PRICE OPINION	2014 HOLD PRICE OPINION	2014 SELL PRICE OPINION	2014 SHORT PRICE OPINION	2014 MYCROFT FREE CASH FLOW PER SHARE ESTIMATE	2014 MYCROFT FREE CASH FLOW RETURN ON TOTAL CAPITAL ESTIMATE (FROIC) >15% = Great	2014 MYCROFT CAPFLOW ESTIMATE <33% = Great BUT NO NEGATIVE RESULTS	2014 MYCROFT MICHAELIS GROWTH RATE ESTIMATE >15% = Great	DIVIDEND YIELD
Step #1 = Look up the company's current stock market price on the day of analysis and compare it to our 2014 Buy, Hold, Sell & Short Price.											
Step #2 =Take the company's current market price; divide it by the "2014 Mycroft Free Cash Flow Per Share estimate." This gives the "Price to Free Cash Flow."											
All results below are based on the 2014 year end estimates using the "2014 Mycroft Michaelis Growth Rate" and are good until December 31, 2014.											
McCormick & Company, Inc.	MKC	Consumer Goods	$20.40	$40.80	$61.20	$122.40	$2.72	12%	25%	8%	2.02%
McDermott International Inc	MDR	Oil & Gas	Negative Free Cash Flow	Negative Free Cash Flow	Negative Free Cash Flow	Negative Free Cash Flow	-$1.17	-15%	1353%	-15%	0.00%
McDonald's Corporation	MCD	Restaurants	$32.55	$65.10	$97.65	$195.30	$4.34	15%	42%	7%	3.18%
McGrath RentCorp	MGRC	Rentals	$0.90	$1.80	$2.70	$5.40	$0.12	1%	98%	-3%	2.72%
McGraw Hill Financial Inc	MHFI	Business Services	$44.10	$88.20	$132.30	$264.60	$5.88	56%	8%	43%	1.81%
McKesson, Inc.	MCK	Medical	$142.05	$284.10	$426.15	$852.30	$18.94	32%	11%	30%	0.76%
MDU Resources Group Inc	MDU	Utilities	Negative Free Cash Flow	Negative Free Cash Flow	Negative Free Cash Flow	Negative Free Cash Flow	-$1.43	-7%	142%	-7%	2.58%
Mead Johnson Nutrition Company	MJN	Consumer Goods	$28.73	$57.45	$86.18	$172.35	$3.83	38%	23%	23%	1.82%
Meade Instruments Corporation	MEAD	Computers	Negative Free Cash Flow	Negative Free Cash Flow	Negative Free Cash Flow	Negative Free Cash Flow	-$2.30	-53%	0%	-53%	0.00%
MeadWestvaco Corporation	MWV	Containers	Negative Free Cash Flow	Negative Free Cash Flow	Negative Free Cash Flow	Negative Free Cash Flow	-$0.72	-2%	129%	-3%	2.63%
Measurement Specialties	MEAS	Computers	$22.50	$45.00	$67.50	$135.00	$3.00	13%	24%	13%	0.00%

NAME	TICKER	INDUSTRY	2014 BUY PRICE OPINION	2014 HOLD PRICE OPINION	2014 SELL PRICE OPINION	2014 SHORT PRICE OPINION	2014 MYCROFT FREE CASH FLOW PER SHARE ESTIMATE	2014 MYCROFT FREE CASH FLOW RETURN ON TOTAL CAPITAL ESTIMATE (FROIC) >15% = Great	2014 MYCROFT CAPFLOW ESTIMATE <33% = Great BUT NO NEGATIVE RESULTS	2014 MYCROFT MICHAELIS GROWTH RATE ESTIMATE >15% = Great	DIVIDEND YIELD
Step #1 = Look up the company's current stock market price on the day of analysis and compare it to our 2014 Buy, Hold, Sell & Short Price.											
Step #2 =Take the company's current market price; divide it by the "2014 Mycroft Free Cash Flow Per Share estimate." This gives the "Price to Free Cash Flow."											
All results below are based on the 2014 year end estimates using the "2014 Mycroft Michaelis Growth Rate" and are good until December 31, 2014.											
MedAssets, Inc.	MDAS	Software	$13.20	$26.40	$39.60	$79.20	$1.76	7%	38%	7%	0.00%
Media General Inc. Class A	MEG	Entertainment	Negative Free Cash Flow	Negative Free Cash Flow	Negative Free Cash Flow	Negative Free Cash Flow	-$0.40	-2%	212%	-2%	0.00%
Medical Action Industries	MDCI	Medical	$3.23	$6.45	$9.68	$19.35	$0.43	4%	17%	4%	0.00%
Medicines	MDCO	Drugs	$2.55	$5.10	$7.65	$15.30	$0.34	2%	42%	2%	0.00%
MediciNova, Inc.	MNOV	Biotech	Negative Free Cash Flow	Negative Free Cash Flow	Negative Free Cash Flow	Negative Free Cash Flow	-$0.42	-41%	-1%	-41%	0.00%
Medidata Solutions, Inc.	MDSO	Software	$8.03	$16.05	$24.08	$48.15	$1.07	15%	27%	15%	0.00%
Medifast, Inc.	MED	Retail	$16.58	$33.15	$49.73	$99.45	$2.21	23%	32%	23%	0.00%
Medivation, Inc.	MDVN	Biotech	Negative Free Cash Flow	Negative Free Cash Flow	Negative Free Cash Flow	Negative Free Cash Flow	-$1.44	-43%	-13%	-43%	0.00%
Mednax, Inc.	MD	Health Care	$56.70	$113.40	$170.10	$340.20	$7.56	15%	5%	15%	0.00%
Medtronic, Inc.	MDT	Medical	$35.03	$70.05	$105.08	$210.15	$4.67	16%	10%	14%	2.08%
MeetMe Inc	MEET	Internet	Negative Free Cash Flow	Negative Free Cash Flow	Negative Free Cash Flow	Negative Free Cash Flow	-$0.02	-1%	-300%	-1%	0.00%

NAME	TICKER	INDUSTRY	2014 BUY PRICE OPINION	2014 HOLD PRICE OPINION	2014 SELL PRICE OPINION	2014 SHORT PRICE OPINION	2014 MYCROFT FREE CASH FLOW PER SHARE ESTIMATE	2014 MYCROFT FREE CASH FLOW RETURN ON TOTAL CAPITAL ESTIMATE (FROIC) >15% = Great	2014 MYCROFT CAPFLOW ESTIMATE <33% = Great BUT NO NEGATIVE RESULTS	2014 MYCROFT MICHAELIS GROWTH RATE ESTIMATE >15% = Great	DIVIDEND YIELD
Step #1 = Look up the company's current stock market price on the day of analysis and compare it to our 2014 Buy, Hold, Sell & Short Price.											
Step #2 =Take the company's current market price; divide it by the "2014 Mycroft Free Cash Flow Per Share estimate." This gives the "Price to Free Cash Flow."											
All results below are based on the 2014 year end estimates using the "2014 Mycroft Michaelis Growth Rate" and are good until December 31, 2014.											
MEI Pharma Inc	MEIP	Drugs	Negative Free Cash Flow	Negative Free Cash Flow	Negative Free Cash Flow	Negative Free Cash Flow	-$0.52	-39%	0%	-39%	0.00%
Memsic, Inc.	MEMS	Semiconductors	$0.30	$0.60	$0.90	$1.80	$0.04	1%	74%	1%	0.00%
Men's Wearhouse	MW	Retail	$18.45	$36.90	$55.35	$110.70	$2.46	10%	51%	9%	1.86%
Mentor Graphics Corporation	MENT	Software	$7.35	$14.70	$22.05	$44.10	$0.98	8%	26%	7%	0.79%
Merck & Co Inc	MRK	Drugs	$21.15	$42.30	$63.45	$126.90	$2.82	12%	20%	8%	3.58%
Mercury Systems Inc	MRCY	Computers	Negative Free Cash Flow	Negative Free Cash Flow	Negative Free Cash Flow	Negative Free Cash Flow	-$0.17	-2%	-207%	-2%	0.00%
Meredith Corporation	MDP	Publishing	$30.68	$61.35	$92.03	$184.05	$4.09	14%	14%	12%	3.65%
Merge Healthcare, Inc.	MRGE	Software	Negative Free Cash Flow	Negative Free Cash Flow	Negative Free Cash Flow	Negative Free Cash Flow	-$0.01	0%	6200%	0%	0.00%
Meridian Bioscience, Inc.	VIVO	Medical	$7.95	$15.90	$23.85	$47.70	$1.06	27%	6%	9%	3.19%
Merit Medical Systems	MMSI	Medical	Negative Free Cash Flow	Negative Free Cash Flow	Negative Free Cash Flow	Negative Free Cash Flow	-$0.51	-5%	155%	-5%	0.00%
Meritage Homes Corporation	MTH	Homebuilding	Negative Free Cash Flow	Negative Free Cash Flow	Negative Free Cash Flow	Negative Free Cash Flow	-$4.07	-11%	-9%	-11%	0.00%

NAME	TICKER	INDUSTRY	2014 BUY PRICE OPINION	2014 HOLD PRICE OPINION	2014 SELL PRICE OPINION	2014 SHORT PRICE OPINION	2014 MYCROFT FREE CASH FLOW PER SHARE ESTIMATE	2014 MYCROFT FREE CASH FLOW RETURN ON TOTAL CAPITAL ESTIMATE (FROIC) >15% = Great	2014 MYCROFT CAPFLOW ESTIMATE <33% = Great BUT NO NEGATIVE RESULTS	2014 MYCROFT MICHAELIS GROWTH RATE ESTIMATE >15% = Great	DIVIDEND YIELD

Step #1 = Look up the company's current stock market price on the day of analysis and compare it to our 2014 Buy, Hold, Sell & Short Price.

Step #2 =Take the company's current market price; divide it by the "2014 Mycroft Free Cash Flow Per Share estimate." This gives the "Price to Free Cash Flow."

All results below are based on the 2014 year end estimates using the "2014 Mycroft Michaelis Growth Rate" and are good until December 31, 2014.

NAME	TICKER	INDUSTRY	2014 BUY PRICE OPINION	2014 HOLD PRICE OPINION	2014 SELL PRICE OPINION	2014 SHORT PRICE OPINION	2014 MYCROFT FCF PER SHARE	FROIC	CAPFLOW	MICHAELIS GROWTH	DIVIDEND YIELD
Merrimack Pharmaceuticals Inc	MACK	Biotech	Negative Free Cash Flow	Negative Free Cash Flow	Negative Free Cash Flow	Negative Free Cash Flow	-$0.89	156%	-7%	156%	0.00%
MERU Networks, Inc.	MERU	Communication	Negative Free Cash Flow	Negative Free Cash Flow	Negative Free Cash Flow	Negative Free Cash Flow	-$0.36	-29%	-19%	-29%	0.00%
Mesa Laboratories, Inc.	MLAB	Medical	$24.90	$49.80	$74.70	$149.40	$3.32	15%	9%	13%	0.85%
Metabolix, Inc.	MBLX	Chemicals	Negative Free Cash Flow	Negative Free Cash Flow	Negative Free Cash Flow	Negative Free Cash Flow	-$0.82	-82%	-1%	-82%	0.00%
Metalico, Inc.	MEA	Industrial	$2.18	$4.35	$6.53	$13.05	$0.29	4%	50%	4%	0.00%
Methode Electronics, Inc. Class A	MEI	Computers	Negative Free Cash Flow	Negative Free Cash Flow	Negative Free Cash Flow	Negative Free Cash Flow	-$0.02	0%	102%	-2%	1.08%
Mettler-Toledo International, Inc.	MTD	Medical	$72.15	$144.30	$216.45	$432.90	$9.62	19%	27%	19%	0.00%
MFRI Inc	MFRI	Industrial	Negative Free Cash Flow	Negative Free Cash Flow	Negative Free Cash Flow	Negative Free Cash Flow	-$0.78	-5%	-151%	-5%	0.00%
MGC Diagnostics Corp	MGCD	Medical	Negative Free Cash Flow	Negative Free Cash Flow	Negative Free Cash Flow	Negative Free Cash Flow	-$0.09	-3%	145%	-3%	0.00%
MGE Energy, Inc.	MGEE	Utilities	$10.05	$20.10	$30.15	$60.30	$1.34	3%	80%	2%	3.14%
MGM Resorts International	MGM	Travel & Leisure	$10.80	$21.60	$32.40	$64.80	$1.44	4%	40%	4%	0.00%

NAME	TICKER	INDUSTRY	2014 BUY PRICE OPINION	2014 HOLD PRICE OPINION	2014 SELL PRICE OPINION	2014 SHORT PRICE OPINION	2014 MYCROFT FREE CASH FLOW PER SHARE ESTIMATE	2014 MYCROFT FREE CASH FLOW RETURN ON TOTAL CAPITAL ESTIMATE (FROIC) >15% = Great	2014 MYCROFT CAPFLOW ESTIMATE <33% = Great BUT NO NEGATIVE RESULTS	2014 MYCROFT MICHAELIS GROWTH RATE ESTIMATE >15% = Great	DIVIDEND YIELD
Step #1 = Look up the company's current stock market price on the day of analysis and compare it to our 2014 Buy, Hold, Sell & Short Price.											
Step #2 =Take the company's current market price; divide it by the "2014 Mycroft Free Cash Flow Per Share estimate." This gives the "Price to Free Cash Flow."											
All results below are based on the 2014 year end estimates using the "2014 Mycroft Michaelis Growth Rate" and are good until December 31, 2014.											
MGP Ingredients, Inc.	MGPI	Consumer Goods	Negative Free Cash Flow	Negative Free Cash Flow	Negative Free Cash Flow	Negative Free Cash Flow	-$0.13	-2%	153%	-2%	1.01%
Michael Baker Corporation	BKR	Engineering	$18.53	$37.05	$55.58	$111.15	$2.47	9%	16%	8%	1.77%
Michael Kors Holdings Ltd	KORS	Retail	$15.45	$30.90	$46.35	$92.70	$2.06	27%	32%	27%	0.00%
Micrel, Inc.	MCRL	Semiconductors	$1.65	$3.30	$4.95	$9.90	$0.22	5%	44%	3%	2.11%
Microchip Technology, Inc.	MCHP	Semiconductors	$17.18	$34.35	$51.53	$103.05	$2.29	18%	14%	9%	3.59%
Micron Technology, Inc.	MU	Semiconductors	$1.80	$3.60	$5.40	$10.80	$0.24	2%	84%	2%	0.00%
Micros Systems, Inc.	MCRS	Software	$19.95	$39.90	$59.85	$119.70	$2.66	16%	14%	16%	0.00%
Microsemi Corp	MSCC	Semiconductors	$10.95	$21.90	$32.85	$65.70	$1.46	7%	24%	7%	0.00%
Microsoft Corporation	MSFT	Software	$26.93	$53.85	$80.78	$161.55	$3.59	27%	15%	22%	2.84%
MicroStrategy, Inc.	MSTR	Software	Negative Free Cash Flow	Negative Free Cash Flow	Negative Free Cash Flow	Negative Free Cash Flow	-$0.72	-3%	161%	-3%	0.00%
Microvision, Inc.	MVIS	Computers	Negative Free Cash Flow	Negative Free Cash Flow	Negative Free Cash Flow	Negative Free Cash Flow	-$0.71	-6418%	-2%	-6418%	0.00%

NAME	TICKER	INDUSTRY	2014 BUY PRICE OPINION	2014 HOLD PRICE OPINION	2014 SELL PRICE OPINION	2014 SHORT PRICE OPINION	2014 MYCROFT FREE CASH FLOW PER SHARE ESTIMATE	2014 MYCROFT FREE CASH FLOW RETURN ON TOTAL CAPITAL ESTIMATE (FROIC) >15% = Great	2014 MYCROFT CAPFLOW ESTIMATE <33% = Great BUT NO NEGATIVE RESULTS	2014 MYCROFT MICHAELIS GROWTH RATE ESTIMATE >15% = Great	DIVIDEND YIELD
Step #1 = Look up the company's current stock market price on the day of analysis and compare it to our 2014 Buy, Hold, Sell & Short Price.											
Step #2 =Take the company's current market price; divide it by the "2014 Mycroft Free Cash Flow Per Share estimate." This gives the "Price to Free Cash Flow."											
All results below are based on the 2014 year end estimates using the "2014 Mycroft Michaelis Growth Rate" and are good until December 31, 2014.											
Middleby Corporation	MIDD	Industrial	$34.13	$68.25	$102.38	$204.75	$4.55	8%	18%	8%	0.00%
Middlesex Water Company	MSEX	Utilities	$5.18	$10.35	$15.53	$31.05	$0.69	3%	64%	3%	3.66%
Midstates Petroleum Co Inc	MPO	Oil & Gas	Negative Free Cash Flow	Negative Free Cash Flow	Negative Free Cash Flow	Negative Free Cash Flow	-$19.27	-166%	980%	-166%	0.00%
Midway Gold Corp.	MDW	Commodities	Negative Free Cash Flow	Negative Free Cash Flow	Negative Free Cash Flow	Negative Free Cash Flow	-$0.04	-30%	-65%	-30%	0.00%
Millennial Media Inc	MM	Advertising	Negative Free Cash Flow	Negative Free Cash Flow	Negative Free Cash Flow	Negative Free Cash Flow	-$0.04	-2%	189%	-2%	0.00%
Miller Energy Resources Inc	MILL	Oil & Gas	Negative Free Cash Flow	Negative Free Cash Flow	Negative Free Cash Flow	Negative Free Cash Flow	-$1.52	-21%	-240%	-21%	0.00%
Miller Industries	MLR	Autos	$4.65	$9.30	$13.95	$27.90	$0.62	4%	33%	4%	3.37%
MiMedx Group, Inc.	MDXG	Medical	Negative Free Cash Flow	Negative Free Cash Flow	Negative Free Cash Flow	Negative Free Cash Flow	-$0.07	-18%	-38%	-18%	0.00%
Mindspeed Technologies, Inc.	MSPD	Semiconductors	Negative Free Cash Flow	Negative Free Cash Flow	Negative Free Cash Flow	Negative Free Cash Flow	-$0.26	-9%	1180%	-9%	0.00%
Mine Safety Appliances	MSA	Medical	$16.20	$32.40	$48.60	$97.20	$2.16	10%	29%	6%	2.39%
Minerals Technologies, Inc.	MTX	Chemicals	$19.35	$38.70	$58.05	$116.10	$2.58	9%	38%	9%	0.43%

NAME	TICKER	INDUSTRY	2014 BUY PRICE OPINION	2014 HOLD PRICE OPINION	2014 SELL PRICE OPINION	2014 SHORT PRICE OPINION	2014 MYCROFT FREE CASH FLOW PER SHARE ESTIMATE	2014 MYCROFT FREE CASH FLOW RETURN ON TOTAL CAPITAL ESTIMATE (FROIC) >15% = Great	2014 MYCROFT CAPFLOW ESTIMATE <33% = Great BUT NO NEGATIVE RESULTS	2014 MYCROFT MICHAELIS GROWTH RATE ESTIMATE >15% = Great	DIVIDEND YIELD
Step #1 = Look up the company's current stock market price on the day of analysis and compare it to our 2014 Buy, Hold, Sell & Short Price.											
Step #2 =Take the company's current market price; divide it by the "2014 Mycroft Free Cash Flow Per Share estimate." This gives the "Price to Free Cash Flow."											
All results below are based on the 2014 year end estimates using the "2014 Mycroft Michaelis Growth Rate" and are good until December 31, 2014.											
Misonix, Inc.	MSON	Medical	Negative Free Cash Flow	Negative Free Cash Flow	Negative Free Cash Flow	Negative Free Cash Flow	-$0.08	-4%	469%	-4%	0.00%
Mistras Group, Inc.	MG	Rentals	$8.93	$17.85	$26.78	$53.55	$1.19	12%	31%	12%	0.00%
Mitcham Industries, Inc.	MIND	Computers	$2.93	$5.85	$8.78	$17.55	$0.39	3%	84%	3%	0.00%
Mitek Systems, Inc.	MITK	Software	Negative Free Cash Flow	Negative Free Cash Flow	Negative Free Cash Flow	Negative Free Cash Flow	-$0.02	-2%	161%	-2%	0.00%
MKS Instruments, Inc.	MKSI	Semiconductors	$6.53	$13.05	$19.58	$39.15	$0.87	4%	26%	4%	2.44%
Mobile Mini Inc	MINI	Containers	$9.60	$19.20	$28.80	$57.60	$1.28	5%	48%	5%	0.00%
Mocon, Inc.	MOCO	Computers	$0.00	$0.00	$0.00	$0.00	$0.00	0%	99%	-3%	3.15%
Model N Inc	MODN	Software	Negative Free Cash Flow	Negative Free Cash Flow	Negative Free Cash Flow	Negative Free Cash Flow	-$0.31	-8%	-209%	-8%	0.00%
Modine Manufacturing Company	MOD	Autos	$1.88	$3.75	$5.63	$11.25	$0.25	3%	81%	3%	0.00%
ModusLink Global Solutions, Inc.	MLNK	Business Services	Negative Free Cash Flow	Negative Free Cash Flow	Negative Free Cash Flow	Negative Free Cash Flow	-$0.62	-19%	-29%	-19%	0.00%
Mohawk Industries, Inc.	MHK	Apparel & Furniture	$37.20	$74.40	$111.60	$223.20	$4.96	6%	44%	6%	0.00%

NAME	TICKER	INDUSTRY	2014 BUY PRICE OPINION	2014 HOLD PRICE OPINION	2014 SELL PRICE OPINION	2014 SHORT PRICE OPINION	2014 MYCROFT FREE CASH FLOW PER SHARE ESTIMATE	2014 MYCROFT FREE CASH FLOW RETURN ON TOTAL CAPITAL ESTIMATE (FROIC) >15% = Great	2014 MYCROFT CAPFLOW ESTIMATE <33% = Great BUT NO NEGATIVE RESULTS	2014 MYCROFT MICHAELIS GROWTH RATE ESTIMATE >15% = Great	DIVIDEND YIELD
Step #1 = Look up the company's current stock market price on the day of analysis and compare it to our 2014 Buy, Hold, Sell & Short Price.											
Step #2 =Take the company's current market price; divide it by the "2014 Mycroft Free Cash Flow Per Share estimate." This gives the "Price to Free Cash Flow."											
All results below are based on the 2014 year end estimates using the "2014 Mycroft Michaelis Growth Rate" and are good until December 31, 2014.											
Molex, Inc.	MOLX	Computers	$5.10	$10.20	$15.30	$30.60	$0.68	4%	69%	1%	2.48%
Molina Healthcare, Inc.	MOH	Health Care	Negative Free Cash Flow	Negative Free Cash Flow	Negative Free Cash Flow	Negative Free Cash Flow	-$1.75	-7%	160140%	-7%	0.00%
Molson Coors Brewing Company	TAP	Beverages	$39.15	$78.30	$117.45	$234.90	$5.22	7%	25%	8%	2.59%
Molycorp, Inc.	MCP	Commodities	Negative Free Cash Flow	Negative Free Cash Flow	Negative Free Cash Flow	Negative Free Cash Flow	-$4.03	-35%	-665%	-35%	0.00%
Momenta Pharmaceuticals, Inc.	MNTA	Drugs	Negative Free Cash Flow	Negative Free Cash Flow	Negative Free Cash Flow	Negative Free Cash Flow	-$1.33	-22%	-12%	-22%	0.00%
Monarch Casino & Resort, Inc.	MCRI	Travel & Leisure	$11.70	$23.40	$35.10	$70.20	$1.56	10%	31%	10%	0.00%
Mondelez International Inc	MDLZ	Consumer Goods	$7.35	$14.70	$22.05	$44.10	$0.98	3%	46%	3%	1.80%
Mosaic Co	MOS	Agriculture	$5.33	$10.65	$15.98	$31.95	$0.71	2%	84%	1%	2.23%
NCI Building Systems, Inc.	NCS	Building Supplies	Negative Free Cash Flow	Negative Free Cash Flow	Negative Free Cash Flow	Negative Free Cash Flow	-$0.07	-1%	128%	-1%	0.00%
NCI, Inc. Class A	NCIT	Software	$19.20	$38.40	$57.60	$115.20	$2.56	25%	4%	25%	0.00%
NCR Corporation	NCR	Software	Negative Free Cash Flow	Negative Free Cash Flow	Negative Free Cash Flow	Negative Free Cash Flow	-$3.65	-28%	-43%	-28%	0.00%

NAME	TICKER	INDUSTRY	2014 BUY PRICE OPINION	2014 HOLD PRICE OPINION	2014 SELL PRICE OPINION	2014 SHORT PRICE OPINION	2014 MYCROFT FREE CASH FLOW PER SHARE ESTIMATE	2014 MYCROFT FREE CASH FLOW RETURN ON TOTAL CAPITAL ESTIMATE (FROIC) >15% = Great	2014 MYCROFT CAPFLOW ESTIMATE <33% = Great BUT NO NEGATIVE RESULTS	2014 MYCROFT MICHAELIS GROWTH RATE ESTIMATE >15% = Great	DIVIDEND YIELD
Step #1 = Look up the company's current stock market price on the day of analysis and compare it to our 2014 Buy, Hold, Sell & Short Price.											
Step #2 =Take the company's current market price; divide it by the "2014 Mycroft Free Cash Flow Per Share estimate." This gives the "Price to Free Cash Flow."											
All results below are based on the 2014 year end estimates using the "2014 Mycroft Michaelis Growth Rate" and are good until December 31, 2014.											
Neenah Paper, Inc.	NP	Forest Products	$28.65	$57.30	$85.95	$171.90	$3.82	13%	32%	12%	2.08%
Neogen Corporation	NEOG	Medical	$5.85	$11.70	$17.55	$35.10	$0.78	7%	34%	7%	0.00%
NeoGenomics, Inc.	NEO	Medical	Negative Free Cash Flow	Negative Free Cash Flow	Negative Free Cash Flow	Negative Free Cash Flow	-$0.05	-11%	11050%	-11%	0.00%
Neonode, Inc.	NEON	Computers	Negative Free Cash Flow	Negative Free Cash Flow	Negative Free Cash Flow	Negative Free Cash Flow	-$0.19	-207%	-1%	-207%	0.00%
NeoPhotonics Corp.	NPTN	Semiconductors	Negative Free Cash Flow	Negative Free Cash Flow	Negative Free Cash Flow	Negative Free Cash Flow	-$0.61	-9%	-1673%	-9%	0.00%
Neostem, Inc.	NBS	Biotech	Negative Free Cash Flow	Negative Free Cash Flow	Negative Free Cash Flow	Negative Free Cash Flow	-$1.32	-80%	-2%	-80%	0.00%
NetApp, Inc.	NTAP	Computers	$31.20	$62.40	$93.60	$187.20	$4.16	28%	21%	25%	1.38%
Netflix, Inc.	NFLX	Retail	Negative Free Cash Flow	Negative Free Cash Flow	Negative Free Cash Flow	Negative Free Cash Flow	-$1.86	-7%	1944%	-7%	0.00%
Netgear, Inc.	NTGR	Communication	$16.88	$33.75	$50.63	$101.25	$2.25	10%	18%	10%	0.00%
NetScout Systems, Inc.	NTCT	Software	$13.88	$27.75	$41.63	$83.25	$1.85	15%	15%	15%	0.00%
Netsol Technologies, Inc.	NTWK	Software	$0.23	$0.45	$0.68	$1.35	$0.03	0%	98%	0%	0.00%

NAME	TICKER	INDUSTRY	2014 BUY PRICE OPINION	2014 HOLD PRICE OPINION	2014 SELL PRICE OPINION	2014 SHORT PRICE OPINION	2014 MYCROFT FREE CASH FLOW PER SHARE ESTIMATE	2014 MYCROFT FREE CASH FLOW RETURN ON TOTAL CAPITAL ESTIMATE (FROIC) >15% = Great	2014 MYCROFT CAPFLOW ESTIMATE <33% = Great BUT NO NEGATIVE RESULTS	2014 MYCROFT MICHAELIS GROWTH RATE ESTIMATE >15% = Great	DIVIDEND YIELD
Step #1 = Look up the company's current stock market price on the day of analysis and compare it to our 2014 Buy, Hold, Sell & Short Price.											
Step #2 =Take the company's current market price; divide it by the "2014 Mycroft Free Cash Flow Per Share estimate." This gives the "Price to Free Cash Flow."											
All results below are based on the 2014 year end estimates using the "2014 Mycroft Michaelis Growth Rate" and are good until December 31, 2014.											
NetSuite, Inc.	N	Software	$5.03	$10.05	$15.08	$30.15	$0.67	20%	30%	20%	0.00%
Neuralstem, Inc.	CUR	Biotech	Negative Free Cash Flow	Negative Free Cash Flow	Negative Free Cash Flow	Negative Free Cash Flow	-$0.14	-230%	-3%	-230%	0.00%
Neurocrine Biosciences, Inc.	NBIX	Drugs	Negative Free Cash Flow	Negative Free Cash Flow	Negative Free Cash Flow	Negative Free Cash Flow	-$0.39	-19%	-3%	-19%	0.00%
NeuStar, Inc.	NSR	Communication	$34.13	$68.25	$102.38	$204.75	$4.55	21%	18%	21%	0.00%
New Jersey Resources Corporation	NJR	Utilities	Negative Free Cash Flow	Negative Free Cash Flow	Negative Free Cash Flow	Negative Free Cash Flow	-$1.09	-3%	139%	-5%	3.80%
New York & Company, Inc.	NWY	Retail	$1.13	$2.25	$3.38	$6.75	$0.15	8%	63%	8%	0.00%
New York Times Company Class A	NYT	Publishing	Negative Free Cash Flow	Negative Free Cash Flow	Negative Free Cash Flow	Negative Free Cash Flow	-$0.29	-6%	-107%	-6%	0.00%
Newell Rubbermaid Inc	NWL	Consumer Goods	$9.90	$19.80	$29.70	$59.40	$1.32	10%	30%	8%	2.25%
Newfield Exploration Company	NFX	Oil & Gas	Negative Free Cash Flow	Negative Free Cash Flow	Negative Free Cash Flow	Negative Free Cash Flow	-$4.44	-9%	151%	-9%	0.00%
NewLink Genetics Corp	NLNK	Biotech	Negative Free Cash Flow	Negative Free Cash Flow	Negative Free Cash Flow	Negative Free Cash Flow	-$0.86	-40%	-2%	-40%	0.00%
NewMarket Corporation	NEU	Chemicals	$180.98	$361.95	$542.93	$1,085.85	$24.13	37%	18%	31%	1.26%

NAME	TICKER	INDUSTRY	2014 BUY PRICE OPINION	2014 HOLD PRICE OPINION	2014 SELL PRICE OPINION	2014 SHORT PRICE OPINION	2014 MYCROFT FREE CASH FLOW PER SHARE ESTIMATE	2014 MYCROFT FREE CASH FLOW RETURN ON TOTAL CAPITAL ESTIMATE (FROIC) >15% = Great	2014 MYCROFT CAPFLOW ESTIMATE <33% = Great BUT NO NEGATIVE RESULTS	2014 MYCROFT MICHAELIS GROWTH RATE ESTIMATE >15% = Great	DIVIDEND YIELD
Step #1 = Look up the company's current stock market price on the day of analysis and compare it to our 2014 Buy, Hold, Sell & Short Price.											
Step #2 =Take the company's current market price; divide it by the "2014 Mycroft Free Cash Flow Per Share estimate." This gives the "Price to Free Cash Flow."											
All results below are based on the 2014 year end estimates using the "2014 Mycroft Michaelis Growth Rate" and are good until December 31, 2014.											
Newmont Mining Corporation	NEM	Commodities	Negative Free Cash Flow	Negative Free Cash Flow	Negative Free Cash Flow	Negative Free Cash Flow	-$1.25	-3%	129%	-3%	3.39%
Newpark Resources, Inc.	NR	Oil & Gas	$7.88	$15.75	$23.63	$47.25	$1.05	11%	40%	11%	0.00%
Newport Corporation	NEWP	Industrial	$15.15	$30.30	$45.45	$90.90	$2.02	15%	17%	15%	0.00%
News Corporation	NWSA	Entertainment	$6.90	$13.80	$20.70	$41.40	$0.92	3%	48%	3%	0.00%
Nexstar Broadcasting Group Inc	NXST	Entertainment	$7.50	$15.00	$22.50	$45.00	$1.00	5%	44%	4%	1.36%
NextEra Energy Inc	NEE	Utilities	$6.68	$13.35	$20.03	$40.05	$0.89	1%	91%	1%	3.32%
NIC, Inc.	EGOV	Software	$3.53	$7.05	$10.58	$21.15	$0.47	24%	35%	24%	0.00%
Nielsen Holdings NV	NLSN	Business Services	$11.78	$23.55	$35.33	$70.65	$1.57	10%	40%	7%	2.26%
NII Holdings Inc	NIHD	Communication	Negative Free Cash Flow	Negative Free Cash Flow	Negative Free Cash Flow	Negative Free Cash Flow	-$5.16	-15%	844%	-15%	0.00%
Nike, Inc. Class B	NKE	Apparel & Furniture	$23.33	$46.65	$69.98	$139.95	$3.11	21%	21%	16%	1.24%
NiSource Inc	NI	Utilities	Negative Free Cash Flow	Negative Free Cash Flow	Negative Free Cash Flow	Negative Free Cash Flow	-$0.91	-2%	120%	-1%	3.38%

NAME	TICKER	INDUSTRY	2014 BUY PRICE OPINION	2014 HOLD PRICE OPINION	2014 SELL PRICE OPINION	2014 SHORT PRICE OPINION	2014 MYCROFT FREE CASH FLOW PER SHARE ESTIMATE	2014 MYCROFT FREE CASH FLOW RETURN ON TOTAL CAPITAL ESTIMATE (FROIC) >15% = Great	2014 MYCROFT CAPFLOW ESTIMATE <33% = Great BUT NO NEGATIVE RESULTS	2014 MYCROFT MICHAELIS GROWTH RATE ESTIMATE >15% = Great	DIVIDEND YIELD
Step #1 = Look up the company's current stock market price on the day of analysis and compare it to our 2014 Buy, Hold, Sell & Short Price.											
Step #2 =Take the company's current market price; divide it by the "2014 Mycroft Free Cash Flow Per Share estimate." This gives the "Price to Free Cash Flow."											
All results below are based on the 2014 year end estimates using the "2014 Mycroft Michaelis Growth Rate" and are good until December 31, 2014.											
NN, Inc.	NNBR	Industrial	$10.35	$20.70	$31.05	$62.10	$1.38	10%	37%	10%	1.59%
Noble Energy Inc	NBL	Oil & Gas	Negative Free Cash Flow	Negative Free Cash Flow	Negative Free Cash Flow	Negative Free Cash Flow	-$2.09	-6%	126%	-6%	0.85%
Noranda Aluminum Holding Corp	NOR	Commodities	Negative Free Cash Flow	Negative Free Cash Flow	Negative Free Cash Flow	Negative Free Cash Flow	-$0.49	-5%	165%	0%	6.90%
Nordic American Tankers Ltd	NAT	Transportation	Negative Free Cash Flow	Negative Free Cash Flow	Negative Free Cash Flow	Negative Free Cash Flow	-$0.65	-4%	-23%	0%	7.90%
Nordson Corporation	NDSN	Industrial	$33.45	$66.90	$100.35	$200.70	$4.46	18%	15%	16%	1.00%
Nordstrom, Inc.	JWN	Retail	$23.55	$47.10	$70.65	$141.30	$3.14	11%	56%	8%	2.10%
Norfolk Southern Corporation	NSC	Transportation	$18.68	$37.35	$56.03	$112.05	$2.49	4%	74%	3%	2.73%
Nortek Inc	NTK	Building Supplies	$50.03	$100.05	$150.08	$300.15	$6.67	8%	27%	8%	0.00%
Northeast Utilities	NU	Utilities	$3.08	$6.15	$9.23	$18.45	$0.41	1%	92%	2%	3.61%
Northern Oil & Gas, Inc.	NOG	Oil & Gas	Negative Free Cash Flow	Negative Free Cash Flow	Negative Free Cash Flow	Negative Free Cash Flow	-$3.32	-23%	195%	-23%	0.00%
Northern Technologies International	NTIC	Containers	Negative Free Cash Flow	Negative Free Cash Flow	Negative Free Cash Flow	Negative Free Cash Flow	-$0.97	-11%	-89%	-11%	0.00%

NAME	TICKER	INDUSTRY	2014 BUY PRICE OPINION	2014 HOLD PRICE OPINION	2014 SELL PRICE OPINION	2014 SHORT PRICE OPINION	2014 MYCROFT FREE CASH FLOW PER SHARE ESTIMATE	2014 MYCROFT FREE CASH FLOW RETURN ON TOTAL CAPITAL ESTIMATE (FROIC) >15% = Great	2014 MYCROFT CAPFLOW ESTIMATE <33% = Great BUT NO NEGATIVE RESULTS	2014 MYCROFT MICHAELIS GROWTH RATE ESTIMATE >15% = Great	DIVIDEND YIELD
Step #1 = Look up the company's current stock market price on the day of analysis and compare it to our 2014 Buy, Hold, Sell & Short Price.											
Step #2 =Take the company's current market price; divide it by the "2014 Mycroft Free Cash Flow Per Share estimate." This gives the "Price to Free Cash Flow."											
All results below are based on the 2014 year end estimates using the "2014 Mycroft Michaelis Growth Rate" and are good until December 31, 2014.											
Northrop Grumman Corp	NOC	Aerospace & Defense	$70.13	$140.25	$210.38	$420.75	$9.35	14%	13%	13%	2.57%
Northwest Natural Gas	NWN	Utilities	$8.03	$16.05	$24.08	$48.15	$1.07	2%	82%	3%	4.40%
Northwest Pipe Company	NWPX	Steel	$4.95	$9.90	$14.85	$29.70	$0.66	2%	82%	2%	0.00%
NorthWestern Corporation	NWE	Utilities	$5.18	$10.35	$15.53	$31.05	$0.69	1%	89%	2%	3.68%
Norwegian Cruise Line Holdings Ltd	NCLH	Travel & Leisure	Negative Free Cash Flow	Negative Free Cash Flow	Negative Free Cash Flow	Negative Free Cash Flow	-$2.41	-10%	224%	-10%	0.00%
NovaBay Pharmaceuticals, Inc.	NBY	Drugs	Negative Free Cash Flow	Negative Free Cash Flow	Negative Free Cash Flow	Negative Free Cash Flow	-$0.23	-123%	-2%	-123%	0.00%
Novatel Wireless, Inc.	NVTL	Communication	Negative Free Cash Flow	Negative Free Cash Flow	Negative Free Cash Flow	Negative Free Cash Flow	-$0.14	-7%	6025%	-7%	0.00%
Novavax, Inc.	NVAX	Biotech	Negative Free Cash Flow	Negative Free Cash Flow	Negative Free Cash Flow	Negative Free Cash Flow	-$0.21	-47%	-25%	-47%	0.00%
NPS Pharmaceuticals Inc	NPSP	Biotech	Negative Free Cash Flow	Negative Free Cash Flow	Negative Free Cash Flow	Negative Free Cash Flow	-$0.29	-11%	-3%	-11%	0.00%
NRG Energy Inc	NRG	Utilities	Negative Free Cash Flow	Negative Free Cash Flow	Negative Free Cash Flow	Negative Free Cash Flow	-$8.05	-27%	635%	-26%	1.83%
NTELOS Holdings Corp	NTLS	Communication	$20.78	$41.55	$62.33	$124.65	$2.77	11%	62%	14%	9.10%

NAME	TICKER	INDUSTRY	2014 BUY PRICE OPINION	2014 HOLD PRICE OPINION	2014 SELL PRICE OPINION	2014 SHORT PRICE OPINION	2014 MYCROFT FREE CASH FLOW PER SHARE ESTIMATE	2014 MYCROFT FREE CASH FLOW RETURN ON TOTAL CAPITAL ESTIMATE (FROIC) >15% = Great	2014 MYCROFT CAPFLOW ESTIMATE <33% = Great BUT NO NEGATIVE RESULTS	2014 MYCROFT MICHAELIS GROWTH RATE ESTIMATE >15% = Great	DIVIDEND YIELD
Step #1 = Look up the company's current stock market price on the day of analysis and compare it to our 2014 Buy, Hold, Sell & Short Price.											
Step #2 =Take the company's current market price; divide it by the "2014 Mycroft Free Cash Flow Per Share estimate." This gives the "Price to Free Cash Flow."											
All results below are based on the 2014 year end estimates using the "2014 Mycroft Michaelis Growth Rate" and are good until December 31, 2014.											
Nu Skin Enterprises, Inc.	NUS	Consumer Goods	$26.63	$53.25	$79.88	$159.75	$3.55	21%	45%	14%	1.28%
Nuance Communications, Inc.	NUAN	Software	$10.80	$21.60	$32.40	$64.80	$1.44	15%	12%	15%	0.00%
Nucor Corp.	NUE	Steel	$1.28	$2.55	$3.83	$7.65	$0.17	0%	96%	-1%	3.02%
Numerex Corp	NMRX	Communication	Negative Free Cash Flow	Negative Free Cash Flow	Negative Free Cash Flow	Negative Free Cash Flow	-$0.21	-5%	423%	-5%	0.00%
NuPathe Inc.	PATH	Biotech	Negative Free Cash Flow	Negative Free Cash Flow	Negative Free Cash Flow	Negative Free Cash Flow	-$0.60	-124%	-14%	-124%	0.00%
Nutraceutical International Corporation	NUTR	Consumer Goods	$11.48	$22.95	$34.43	$68.85	$1.53	8%	39%	8%	0.00%
NutriSystem, Inc.	NTRI	Services	$4.05	$8.10	$12.15	$24.30	$0.54	18%	34%	0%	4.70%
NuVasive, Inc.	NUVA	Medical	$9.53	$19.05	$28.58	$57.15	$1.27	6%	45%	6%	0.00%
Nuverra Environmental Solutions Inc	NES	Waste Management	$0.53	$1.05	$1.58	$3.15	$0.07	2%	71%	2%	0.00%
NV Energy Inc	NVE	Utilities	$12.75	$25.50	$38.25	$76.50	$1.70	4%	53%	6%	3.24%
NVE Corporation	NVEC	Semiconductors	$20.85	$41.70	$62.55	$125.10	$2.78	13%	0%	13%	0.00%

NAME	TICKER	INDUSTRY	2014 BUY PRICE OPINION	2014 HOLD PRICE OPINION	2014 SELL PRICE OPINION	2014 SHORT PRICE OPINION	2014 MYCROFT FREE CASH FLOW PER SHARE ESTIMATE	2014 MYCROFT FREE CASH FLOW RETURN ON TOTAL CAPITAL ESTIMATE (FROIC) >15% = Great	2014 MYCROFT CAPFLOW ESTIMATE <33% = Great BUT NO NEGATIVE RESULTS	2014 MYCROFT MICHAELIS GROWTH RATE ESTIMATE >15% = Great	DIVIDEND YIELD
Step #1 = Look up the company's current stock market price on the day of analysis and compare it to our 2014 Buy, Hold, Sell & Short Price.											
Step #2 =Take the company's current market price; divide it by the "2014 Mycroft Free Cash Flow Per Share estimate." This gives the "Price to Free Cash Flow."											
All results below are based on the 2014 year end estimates using the "2014 Mycroft Michaelis Growth Rate" and are good until December 31, 2014.											
NVIDIA Corporation	NVDA	Semiconductors	$9.75	$19.50	$29.25	$58.50	$1.30	16%	27%	14%	1.91%
NVR, Inc.	NVR	Homebuilding	$150.15	$300.30	$450.45	$900.90	$20.02	7%	14%	7%	0.00%
NxStage Medical, Inc.	NXTM	Medical	Negative Free Cash Flow	Negative Free Cash Flow	Negative Free Cash Flow	Negative Free Cash Flow	-$0.23	-7%	-195%	-7%	0.00%
Oasis Petroleum Inc	OAS	Oil & Gas	Negative Free Cash Flow	Negative Free Cash Flow	Negative Free Cash Flow	Negative Free Cash Flow	-$4.96	-27%	180%	-27%	0.00%
Occidental Petroleum Corporation	OXY	Oil & Gas	$21.08	$42.15	$63.23	$126.45	$2.81	4%	81%	3%	2.82%
Ocean Power Technologies	OPTT	Utilities	Negative Free Cash Flow	Negative Free Cash Flow	Negative Free Cash Flow	Negative Free Cash Flow	-$1.09	-60%	-4%	-60%	0.00%
Oceaneering International	OII	Oil & Gas	$11.48	$22.95	$34.43	$68.85	$1.53	8%	67%	4%	1.07%
Ocera Therapeutics Inc	OCRX	Biotech	Negative Free Cash Flow	Negative Free Cash Flow	Negative Free Cash Flow	Negative Free Cash Flow	-$1.50	-64%	0%	-64%	0.00%
OCZ Technology Group Inc.	OCZ	Computers	Negative Free Cash Flow	Negative Free Cash Flow	Negative Free Cash Flow	Negative Free Cash Flow	-$1.93	-52%	-6%	-52%	0.00%
Odyssey Marine Exploration, Inc.	OMEX	Business Services	Negative Free Cash Flow	Negative Free Cash Flow	Negative Free Cash Flow	Negative Free Cash Flow	-$0.30	-1038%	-15%	-1038%	0.00%
Office Depot Inc	ODP	Retail	$2.70	$5.40	$8.10	$16.20	$0.36	8%	55%	8%	0.00%

NAME	TICKER	INDUSTRY	2014 BUY PRICE OPINION	2014 HOLD PRICE OPINION	2014 SELL PRICE OPINION	2014 SHORT PRICE OPINION	2014 MYCROFT FREE CASH FLOW PER SHARE ESTIMATE	2014 MYCROFT FREE CASH FLOW RETURN ON TOTAL CAPITAL ESTIMATE (FROIC) >15% = Great	2014 MYCROFT CAPFLOW ESTIMATE <33% = Great BUT NO NEGATIVE RESULTS	2014 MYCROFT MICHAELIS GROWTH RATE ESTIMATE >15% = Great	DIVIDEND YIELD
Step #1 = Look up the company's current stock market price on the day of analysis and compare it to our 2014 Buy, Hold, Sell & Short Price.											
Step #2 =Take the company's current market price; divide it by the "2014 Mycroft Free Cash Flow Per Share estimate." This gives the "Price to Free Cash Flow."											
All results below are based on the 2014 year end estimates using the "2014 Mycroft Michaelis Growth Rate" and are good until December 31, 2014.											
OfficeMax Inc	OMX	Retail	$1.80	$3.60	$5.40	$10.80	$0.24	1%	83%	1%	0.69%
Official Payments Holdings Inc	OPAY	Software	Negative Free Cash Flow	Negative Free Cash Flow	Negative Free Cash Flow	Negative Free Cash Flow	-$0.04	-1%	110%	-1%	0.00%
OGE Energy Corp	OGE	Utilities	Negative Free Cash Flow	Negative Free Cash Flow	Negative Free Cash Flow	Negative Free Cash Flow	-$1.44	-5%	134%	-6%	2.39%
Oil States International, Inc.	OIS	Oil & Gas	$32.10	$64.20	$96.30	$192.60	$4.28	9%	71%	9%	0.00%
Oil-Dri Corporation of America	ODC	Chemicals	$21.30	$42.60	$63.90	$127.80	$2.84	15%	35%	13%	2.41%
Old Dominion Freight Lines	ODFL	Transportation	$1.58	$3.15	$4.73	$9.45	$0.21	1%	95%	1%	0.00%
Olin Corporation	OLN	Chemicals	$14.03	$28.05	$42.08	$84.15	$1.87	9%	54%	8%	3.46%
Olympic Steel	ZEUS	Industrial	$64.05	$128.10	$192.15	$384.30	$8.54	14%	12%	14%	0.29%
OM Group, Inc.	OMG	Chemicals	$17.93	$35.85	$53.78	$107.55	$2.39	4%	47%	4%	0.00%
Omega Flex, Inc.	OFLX	Industrial	$4.05	$8.10	$12.15	$24.30	$0.54	19%	9%	19%	0.00%
Omega Protein Corporation	OME	Consumer Goods	$10.13	$20.25	$30.38	$60.75	$1.35	10%	46%	10%	0.00%

NAME	TICKER	INDUSTRY	2014 BUY PRICE OPINION	2014 HOLD PRICE OPINION	2014 SELL PRICE OPINION	2014 SHORT PRICE OPINION	2014 MYCROFT FREE CASH FLOW PER SHARE ESTIMATE	2014 MYCROFT FREE CASH FLOW RETURN ON TOTAL CAPITAL ESTIMATE (FROIC) >15% = Great	2014 MYCROFT CAPFLOW ESTIMATE <33% = Great BUT NO NEGATIVE RESULTS	2014 MYCROFT MICHAELIS GROWTH RATE ESTIMATE >15% = Great	DIVIDEND YIELD
Step #1 = Look up the company's current stock market price on the day of analysis and compare it to our 2014 Buy, Hold, Sell & Short Price.												
Step #2 =Take the company's current market price; divide it by the "2014 Mycroft Free Cash Flow Per Share estimate." This gives the "Price to Free Cash Flow."												
All results below are based on the 2014 year end estimates using the "2014 Mycroft Michaelis Growth Rate" and are good until December 31, 2014.												
Omnicare Inc	OCR	Health Care	$38.33	$76.65	$114.98	$229.95	$5.11	9%	17%	9%	1.00%
Omnicell, Inc.	OMCL	Software	$4.13	$8.25	$12.38	$24.75	$0.55	5%	57%	5%	0.00%
Omnicom Group, Inc.	OMC	Advertising	$38.63	$77.25	$115.88	$231.75	$5.15	15%	13%	13%	2.48%
OmniVision Technologies, Inc.	OVTI	Semiconductors	$0.15	$0.30	$0.45	$0.90	$0.02	0%	98%	0%	0.00%
Omnova Solutions, Inc.	OMN	Chemicals	$0.23	$0.45	$0.68	$1.35	$0.03	0%	96%	0%	0.00%
On Assignment, Inc.	ASGN	Services	$9.75	$19.50	$29.25	$58.50	$1.30	6%	18%	6%	0.00%
ON Semiconductor Corporation	ONNN	Semiconductors	$1.05	$2.10	$3.15	$6.30	$0.14	3%	78%	3%	0.00%
OncoGenex Pharmaceuticals, Inc.	OGXI	Biotech	Negative Free Cash Flow	Negative Free Cash Flow	Negative Free Cash Flow	Negative Free Cash Flow	-$2.79	-78%	-1%	-78%	0.00%
ONEOK, Inc.	OKE	Oil & Gas	Negative Free Cash Flow	Negative Free Cash Flow	Negative Free Cash Flow	Negative Free Cash Flow	-$4.94	-14%	190%	-15%	2.96%
Onvia, Inc.	ONVI	Business Services	$0.45	$0.90	$1.35	$2.70	$0.06	5%	85%	5%	0.00%
Onyx Pharmaceuticals, Inc.	ONXX	Biotech	Negative Free Cash Flow	Negative Free Cash Flow	Negative Free Cash Flow	Negative Free Cash Flow	-$3.59	-20%	-2%	-20%	0.00%

NAME	TICKER	INDUSTRY	2014 BUY PRICE OPINION	2014 HOLD PRICE OPINION	2014 SELL PRICE OPINION	2014 SHORT PRICE OPINION	2014 MYCROFT FREE CASH FLOW PER SHARE ESTIMATE	2014 MYCROFT FREE CASH FLOW RETURN ON TOTAL CAPITAL ESTIMATE (FROIC) >15% = Great	2014 MYCROFT CAPFLOW ESTIMATE <33% = Great BUT NO NEGATIVE RESULTS	2014 MYCROFT MICHAELIS GROWTH RATE ESTIMATE >15% = Great	DIVIDEND YIELD
Step #1 = Look up the company's current stock market price on the day of analysis and compare it to our 2014 Buy, Hold, Sell & Short Price.											
Step #2 =Take the company's current market price; divide it by the "2014 Mycroft Free Cash Flow Per Share estimate." This gives the "Price to Free Cash Flow."											
All results below are based on the 2014 year end estimates using the "2014 Mycroft Michaelis Growth Rate" and are good until December 31, 2014.											
Opentable, Inc.	OPEN	Internet	$17.55	$35.10	$52.65	$105.30	$2.34	24%	28%	24%	0.00%
Opexa Therapeutics, Inc.	OPXA	Biotech	Negative Free Cash Flow	Negative Free Cash Flow	Negative Free Cash Flow	Negative Free Cash Flow	-$0.18	-263%	-3%	-263%	0.00%
Opko Health, Inc.	OPK	Medical	Negative Free Cash Flow	Negative Free Cash Flow	Negative Free Cash Flow	Negative Free Cash Flow	-$0.09	-10%	-11%	-10%	0.00%
Oplink Communications, Inc.	OPLK	Communication	$5.18	$10.35	$15.53	$31.05	$0.69	5%	48%	5%	0.00%
Optical Cable Corporation	OCC	Communication	$0.23	$0.45	$0.68	$1.35	$0.03	0%	95%	1%	1.82%
Optimer Pharmaceuticals, Inc.	OPTR	Biotech	Negative Free Cash Flow	Negative Free Cash Flow	Negative Free Cash Flow	Negative Free Cash Flow	-$2.57	-141%	-1%	-141%	0.00%
Oracle Corporation	ORCL	Software	$26.63	$53.25	$79.88	$159.75	$3.55	23%	5%	21%	1.45%
OraSure Technologies, Inc.	OSUR	Medical	Negative Free Cash Flow	Negative Free Cash Flow	Negative Free Cash Flow	Negative Free Cash Flow	-$0.27	-10%	-19%	-10%	0.00%
ORBCOMM, Inc.	ORBC	Communication	Negative Free Cash Flow	Negative Free Cash Flow	Negative Free Cash Flow	Negative Free Cash Flow	-$0.81	-20%	452%	-20%	0.00%
Orbit International Corp.	ORBT	Computers	$3.23	$6.45	$9.68	$19.35	$0.43	9%	12%	9%	0.00%
Orbital Sciences Corporation	ORB	Aerospace & Defense	Negative Free Cash Flow	Negative Free Cash Flow	Negative Free Cash Flow	Negative Free Cash Flow	-$1.22	-8%	-122%	-8%	0.00%

NAME	TICKER	INDUSTRY	2014 BUY PRICE OPINION	2014 HOLD PRICE OPINION	2014 SELL PRICE OPINION	2014 SHORT PRICE OPINION	2014 MYCROFT FREE CASH FLOW PER SHARE ESTIMATE	2014 MYCROFT FREE CASH FLOW RETURN ON TOTAL CAPITAL ESTIMATE (FROIC) >15% = Great	2014 MYCROFT CAPFLOW ESTIMATE <33% = Great BUT NO NEGATIVE RESULTS	2014 MYCROFT MICHAELIS GROWTH RATE ESTIMATE >15% = Great	DIVIDEND YIELD
Step #1 = Look up the company's current stock market price on the day of analysis and compare it to our 2014 Buy, Hold, Sell & Short Price.											
Step #2 =Take the company's current market price; divide it by the "2014 Mycroft Free Cash Flow Per Share estimate." This gives the "Price to Free Cash Flow."											
All results below are based on the 2014 year end estimates using the "2014 Mycroft Michaelis Growth Rate" and are good until December 31, 2014.											
Orbitz Worldwide, Inc.	OWW	Travel & Leisure	$16.05	$32.10	$48.15	$96.30	$2.14	38%	20%	38%	0.00%
Orchids Paper Products Company	TIS	Forest Products	$5.93	$11.85	$17.78	$35.55	$0.79	7%	59%	0%	5.10%
O'Reilly Automotive Inc	ORLY	Autos	$57.75	$115.50	$173.25	$346.50	$7.70	24%	33%	24%	0.00%
Orexigen Therapeutics, Inc.	OREX	Drugs	Negative Free Cash Flow	Negative Free Cash Flow	Negative Free Cash Flow	Negative Free Cash Flow	-$0.89	-201%	0%	-201%	0.00%
Orient-Express Hotels, Ltd.	OEH	Travel & Leisure	Negative Free Cash Flow	Negative Free Cash Flow	Negative Free Cash Flow	Negative Free Cash Flow	-$0.29	-4%	165%	-4%	0.00%
Orion Energy Systems, Inc.	OESX	Computers	$1.05	$2.10	$3.15	$6.30	$0.14	3%	34%	3%	0.00%
Orion Marine Group, Inc.	ORN	Engineering	$6.08	$12.15	$18.23	$36.45	$0.81	9%	39%	9%	0.00%
Ormat Technologies, Inc.	ORA	Utilities	Negative Free Cash Flow	Negative Free Cash Flow	Negative Free Cash Flow	Negative Free Cash Flow	-$3.69	-10%	549%	-10%	0.60%
Orthofix International N.V.	OFIX	Medical	Negative Free Cash Flow	Negative Free Cash Flow	Negative Free Cash Flow	Negative Free Cash Flow	-$2.63	-12%	-128%	-12%	0.00%
Oshkosh Corporation	OSK	Truck Manufacturing	$36.83	$73.65	$110.48	$220.95	$4.91	13%	14%	13%	0.00%
OSI Systems, Inc.	OSIS	Computers	Negative Free Cash Flow	Negative Free Cash Flow	Negative Free Cash Flow	Negative Free Cash Flow	-$5.16	-21%	276%	-21%	0.00%

NAME	TICKER	INDUSTRY	2014 BUY PRICE OPINION	2014 HOLD PRICE OPINION	2014 SELL PRICE OPINION	2014 SHORT PRICE OPINION	2014 MYCROFT FREE CASH FLOW PER SHARE ESTIMATE	2014 MYCROFT FREE CASH FLOW RETURN ON TOTAL CAPITAL ESTIMATE (FROIC) >15% = Great	2014 MYCROFT CAPFLOW ESTIMATE <33% = Great BUT NO NEGATIVE RESULTS	2014 MYCROFT MICHAELIS GROWTH RATE ESTIMATE >15% = Great	DIVIDEND YIELD
Step #1 = Look up the company's current stock market price on the day of analysis and compare it to our 2014 Buy, Hold, Sell & Short Price.											
Step #2 =Take the company's current market price; divide it by the "2014 Mycroft Free Cash Flow Per Share estimate." This gives the "Price to Free Cash Flow."											
All results below are based on the 2014 year end estimates using the "2014 Mycroft Michaelis Growth Rate" and are good until December 31, 2014.											
Osiris Therapeutics, Inc.	OSIR	Biotech	Negative Free Cash Flow	Negative Free Cash Flow	Negative Free Cash Flow	Negative Free Cash Flow	-$0.37	-40%	-3%	-40%	0.00%
Otter Tail Corporation	OTTR	Utilities	$31.28	$62.55	$93.83	$187.65	$4.17	14%	43%	14%	4.40%
Outerwall Inc	OUTR	Retail	$45.00	$90.00	$135.00	$270.00	$6.00	20%	59%	20%	0.00%
OvaScience Inc	OVAS	Biotech	Negative Free Cash Flow	Negative Free Cash Flow	Negative Free Cash Flow	Negative Free Cash Flow	-$0.89	-30%	-4%	-30%	0.00%
Overstock.com, Inc.	OSTK	Retail	$30.15	$60.30	$90.45	$180.90	$4.02	106%	25%	106%	0.00%
Owens & Minor, Inc.	OMI	Medical	$27.60	$55.20	$82.80	$165.60	$3.68	17%	20%	15%	2.74%
Owens-Corning, Inc.	OC	Building Supplies	$4.05	$8.10	$12.15	$24.30	$0.54	1%	82%	1%	0.00%
Owens-Illinois Inc	OI	Containers	$12.45	$24.90	$37.35	$74.70	$1.66	6%	56%	6%	0.00%
Oxford Industries, Inc.	OXM	Apparel & Furniture	$0.45	$0.90	$1.35	$2.70	$0.06	0%	98%	-2%	1.11%
P & F Industries, Inc. Class A	PFIN	Industrial	Negative Free Cash Flow	Negative Free Cash Flow	Negative Free Cash Flow	Negative Free Cash Flow	-$0.80	-7%	-97%	-7%	0.00%
PACCAR Inc	PCAR	Truck Manufacturing	$43.13	$86.25	$129.38	$258.75	$5.75	26%	26%	23%	1.43%

NAME	TICKER	INDUSTRY	2014 BUY PRICE OPINION	2014 HOLD PRICE OPINION	2014 SELL PRICE OPINION	2014 SHORT PRICE OPINION	2014 MYCROFT FREE CASH FLOW PER SHARE ESTIMATE	2014 MYCROFT FREE CASH FLOW RETURN ON TOTAL CAPITAL ESTIMATE (FROIC) >15% = Great	2014 MYCROFT CAPFLOW ESTIMATE <33% = Great BUT NO NEGATIVE RESULTS	2014 MYCROFT MICHAELIS GROWTH RATE ESTIMATE >15% = Great	DIVIDEND YIELD
Step #1 = Look up the company's current stock market price on the day of analysis and compare it to our 2014 Buy, Hold, Sell & Short Price.											
Step #2 =Take the company's current market price; divide it by the "2014 Mycroft Free Cash Flow Per Share estimate." This gives the "Price to Free Cash Flow."											
All results below are based on the 2014 year end estimates using the "2014 Mycroft Michaelis Growth Rate" and are good until December 31, 2014.											
Pacer International, Inc.	PACR	Transportation	$4.43	$8.85	$13.28	$26.55	$0.59	15%	34%	15%	0.00%
Pacific Biosciences of California, Inc.	PACB	Biotech	Negative Free Cash Flow	Negative Free Cash Flow	Negative Free Cash Flow	Negative Free Cash Flow	-$1.09	-69%	-2%	-69%	0.00%
Pacific Ethanol, Inc.	PEIX	Chemicals	Negative Free Cash Flow	Negative Free Cash Flow	Negative Free Cash Flow	Negative Free Cash Flow	-$1.40	-16%	-9%	-16%	0.00%
Pacific Sunwear	PSUN	Retail	Negative Free Cash Flow	Negative Free Cash Flow	Negative Free Cash Flow	Negative Free Cash Flow	-$0.12	-8%	373%	-8%	0.00%
Pacira Pharmaceuticals, Inc.	PCRX	Drugs	Negative Free Cash Flow	Negative Free Cash Flow	Negative Free Cash Flow	Negative Free Cash Flow	-$2.26	-90%	-26%	-90%	0.00%
Packaging Corporation of America	PKG	Containers	$35.10	$70.20	$105.30	$210.60	$4.68	22%	26%	16%	2.92%
Pall Corporation	PLL	Industrial	$15.38	$30.75	$46.13	$92.25	$2.05	9%	42%	6%	1.34%
Palo Alto Networks Inc	PANW	Communication	$9.60	$19.20	$28.80	$57.60	$1.28	27%	22%	27%	0.00%
Pandora Media Inc	P	Entertainment	Negative Free Cash Flow	Negative Free Cash Flow	Negative Free Cash Flow	Negative Free Cash Flow	-$0.17	-34%	-300%	-34%	0.00%
Panera Bread Company, Inc. Class A	PNRA	Restaurants	$34.95	$69.90	$104.85	$209.70	$4.66	13%	58%	13%	0.00%
Panhandle Oil and Gas Inc. Class A	PHX	Oil & Gas	Negative Free Cash Flow	Negative Free Cash Flow	Negative Free Cash Flow	Negative Free Cash Flow	-$0.25	-2%	107%	-3%	0.96%

NAME	TICKER	INDUSTRY	2014 BUY PRICE OPINION	2014 HOLD PRICE OPINION	2014 SELL PRICE OPINION	2014 SHORT PRICE OPINION	2014 MYCROFT FREE CASH FLOW PER SHARE ESTIMATE	2014 MYCROFT FREE CASH FLOW RETURN ON TOTAL CAPITAL ESTIMATE (FROIC) >15% = Great	2014 MYCROFT CAPFLOW ESTIMATE <33% = Great BUT NO NEGATIVE RESULTS	2014 MYCROFT MICHAELIS GROWTH RATE ESTIMATE >15% = Great	DIVIDEND YIELD
colspan across		Step #1 = Look up the company's current stock market price on the day of analysis and compare it to our 2014 Buy, Hold, Sell & Short Price.									
		Step #2 =Take the company's current market price; divide it by the "2014 Mycroft Free Cash Flow Per Share estimate." This gives the "Price to Free Cash Flow."									
		All results below are based on the 2014 year end estimates using the "2014 Mycroft Michaelis Growth Rate" and are good until December 31, 2014.									
Pantry, Inc.	PTRY	Retail	$13.13	$26.25	$39.38	$78.75	$1.75	4%	64%	4%	0.00%
Papa John's International Inc.	PZZA	Restaurants	$12.30	$24.60	$36.90	$73.80	$1.64	15%	61%	7%	1.46%
PAR Technology Corp.	PAR	Software	Negative Free Cash Flow	Negative Free Cash Flow	Negative Free Cash Flow	Negative Free Cash Flow	-$0.38	-8%	-270%	-8%	0.00%
Paramount Gold and Silver Corporation	PZG	Commodities	Negative Free Cash Flow	Negative Free Cash Flow	Negative Free Cash Flow	Negative Free Cash Flow	-$0.11	-25%	-10%	-25%	0.00%
Parexel International Corporation	PRXL	Medical	$15.60	$31.20	$46.80	$93.60	$2.08	14%	44%	14%	0.00%
Park Electrochemical Corp.	PKE	Semiconductors	$8.33	$16.65	$24.98	$49.95	$1.11	7%	7%	6%	1.41%
Parker Drilling Company	PKD	Oil & Gas	Negative Free Cash Flow	Negative Free Cash Flow	Negative Free Cash Flow	Negative Free Cash Flow	-$0.05	-1%	104%	-1%	0.00%
Parker Hannifin Corporation	PH	Industrial	$51.53	$103.05	$154.58	$309.15	$6.87	13%	22%	11%	1.71%
Parkervision, Inc.	PRKR	Semiconductors	Negative Free Cash Flow	Negative Free Cash Flow	Negative Free Cash Flow	Negative Free Cash Flow	-$0.19	-81%	-5%	-81%	0.00%
Park-Ohio Holdings Corp	PKOH	Industrial	$20.48	$40.95	$61.43	$122.85	$2.73	6%	55%	6%	0.00%
Patrick Industries, Inc.	PATK	Forest Products	$10.05	$20.10	$30.15	$60.30	$1.34	13%	42%	13%	0.00%

NAME	TICKER	INDUSTRY	2014 BUY PRICE OPINION	2014 HOLD PRICE OPINION	2014 SELL PRICE OPINION	2014 SHORT PRICE OPINION	2014 MYCROFT FREE CASH FLOW PER SHARE ESTIMATE	2014 MYCROFT FREE CASH FLOW RETURN ON TOTAL CAPITAL ESTIMATE (FROIC) >15% = Great	2014 MYCROFT CAPFLOW ESTIMATE <33% = Great BUT NO NEGATIVE RESULTS	2014 MYCROFT MICHAELIS GROWTH RATE ESTIMATE >15% = Great	DIVIDEND YIELD
Step #1 = Look up the company's current stock market price on the day of analysis and compare it to our 2014 Buy, Hold, Sell & Short Price.											
Step #2 =Take the company's current market price; divide it by the "2014 Mycroft Free Cash Flow Per Share estimate." This gives the "Price to Free Cash Flow."											
All results below are based on the 2014 year end estimates using the "2014 Mycroft Michaelis Growth Rate" and are good until December 31, 2014.											
Patriot Transportation Holdings, Inc.	PATR	Transportation	$0.53	$1.05	$1.58	$3.15	$0.07	0%	97%	0%	0.00%
Patterson Companies, Inc.	PDCO	Medical	$18.45	$36.90	$55.35	$110.70	$2.46	11%	9%	10%	1.56%
Patterson-UTI Energy, Inc.	PTEN	Oil & Gas	$5.18	$10.35	$15.53	$31.05	$0.69	3%	89%	3%	0.96%
Paychex, Inc.	PAYX	Services	$12.68	$25.35	$38.03	$76.05	$1.69	33%	15%	7%	3.46%
PBF Energy Inc	PBF	Oil & Gas	$97.58	$195.15	$292.73	$585.45	$13.01	28%	40%	30%	5.30%
PC Connection, Inc.	PCCC	Retail	$4.95	$9.90	$14.85	$29.70	$0.66	5%	34%	5%	0.00%
PCM Inc	PCMI	Retail	Negative Free Cash Flow	Negative Free Cash Flow	Negative Free Cash Flow	Negative Free Cash Flow	-$2.44	-21%	-56%	-21%	0.00%
PCTEL, Inc.	PCTI	Communication	$1.88	$3.75	$5.63	$11.25	$0.25	4%	41%	3%	1.62%
PDC Energy Inc	PDCE	Oil & Gas	Negative Free Cash Flow	Negative Free Cash Flow	Negative Free Cash Flow	Negative Free Cash Flow	-$15.99	-38%	431%	-38%	0.00%
PDF Solutions, Inc.	PDFS	Software	$5.63	$11.25	$16.88	$33.75	$0.75	17%	18%	17%	0.00%
PDI, Inc.	PDII	Business Services	Negative Free Cash Flow	Negative Free Cash Flow	Negative Free Cash Flow	Negative Free Cash Flow	-$0.37	-15%	-40%	-15%	0.00%

NAME	TICKER	INDUSTRY	2014 BUY PRICE OPINION	2014 HOLD PRICE OPINION	2014 SELL PRICE OPINION	2014 SHORT PRICE OPINION	2014 MYCROFT FREE CASH FLOW PER SHARE ESTIMATE	2014 MYCROFT FREE CASH FLOW RETURN ON TOTAL CAPITAL ESTIMATE (FROIC) >15% = Great	2014 MYCROFT CAPFLOW ESTIMATE <33% = Great BUT NO NEGATIVE RESULTS	2014 MYCROFT MICHAELIS GROWTH RATE ESTIMATE >15% = Great	DIVIDEND YIELD
Step #1 = Look up the company's current stock market price on the day of analysis and compare it to our 2014 Buy, Hold, Sell & Short Price.										
Step #2 =Take the company's current market price; divide it by the "2014 Mycroft Free Cash Flow Per Share estimate." This gives the "Price to Free Cash Flow."										
All results below are based on the 2014 year end estimates using the "2014 Mycroft Michaelis Growth Rate" and are good until December 31, 2014.										
PDL BioPharma, Inc.	PDLI	Biotech	$24.75	$49.50	$74.25	$148.50	$3.30	83%	0%	65%	7.70%
Peabody Energy Corporation	BTU	Coal	$4.80	$9.60	$14.40	$28.80	$0.64	2%	86%	3%	1.82%
Pegasystems, Inc.	PEGA	Software	$22.28	$44.55	$66.83	$133.65	$2.97	35%	11%	33%	0.32%
Pendrell Corp Class A	PCO	Communication	Negative Free Cash Flow	Negative Free Cash Flow	Negative Free Cash Flow	Negative Free Cash Flow	-$0.01	-1%	-2630%	-1%	0.00%
Penford Corporation	PENX	Chemicals	Negative Free Cash Flow	Negative Free Cash Flow	Negative Free Cash Flow	Negative Free Cash Flow	-$0.20	-3%	123%	-3%	0.00%
Penn National Gaming	PENN	Travel & Leisure	$28.58	$57.15	$85.73	$171.45	$3.81	6%	50%	6%	0.00%
Penn Virginia Corporation	PVA	Oil & Gas	Negative Free Cash Flow	Negative Free Cash Flow	Negative Free Cash Flow	Negative Free Cash Flow	-$2.39	-9%	161%	-9%	0.00%
Penske Automotive Group Inc	PAG	Autos	$5.63	$11.25	$16.88	$33.75	$0.75	3%	79%	2%	1.50%
Pentair Ltd	PNR	Industrial	$5.18	$10.35	$15.53	$31.05	$0.69	2%	53%	1%	1.55%
Pep Boys - Manny, Moe & Jack	PBY	Autos	$0.60	$1.20	$1.80	$3.60	$0.08	1%	93%	1%	0.00%
Pepco Holdings Inc	POM	Utilities	Negative Free Cash Flow	Negative Free Cash Flow	Negative Free Cash Flow	Negative Free Cash Flow	-$3.25	-9%	287%	-6%	5.90%

NAME	TICKER	INDUSTRY	2014 BUY PRICE OPINION	2014 HOLD PRICE OPINION	2014 SELL PRICE OPINION	2014 SHORT PRICE OPINION	2014 MYCROFT FREE CASH FLOW PER SHARE ESTIMATE	2014 MYCROFT FREE CASH FLOW RETURN ON TOTAL CAPITAL ESTIMATE (FROIC) >15% = Great	2014 MYCROFT CAPFLOW ESTIMATE <33% = Great BUT NO NEGATIVE RESULTS	2014 MYCROFT MICHAELIS GROWTH RATE ESTIMATE >15% = Great	DIVIDEND YIELD
Step #1 = Look up the company's current stock market price on the day of analysis and compare it to our 2014 Buy, Hold, Sell & Short Price.												
Step #2 =Take the company's current market price; divide it by the "2014 Mycroft Free Cash Flow Per Share estimate." This gives the "Price to Free Cash Flow."												
All results below are based on the 2014 year end estimates using the "2014 Mycroft Michaelis Growth Rate" and are good until December 31, 2014.												
PepsiCo Inc	PEP	Beverages	$40.95	$81.90	$122.85	$245.70	$5.46	17%	27%	12%	2.84%
Perceptron, Inc.	PRCP	Computers	$5.70	$11.40	$17.10	$34.20	$0.76	11%	13%	10%	1.37%
Peregrine Pharmaceuticals, Inc.	PPHM	Biotech	Negative Free Cash Flow	Negative Free Cash Flow	Negative Free Cash Flow	Negative Free Cash Flow	-$0.19	-91%	-2%	-91%	0.00%
Peregrine Semiconductor Corp	PSMI	Semiconductors	Negative Free Cash Flow	Negative Free Cash Flow	Negative Free Cash Flow	Negative Free Cash Flow	-$1.53	-41%	-44%	-41%	0.00%
Perficient, Inc.	PRFT	Software	$10.50	$21.00	$31.50	$63.00	$1.40	16%	11%	16%	0.00%
Performance Technologies, Inc.	PTIX	Computers	Negative Free Cash Flow	Negative Free Cash Flow	Negative Free Cash Flow	Negative Free Cash Flow	-$0.33	-15%	-242%	-15%	0.00%
Performant Financial Corp	PFMT	Business Services	$4.13	$8.25	$12.38	$24.75	$0.55	12%	37%	12%	0.00%
Pericom Semiconductor Corporation	PSEM	Semiconductors	Negative Free Cash Flow	Negative Free Cash Flow	Negative Free Cash Flow	Negative Free Cash Flow	-$0.10	-1%	120%	-1%	0.00%
PerkinElmer Inc	PKI	Medical	$3.08	$6.15	$9.23	$18.45	$0.41	2%	54%	1%	0.74%
Pernix Therapeutics Holdings, Inc.	PTX	Drugs	Negative Free Cash Flow	Negative Free Cash Flow	Negative Free Cash Flow	Negative Free Cash Flow	-$0.07	-3%	161%	-3%	0.00%
Perrigo Company	PRGO	Drugs	$39.98	$79.95	$119.93	$239.85	$5.33	12%	19%	12%	0.29%

NAME	TICKER	INDUSTRY	2014 BUY PRICE OPINION	2014 HOLD PRICE OPINION	2014 SELL PRICE OPINION	2014 SHORT PRICE OPINION	2014 MYCROFT FREE CASH FLOW PER SHARE ESTIMATE	2014 MYCROFT FREE CASH FLOW RETURN ON TOTAL CAPITAL ESTIMATE (FROIC) >15% = Great	2014 MYCROFT CAPFLOW ESTIMATE <33% = Great BUT NO NEGATIVE RESULTS	2014 MYCROFT MICHAELIS GROWTH RATE ESTIMATE >15% = Great	DIVIDEND YIELD
Step #1 = Look up the company's current stock market price on the day of analysis and compare it to our 2014 Buy, Hold, Sell & Short Price.											
Step #2 =Take the company's current market price; divide it by the "2014 Mycroft Free Cash Flow Per Share estimate." This gives the "Price to Free Cash Flow."											
All results below are based on the 2014 year end estimates using the "2014 Mycroft Michaelis Growth Rate" and are good until December 31, 2014.											
Perry Ellis International, Inc.	PERY	Apparel & Furniture	Negative Free Cash Flow	Negative Free Cash Flow	Negative Free Cash Flow	Negative Free Cash Flow	-$0.99	-3%	372%	-3%	0.00%
PetMed Express, Inc.	PETS	Retail	$7.88	$15.75	$23.63	$47.25	$1.05	29%	2%	12%	4.10%
Petroquest Energy, Inc.	PQ	Oil & Gas	Negative Free Cash Flow	Negative Free Cash Flow	Negative Free Cash Flow	Negative Free Cash Flow	-$0.93	-23%	189%	-23%	0.00%
PetSmart Inc.	PETM	Retail	$53.48	$106.95	$160.43	$320.85	$7.13	46%	20%	41%	0.90%
Pfizer Inc	PFE	Drugs	$18.98	$37.95	$56.93	$113.85	$2.53	14%	8%	11%	3.35%
PFSweb, Inc.	PFSW	Business Services	$2.48	$4.95	$7.43	$14.85	$0.33	12%	64%	12%	0.00%
PG&E Corp	PCG	Utilities	Negative Free Cash Flow	Negative Free Cash Flow	Negative Free Cash Flow	Negative Free Cash Flow	-$1.71	-3%	118%	-2%	4.50%
PGT, Inc.	PGTI	Building Supplies	$4.50	$9.00	$13.50	$27.00	$0.60	52%	16%	52%	0.00%
PH Glatfelter Company	GLT	Forest Products	$7.95	$15.90	$23.85	$47.70	$1.06	6%	67%	5%	1.53%
Pharmacyclics, Inc.	PCYC	Drugs	$24.68	$49.35	$74.03	$148.05	$3.29	38%	2%	38%	0.00%
PharmAthene, Inc.	PIP	Biotech	Negative Free Cash Flow	Negative Free Cash Flow	Negative Free Cash Flow	Negative Free Cash Flow	-$0.02	-7%	0%	-7%	0.00%

NAME	TICKER	INDUSTRY	2014 BUY PRICE OPINION	2014 HOLD PRICE OPINION	2014 SELL PRICE OPINION	2014 SHORT PRICE OPINION	2014 MYCROFT FREE CASH FLOW PER SHARE ESTIMATE	2014 MYCROFT FREE CASH FLOW RETURN ON TOTAL CAPITAL ESTIMATE (FROIC) >15% = Great	2014 MYCROFT CAPFLOW ESTIMATE <33% = Great BUT NO NEGATIVE RESULTS	2014 MYCROFT MICHAELIS GROWTH RATE ESTIMATE >15% = Great	DIVIDEND YIELD
Step #1 = Look up the company's current stock market price on the day of analysis and compare it to our 2014 Buy, Hold, Sell & Short Price.											
Step #2 =Take the company's current market price; divide it by the "2014 Mycroft Free Cash Flow Per Share estimate." This gives the "Price to Free Cash Flow."											
All results below are based on the 2014 year end estimates using the "2014 Mycroft Michaelis Growth Rate" and are good until December 31, 2014.											
Pharmerica Corporation	PMC	Retail	$22.50	$45.00	$67.50	$135.00	$3.00	11%	26%	11%	0.00%
PHI, Inc.	PHIIK	Oil & Gas	Negative Free Cash Flow	Negative Free Cash Flow	Negative Free Cash Flow	Negative Free Cash Flow	-$4.05	-7%	175%	-7%	0.00%
Philip Morris International, Inc.	PM	Tobacco	$41.03	$82.05	$123.08	$246.15	$5.47	80%	13%	19%	4.30%
Phillips 66	PSX	Oil & Gas	$62.18	$124.35	$186.53	$373.05	$8.29	15%	31%	15%	2.20%
PhotoMedex, Inc.	PHMD	Medical	$13.35	$26.70	$40.05	$80.10	$1.78	18%	3%	18%	0.00%
Photronics Inc.	PLAB	Semiconductors	$5.18	$10.35	$15.53	$31.05	$0.69	5%	56%	5%	0.00%
PICO Holdings, Inc.	PICO	Conglomerates	Negative Free Cash Flow	Negative Free Cash Flow	Negative Free Cash Flow	Negative Free Cash Flow	-$1.93	-8%	-21%	-8%	0.00%
Piedmont Natural Gas Company	PNY	Utilities	Negative Free Cash Flow	Negative Free Cash Flow	Negative Free Cash Flow	Negative Free Cash Flow	-$3.92	-14%	192%	-14%	3.78%
Pier 1 Imports, Inc.	PIR	Retail	$6.75	$13.50	$20.25	$40.50	$0.90	15%	49%	13%	0.88%
Pike Electric Corporation	PIKE	Engineering	$11.18	$22.35	$33.53	$67.05	$1.49	12%	49%	12%	0.00%
Pilgrims Pride Corp.	PPC	Consumer Goods	$10.80	$21.60	$32.40	$64.80	$1.44	14%	24%	14%	0.00%

NAME	TICKER	INDUSTRY	2014 BUY PRICE OPINION	2014 HOLD PRICE OPINION	2014 SELL PRICE OPINION	2014 SHORT PRICE OPINION	2014 MYCROFT FREE CASH FLOW PER SHARE ESTIMATE	2014 MYCROFT FREE CASH FLOW RETURN ON TOTAL CAPITAL ESTIMATE (FROIC) >15% = Great	2014 MYCROFT CAPFLOW ESTIMATE <33% = Great BUT NO NEGATIVE RESULTS	2014 MYCROFT MICHAELIS GROWTH RATE ESTIMATE >15% = Great	DIVIDEND YIELD
Step #1 = Look up the company's current stock market price on the day of analysis and compare it to our 2014 Buy, Hold, Sell & Short Price.											
Step #2 =Take the company's current market price; divide it by the "2014 Mycroft Free Cash Flow Per Share estimate." This gives the "Price to Free Cash Flow."											
All results below are based on the 2014 year end estimates using the "2014 Mycroft Michaelis Growth Rate" and are good until December 31, 2014.											
Pinnacle Entertainment Inc.	PNK	Travel & Leisure	Negative Free Cash Flow	Negative Free Cash Flow	Negative Free Cash Flow	Negative Free Cash Flow	-$1.60	-5%	160%	-5%	0.00%
Pinnacle Foods Inc	PF	Consumer Goods	$11.03	$22.05	$33.08	$66.15	$1.47	11%	35%	8%	2.67%
Pinnacle West Capital	PNW	Utilities	$23.40	$46.80	$70.20	$140.40	$3.12	4%	72%	5%	4.00%
Pioneer Energy Services Corp	PES	Oil & Gas	Negative Free Cash Flow	Negative Free Cash Flow	Negative Free Cash Flow	Negative Free Cash Flow	-$1.67	-11%	158%	-11%	0.00%
Pioneer Natural Resources Company	PXD	Oil & Gas	Negative Free Cash Flow	Negative Free Cash Flow	Negative Free Cash Flow	Negative Free Cash Flow	-$7.99	-10%	160%	-10%	0.04%
Pitney Bowes Inc	PBI	Industrial	$18.30	$36.60	$54.90	$109.80	$2.44	13%	27%	13%	4.00%
Pixelworks, Inc.	PXLW	Semiconductors	Negative Free Cash Flow	Negative Free Cash Flow	Negative Free Cash Flow	Negative Free Cash Flow	-$0.26	-102%	-40%	-102%	0.00%
Pizza Inn Holdings Inc	PZZI	Restaurants	Negative Free Cash Flow	Negative Free Cash Flow	Negative Free Cash Flow	Negative Free Cash Flow	-$0.11	-12%	188%	-12%	0.00%
Planar Systems, Inc.	PLNR	Computers	Negative Free Cash Flow	Negative Free Cash Flow	Negative Free Cash Flow	Negative Free Cash Flow	-$0.36	-18%	-101%	-18%	0.00%
Planet Payment Inc	PLPM	Business Services	Negative Free Cash Flow	Negative Free Cash Flow	Negative Free Cash Flow	Negative Free Cash Flow	-$0.04	-12%	2042%	-12%	0.00%
Plantronics	PLT	Communication	$18.30	$36.60	$54.90	$109.80	$2.44	13%	27%	12%	0.90%

178

NAME	TICKER	INDUSTRY	2014 BUY PRICE OPINION	2014 HOLD PRICE OPINION	2014 SELL PRICE OPINION	2014 SHORT PRICE OPINION	2014 MYCROFT FREE CASH FLOW PER SHARE ESTIMATE	2014 MYCROFT FREE CASH FLOW RETURN ON TOTAL CAPITAL ESTIMATE (FROIC) >15% = Great	2014 MYCROFT CAPFLOW ESTIMATE <33% = Great BUT NO NEGATIVE RESULTS	2014 MYCROFT MICHAELIS GROWTH RATE ESTIMATE >15% = Great	DIVIDEND YIELD
Step #1 = Look up the company's current stock market price on the day of analysis and compare it to our 2014 Buy, Hold, Sell & Short Price.										
Step #2 =Take the company's current market price; divide it by the "2014 Mycroft Free Cash Flow Per Share estimate." This gives the "Price to Free Cash Flow."										
All results below are based on the 2014 year end estimates using the "2014 Mycroft Michaelis Growth Rate" and are good until December 31, 2014.										
Plexus Corp.	PLXS	Computers	$13.13	$26.25	$39.38	$78.75	$1.75	8%	65%	8%	0.00%
PLX Technology, Inc.	PLXT	Semiconductors	Negative Free Cash Flow	Negative Free Cash Flow	Negative Free Cash Flow	Negative Free Cash Flow	-$0.13	-10%	-28%	-10%	0.00%
Ply Gem Holdings Inc	PGEM	Building Supplies	Negative Free Cash Flow	Negative Free Cash Flow	Negative Free Cash Flow	Negative Free Cash Flow	-$1.10	-8%	-61%	-8%	0.00%
PMC-Sierra, Inc.	PMCS	Semiconductors	$2.40	$4.80	$7.20	$14.40	$0.32	9%	33%	9%	0.00%
PMFG, Inc.	PMFG	Industrial	Negative Free Cash Flow	Negative Free Cash Flow	Negative Free Cash Flow	Negative Free Cash Flow	-$0.51	-8%	297%	-8%	0.00%
PNM Resources Inc	PNM	Utilities	$9.23	$18.45	$27.68	$55.35	$1.23	3%	76%	4%	3.06%
Polaris Industries, Inc.	PII	Autos	$37.43	$74.85	$112.28	$224.55	$4.99	32%	35%	20%	1.39%
Polycom, Inc.	PLCM	Communication	$6.60	$13.20	$19.80	$39.60	$0.88	10%	30%	10%	0.00%
PolyOne Corporation	POL	Chemicals	Negative Free Cash Flow	Negative Free Cash Flow	Negative Free Cash Flow	Negative Free Cash Flow	-$0.19	-1%	136%	-2%	0.84%
Polypore International, Inc.	PPO	Industrial	Negative Free Cash Flow	Negative Free Cash Flow	Negative Free Cash Flow	Negative Free Cash Flow	-$0.22	-1%	108%	-1%	0.00%
Pool Corp	POOL	Travel & Leisure	$5.78	$11.55	$17.33	$34.65	$0.77	5%	33%	1%	1.38%

NAME	TICKER	INDUSTRY	2014 BUY PRICE OPINION	2014 HOLD PRICE OPINION	2014 SELL PRICE OPINION	2014 SHORT PRICE OPINION	2014 MYCROFT FREE CASH FLOW PER SHARE ESTIMATE	2014 MYCROFT FREE CASH FLOW RETURN ON TOTAL CAPITAL ESTIMATE (FROIC) >15% = Great	2014 MYCROFT CAPFLOW ESTIMATE <33% = Great BUT NO NEGATIVE RESULTS	2014 MYCROFT MICHAELIS GROWTH RATE ESTIMATE >15% = Great	DIVIDEND YIELD
Step #1 = Look up the company's current stock market price on the day of analysis and compare it to our 2014 Buy, Hold, Sell & Short Price.										
Step #2 =Take the company's current market price; divide it by the "2014 Mycroft Free Cash Flow Per Share estimate." This gives the "Price to Free Cash Flow."										
All results below are based on the 2014 year end estimates using the "2014 Mycroft Michaelis Growth Rate" and are good until December 31, 2014.										
Portfolio Recovery Associates, Inc.	PRAA	Business Services	$29.18	$58.35	$87.53	$175.05	$3.89	21%	6%	21%	0.00%
Portland General Electric Company	POR	Utilities	$8.03	$16.05	$24.08	$48.15	$1.07	2%	84%	4%	3.90%
Portola Pharmaceuticals Inc	PTLA	Biotech	Negative Free Cash Flow	Negative Free Cash Flow	Negative Free Cash Flow	Negative Free Cash Flow	-$1.46	-24%	-1%	-24%	0.00%
Post Holdings Inc	POST	Consumer Goods	$18.60	$37.20	$55.80	$111.60	$2.48	3%	25%	3%	0.00%
PostRock Energy Corp	PSTR	Oil & Gas	$1.58	$3.15	$4.73	$9.45	$0.21	-43%	79%	-43%	0.00%
Powell Industries, Inc.	POWL	Industrial	$12.60	$25.20	$37.80	$75.60	$1.68	6%	75%	6%	0.00%
Power Integrations, Inc.	POWI	Semiconductors	$9.30	$18.60	$27.90	$55.80	$1.24	9%	30%	7%	0.57%
Power Solutions International Inc	PSIX	Industrial	Negative Free Cash Flow	Negative Free Cash Flow	Negative Free Cash Flow	Negative Free Cash Flow	-$1.36	-29%	-58%	-29%	0.00%
PowerSecure International, Inc.	POWR	Business Services	Negative Free Cash Flow	Negative Free Cash Flow	Negative Free Cash Flow	Negative Free Cash Flow	-$0.39	-7%	387%	-7%	0.00%
POZEN, Inc.	POZN	Drugs	Negative Free Cash Flow	Negative Free Cash Flow	Negative Free Cash Flow	Negative Free Cash Flow	-$0.60	-24%	0%	-24%	0.00%
PPG Industries, Inc.	PPG	Chemicals	$84.53	$169.05	$253.58	$507.15	$11.27	18%	24%	15%	1.48%

NAME	TICKER	INDUSTRY	2014 BUY PRICE OPINION	2014 HOLD PRICE OPINION	2014 SELL PRICE OPINION	2014 SHORT PRICE OPINION	2014 MYCROFT FREE CASH FLOW PER SHARE ESTIMATE	2014 MYCROFT FREE CASH FLOW RETURN ON TOTAL CAPITAL ESTIMATE (FROIC) >15% = Great	2014 MYCROFT CAPFLOW ESTIMATE <33% = Great BUT NO NEGATIVE RESULTS	2014 MYCROFT MICHAELIS GROWTH RATE ESTIMATE >15% = Great	DIVIDEND YIELD
Step #1 = Look up the company's current stock market price on the day of analysis and compare it to our 2014 Buy, Hold, Sell & Short Price.											
Step #2 =Take the company's current market price; divide it by the "2014 Mycroft Free Cash Flow Per Share estimate." This gives the "Price to Free Cash Flow."											
All results below are based on the 2014 year end estimates using the "2014 Mycroft Michaelis Growth Rate" and are good until December 31, 2014.											
PPL Corp	PPL	Utilities	Negative Free Cash Flow	Negative Free Cash Flow	Negative Free Cash Flow	Negative Free Cash Flow	-$1.31	-3%	130%	-1%	4.90%
Praxair, Inc.	PX	Chemicals	$14.18	$28.35	$42.53	$85.05	$1.89	5%	79%	1%	1.98%
Precision Castparts Corp.	PCP	Industrial	$70.80	$141.60	$212.40	$424.80	$9.44	12%	22%	12%	0.05%
Preformed Line Products Company	PLPC	Computers	$32.18	$64.35	$96.53	$193.05	$4.29	8%	47%	8%	1.14%
Premier Exhibitions, Inc.	PRXI	Travel & Leisure	$0.38	$0.75	$1.13	$2.25	$0.05	10%	35%	10%	0.00%
Premiere Global Services, Inc.	PGI	Communication	$6.45	$12.90	$19.35	$38.70	$0.86	14%	49%	14%	0.00%
Prestige Brands Holdings Inc	PBH	Consumer Goods	$21.45	$42.90	$64.35	$128.70	$2.86	8%	7%	8%	0.00%
PRGX Global, Inc.	PRGX	Business Services	$1.95	$3.90	$5.85	$11.70	$0.26	7%	53%	7%	0.00%
Priceline.com, Inc.	PCLN	Travel & Leisure	$350.70	$701.40	$1,052.10	$2,104.20	$46.76	28%	3%	28%	0.00%
Pricesmart, Inc.	PSMT	Retail	$3.68	$7.35	$11.03	$22.05	$0.49	3%	82%	0%	0.66%
Primo Water Corp	PRMW	Beverages	$2.18	$4.35	$6.53	$13.05	$0.29	16%	42%	16%	0.00%

NAME	TICKER	INDUSTRY	2014 BUY PRICE OPINION	2014 HOLD PRICE OPINION	2014 SELL PRICE OPINION	2014 SHORT PRICE OPINION	2014 MYCROFT FREE CASH FLOW PER SHARE ESTIMATE	2014 MYCROFT FREE CASH FLOW RETURN ON TOTAL CAPITAL ESTIMATE (FROIC) >15% = Great	2014 MYCROFT CAPFLOW ESTIMATE <33% = Great BUT NO NEGATIVE RESULTS	2014 MYCROFT MICHAELIS GROWTH RATE ESTIMATE >15% = Great	DIVIDEND YIELD
Step #1 = Look up the company's current stock market price on the day of analysis and compare it to our 2014 Buy, Hold, Sell & Short Price.												
Step #2 =Take the company's current market price; divide it by the "2014 Mycroft Free Cash Flow Per Share estimate." This gives the "Price to Free Cash Flow."												
All results below are based on the 2014 year end estimates using the "2014 Mycroft Michaelis Growth Rate" and are good until December 31, 2014.												
Primoris Services Corporation	PRIM	Engineering	Negative Free Cash Flow	Negative Free Cash Flow	Negative Free Cash Flow	Negative Free Cash Flow	-$0.53	-7%	158%	-8%	0.57%
Procera Networks, Inc.	PKT	Software	Negative Free Cash Flow	Negative Free Cash Flow	Negative Free Cash Flow	Negative Free Cash Flow	-$0.61	-8%	-56%	-8%	0.00%
Procter & Gamble Co	PG	Consumer Goods	$31.50	$63.00	$94.50	$189.00	$4.20	12%	27%	8%	3.07%
Pro-Dex, Inc.	PDEX	Medical	Negative Free Cash Flow	Negative Free Cash Flow	Negative Free Cash Flow	Negative Free Cash Flow	-$0.60	-23%	-9%	-23%	0.00%
Progenics Pharmaceuticals, Inc.	PGNX	Biotech	Negative Free Cash Flow	Negative Free Cash Flow	Negative Free Cash Flow	Negative Free Cash Flow	-$0.49	-33%	0%	-33%	0.00%
Progress Software	PRGS	Software	$5.18	$10.35	$15.53	$31.05	$0.69	6%	10%	6%	0.00%
Proofpoint Inc	PFPT	Software	$0.15	$0.30	$0.45	$0.90	$0.02	2%	88%	2%	0.00%
ProPhase Labs, Inc.	PRPH	Drugs	Negative Free Cash Flow	Negative Free Cash Flow	Negative Free Cash Flow	Negative Free Cash Flow	-$0.11	-18%	-22%	-18%	0.00%
Pros Holdings, Inc.	PRO	Software	$5.10	$10.20	$15.30	$30.60	$0.68	17%	36%	17%	0.00%
Prothena Corporation PLC	PRTA	Biotech	Negative Free Cash Flow	Negative Free Cash Flow	Negative Free Cash Flow	Negative Free Cash Flow	-$2.07	-34%	-4%	-34%	0.00%
Proto Labs Inc	PRLB	Industrial	$7.43	$14.85	$22.28	$44.55	$0.99	12%	32%	12%	0.00%

NAME	TICKER	INDUSTRY	2014 BUY PRICE OPINION	2014 HOLD PRICE OPINION	2014 SELL PRICE OPINION	2014 SHORT PRICE OPINION	2014 MYCROFT FREE CASH FLOW PER SHARE ESTIMATE	2014 MYCROFT FREE CASH FLOW RETURN ON TOTAL CAPITAL ESTIMATE (FROIC) >15% = Great	2014 MYCROFT CAPFLOW ESTIMATE <33% = Great BUT NO NEGATIVE RESULTS	2014 MYCROFT MICHAELIS GROWTH RATE ESTIMATE >15% = Great	DIVIDEND YIELD
Step #1 = Look up the company's current stock market price on the day of analysis and compare it to our 2014 Buy, Hold, Sell & Short Price.											
Step #2 =Take the company's current market price; divide it by the "2014 Mycroft Free Cash Flow Per Share estimate." This gives the "Price to Free Cash Flow."											
All results below are based on the 2014 year end estimates using the "2014 Mycroft Michaelis Growth Rate" and are good until December 31, 2014.											
Providence & Worcester Railroad Company	PWX	Transportation	Negative Free Cash Flow	Negative Free Cash Flow	Negative Free Cash Flow	Negative Free Cash Flow	-$0.13	-1%	125%	-1%	0.88%
Providence Service Corporation	PRSC	Health Care	$32.33	$64.65	$96.98	$193.95	$4.31	18%	12%	18%	0.00%
Psychemedics Corporation	PMD	Medical	$1.80	$3.60	$5.40	$10.80	$0.24	12%	62%	-11%	4.50%
PTC Inc	PMTC	Software	$12.90	$25.80	$38.70	$77.40	$1.72	18%	14%	18%	0.00%
PTC Therapeutics Inc	PTCT	Biotech	Negative Free Cash Flow	Negative Free Cash Flow	Negative Free Cash Flow	Negative Free Cash Flow	-$1.79	-29%	0%	-29%	0.00%
Public Service Enterprise Group Inc	PEG	Utilities	$0.75	$1.50	$2.25	$4.50	$0.10	0%	98%	1%	4.40%
Pulse Electronics Corp	PULS	Computers	Negative Free Cash Flow	Negative Free Cash Flow	Negative Free Cash Flow	Negative Free Cash Flow	-$1.42	-283%	-187%	-283%	0.00%
PulteGroup Inc	PHM	Homebuilding	$19.35	$38.70	$58.05	$116.10	$2.58	16%	2%	16%	1.21%
Puma Biotechnology Inc	PBYI	Biotech	Negative Free Cash Flow	Negative Free Cash Flow	Negative Free Cash Flow	Negative Free Cash Flow	-$2.18	-59%	-1%	-59%	0.00%
Pure Cycle Corporation	PCYO	Utilities	Negative Free Cash Flow	Negative Free Cash Flow	Negative Free Cash Flow	Negative Free Cash Flow	-$0.08	-7%	-16%	-7%	0.00%
PVH Corp	PVH	Apparel & Furniture	$22.73	$45.45	$68.18	$136.35	$3.03	4%	48%	4%	0.12%

NAME	TICKER	INDUSTRY	2014 BUY PRICE OPINION	2014 HOLD PRICE OPINION	2014 SELL PRICE OPINION	2014 SHORT PRICE OPINION	2014 MYCROFT FREE CASH FLOW PER SHARE ESTIMATE	2014 MYCROFT FREE CASH FLOW RETURN ON TOTAL CAPITAL ESTIMATE (FROIC) >15% = Great	2014 MYCROFT CAPFLOW ESTIMATE <33% = Great BUT NO NEGATIVE RESULTS	2014 MYCROFT MICHAELIS GROWTH RATE ESTIMATE >15% = Great	DIVIDEND YIELD
Step #1 = Look up the company's current stock market price on the day of analysis and compare it to our 2014 Buy, Hold, Sell & Short Price.										
Step #2 =Take the company's current market price; divide it by the "2014 Mycroft Free Cash Flow Per Share estimate." This gives the "Price to Free Cash Flow."										
All results below are based on the 2014 year end estimates using the "2014 Mycroft Michaelis Growth Rate" and are good until December 31, 2014.										
Pyramid Oil Company	PDO	Oil & Gas	$1.73	$3.45	$5.18	$10.35	$0.23	9%	26%	9%	0.00%
QAD, Inc.	QADA	Software	$7.20	$14.40	$21.60	$43.20	$0.96	18%	25%	14%	2.18%
QEP Resources Inc	QEP	Oil & Gas	Negative Free Cash Flow	Negative Free Cash Flow	Negative Free Cash Flow	Negative Free Cash Flow	-$9.80	-33%	260%	-33%	0.28%
Qiagen NV	QGEN	Medical	$3.60	$7.20	$10.80	$21.60	$0.48	4%	55%	4%	0.00%
Qlik Technologies, Inc.	QLIK	Software	$1.13	$2.25	$3.38	$6.75	$0.15	6%	43%	6%	0.00%
QLogic Corporation	QLGC	Computers	$3.53	$7.05	$10.58	$21.15	$0.47	6%	55%	6%	0.00%
Quad/Graphics, Inc. Class A	QUAD	Business Services	$50.10	$100.20	$150.30	$300.60	$6.68	12%	30%	13%	4.00%
Quaker Chemical Corporation	KWR	Chemicals	$36.98	$73.95	$110.93	$221.85	$4.93	16%	17%	14%	1.47%
Qualcomm, Inc.	QCOM	Communication	$32.78	$65.55	$98.33	$196.65	$4.37	18%	14%	13%	2.06%
Quality Distribution, Inc.	QLTY	Transportation	$0.23	$0.45	$0.68	$1.35	$0.03	0%	97%	0%	0.00%
Quality Systems, Inc.	QSII	Software	$5.03	$10.05	$15.08	$30.15	$0.67	13%	51%	2%	3.33%

NAME	TICKER	INDUSTRY	2014 BUY PRICE OPINION	2014 HOLD PRICE OPINION	2014 SELL PRICE OPINION	2014 SHORT PRICE OPINION	2014 MYCROFT FREE CASH FLOW PER SHARE ESTIMATE	2014 MYCROFT FREE CASH FLOW RETURN ON TOTAL CAPITAL ESTIMATE (FROIC) >15% = Great	2014 MYCROFT CAPFLOW ESTIMATE <33% = Great BUT NO NEGATIVE RESULTS	2014 MYCROFT MICHAELIS GROWTH RATE ESTIMATE >15% = Great	DIVIDEND YIELD
Step #1 = Look up the company's current stock market price on the day of analysis and compare it to our 2014 Buy, Hold, Sell & Short Price.											
Step #2 =Take the company's current market price; divide it by the "2014 Mycroft Free Cash Flow Per Share estimate." This gives the "Price to Free Cash Flow."											
All results below are based on the 2014 year end estimates using the "2014 Mycroft Michaelis Growth Rate" and are good until December 31, 2014.											
Qualstar Corporation	QBAK	Computers	Negative Free Cash Flow	Negative Free Cash Flow	Negative Free Cash Flow	Negative Free Cash Flow	-$0.39	-26%	-11%	-26%	0.00%
Qualys Inc	QLYS	Software	$3.53	$7.05	$10.58	$21.15	$0.47	14%	46%	14%	0.00%
Quanex Building Products Corp	NX	Building Supplies	Negative Free Cash Flow	Negative Free Cash Flow	Negative Free Cash Flow	Negative Free Cash Flow	-$0.50	-4%	169%	-5%	0.83%
Quanta Services, Inc.	PWR	Engineering	Negative Free Cash Flow	Negative Free Cash Flow	Negative Free Cash Flow	Negative Free Cash Flow	-$0.15	-1%	113%	-1%	0.00%
Quantum Corporation	QTM	Computers	$0.38	$0.75	$1.13	$2.25	$0.05	10%	41%	10%	0.00%
Quantum Fuel Systems Technologies Worldwide	QTWW	Autos	Negative Free Cash Flow	Negative Free Cash Flow	Negative Free Cash Flow	Negative Free Cash Flow	-$0.71	-32%	-30%	-32%	0.00%
Quest Diagnostics Inc	DGX	Medical	$44.85	$89.70	$134.55	$269.10	$5.98	11%	20%	11%	1.94%
Questar Corp	STR	Utilities	$5.63	$11.25	$16.88	$33.75	$0.75	6%	75%	3%	3.24%
Questcor Pharmaceuticals, Inc.	QCOR	Biotech	$56.48	$112.95	$169.43	$338.85	$7.53	98%	1%	76%	1.56%
Quicklogic Corporation	QUIK	Semiconductors	Negative Free Cash Flow	Negative Free Cash Flow	Negative Free Cash Flow	Negative Free Cash Flow	-$0.22	-46%	-12%	-46%	0.00%
Quicksilver Resources, Inc.	KWK	Oil & Gas	Negative Free Cash Flow	Negative Free Cash Flow	Negative Free Cash Flow	Negative Free Cash Flow	-$1.04	-17%	467%	-17%	0.00%

NAME	TICKER	INDUSTRY	2014 BUY PRICE OPINION	2014 HOLD PRICE OPINION	2014 SELL PRICE OPINION	2014 SHORT PRICE OPINION	2014 MYCROFT FREE CASH FLOW PER SHARE ESTIMATE	2014 MYCROFT FREE CASH FLOW RETURN ON TOTAL CAPITAL ESTIMATE (FROIC) >15% = Great	2014 MYCROFT CAPFLOW ESTIMATE <33% = Great BUT NO NEGATIVE RESULTS	2014 MYCROFT MICHAELIS GROWTH RATE ESTIMATE >15% = Great	DIVIDEND YIELD
Step #1 = Look up the company's current stock market price on the day of analysis and compare it to our 2014 Buy, Hold, Sell & Short Price.											
Step #2 =Take the company's current market price; divide it by the "2014 Mycroft Free Cash Flow Per Share estimate." This gives the "Price to Free Cash Flow."											
All results below are based on the 2014 year end estimates using the "2014 Mycroft Michaelis Growth Rate" and are good until December 31, 2014.											
Quidel Corporation	QDEL	Medical	$5.40	$10.80	$16.20	$32.40	$0.72	9%	49%	9%	0.00%
Quiksilver Inc	ZQK	Apparel & Furniture	Negative Free Cash Flow	Negative Free Cash Flow	Negative Free Cash Flow	Negative Free Cash Flow	-$0.40	-5%	-635%	-5%	0.00%
QuinStreet, Inc.	QNST	Internet	$8.85	$17.70	$26.55	$53.10	$1.18	12%	12%	12%	0.00%
Quintiles Transnational Holdings Inc	Q	Medical	$7.13	$14.25	$21.38	$42.75	$0.95	-19%	40%	-19%	0.00%
R.R. Donnelley & Sons Company	RRD	Business Services	$26.70	$53.40	$80.10	$160.20	$3.56	16%	27%	17%	6.50%
Rackspace Hosting, Inc.	RAX	Software	$4.58	$9.15	$13.73	$27.45	$0.61	8%	82%	8%	0.00%
Radio One, Inc. Class D	ROIAK	Entertainment	$3.30	$6.60	$9.90	$19.80	$0.44	2%	36%	2%	0.00%
RadioShack Corp	RSH	Retail	Negative Free Cash Flow	Negative Free Cash Flow	Negative Free Cash Flow	Negative Free Cash Flow	-$0.55	-7%	-1786%	-7%	0.00%
Radisys Corporation	RSYS	Computers	Negative Free Cash Flow	Negative Free Cash Flow	Negative Free Cash Flow	Negative Free Cash Flow	-$0.04	-1%	116%	-1%	0.00%
RadNet, Inc.	RDNT	Medical	Negative Free Cash Flow	Negative Free Cash Flow	Negative Free Cash Flow	Negative Free Cash Flow	-$0.58	-4%	137%	-4%	0.00%
Rally Software Development Corp	RALY	Software	Negative Free Cash Flow	Negative Free Cash Flow	Negative Free Cash Flow	Negative Free Cash Flow	-$0.10	-3%	229%	-3%	0.00%

NAME	TICKER	INDUSTRY	2014 BUY PRICE OPINION	2014 HOLD PRICE OPINION	2014 SELL PRICE OPINION	2014 SHORT PRICE OPINION	2014 MYCROFT FREE CASH FLOW PER SHARE ESTIMATE	2014 MYCROFT FREE CASH FLOW RETURN ON TOTAL CAPITAL ESTIMATE (FROIC) >15% = Great	2014 MYCROFT CAPFLOW ESTIMATE <33% = Great BUT NO NEGATIVE RESULTS	2014 MYCROFT MICHAELIS GROWTH RATE ESTIMATE >15% = Great	DIVIDEND YIELD
Step #1 = Look up the company's current stock market price on the day of analysis and compare it to our 2014 Buy, Hold, Sell & Short Price.											
Step #2 =Take the company's current market price; divide it by the "2014 Mycroft Free Cash Flow Per Share estimate." This gives the "Price to Free Cash Flow."											
All results below are based on the 2014 year end estimates using the "2014 Mycroft Michaelis Growth Rate" and are good until December 31, 2014.											
Ralph Lauren Corp	RL	Apparel & Furniture	$73.73	$147.45	$221.18	$442.35	$9.83	19%	27%	16%	0.98%
Rambus, Inc.	RMBS	Semiconductors	Negative Free Cash Flow	Negative Free Cash Flow	Negative Free Cash Flow	Negative Free Cash Flow	-$0.03	-1%	117%	-1%	0.00%
Rand Logistics, Inc.	RLOG	Transportation	Negative Free Cash Flow	Negative Free Cash Flow	Negative Free Cash Flow	Negative Free Cash Flow	-$0.33	-4%	136%	-4%	0.00%
Range Resources Corporation	RRC	Oil & Gas	Negative Free Cash Flow	Negative Free Cash Flow	Negative Free Cash Flow	Negative Free Cash Flow	-$4.53	-15%	215%	-15%	0.20%
Raptor Pharmaceutical Corp	RPTP	Drugs	Negative Free Cash Flow	Negative Free Cash Flow	Negative Free Cash Flow	Negative Free Cash Flow	-$0.61	-171%	-1%	-171%	0.00%
Raven Industries, Inc.	RAVN	Industrial	$7.88	$15.75	$23.63	$47.25	$1.05	15%	43%	9%	1.47%
Raytheon Company	RTN	Aerospace & Defense	$56.03	$112.05	$168.08	$336.15	$7.47	16%	14%	14%	2.84%
RBC Bearings, Inc.	ROLL	Industrial	$5.18	$10.35	$15.53	$31.05	$0.69	3%	73%	3%	0.00%
RCM Technologies	RCMT	Services	Negative Free Cash Flow	Negative Free Cash Flow	Negative Free Cash Flow	Negative Free Cash Flow	-$0.21	-4%	-96%	-4%	0.00%
ReachLocal, Inc.	RLOC	Advertising	$3.83	$7.65	$11.48	$22.95	$0.51	16%	61%	16%	0.00%
Reading International, Inc.	RDI	Entertainment	$8.25	$16.50	$24.75	$49.50	$1.10	8%	11%	8%	0.00%

NAME	TICKER	INDUSTRY	2014 BUY PRICE OPINION	2014 HOLD PRICE OPINION	2014 SELL PRICE OPINION	2014 SHORT PRICE OPINION	2014 MYCROFT FREE CASH FLOW PER SHARE ESTIMATE	2014 MYCROFT FREE CASH FLOW RETURN ON TOTAL CAPITAL ESTIMATE (FROIC) >15% = Great	2014 MYCROFT CAPFLOW ESTIMATE <33% = Great BUT NO NEGATIVE RESULTS	2014 MYCROFT MICHAELIS GROWTH RATE ESTIMATE >15% = Great	DIVIDEND YIELD
Step #1 = Look up the company's current stock market price on the day of analysis and compare it to our 2014 Buy, Hold, Sell & Short Price.											
Step #2 =Take the company's current market price; divide it by the "2014 Mycroft Free Cash Flow Per Share estimate." This gives the "Price to Free Cash Flow."											
All results below are based on the 2014 year end estimates using the "2014 Mycroft Michaelis Growth Rate" and are good until December 31, 2014.											
RealD Inc.	RLD	Entertainment	$0.08	$0.15	$0.23	$0.45	$0.01	0%	99%	0%	0.00%
RealNetworks, Inc.	RNWK	Software	Negative Free Cash Flow	Negative Free Cash Flow	Negative Free Cash Flow	Negative Free Cash Flow	-$0.96	-11%	-19%	-11%	0.00%
Realogy Holdings Corp	RLGY	Real Estate	$1.58	$3.15	$4.73	$9.45	$0.21	0%	65%	0%	0.00%
Realpage, Inc.	RP	Software	$3.75	$7.50	$11.25	$22.50	$0.50	11%	43%	11%	0.00%
Receptos Inc	RCPT	Biotech	Negative Free Cash Flow	Negative Free Cash Flow	Negative Free Cash Flow	Negative Free Cash Flow	-$1.43	-33%	0%	-33%	0.00%
Red Hat, Inc.	RHT	Software	$17.48	$34.95	$52.43	$104.85	$2.33	25%	27%	25%	0.00%
Red Lion Hotels Corporation	RLH	Travel & Leisure	$0.00	$0.00	$0.00	$0.00	$0.00	0%	99%	0%	0.00%
Red Robin Gourmet Burgers, Inc.	RRGB	Restaurants	$27.98	$55.95	$83.93	$167.85	$3.73	11%	58%	11%	0.00%
Reeds, Inc.	REED	Beverages	Negative Free Cash Flow	Negative Free Cash Flow	Negative Free Cash Flow	Negative Free Cash Flow	-$0.14	-44%	-50%	-44%	0.00%
Regal Entertainment Group	RGC	Entertainment	$17.93	$35.85	$53.78	$107.55	$2.39	26%	25%	19%	4.50%
Regal-Beloit Corporation	RBC	Computers	$39.38	$78.75	$118.13	$236.25	$5.25	8%	28%	8%	1.23%

NAME	TICKER	INDUSTRY	2014 BUY PRICE OPINION	2014 HOLD PRICE OPINION	2014 SELL PRICE OPINION	2014 SHORT PRICE OPINION	2014 MYCROFT FREE CASH FLOW PER SHARE ESTIMATE	2014 MYCROFT FREE CASH FLOW RETURN ON TOTAL CAPITAL ESTIMATE (FROIC) >15% = Great	2014 MYCROFT CAPFLOW ESTIMATE <33% = Great BUT NO NEGATIVE RESULTS	2014 MYCROFT MICHAELIS GROWTH RATE ESTIMATE >15% = Great	DIVIDEND YIELD
Step #1 = Look up the company's current stock market price on the day of analysis and compare it to our 2014 Buy, Hold, Sell & Short Price.										
Step #2 =Take the company's current market price; divide it by the "2014 Mycroft Free Cash Flow Per Share estimate." This gives the "Price to Free Cash Flow."										
All results below are based on the 2014 year end estimates using the "2014 Mycroft Michaelis Growth Rate" and are good until December 31, 2014.										
Regeneron Pharmaceuticals, Inc.	REGN	Biotech	$19.13	$38.25	$57.38	$114.75	$2.55	13%	27%	13%	0.00%
Regis Corporation	RGS	Services	Negative Free Cash Flow	Negative Free Cash Flow	Negative Free Cash Flow	Negative Free Cash Flow	-$0.65	-4%	153%	-4%	1.54%
Regulus Therapeutics Inc	RGLS	Biotech	Negative Free Cash Flow	Negative Free Cash Flow	Negative Free Cash Flow	Negative Free Cash Flow	-$0.35	-29%	-7%	-29%	0.00%
Reis, Inc.	REIS	Business Services	Negative Free Cash Flow	Negative Free Cash Flow	Negative Free Cash Flow	Negative Free Cash Flow	-$0.94	-14%	-73%	-14%	0.00%
Reliance Steel and Aluminum	RS	Industrial	$72.68	$145.35	$218.03	$436.05	$9.69	13%	23%	13%	1.83%
Reliv' International, Inc.	RELV	Biotech	Negative Free Cash Flow	Negative Free Cash Flow	Negative Free Cash Flow	Negative Free Cash Flow	$0.00	0%	105%	-1%	1.79%
RELM Wireless Corporation	RWC	Communication	$0.83	$1.65	$2.48	$4.95	$0.11	4%	42%	4%	0.00%
Remy International, Inc.	REMY	Autos	$6.60	$13.20	$19.80	$39.60	$0.88	4%	47%	4%	2.01%
Renewable Energy Group Inc	REGI	Oil & Gas	$10.50	$21.00	$31.50	$63.00	$1.40	11%	36%	11%	0.00%
Rent-A-Center, Inc.	RCII	Retail	$10.65	$21.30	$31.95	$63.90	$1.42	4%	57%	4%	2.20%
Rentech Inc.	RTK	Chemicals	Negative Free Cash Flow	Negative Free Cash Flow	Negative Free Cash Flow	Negative Free Cash Flow	-$0.06	-6%	126%	-6%	0.00%

NAME	TICKER	INDUSTRY	2014 BUY PRICE OPINION	2014 HOLD PRICE OPINION	2014 SELL PRICE OPINION	2014 SHORT PRICE OPINION	2014 MYCROFT FREE CASH FLOW PER SHARE ESTIMATE	2014 MYCROFT FREE CASH FLOW RETURN ON TOTAL CAPITAL ESTIMATE (FROIC) >15% = Great	2014 MYCROFT CAPFLOW ESTIMATE <33% = Great BUT NO NEGATIVE RESULTS	2014 MYCROFT MICHAELIS GROWTH RATE ESTIMATE >15% = Great	DIVIDEND YIELD
Step #1 = Look up the company's current stock market price on the day of analysis and compare it to our 2014 Buy, Hold, Sell & Short Price.											
Step #2 =Take the company's current market price; divide it by the "2014 Mycroft Free Cash Flow Per Share estimate." This gives the "Price to Free Cash Flow."											
All results below are based on the 2014 year end estimates using the "2014 Mycroft Michaelis Growth Rate" and are good until December 31, 2014.											
Rentrak Corporation	RENT	Entertainment	Negative Free Cash Flow	Negative Free Cash Flow	Negative Free Cash Flow	Negative Free Cash Flow	-$0.52	-13%	563%	-13%	0.00%
Repligen Corporation	RGEN	Biotech	$5.85	$11.70	$17.55	$35.10	$0.78	22%	8%	22%	0.00%
Repros Therapeutics, Inc.	RPRX	Biotech	Negative Free Cash Flow	Negative Free Cash Flow	Negative Free Cash Flow	Negative Free Cash Flow	-$0.98	-26%	-3%	-26%	0.00%
Republic Airways Holdings, Inc.	RJET	Airlines	$43.73	$87.45	$131.18	$262.35	$5.83	10%	11%	10%	0.00%
Republic Services Inc Class A	RSG	Waste Management	$14.78	$29.55	$44.33	$88.65	$1.97	5%	57%	5%	3.13%
Research Frontiers	REFR	Computers	Negative Free Cash Flow	Negative Free Cash Flow	Negative Free Cash Flow	Negative Free Cash Flow	-$0.13	-24%	-1%	-24%	0.00%
ResMed Inc.	RMD	Medical	$19.58	$39.15	$58.73	$117.45	$2.61	18%	18%	12%	1.92%
Resolute Energy Corp	REN	Oil & Gas	Negative Free Cash Flow	Negative Free Cash Flow	Negative Free Cash Flow	Negative Free Cash Flow	-$5.20	-43%	496%	-43%	0.00%
Resolute Forest Products Inc	RFP	Forest Products	Negative Free Cash Flow	Negative Free Cash Flow	Negative Free Cash Flow	Negative Free Cash Flow	-$0.59	-2%	140%	-2%	0.00%
Resources Connection Inc	RECN	Services	$6.45	$12.90	$19.35	$38.70	$0.86	9%	9%	8%	2.18%
Response Genetics, Inc.	RGDX	Medical	Negative Free Cash Flow	Negative Free Cash Flow	Negative Free Cash Flow	Negative Free Cash Flow	-$0.17	-139%	-18%	-139%	0.00%

NAME	TICKER	INDUSTRY	2014 BUY PRICE OPINION	2014 HOLD PRICE OPINION	2014 SELL PRICE OPINION	2014 SHORT PRICE OPINION	2014 MYCROFT FREE CASH FLOW PER SHARE ESTIMATE	2014 MYCROFT FREE CASH FLOW RETURN ON TOTAL CAPITAL ESTIMATE (FROIC) >15% = Great	2014 MYCROFT CAPFLOW ESTIMATE <33% = Great BUT NO NEGATIVE RESULTS	2014 MYCROFT MICHAELIS GROWTH RATE ESTIMATE >15% = Great	DIVIDEND YIELD
Step #1 = Look up the company's current stock market price on the day of analysis and compare it to our 2014 Buy, Hold, Sell & Short Price.											
Step #2 =Take the company's current market price; divide it by the "2014 Mycroft Free Cash Flow Per Share estimate." This gives the "Price to Free Cash Flow."											
All results below are based on the 2014 year end estimates using the "2014 Mycroft Michaelis Growth Rate" and are good until December 31, 2014.											
Responsys Inc	MKTG	Software	$1.20	$2.40	$3.60	$7.20	$0.16	5%	70%	5%	0.00%
Restoration Hardware Holdings Inc	RH	Retail	Negative Free Cash Flow	Negative Free Cash Flow	Negative Free Cash Flow	Negative Free Cash Flow	-$1.73	-11%	-364%	-11%	0.00%
Revlon Inc	REV	Consumer Goods	$19.65	$39.30	$58.95	$117.90	$2.62	21%	18%	21%	0.00%
Revolution Lighting Technologies Inc	RVLT	Computers	Negative Free Cash Flow	Negative Free Cash Flow	Negative Free Cash Flow	Negative Free Cash Flow	-$0.06	-36%	0%	-36%	0.00%
REX American Resources Corp	REX	Chemicals	$19.88	$39.75	$59.63	$119.25	$2.65	6%	7%	6%	0.00%
Rex Energy Corporation	REXX	Oil & Gas	Negative Free Cash Flow	Negative Free Cash Flow	Negative Free Cash Flow	Negative Free Cash Flow	-$2.57	-25%	253%	-25%	0.00%
Rexnord Corp	RXN	Industrial	$8.18	$16.35	$24.53	$49.05	$1.09	4%	34%	4%	0.00%
Reynolds American Inc	RAI	Tobacco	$19.35	$38.70	$58.05	$116.10	$2.58	17%	6%	5%	5.10%
RF Industries, Ltd.	RFIL	Computers	$3.15	$6.30	$9.45	$18.90	$0.42	12%	7%	8%	3.80%
RF Micro Devices, Inc.	RFMD	Semiconductors	Negative Free Cash Flow	Negative Free Cash Flow	Negative Free Cash Flow	Negative Free Cash Flow	-$0.04	-1%	116%	-1%	0.00%
RG Barry Corporation	DFZ	Apparel & Furniture	$10.35	$20.70	$31.05	$62.10	$1.38	13%	6%	11%	2.14%

NAME	TICKER	INDUSTRY	2014 BUY PRICE OPINION	2014 HOLD PRICE OPINION	2014 SELL PRICE OPINION	2014 SHORT PRICE OPINION	2014 MYCROFT FREE CASH FLOW PER SHARE ESTIMATE	2014 MYCROFT FREE CASH FLOW RETURN ON TOTAL CAPITAL ESTIMATE (FROIC) >15% = Great	2014 MYCROFT CAPFLOW ESTIMATE <33% = Great BUT NO NEGATIVE RESULTS	2014 MYCROFT MICHAELIS GROWTH RATE ESTIMATE >15% = Great	DIVIDEND YIELD

Step #1 = Look up the company's current stock market price on the day of analysis and compare it to our 2014 Buy, Hold, Sell & Short Price.

Step #2 =Take the company's current market price; divide it by the "2014 Mycroft Free Cash Flow Per Share estimate." This gives the "Price to Free Cash Flow."

All results below are based on the 2014 year end estimates using the "2014 Mycroft Michaelis Growth Rate" and are good until December 31, 2014.

NAME	TICKER	INDUSTRY	BUY	HOLD	SELL	SHORT	FCF/SHARE	FROIC	CAPFLOW	MICHAELIS	DIV YIELD
RGC Resources	RGCO	Utilities	$1.50	$3.00	$4.50	$9.00	$0.20	2%	90%	0%	3.83%
Richardson Electronics	RELL	Computers	$3.83	$7.65	$11.48	$22.95	$0.51	4%	19%	4%	2.11%
Rick's Cabaret International, Inc.	RICK	Restaurants	$9.53	$19.05	$28.58	$57.15	$1.27	9%	40%	9%	0.00%
Rigel Pharmaceuticals, Inc.	RIGL	Drugs	Negative Free Cash Flow	Negative Free Cash Flow	Negative Free Cash Flow	Negative Free Cash Flow	-$1.02	-37%	-2%	-37%	0.00%
RigNet, Inc.	RNET	Communication	$0.75	$1.50	$2.25	$4.50	$0.10	1%	94%	1%	0.00%
Rimage Corporation	RIMG	Computers	Negative Free Cash Flow	Negative Free Cash Flow	Negative Free Cash Flow	Negative Free Cash Flow	-$0.59	-8%	-49%	-8%	0.00%
Rite Aid Corporation	RAD	Retail	$2.40	$4.80	$7.20	$14.40	$0.32	7%	61%	7%	0.00%
Riverbed Technology, Inc.	RVBD	Software	$14.70	$29.40	$44.10	$88.20	$1.96	28%	8%	28%	0.00%
Roadrunner Transportation Systems, Inc.	RRTS	Transportation	$3.15	$6.30	$9.45	$18.90	$0.42	3%	64%	3%	0.00%
Robert Half International Inc.	RHI	Services	$15.90	$31.80	$47.70	$95.40	$2.12	28%	19%	20%	1.67%
Rochester Medical Corporation	ROCM	Medical	$4.50	$9.00	$13.50	$27.00	$0.60	9%	31%	9%	0.00%

NAME	TICKER	INDUSTRY	2014 BUY PRICE OPINION	2014 HOLD PRICE OPINION	2014 SELL PRICE OPINION	2014 SHORT PRICE OPINION	2014 MYCROFT FREE CASH FLOW PER SHARE ESTIMATE	2014 MYCROFT FREE CASH FLOW RETURN ON TOTAL CAPITAL ESTIMATE (FROIC) >15% = Great	2014 MYCROFT CAPFLOW ESTIMATE <33% = Great BUT NO NEGATIVE RESULTS	2014 MYCROFT MICHAELIS GROWTH RATE ESTIMATE >15% = Great	DIVIDEND YIELD
Step #1 = Look up the company's current stock market price on the day of analysis and compare it to our 2014 Buy, Hold, Sell & Short Price.											
Step #2 =Take the company's current market price; divide it by the "2014 Mycroft Free Cash Flow Per Share estimate." This gives the "Price to Free Cash Flow."											
All results below are based on the 2014 year end estimates using the "2014 Mycroft Michaelis Growth Rate" and are good until December 31, 2014.											
Rock-Tenn Company	RKT	Containers	$45.08	$90.15	$135.23	$270.45	$6.01	6%	51%	6%	1.02%
Rockwell Automation	ROK	Industrial	$61.73	$123.45	$185.18	$370.35	$8.23	32%	12%	24%	2.01%
Rockwell Collins, Inc.	COL	Aerospace & Defense	$35.18	$70.35	$105.53	$211.05	$4.69	27%	19%	20%	1.65%
Rockwell Medical Inc	RMTI	Drugs	Negative Free Cash Flow	Negative Free Cash Flow	Negative Free Cash Flow	Negative Free Cash Flow	-$1.23	-286%	-1%	-286%	0.00%
Rockwood Holdings Inc	ROC	Chemicals	$15.15	$30.30	$45.45	$90.90	$2.02	5%	66%	3%	2.76%
Rocky Brands, Inc.	RCKY	Apparel & Furniture	$0.15	$0.30	$0.45	$0.90	$0.02	0%	97%	1%	2.41%
Rocky Mountain Chocolate	RMCF	Consumer Goods	$5.03	$10.05	$15.08	$30.15	$0.67	22%	27%	10%	3.60%
Rofin-Sinar Technologies, Inc.	RSTI	Computers	$8.48	$16.95	$25.43	$50.85	$1.13	6%	39%	6%	0.00%
Rogers Corporation	ROG	Computers	$19.88	$39.75	$59.63	$119.25	$2.65	8%	36%	8%	0.00%
Rollins, Inc.	ROL	Business Services	$7.35	$14.70	$22.05	$44.10	$0.98	31%	15%	19%	1.42%
Roper Industries, Inc.	ROP	Industrial	$58.95	$117.90	$176.85	$353.70	$7.86	14%	5%	13%	0.51%

NAME	TICKER	INDUSTRY	2014 BUY PRICE OPINION	2014 HOLD PRICE OPINION	2014 SELL PRICE OPINION	2014 SHORT PRICE OPINION	2014 MYCROFT FREE CASH FLOW PER SHARE ESTIMATE	2014 MYCROFT FREE CASH FLOW RETURN ON TOTAL CAPITAL ESTIMATE (FROIC) >15% = Great	2014 MYCROFT CAPFLOW ESTIMATE <33% = Great BUT NO NEGATIVE RESULTS	2014 MYCROFT MICHAELIS GROWTH RATE ESTIMATE >15% = Great	DIVIDEND YIELD
Step #1 = Look up the company's current stock market price on the day of analysis and compare it to our 2014 Buy, Hold, Sell & Short Price.											
Step #2 =Take the company's current market price; divide it by the "2014 Mycroft Free Cash Flow Per Share estimate." This gives the "Price to Free Cash Flow."											
All results below are based on the 2014 year end estimates using the "2014 Mycroft Michaelis Growth Rate" and are good until December 31, 2014.											
Rosetta Resources, Inc.	ROSE	Oil & Gas	Negative Free Cash Flow	Negative Free Cash Flow	Negative Free Cash Flow	Negative Free Cash Flow	-$18.55	-73%	328%	-73%	0.00%
Rosetta Stone, Inc.	RST	Software	$7.58	$15.15	$22.73	$45.45	$1.01	14%	25%	14%	0.00%
Ross Stores, Inc.	ROST	Retail	$23.85	$47.70	$71.55	$143.10	$3.18	28%	45%	22%	0.96%
Roundys Inc	RNDY	Retail	$9.08	$18.15	$27.23	$54.45	$1.21	23%	59%	18%	5.50%
Rovi Corp	ROVI	Software	$15.83	$31.65	$47.48	$94.95	$2.11	7%	7%	7%	0.00%
Rowan Companies PLC	RDC	Oil & Gas	Negative Free Cash Flow	Negative Free Cash Flow	Negative Free Cash Flow	Negative Free Cash Flow	-$1.84	-4%	149%	-4%	0.00%
Royal Caribbean Cruises, Ltd.	RCL	Travel & Leisure	$3.68	$7.35	$11.03	$22.05	$0.49	1%	93%	1%	1.24%
Royal Gold, Inc.	RGLD	Commodities	Negative Free Cash Flow	Negative Free Cash Flow	Negative Free Cash Flow	Negative Free Cash Flow	-$2.18	-5%	182%	-6%	1.49%
Royale Energy, Inc.	ROYL	Oil & Gas	Negative Free Cash Flow	Negative Free Cash Flow	Negative Free Cash Flow	Negative Free Cash Flow	-$0.39	-150%	-482%	-150%	0.00%
RPC, Inc.	RES	Oil & Gas	$8.85	$17.70	$26.55	$53.10	$1.18	21%	51%	15%	2.67%
RPM International Inc	RPM	Chemicals	$17.10	$34.20	$51.30	$102.60	$2.28	12%	25%	9%	2.53%

NAME	TICKER	INDUSTRY	2014 BUY PRICE OPINION	2014 HOLD PRICE OPINION	2014 SELL PRICE OPINION	2014 SHORT PRICE OPINION	2014 MYCROFT FREE CASH FLOW PER SHARE ESTIMATE	2014 MYCROFT FREE CASH FLOW RETURN ON TOTAL CAPITAL ESTIMATE (FROIC) >15% = Great	2014 MYCROFT CAPFLOW ESTIMATE <33% = Great BUT NO NEGATIVE RESULTS	2014 MYCROFT MICHAELIS GROWTH RATE ESTIMATE >15% = Great	DIVIDEND YIELD
Step #1 = Look up the company's current stock market price on the day of analysis and compare it to our 2014 Buy, Hold, Sell & Short Price.											
Step #2 =Take the company's current market price; divide it by the "2014 Mycroft Free Cash Flow Per Share estimate." This gives the "Price to Free Cash Flow."											
All results below are based on the 2014 year end estimates using the "2014 Mycroft Michaelis Growth Rate" and are good until December 31, 2014.											
RPX Corp	RPXC	Business Services	$4.73	$9.45	$14.18	$28.35	$0.63	8%	80%	8%	0.00%
RTI International Metals, Inc.	RTI	Industrial	Negative Free Cash Flow	Negative Free Cash Flow	Negative Free Cash Flow	Negative Free Cash Flow	-$2.02	-7%	-552%	-7%	0.00%
RTI Surgical Inc	RTIX	Medical	Negative Free Cash Flow	Negative Free Cash Flow	Negative Free Cash Flow	Negative Free Cash Flow	-$0.14	-4%	219%	-4%	0.00%
Rubicon Technology, Inc.	RBCN	Semiconductors	Negative Free Cash Flow	Negative Free Cash Flow	Negative Free Cash Flow	Negative Free Cash Flow	-$0.59	-6%	-140%	-6%	0.00%
Ruby Tuesday, Inc.	RT	Restaurants	Negative Free Cash Flow	Negative Free Cash Flow	Negative Free Cash Flow	Negative Free Cash Flow	-$0.02	0%	103%	0%	0.00%
Ruckus Wireless Inc	RKUS	Computers	$0.45	$0.90	$1.35	$2.70	$0.06	3%	61%	3%	0.00%
Rudolph Technologies, Inc.	RTEC	Computers	$0.53	$1.05	$1.58	$3.15	$0.07	1%	64%	1%	0.00%
rue21, Inc.	RUE	Retail	$2.85	$5.70	$8.55	$17.10	$0.38	5%	88%	5%	0.00%
Rush Enterprises, Inc. Class A	RUSHA	Autos	$32.63	$65.25	$97.88	$195.75	$4.35	16%	54%	16%	0.00%
Ruth's Hospitality Group, Inc.	RUTH	Restaurants	$8.10	$16.20	$24.30	$48.60	$1.08	20%	28%	18%	1.35%
Ryder System Inc	R	Rentals	Negative Free Cash Flow	Negative Free Cash Flow	Negative Free Cash Flow	Negative Free Cash Flow	-$12.51	-13%	154%	-13%	2.26%

NAME	TICKER	INDUSTRY	2014 BUY PRICE OPINION	2014 HOLD PRICE OPINION	2014 SELL PRICE OPINION	2014 SHORT PRICE OPINION	2014 MYCROFT FREE CASH FLOW PER SHARE ESTIMATE	2014 MYCROFT FREE CASH FLOW RETURN ON TOTAL CAPITAL ESTIMATE (FROIC) >15% = Great	2014 MYCROFT CAPFLOW ESTIMATE <33% = Great BUT NO NEGATIVE RESULTS	2014 MYCROFT MICHAELIS GROWTH RATE ESTIMATE >15% = Great	DIVIDEND YIELD

Step #1 = Look up the company's current stock market price on the day of analysis and compare it to our 2014 Buy, Hold, Sell & Short Price.

Step #2 =Take the company's current market price; divide it by the "2014 Mycroft Free Cash Flow Per Share estimate." This gives the "Price to Free Cash Flow."

All results below are based on the 2014 year end estimates using the "2014 Mycroft Michaelis Growth Rate" and are good until December 31, 2014.

NAME	TICKER	INDUSTRY	BUY	HOLD	SELL	SHORT	FCF/SHARE	FROIC	CAPFLOW	MICHAELIS	DIV YIELD
Ryland Group, Inc.	RYL	Homebuilding	Negative Free Cash Flow	Negative Free Cash Flow	Negative Free Cash Flow	Negative Free Cash Flow	-$6.84	-17%	-5%	-17%	0.31%
Safeguard Scientifics, Inc.	SFE	Business Services	Negative Free Cash Flow	Negative Free Cash Flow	Negative Free Cash Flow	Negative Free Cash Flow	-$0.88	-6%	0%	-6%	0.00%
Safeway Inc.	SWY	Retail	$32.70	$65.40	$98.10	$196.20	$4.36	11%	42%	12%	3.01%
Saga Communications, Inc.	SGA	Entertainment	$33.53	$67.05	$100.58	$201.15	$4.47	13%	18%	13%	0.00%
Sagent Pharmaceuticals Co	SGNT	Drugs	$7.43	$14.85	$22.28	$44.55	$0.99	16%	10%	16%	0.00%
Saia, Inc.	SAIA	Transportation	Negative Free Cash Flow	Negative Free Cash Flow	Negative Free Cash Flow	Negative Free Cash Flow	-$0.18	-1%	105%	-1%	0.00%
SAIC, Inc.	SAI	Software	$13.73	$27.45	$41.18	$82.35	$1.83	15%	8%	14%	3.25%
Saks Incorporated	SKS	Retail	Negative Free Cash Flow	Negative Free Cash Flow	Negative Free Cash Flow	Negative Free Cash Flow	-$0.03	0%	103%	0%	0.00%
Salem Communications Corporation	SALM	Entertainment	$4.88	$9.75	$14.63	$29.25	$0.65	8%	50%	8%	2.45%
Salesforce.com, Inc.	CRM	Software	$9.08	$18.15	$27.23	$54.45	$1.21	21%	30%	21%	0.00%
Salix Pharmaceuticals, Ltd.	SLXP	Drugs	$15.53	$31.05	$46.58	$93.15	$2.07	8%	3%	8%	0.00%

NAME	TICKER	INDUSTRY	2014 BUY PRICE OPINION	2014 HOLD PRICE OPINION	2014 SELL PRICE OPINION	2014 SHORT PRICE OPINION	2014 MYCROFT FREE CASH FLOW PER SHARE ESTIMATE	2014 MYCROFT FREE CASH FLOW RETURN ON TOTAL CAPITAL ESTIMATE (FROIC) >15% = Great	2014 MYCROFT CAPFLOW ESTIMATE <33% = Great BUT NO NEGATIVE RESULTS	2014 MYCROFT MICHAELIS GROWTH RATE ESTIMATE >15% = Great	DIVIDEND YIELD
Step #1 = Look up the company's current stock market price on the day of analysis and compare it to our 2014 Buy, Hold, Sell & Short Price.												
Step #2 =Take the company's current market price; divide it by the "2014 Mycroft Free Cash Flow Per Share estimate." This gives the "Price to Free Cash Flow."												
All results below are based on the 2014 year end estimates using the "2014 Mycroft Michaelis Growth Rate" and are good until December 31, 2014.												
Sally Beauty Holdings Inc	SBH	Retail	$11.03	$22.05	$33.08	$66.15	$1.47	18%	30%	18%	0.00%
Sanchez Energy Corp	SN	Oil & Gas	Negative Free Cash Flow	Negative Free Cash Flow	Negative Free Cash Flow	Negative Free Cash Flow	-$14.67	-87%	707%	-87%	0.00%
Sanderson Farms, Inc.	SAFM	Consumer Goods	$45.38	$90.75	$136.13	$272.25	$6.05	16%	30%	15%	1.05%
SanDisk Corp	SNDK	Computers	$32.40	$64.80	$97.20	$194.40	$4.32	12%	28%	10%	1.48%
SandRidge Energy Inc	SD	Oil & Gas	Negative Free Cash Flow	Negative Free Cash Flow	Negative Free Cash Flow	Negative Free Cash Flow	-$2.25	-20%	247%	-20%	0.00%
Sangamo BioSciences, Inc.	SGMO	Biotech	Negative Free Cash Flow	Negative Free Cash Flow	Negative Free Cash Flow	Negative Free Cash Flow	-$0.35	-32%	-4%	-32%	0.00%
Sanmina Corp	SANM	Computers	$27.83	$55.65	$83.48	$166.95	$3.71	14%	22%	14%	0.00%
Santarus, Inc.	SNTS	Biotech	$8.63	$17.25	$25.88	$51.75	$1.15	29%	12%	29%	0.00%
Sapiens International Corporation	SPNS	Software	$3.00	$6.00	$9.00	$18.00	$0.40	12%	25%	12%	0.00%
Sapient Corporation	SAPE	Software	$7.20	$14.40	$21.60	$43.20	$0.96	21%	23%	21%	0.00%
Saratoga Resources, Inc.	SARA	Oil & Gas	Negative Free Cash Flow	Negative Free Cash Flow	Negative Free Cash Flow	Negative Free Cash Flow	-$0.95	-16%	326%	-16%	0.00%

NAME	TICKER	INDUSTRY	2014 BUY PRICE OPINION	2014 HOLD PRICE OPINION	2014 SELL PRICE OPINION	2014 SHORT PRICE OPINION	2014 MYCROFT FREE CASH FLOW PER SHARE ESTIMATE	2014 MYCROFT FREE CASH FLOW RETURN ON TOTAL CAPITAL ESTIMATE (FROIC) >15% = Great	2014 MYCROFT CAPFLOW ESTIMATE <33% = Great BUT NO NEGATIVE RESULTS	2014 MYCROFT MICHAELIS GROWTH RATE ESTIMATE >15% = Great	DIVIDEND YIELD
Step #1 = Look up the company's current stock market price on the day of analysis and compare it to our 2014 Buy, Hold, Sell & Short Price.											
Step #2 =Take the company's current market price; divide it by the "2014 Mycroft Free Cash Flow Per Share estimate." This gives the "Price to Free Cash Flow."											
All results below are based on the 2014 year end estimates using the "2014 Mycroft Michaelis Growth Rate" and are good until December 31, 2014.											
Sarepta Therapeutics Inc	SRPT	Biotech	Negative Free Cash Flow	Negative Free Cash Flow	Negative Free Cash Flow	Negative Free Cash Flow	-$1.31	-48%	-4%	-48%	0.00%
SBA Communications Corp	SBAC	Communication	$18.08	$36.15	$54.23	$108.45	$2.41	8%	32%	8%	0.00%
SCANA Corp	SCG	Utilities	Negative Free Cash Flow	Negative Free Cash Flow	Negative Free Cash Flow	Negative Free Cash Flow	-$0.85	-1%	113%	0%	4.50%
ScanSource	SCSC	Computers	$39.23	$78.45	$117.68	$235.35	$5.23	18%	4%	18%	0.00%
Schawk, Inc.	SGK	Business Services	$2.85	$5.70	$8.55	$17.10	$0.38	3%	63%	3%	2.42%
Schlumberger NV	SLB	Oil & Gas	$24.45	$48.90	$73.35	$146.70	$3.26	9%	54%	7%	1.44%
Schnitzer Steel Industries, Inc.	SCHN	Industrial	$5.70	$11.40	$17.10	$34.20	$0.76	1%	82%	3%	2.76%
Scholastic Corporation	SCHL	Publishing	$35.85	$71.70	$107.55	$215.10	$4.78	13%	29%	13%	1.67%
Schweitzer-Mauduit International, Inc.	SWM	Forest Products	$45.08	$90.15	$135.23	$270.45	$6.01	23%	13%	19%	1.97%
SciClone Pharmaceuticals	SCLN	Drugs	$2.10	$4.20	$6.30	$12.60	$0.28	9%	2%	9%	0.00%
Scientific Games Corporation	SGMS	Travel & Leisure	$0.15	$0.30	$0.45	$0.90	$0.02	0%	99%	0%	0.00%

NAME	TICKER	INDUSTRY	2014 BUY PRICE OPINION	2014 HOLD PRICE OPINION	2014 SELL PRICE OPINION	2014 SHORT PRICE OPINION	2014 MYCROFT FREE CASH FLOW PER SHARE ESTIMATE	2014 MYCROFT FREE CASH FLOW RETURN ON TOTAL CAPITAL ESTIMATE (FROIC) >15% = Great	2014 MYCROFT CAPFLOW ESTIMATE <33% = Great BUT NO NEGATIVE RESULTS	2014 MYCROFT MICHAELIS GROWTH RATE ESTIMATE >15% = Great	DIVIDEND YIELD
Step #1 = Look up the company's current stock market price on the day of analysis and compare it to our 2014 Buy, Hold, Sell & Short Price.											
Step #2 =Take the company's current market price; divide it by the "2014 Mycroft Free Cash Flow Per Share estimate." This gives the "Price to Free Cash Flow."											
All results below are based on the 2014 year end estimates using the "2014 Mycroft Michaelis Growth Rate" and are good until December 31, 2014.											
SciQuest, Inc.	SQI	Software	$4.28	$8.55	$12.83	$25.65	$0.57	16%	34%	16%	0.00%
Scorpio Tankers, Inc.	STNG	Transportation	Negative Free Cash Flow	Negative Free Cash Flow	Negative Free Cash Flow	Negative Free Cash Flow	-$2.57	-38%	-3278%	-39%	1.40%
Scotts Miracle Gro Co	SMG	Agriculture	$13.58	$27.15	$40.73	$81.45	$1.81	8%	40%	3%	3.19%
Scripps Networks Interactive Inc	SNI	Entertainment	$44.33	$88.65	$132.98	$265.95	$5.91	22%	10%	20%	0.81%
Seaboard Corporation	SEB	Consumer Goods	Negative Free Cash Flow	Negative Free Cash Flow	Negative Free Cash Flow	Negative Free Cash Flow	-$6.69	0%	105%	0%	0.00%
SeaChange International, Inc.	SEAC	Software	$6.08	$12.15	$18.23	$36.45	$0.81	12%	16%	12%	0.00%
Seacor Holdings Inc	CKH	Oil & Gas	Negative Free Cash Flow	Negative Free Cash Flow	Negative Free Cash Flow	Negative Free Cash Flow	-$8.75	-8%	208%	-8%	0.00%
Seadrill Ltd	SDRL	Oil & Gas	Negative Free Cash Flow	Negative Free Cash Flow	Negative Free Cash Flow	Negative Free Cash Flow	-$2.02	-6%	170%	-8%	5.90%
Sealed Air Corporation	SEE	Containers	$16.43	$32.85	$49.28	$98.55	$2.19	6%	21%	6%	1.73%
Sears Holdings Corporation	SHLD	Retail	Negative Free Cash Flow	Negative Free Cash Flow	Negative Free Cash Flow	Negative Free Cash Flow	-$12.02	-30%	-35%	-30%	0.00%
Sears Hometown & Outlet Stores Inc	SHOS	Retail	$24.08	$48.15	$72.23	$144.45	$3.21	11%	10%	11%	0.00%

NAME	TICKER	INDUSTRY	2014 BUY PRICE OPINION	2014 HOLD PRICE OPINION	2014 SELL PRICE OPINION	2014 SHORT PRICE OPINION	2014 MYCROFT FREE CASH FLOW PER SHARE ESTIMATE	2014 MYCROFT FREE CASH FLOW RETURN ON TOTAL CAPITAL ESTIMATE (FROIC) >15% = Great	2014 MYCROFT CAPFLOW ESTIMATE <33% = Great BUT NO NEGATIVE RESULTS	2014 MYCROFT MICHAELIS GROWTH RATE ESTIMATE >15% = Great	DIVIDEND YIELD
Step #1 = Look up the company's current stock market price on the day of analysis and compare it to our 2014 Buy, Hold, Sell & Short Price.											
Step #2 =Take the company's current market price; divide it by the "2014 Mycroft Free Cash Flow Per Share estimate." This gives the "Price to Free Cash Flow."											
All results below are based on the 2014 year end estimates using the "2014 Mycroft Michaelis Growth Rate" and are good until December 31, 2014.											
Seattle Genetics, Inc.	SGEN	Biotech	Negative Free Cash Flow	Negative Free Cash Flow	Negative Free Cash Flow	Negative Free Cash Flow	-$0.23	-12%	-150%	-12%	0.00%
SeaWorld Entertainment Inc	SEAS	Travel & Leisure	$8.03	$16.05	$24.08	$48.15	$1.07	4%	63%	4%	2.79%
Select Comfort Corporation	SCSS	Apparel & Furniture	$4.13	$8.25	$12.38	$24.75	$0.55	13%	71%	13%	0.00%
Select Medical Holdings Corporation	SEM	Health Care	$7.80	$15.60	$23.40	$46.80	$1.04	6%	34%	9%	4.90%
Semgroup Corp	SEMG	Oil & Gas	Negative Free Cash Flow	Negative Free Cash Flow	Negative Free Cash Flow	Negative Free Cash Flow	-$0.59	-2%	123%	-4%	1.48%
Sempra Energy	SRE	Utilities	Negative Free Cash Flow	Negative Free Cash Flow	Negative Free Cash Flow	Negative Free Cash Flow	-$5.48	-6%	168%	-6%	3.00%
Semtech Corporation	SMTC	Semiconductors	$13.20	$26.40	$39.60	$79.20	$1.76	10%	27%	10%	0.00%
Seneca Foods Corp. Class A	SENEA	Consumer Goods	$4.05	$8.10	$12.15	$24.30	$0.54	1%	66%	1%	0.00%
Senomyx, Inc.	SNMX	Chemicals	Negative Free Cash Flow	Negative Free Cash Flow	Negative Free Cash Flow	Negative Free Cash Flow	-$0.27	-49%	-5%	-49%	0.00%
Sensient Technologies Corporation	SXT	Chemicals	$7.50	$15.00	$22.50	$45.00	$1.00	3%	69%	2%	2.11%
Service Corporation International, Inc.	SCI	Services	$12.53	$25.05	$37.58	$75.15	$1.67	10%	26%	10%	1.52%

NAME	TICKER	INDUSTRY	2014 BUY PRICE OPINION	2014 HOLD PRICE OPINION	2014 SELL PRICE OPINION	2014 SHORT PRICE OPINION	2014 MYCROFT FREE CASH FLOW PER SHARE ESTIMATE	2014 MYCROFT FREE CASH FLOW RETURN ON TOTAL CAPITAL ESTIMATE (FROIC) >15% = Great	2014 MYCROFT CAPFLOW ESTIMATE <33% = Great BUT NO NEGATIVE RESULTS	2014 MYCROFT MICHAELIS GROWTH RATE ESTIMATE >15% = Great	DIVIDEND YIELD
Step #1 = Look up the company's current stock market price on the day of analysis and compare it to our 2014 Buy, Hold, Sell & Short Price.										
Step #2 =Take the company's current market price; divide it by the "2014 Mycroft Free Cash Flow Per Share estimate." This gives the "Price to Free Cash Flow."										
All results below are based on the 2014 year end estimates using the "2014 Mycroft Michaelis Growth Rate" and are good until December 31, 2014.										
ServiceNow Inc	NOW	Software	$0.38	$0.75	$1.13	$2.25	$0.05	2%	87%	2%	0.00%
ServiceSource International Inc	SREV	Software	$0.08	$0.15	$0.23	$0.45	$0.01	1%	92%	1%	0.00%
Shenandoah Telecommunications Co	SHEN	Communication	Negative Free Cash Flow	Negative Free Cash Flow	Negative Free Cash Flow	Negative Free Cash Flow	-$0.02	0%	101%	0%	1.83%
Sherwin-Williams Company	SHW	Chemicals	$73.28	$146.55	$219.83	$439.65	$9.77	33%	16%	26%	1.13%
SHFL Entertainment Inc	SHFL	Travel & Leisure	$4.65	$9.30	$13.95	$27.90	$0.62	10%	36%	10%	0.00%
Shiloh Industries, Inc.	SHLO	Autos	$3.98	$7.95	$11.93	$23.85	$0.53	6%	74%	6%	0.00%
Ship Finance International Ltd	SFL	Transportation	Negative Free Cash Flow	Negative Free Cash Flow	Negative Free Cash Flow	Negative Free Cash Flow	-$0.44	-1%	131%	4%	9.90%
Shoe Carnival	SCVL	Retail	Negative Free Cash Flow	Negative Free Cash Flow	Negative Free Cash Flow	Negative Free Cash Flow	-$1.47	-10%	-432%	-11%	0.90%
ShoreTel, Inc.	SHOR	Communication	Negative Free Cash Flow	Negative Free Cash Flow	Negative Free Cash Flow	Negative Free Cash Flow	-$0.11	-4%	237%	-4%	0.00%
Shutterfly, Inc.	SFLY	Services	$11.33	$22.65	$33.98	$67.95	$1.51	7%	55%	7%	0.00%
Shutterstock Inc	SSTK	Business Services	$12.75	$25.50	$38.25	$76.50	$1.70	42%	9%	42%	0.00%

NAME	TICKER	INDUSTRY	2014 BUY PRICE OPINION	2014 HOLD PRICE OPINION	2014 SELL PRICE OPINION	2014 SHORT PRICE OPINION	2014 MYCROFT FREE CASH FLOW PER SHARE ESTIMATE	2014 MYCROFT FREE CASH FLOW RETURN ON TOTAL CAPITAL ESTIMATE (FROIC) >15% = Great	2014 MYCROFT CAPFLOW ESTIMATE <33% = Great BUT NO NEGATIVE RESULTS	2014 MYCROFT MICHAELIS GROWTH RATE ESTIMATE >15% = Great	DIVIDEND YIELD
Step #1 = Look up the company's current stock market price on the day of analysis and compare it to our 2014 Buy, Hold, Sell & Short Price.											
Step #2 =Take the company's current market price; divide it by the "2014 Mycroft Free Cash Flow Per Share estimate." This gives the "Price to Free Cash Flow."											
All results below are based on the 2014 year end estimates using the "2014 Mycroft Michaelis Growth Rate" and are good until December 31, 2014.											
Sifco Industries, Inc.	SIF	Industrial	$4.73	$9.45	$14.18	$28.35	$0.63	4%	59%	4%	0.00%
Siga Technologies, Inc.	SIGA	Drugs	Negative Free Cash Flow	Negative Free Cash Flow	Negative Free Cash Flow	Negative Free Cash Flow	-$0.29	-64%	-5%	-64%	0.00%
Sigma Designs, Inc.	SIGM	Semiconductors	Negative Free Cash Flow	Negative Free Cash Flow	Negative Free Cash Flow	Negative Free Cash Flow	-$0.66	-14%	-976%	-14%	0.00%
Sigma-Aldrich Corporation	SIAL	Chemicals	$36.08	$72.15	$108.23	$216.45	$4.81	17%	17%	15%	1.01%
Signet Jewelers Ltd	SIG	Retail	$11.78	$23.55	$35.33	$70.65	$1.57	5%	52%	4%	0.87%
Silgan Holdings, Inc.	SLGN	Containers	$36.60	$73.20	$109.80	$219.60	$4.88	13%	29%	13%	1.17%
Silicon Graphics International Corp	SGI	Computers	$24.90	$49.80	$74.70	$149.40	$3.32	56%	5%	56%	0.00%
Silicon Image, Inc.	SIMG	Semiconductors	$2.55	$5.10	$7.65	$15.30	$0.34	13%	29%	13%	0.00%
Silicon Laboratories, Inc.	SLAB	Semiconductors	$3.30	$6.60	$9.90	$19.80	$0.44	3%	85%	3%	0.00%
Simpson Manufacturing	SSD	Industrial	$8.03	$16.05	$24.08	$48.15	$1.07	6%	29%	5%	1.56%
Simulations Plus, Inc.	SLP	Software	$0.60	$1.20	$1.80	$3.60	$0.08	9%	45%	-1%	2.51%

NAME	TICKER	INDUSTRY	2014 BUY PRICE OPINION	2014 HOLD PRICE OPINION	2014 SELL PRICE OPINION	2014 SHORT PRICE OPINION	2014 MYCROFT FREE CASH FLOW PER SHARE ESTIMATE	2014 MYCROFT FREE CASH FLOW RETURN ON TOTAL CAPITAL ESTIMATE (FROIC) >15% = Great	2014 MYCROFT CAPFLOW ESTIMATE <33% = Great BUT NO NEGATIVE RESULTS	2014 MYCROFT MICHAELIS GROWTH RATE ESTIMATE >15% = Great	DIVIDEND YIELD
Step #1 = Look up the company's current stock market price on the day of analysis and compare it to our 2014 Buy, Hold, Sell & Short Price.											
Step #2 =Take the company's current market price; divide it by the "2014 Mycroft Free Cash Flow Per Share estimate." This gives the "Price to Free Cash Flow."											
All results below are based on the 2014 year end estimates using the "2014 Mycroft Michaelis Growth Rate" and are good until December 31, 2014.											
Sinclair Broadcast Group, Inc.	SBGI	Entertainment	$15.75	$31.50	$47.25	$94.50	$2.10	43%	23%	29%	2.09%
Sirius XM Radio Inc.	SIRI	Entertainment	$1.20	$2.40	$3.60	$7.20	$0.16	15%	12%	15%	0.00%
Sirona Dental Systems, Inc.	SIRO	Medical	$29.03	$58.05	$87.08	$174.15	$3.87	16%	23%	16%	0.00%
Six Flags Entertainment Corp	SIX	Travel & Leisure	$23.78	$47.55	$71.33	$142.65	$3.17	20%	28%	13%	5.40%
SJW Corporation	SJW	Utilities	Negative Free Cash Flow	Negative Free Cash Flow	Negative Free Cash Flow	Negative Free Cash Flow	-$1.78	-6%	151%	-5%	2.75%
Skechers USA, Inc.	SKX	Apparel & Furniture	Negative Free Cash Flow	Negative Free Cash Flow	Negative Free Cash Flow	Negative Free Cash Flow	-$1.20	-6%	-360%	-6%	0.00%
Skilled Healthcare Group, Inc.	SKH	Health Care	$4.80	$9.60	$14.40	$28.80	$0.64	4%	43%	4%	0.00%
Skullcandy, Inc.	SKUL	Computers	$8.03	$16.05	$24.08	$48.15	$1.07	18%	25%	18%	0.00%
Skyline Corporation	SKY	Homebuilding	Negative Free Cash Flow	Negative Free Cash Flow	Negative Free Cash Flow	Negative Free Cash Flow	-$1.68	-31%	-1%	-31%	0.00%
SkyWest, Inc.	SKYW	Airlines	$31.28	$62.55	$93.83	$187.65	$4.17	7%	35%	8%	1.14%
Skyworks Solutions, Inc.	SWKS	Semiconductors	$12.60	$25.20	$37.80	$75.60	$1.68	14%	30%	14%	0.00%

NAME	TICKER	INDUSTRY	2014 BUY PRICE OPINION	2014 HOLD PRICE OPINION	2014 SELL PRICE OPINION	2014 SHORT PRICE OPINION	2014 MYCROFT FREE CASH FLOW PER SHARE ESTIMATE	2014 MYCROFT FREE CASH FLOW RETURN ON TOTAL CAPITAL ESTIMATE (FROIC) >15% = Great	2014 MYCROFT CAPFLOW ESTIMATE <33% = Great BUT NO NEGATIVE RESULTS	2014 MYCROFT MICHAELIS GROWTH RATE ESTIMATE >15% = Great	DIVIDEND YIELD
Step #1 = Look up the company's current stock market price on the day of analysis and compare it to our 2014 Buy, Hold, Sell & Short Price.										
Step #2 =Take the company's current market price; divide it by the "2014 Mycroft Free Cash Flow Per Share estimate." This gives the "Price to Free Cash Flow."										
All results below are based on the 2014 year end estimates using the "2014 Mycroft Michaelis Growth Rate" and are good until December 31, 2014.										
SL Industries, Inc.	SLI	Computers	Negative Free Cash Flow	Negative Free Cash Flow	Negative Free Cash Flow	Negative Free Cash Flow	-$0.06	0%	110%	0%	0.00%
SM Energy Co	SM	Oil & Gas	Negative Free Cash Flow	Negative Free Cash Flow	Negative Free Cash Flow	Negative Free Cash Flow	-$7.29	-18%	144%	-18%	0.13%
SmartPros Ltd.	SPRO	Education	$0.23	$0.45	$0.68	$1.35	$0.03	2%	81%	2%	3.51%
Smith & Wesson Holding Corporation	SWHC	Aerospace & Defense	$9.08	$18.15	$27.23	$54.45	$1.21	25%	44%	25%	0.00%
Smithfield Foods, Inc.	SFD	Consumer Goods	Negative Free Cash Flow	Negative Free Cash Flow	Negative Free Cash Flow	Negative Free Cash Flow	-$1.26	-6%	247%	-6%	0.00%
Snap-on, Inc.	SNA	Industrial	$40.20	$80.40	$120.60	$241.20	$5.36	10%	20%	9%	1.54%
Snyders-Lance, Inc.	LNCE	Consumer Goods	$3.00	$6.00	$9.00	$18.00	$0.40	3%	76%	1%	2.23%
SolarCity Corp	SCTY	Semiconductors	Negative Free Cash Flow	Negative Free Cash Flow	Negative Free Cash Flow	Negative Free Cash Flow	-$4.94	-151%	313%	-151%	0.00%
SolarWinds, Inc.	SWI	Software	$19.80	$39.60	$59.40	$118.80	$2.64	33%	3%	33%	0.00%
Solazyme Inc	SZYM	Oil & Gas	Negative Free Cash Flow	Negative Free Cash Flow	Negative Free Cash Flow	Negative Free Cash Flow	-$1.20	-48%	-10%	-48%	0.00%
Solera Holdings, Inc.	SLH	Software	$22.05	$44.10	$66.15	$132.30	$2.94	10%	18%	9%	1.28%

NAME	TICKER	INDUSTRY	2014 BUY PRICE OPINION	2014 HOLD PRICE OPINION	2014 SELL PRICE OPINION	2014 SHORT PRICE OPINION	2014 MYCROFT FREE CASH FLOW PER SHARE ESTIMATE	2014 MYCROFT FREE CASH FLOW RETURN ON TOTAL CAPITAL ESTIMATE (FROIC) >15% = Great	2014 MYCROFT CAPFLOW ESTIMATE <33% = Great BUT NO NEGATIVE RESULTS	2014 MYCROFT MICHAELIS GROWTH RATE ESTIMATE >15% = Great	DIVIDEND YIELD
Step #1 = Look up the company's current stock market price on the day of analysis and compare it to our 2014 Buy, Hold, Sell & Short Price.											
Step #2 =Take the company's current market price; divide it by the "2014 Mycroft Free Cash Flow Per Share estimate." This gives the "Price to Free Cash Flow."											
All results below are based on the 2014 year end estimates using the "2014 Mycroft Michaelis Growth Rate" and are good until December 31, 2014.											
Solitario Exploration & Royalty Corp	XPL	Commodities	Negative Free Cash Flow	Negative Free Cash Flow	Negative Free Cash Flow	Negative Free Cash Flow	-$0.17	-93%	-101%	-93%	0.00%
Solta Medical, Inc.	SLTM	Medical	Negative Free Cash Flow	Negative Free Cash Flow	Negative Free Cash Flow	Negative Free Cash Flow	-$0.19	-10%	-24%	-10%	0.00%
Sonic Automotive Inc	SAH	Autos	Negative Free Cash Flow	Negative Free Cash Flow	Negative Free Cash Flow	Negative Free Cash Flow	-$2.64	-13%	1383%	-13%	0.41%
Sonic Corporation	SONC	Restaurants	$6.90	$13.80	$20.70	$41.40	$0.92	9%	46%	9%	0.00%
Sonoco Products Company	SON	Containers	$24.38	$48.75	$73.13	$146.25	$3.25	11%	41%	9%	3.20%
Sonus Networks, Inc.	SONS	Communication	Negative Free Cash Flow	Negative Free Cash Flow	Negative Free Cash Flow	Negative Free Cash Flow	-$0.02	-1%	203%	-1%	0.00%
Sothebys Class A	BID	Retail	$28.35	$56.70	$85.05	$170.10	$3.78	17%	8%	15%	0.83%
Sourcefire, Inc.	FIRE	Software	$8.63	$17.25	$25.88	$51.75	$1.15	12%	22%	12%	0.00%
South Jersey Industries	SJI	Utilities	Negative Free Cash Flow	Negative Free Cash Flow	Negative Free Cash Flow	Negative Free Cash Flow	-$3.79	-9%	198%	-10%	3.08%
Southern Co	SO	Utilities	$0.30	$0.60	$0.90	$1.80	$0.04	0%	99%	0%	5.00%
Southern Copper Corporation	SCCO	Commodities	$4.20	$8.40	$12.60	$25.20	$0.56	6%	75%	2%	1.66%

NAME	TICKER	INDUSTRY	2014 BUY PRICE OPINION	2014 HOLD PRICE OPINION	2014 SELL PRICE OPINION	2014 SHORT PRICE OPINION	2014 MYCROFT FREE CASH FLOW PER SHARE ESTIMATE	2014 MYCROFT FREE CASH FLOW RETURN ON TOTAL CAPITAL ESTIMATE (FROIC) >15% = Great	2014 MYCROFT CAPFLOW ESTIMATE <33% = Great BUT NO NEGATIVE RESULTS	2014 MYCROFT MICHAELIS GROWTH RATE ESTIMATE >15% = Great	DIVIDEND YIELD
Step #1 = Look up the company's current stock market price on the day of analysis and compare it to our 2014 Buy, Hold, Sell & Short Price.												
Step #2 =Take the company's current market price; divide it by the "2014 Mycroft Free Cash Flow Per Share estimate." This gives the "Price to Free Cash Flow."												
All results below are based on the 2014 year end estimates using the "2014 Mycroft Michaelis Growth Rate" and are good until December 31, 2014.												
Southwest Airlines Co	LUV	Airlines	$10.73	$21.45	$32.18	$64.35	$1.43	9%	62%	9%	1.16%
Southwest Gas Corporation	SWX	Utilities	Negative Free Cash Flow	Negative Free Cash Flow	Negative Free Cash Flow	Negative Free Cash Flow	-$0.67	-1%	109%	-1%	2.82%
Southwestern Energy Company	SWN	Oil & Gas	Negative Free Cash Flow	Negative Free Cash Flow	Negative Free Cash Flow	Negative Free Cash Flow	-$1.28	-9%	126%	-9%	0.00%
Spanish Broadcasting System Inc	SBSA	Entertainment	$6.30	$12.60	$18.90	$37.80	$0.84	2%	26%	2%	0.00%
Spansion Inc	CODE	Semiconductors	$7.28	$14.55	$21.83	$43.65	$0.97	5%	47%	5%	0.00%
Spark Networks, Inc.	LOV	Services	Negative Free Cash Flow	Negative Free Cash Flow	Negative Free Cash Flow	Negative Free Cash Flow	-$0.38	-46%	-34%	-46%	0.00%
Spartan Motors	SPAR	Truck Manufacturing	Negative Free Cash Flow	Negative Free Cash Flow	Negative Free Cash Flow	Negative Free Cash Flow	-$0.50	-9%	-132%	-10%	1.65%
Spartan Stores, Inc.	SPTN	Retail	$15.75	$31.50	$47.25	$94.50	$2.10	12%	52%	12%	1.73%
Sparton Corporation	SPA	Computers	Negative Free Cash Flow	Negative Free Cash Flow	Negative Free Cash Flow	Negative Free Cash Flow	-$0.09	-1%	132%	-1%	0.00%
Spectra Energy Corp	SE	Oil & Gas	Negative Free Cash Flow	Negative Free Cash Flow	Negative Free Cash Flow	Negative Free Cash Flow	-$0.32	-1%	111%	-2%	3.68%
Spectranetics Corporation	SPNC	Medical	$0.38	$0.75	$1.13	$2.25	$0.05	1%	60%	1%	0.00%

NAME	TICKER	INDUSTRY	2014 BUY PRICE OPINION	2014 HOLD PRICE OPINION	2014 SELL PRICE OPINION	2014 SHORT PRICE OPINION	2014 MYCROFT FREE CASH FLOW PER SHARE ESTIMATE	2014 MYCROFT FREE CASH FLOW RETURN ON TOTAL CAPITAL ESTIMATE (FROIC) >15% = Great	2014 MYCROFT CAPFLOW ESTIMATE <33% = Great BUT NO NEGATIVE RESULTS	2014 MYCROFT MICHAELIS GROWTH RATE ESTIMATE >15% = Great	DIVIDEND YIELD
Step #1 = Look up the company's current stock market price on the day of analysis and compare it to our 2014 Buy, Hold, Sell & Short Price.											
Step #2 =Take the company's current market price; divide it by the "2014 Mycroft Free Cash Flow Per Share estimate." This gives the "Price to Free Cash Flow."											
All results below are based on the 2014 year end estimates using the "2014 Mycroft Michaelis Growth Rate" and are good until December 31, 2014.											
Spectrum Brands Holdings Inc	SPB	Apparel & Furniture	$27.83	$55.65	$83.48	$166.95	$3.71	7%	24%	6%	1.50%
Spectrum Pharmaceuticals Inc	SPPI	Biotech	$3.98	$7.95	$11.93	$23.85	$0.53	11%	0%	11%	0.00%
Speedway Motorsports Inc	TRK	Travel & Leisure	$17.33	$34.65	$51.98	$103.95	$2.31	7%	14%	8%	3.20%
Spirit AeroSystems Holdings, Inc.	SPR	Aerospace & Defense	$7.95	$15.90	$23.85	$47.70	$1.06	5%	66%	5%	0.00%
Spirit Airlines Inc	SAVE	Airlines	$14.55	$29.10	$43.65	$87.30	$1.94	18%	21%	18%	0.00%
Splunk Inc	SPLK	Software	$3.98	$7.95	$11.93	$23.85	$0.53	20%	15%	20%	0.00%
Sprint Corp	S	Communication	Negative Free Cash Flow	Negative Free Cash Flow	Negative Free Cash Flow	Negative Free Cash Flow	-$0.69	-9%	189%	-9%	0.00%
SPS Commerce, Inc.	SPSC	Software	$2.63	$5.25	$7.88	$15.75	$0.35	4%	54%	4%	0.00%
SPX Corporation	SPW	Industrial	Negative Free Cash Flow	Negative Free Cash Flow	Negative Free Cash Flow	Negative Free Cash Flow	-$2.29	-3%	-440%	-3%	1.24%
SS&C Technologies Holdings	SSNC	Software	$14.48	$28.95	$43.43	$86.85	$1.93	7%	13%	7%	0.00%
St Jude Medical, Inc.	STJ	Medical	$25.20	$50.40	$75.60	$151.20	$3.36	13%	24%	11%	1.89%

NAME	TICKER	INDUSTRY	2014 BUY PRICE OPINION	2014 HOLD PRICE OPINION	2014 SELL PRICE OPINION	2014 SHORT PRICE OPINION	2014 MYCROFT FREE CASH FLOW PER SHARE ESTIMATE	2014 MYCROFT FREE CASH FLOW RETURN ON TOTAL CAPITAL ESTIMATE (FROIC) >15% = Great	2014 MYCROFT CAPFLOW ESTIMATE <33% = Great BUT NO NEGATIVE RESULTS	2014 MYCROFT MICHAELIS GROWTH RATE ESTIMATE >15% = Great	DIVIDEND YIELD
Step #1 = Look up the company's current stock market price on the day of analysis and compare it to our 2014 Buy, Hold, Sell & Short Price.											
Step #2 =Take the company's current market price; divide it by the "2014 Mycroft Free Cash Flow Per Share estimate." This gives the "Price to Free Cash Flow."											
All results below are based on the 2014 year end estimates using the "2014 Mycroft Michaelis Growth Rate" and are good until December 31, 2014.											
St. Joe Corporation	JOE	Real Estate	$1.88	$3.75	$5.63	$11.25	$0.25	4%	9%	4%	0.00%
Staar Surgical	STAA	Medical	Negative Free Cash Flow	Negative Free Cash Flow	Negative Free Cash Flow	Negative Free Cash Flow	-$0.03	-3%	147%	-3%	0.00%
Stage Stores, Inc.	SSI	Retail	Negative Free Cash Flow	Negative Free Cash Flow	Negative Free Cash Flow	Negative Free Cash Flow	-$0.87	-6%	201%	-6%	2.53%
Stamps.com, Inc.	STMP	Retail	$15.38	$30.75	$46.13	$92.25	$2.05	20%	22%	20%	0.00%
Standard Motor Products	SMP	Autos	$17.63	$35.25	$52.88	$105.75	$2.35	14%	20%	13%	1.44%
Standard Pacific Corp	SPF	Homebuilding	Negative Free Cash Flow	Negative Free Cash Flow	Negative Free Cash Flow	Negative Free Cash Flow	-$1.21	-12%	0%	-12%	0.00%
Standard Parking Corporation	STAN	Business Services	Negative Free Cash Flow	Negative Free Cash Flow	Negative Free Cash Flow	Negative Free Cash Flow	-$0.16	-1%	141%	-1%	0.00%
Standard Register Company	SR	Industrial	$11.85	$23.70	$35.55	$71.10	$1.58	-22%	46%	-22%	0.00%
Standex International Corporation	SXI	Industrial	$30.38	$60.75	$91.13	$182.25	$4.05	13%	24%	13%	0.57%
Stanley Black & Decker Inc	SWK	Industrial	$16.95	$33.90	$50.85	$101.70	$2.26	4%	52%	3%	2.24%
Stanley Furniture Company Inc.	STLY	Apparel & Furniture	Negative Free Cash Flow	Negative Free Cash Flow	Negative Free Cash Flow	Negative Free Cash Flow	-$1.48	-26%	-25%	-26%	0.00%

NAME	TICKER	INDUSTRY	2014 BUY PRICE OPINION	2014 HOLD PRICE OPINION	2014 SELL PRICE OPINION	2014 SHORT PRICE OPINION	2014 MYCROFT FREE CASH FLOW PER SHARE ESTIMATE	2014 MYCROFT FREE CASH FLOW RETURN ON TOTAL CAPITAL ESTIMATE (FROIC) >15% = Great	2014 MYCROFT CAPFLOW ESTIMATE <33% = Great BUT NO NEGATIVE RESULTS	2014 MYCROFT MICHAELIS GROWTH RATE ESTIMATE >15% = Great	DIVIDEND YIELD
Step #1 = Look up the company's current stock market price on the day of analysis and compare it to our 2014 Buy, Hold, Sell & Short Price.											
Step #2 =Take the company's current market price; divide it by the "2014 Mycroft Free Cash Flow Per Share estimate." This gives the "Price to Free Cash Flow."											
All results below are based on the 2014 year end estimates using the "2014 Mycroft Michaelis Growth Rate" and are good until December 31, 2014.											
Staples, Inc.	SPLS	Retail	$12.23	$24.45	$36.68	$73.35	$1.63	13%	27%	12%	3.26%
Star Scientific, Inc.	STSI	Drugs	Negative Free Cash Flow	Negative Free Cash Flow	Negative Free Cash Flow	Negative Free Cash Flow	-$0.10	-173%	0%	-173%	0.00%
Starbucks Corporation	SBUX	Restaurants	$17.78	$35.55	$53.33	$106.65	$2.37	24%	42%	16%	1.11%
StarTek, Inc.	SRT	Business Services	Negative Free Cash Flow	Negative Free Cash Flow	Negative Free Cash Flow	Negative Free Cash Flow	-$0.28	-7%	248%	-7%	0.00%
Starwood Hotels & Resorts Worldwide Inc	HOT	Travel & Leisure	$35.33	$70.65	$105.98	$211.95	$4.71	15%	30%	12%	1.82%
Starz Class A	STRZA	Entertainment	$34.95	$69.90	$104.85	$209.70	$4.66	54%	5%	54%	0.00%
STEC, Inc.	STEC	Computers	Negative Free Cash Flow	Negative Free Cash Flow	Negative Free Cash Flow	Negative Free Cash Flow	-$1.50	-40%	-11%	-40%	0.00%
Steel Dynamics Inc	STLD	Steel	$5.93	$11.85	$17.78	$35.55	$0.79	4%	56%	4%	2.62%
Steelcase, Inc.	SCS	Industrial	$6.75	$13.50	$20.25	$40.50	$0.90	11%	45%	8%	2.68%
Stein Mart	SMRT	Retail	$0.75	$1.50	$2.25	$4.50	$0.10	2%	90%	0%	1.53%
Steiner Leisure Ltd	STNR	Services	$50.18	$100.35	$150.53	$301.05	$6.69	16%	23%	16%	0.00%

NAME	TICKER	INDUSTRY	2014 BUY PRICE OPINION	2014 HOLD PRICE OPINION	2014 SELL PRICE OPINION	2014 SHORT PRICE OPINION	2014 MYCROFT FREE CASH FLOW PER SHARE ESTIMATE	2014 MYCROFT FREE CASH FLOW RETURN ON TOTAL CAPITAL ESTIMATE (FROIC) >15% = Great	2014 MYCROFT CAPFLOW ESTIMATE <33% = Great BUT NO NEGATIVE RESULTS	2014 MYCROFT MICHAELIS GROWTH RATE ESTIMATE >15% = Great	DIVIDEND YIELD
Steinway Musical Instruments, Inc.	LVB	Travel & Leisure	$17.33	$34.65	$51.98	$103.95	$2.31	8%	19%	8%	0.00%
StemCells, Inc.	STEM	Biotech	Negative Free Cash Flow	Negative Free Cash Flow	Negative Free Cash Flow	Negative Free Cash Flow	-$0.53	-246%	-13%	-246%	0.00%
Stemline Therapeutics Inc	STML	Biotech	Negative Free Cash Flow	Negative Free Cash Flow	Negative Free Cash Flow	Negative Free Cash Flow	-$0.80	-11%	0%	-11%	0.00%
Stepan Company	SCL	Chemicals	$10.35	$20.70	$31.05	$62.10	$1.38	4%	74%	3%	1.13%
Stericycle, Inc.	SRCL	Waste Management	$29.55	$59.10	$88.65	$177.30	$3.94	11%	18%	11%	0.00%
Steris Corporation	STE	Medical	$14.33	$28.65	$42.98	$85.95	$1.91	9%	47%	7%	1.98%
Sterling Construction Company, Inc.	STRL	Engineering	Negative Free Cash Flow	Negative Free Cash Flow	Negative Free Cash Flow	Negative Free Cash Flow	-$3.09	-27%	-104%	-27%	0.00%
Steven Madden	SHOO	Apparel & Furniture	$28.28	$56.55	$84.83	$169.65	$3.77	22%	14%	22%	0.00%
Stewart Enterprises, Inc.	STEI	Services	$5.70	$11.40	$17.10	$34.20	$0.76	8%	30%	7%	1.37%
Stillwater Mining Company	SWC	Commodities	Negative Free Cash Flow	Negative Free Cash Flow	Negative Free Cash Flow	Negative Free Cash Flow	-$0.27	-3%	140%	-3%	0.00%
Stone Energy Corporation	SGY	Oil & Gas	Negative Free Cash Flow	Negative Free Cash Flow	Negative Free Cash Flow	Negative Free Cash Flow	-$1.54	-4%	114%	-4%	0.00%

Step #1 = Look up the company's current stock market price on the day of analysis and compare it to our 2014 Buy, Hold, Sell & Short Price.

Step #2 =Take the company's current market price; divide it by the "2014 Mycroft Free Cash Flow Per Share estimate." This gives the "Price to Free Cash Flow."

All results below are based on the 2014 year end estimates using the "2014 Mycroft Michaelis Growth Rate" and are good until December 31, 2014.

NAME	TICKER	INDUSTRY	2014 BUY PRICE OPINION	2014 HOLD PRICE OPINION	2014 SELL PRICE OPINION	2014 SHORT PRICE OPINION	2014 MYCROFT FREE CASH FLOW PER SHARE ESTIMATE	2014 MYCROFT FREE CASH FLOW RETURN ON TOTAL CAPITAL ESTIMATE (FROIC) >15% = Great	2014 MYCROFT CAPFLOW ESTIMATE <33% = Great BUT NO NEGATIVE RESULTS	2014 MYCROFT MICHAELIS GROWTH RATE ESTIMATE >15% = Great	DIVIDEND YIELD
Step #1 = Look up the company's current stock market price on the day of analysis and compare it to our 2014 Buy, Hold, Sell & Short Price.											
Step #2 =Take the company's current market price; divide it by the "2014 Mycroft Free Cash Flow Per Share estimate." This gives the "Price to Free Cash Flow."											
All results below are based on the 2014 year end estimates using the "2014 Mycroft Michaelis Growth Rate" and are good until December 31, 2014.											
Stoneridge, Inc.	SRI	Autos	$12.08	$24.15	$36.23	$72.45	$1.61	12%	36%	12%	0.00%
STR Holdings, Inc.	STRI	Autos	Negative Free Cash Flow	Negative Free Cash Flow	Negative Free Cash Flow	Negative Free Cash Flow	-$0.01	0%	120%	0%	0.00%
Stratasys Ltd	SSYS	Computers	Negative Free Cash Flow	Negative Free Cash Flow	Negative Free Cash Flow	Negative Free Cash Flow	-$0.71	-2%	-143%	-2%	0.00%
Strategic Diagnostics, Inc.	SDIX	Biotech	Negative Free Cash Flow	Negative Free Cash Flow	Negative Free Cash Flow	Negative Free Cash Flow	-$0.27	-25%	-20%	-25%	0.00%
Strattec Security Corporation	STRT	Autos	$7.05	$14.10	$21.15	$42.30	$0.94	3%	80%	3%	1.16%
Strayer Education, Inc.	STRA	Education	$77.93	$155.85	$233.78	$467.55	$10.39	59%	22%	59%	0.00%
Streamline Health Solutions, Inc.	STRM	Software	Negative Free Cash Flow	Negative Free Cash Flow	Negative Free Cash Flow	Negative Free Cash Flow	-$0.52	-47%	-53%	-47%	0.00%
Stryker Corporation	SYK	Medical	$34.73	$69.45	$104.18	$208.35	$4.63	15%	12%	13%	1.52%
Sturm, Ruger & Company	RGR	Aerospace & Defense	$43.43	$86.85	$130.28	$260.55	$5.79	63%	28%	31%	4.00%
Sucampo Pharmaceuticals, Inc. Class A	SCMP	Drugs	$0.90	$1.80	$2.70	$5.40	$0.12	6%	6%	6%	0.00%
Sun Hydraulics Corp	SNHY	Industrial	$11.10	$22.20	$33.30	$66.60	$1.48	20%	35%	15%	1.06%

NAME	TICKER	INDUSTRY	2014 BUY PRICE OPINION	2014 HOLD PRICE OPINION	2014 SELL PRICE OPINION	2014 SHORT PRICE OPINION	2014 MYCROFT FREE CASH FLOW PER SHARE ESTIMATE	2014 MYCROFT FREE CASH FLOW RETURN ON TOTAL CAPITAL ESTIMATE (FROIC) >15% = Great	2014 MYCROFT CAPFLOW ESTIMATE <33% = Great BUT NO NEGATIVE RESULTS	2014 MYCROFT MICHAELIS GROWTH RATE ESTIMATE >15% = Great	DIVIDEND YIELD
Step #1 = Look up the company's current stock market price on the day of analysis and compare it to our 2014 Buy, Hold, Sell & Short Price.											
Step #2 =Take the company's current market price; divide it by the "2014 Mycroft Free Cash Flow Per Share estimate." This gives the "Price to Free Cash Flow."											
All results below are based on the 2014 year end estimates using the "2014 Mycroft Michaelis Growth Rate" and are good until December 31, 2014.											
SunCoke Energy Inc	SXC	Steel	$9.98	$19.95	$29.93	$59.85	$1.33	7%	58%	7%	0.00%
SunEdison Inc	SUNE	Semiconductors	Negative Free Cash Flow	Negative Free Cash Flow	Negative Free Cash Flow	Negative Free Cash Flow	-$2.70	-70%	-244%	-70%	0.00%
Sunesis Pharmaceuticals Inc	SNSS	Biotech	Negative Free Cash Flow	Negative Free Cash Flow	Negative Free Cash Flow	Negative Free Cash Flow	-$0.28	-508%	0%	-508%	0.00%
SunPower Corporation	SPWR	Semiconductors	$12.53	$25.05	$37.58	$75.15	$1.67	10%	29%	10%	0.00%
Super Micro Computer, Inc.	SMCI	Communication	$0.15	$0.30	$0.45	$0.90	$0.02	0%	94%	0%	0.00%
Superconductor Technologies, Inc.	SCON	Semiconductors	Negative Free Cash Flow	Negative Free Cash Flow	Negative Free Cash Flow	Negative Free Cash Flow	-$0.80	-110%	-29%	-110%	0.00%
Superior Energy Services Inc	SPN	Oil & Gas	$6.08	$12.15	$18.23	$36.45	$0.81	2%	88%	2%	0.00%
Superior Industries International	SUP	Autos	$4.20	$8.40	$12.60	$25.20	$0.56	3%	68%	3%	4.10%
Supernus Pharmaceuticals Inc	SUPN	Drugs	Negative Free Cash Flow	Negative Free Cash Flow	Negative Free Cash Flow	Negative Free Cash Flow	-$2.01	-117%	-3%	-117%	0.00%
Supertex, Inc.	SUPX	Semiconductors	$12.00	$24.00	$36.00	$72.00	$1.60	10%	4%	10%	0.00%
SUPERVALU Inc	SVU	Retail	$14.63	$29.25	$43.88	$87.75	$1.95	9%	4%	9%	0.00%

NAME	TICKER	INDUSTRY	2014 BUY PRICE OPINION	2014 HOLD PRICE OPINION	2014 SELL PRICE OPINION	2014 SHORT PRICE OPINION	2014 MYCROFT FREE CASH FLOW PER SHARE ESTIMATE	2014 MYCROFT FREE CASH FLOW RETURN ON TOTAL CAPITAL ESTIMATE (FROIC) >15% = Great	2014 MYCROFT CAPFLOW ESTIMATE <33% = Great BUT NO NEGATIVE RESULTS	2014 MYCROFT MICHAELIS GROWTH RATE ESTIMATE >15% = Great	DIVIDEND YIELD
Step #1 = Look up the company's current stock market price on the day of analysis and compare it to our 2014 Buy, Hold, Sell & Short Price.											
Step #2 =Take the company's current market price; divide it by the "2014 Mycroft Free Cash Flow Per Share estimate." This gives the "Price to Free Cash Flow."											
All results below are based on the 2014 year end estimates using the "2014 Mycroft Michaelis Growth Rate" and are good until December 31, 2014.											
support.com, Inc.	SPRT	Software	$2.03	$4.05	$6.08	$12.15	$0.27	15%	2%	15%	0.00%
Supreme Industries Inc.	STS	Truck Manufacturing	$3.08	$6.15	$9.23	$18.45	$0.41	7%	67%	7%	0.00%
SurModics, Inc.	SRDX	Medical	$8.55	$17.10	$25.65	$51.30	$1.14	15%	11%	15%	0.00%
Susser Holdings Corporation	SUSS	Retail	Negative Free Cash Flow	Negative Free Cash Flow	Negative Free Cash Flow	Negative Free Cash Flow	-$6.10	-16%	266%	-16%	0.00%
Sutron Corporation	STRN	Computers	$1.50	$3.00	$4.50	$9.00	$0.20	4%	24%	4%	0.00%
Swift Energy Company	SFY	Oil & Gas	Negative Free Cash Flow	Negative Free Cash Flow	Negative Free Cash Flow	Negative Free Cash Flow	-$7.83	-19%	210%	-19%	0.00%
Swift Transportation Co	SWFT	Transportation	$10.65	$21.30	$31.95	$63.90	$1.42	45%	70%	45%	0.00%
Sykes Enterprises, Inc.	SYKE	Software	$0.90	$1.80	$2.70	$5.40	$0.12	1%	91%	1%	0.00%
Symantec Corp	SYMC	Software	$15.15	$30.30	$45.45	$90.90	$2.02	16%	20%	13%	2.38%
Symmetricom Inc.	SYMM	Communication	$3.60	$7.20	$10.80	$21.60	$0.48	10%	24%	10%	0.00%
Symmetry Medical, Inc.	SMA	Medical	$7.65	$15.30	$22.95	$45.90	$1.02	7%	22%	7%	0.00%

NAME	TICKER	INDUSTRY	2014 BUY PRICE OPINION	2014 HOLD PRICE OPINION	2014 SELL PRICE OPINION	2014 SHORT PRICE OPINION	2014 MYCROFT FREE CASH FLOW PER SHARE ESTIMATE	2014 MYCROFT FREE CASH FLOW RETURN ON TOTAL CAPITAL ESTIMATE (FROIC) >15% = Great	2014 MYCROFT CAPFLOW ESTIMATE <33% = Great BUT NO NEGATIVE RESULTS	2014 MYCROFT MICHAELIS GROWTH RATE ESTIMATE >15% = Great	DIVIDEND YIELD
Step #1 = Look up the company's current stock market price on the day of analysis and compare it to our 2014 Buy, Hold, Sell & Short Price.											
Step #2 =Take the company's current market price; divide it by the "2014 Mycroft Free Cash Flow Per Share estimate." This gives the "Price to Free Cash Flow."											
All results below are based on the 2014 year end estimates using the "2014 Mycroft Michaelis Growth Rate" and are good until December 31, 2014.											
Synacor Inc	SYNC	Internet	$1.50	$3.00	$4.50	$9.00	$0.20	10%	49%	10%	0.00%
Synageva BioPharma Corp	GEVA	Biotech	Negative Free Cash Flow	Negative Free Cash Flow	Negative Free Cash Flow	Negative Free Cash Flow	-$2.54	-22%	-19%	-22%	0.00%
Synalloy Corporation	SYNL	Steel	Negative Free Cash Flow	Negative Free Cash Flow	Negative Free Cash Flow	Negative Free Cash Flow	-$1.15	-9%	-719%	-9%	1.53%
Synaptics, Inc.	SYNA	Computers	$13.28	$26.55	$39.83	$79.65	$1.77	10%	47%	10%	0.00%
Synchronoss Technologies, Inc.	SNCR	Software	$4.73	$9.45	$14.18	$28.35	$0.63	6%	67%	6%	0.00%
Synergetics USA, Inc.	SURG	Medical	$0.23	$0.45	$0.68	$1.35	$0.03	1%	55%	1%	0.00%
Synergy Pharmaceuticals, Inc.	SGYP	Drugs	Negative Free Cash Flow	Negative Free Cash Flow	Negative Free Cash Flow	Negative Free Cash Flow	-$0.51	-53%	0%	-53%	0.00%
Synergy Resources Corporation	SYRG	Oil & Gas	Negative Free Cash Flow	Negative Free Cash Flow	Negative Free Cash Flow	Negative Free Cash Flow	-$0.73	-39%	256%	-39%	0.00%
Synnex Corporation	SNX	Business Services	$44.63	$89.25	$133.88	$267.75	$5.95	14%	7%	14%	0.00%
Synopsys	SNPS	Semiconductors	$18.23	$36.45	$54.68	$109.35	$2.43	12%	18%	12%	0.00%
Synta Pharmaceuticals, Inc.	SNTA	Biotech	Negative Free Cash Flow	Negative Free Cash Flow	Negative Free Cash Flow	Negative Free Cash Flow	-$0.99	-157%	-1%	-157%	0.00%

NAME	TICKER	INDUSTRY	2014 BUY PRICE OPINION	2014 HOLD PRICE OPINION	2014 SELL PRICE OPINION	2014 SHORT PRICE OPINION	2014 MYCROFT FREE CASH FLOW PER SHARE ESTIMATE	2014 MYCROFT FREE CASH FLOW RETURN ON TOTAL CAPITAL ESTIMATE (FROIC) >15% = Great	2014 MYCROFT CAPFLOW ESTIMATE <33% = Great BUT NO NEGATIVE RESULTS	2014 MYCROFT MICHAELIS GROWTH RATE ESTIMATE >15% = Great	DIVIDEND YIELD
Step #1 = Look up the company's current stock market price on the day of analysis and compare it to our 2014 Buy, Hold, Sell & Short Price.											
Step #2 =Take the company's current market price; divide it by the "2014 Mycroft Free Cash Flow Per Share estimate." This gives the "Price to Free Cash Flow."											
All results below are based on the 2014 year end estimates using the "2014 Mycroft Michaelis Growth Rate" and are good until December 31, 2014.											
Syntel, Inc.	SYNT	Software	$36.15	$72.30	$108.45	$216.90	$4.82	27%	16%	25%	0.32%
Synthetic Biologics Inc	SYN	Biotech	Negative Free Cash Flow	Negative Free Cash Flow	Negative Free Cash Flow	Negative Free Cash Flow	-$0.22	-106%	0%	-106%	0.00%
Syntroleum Corporation	SYNM	Oil & Gas	Negative Free Cash Flow	Negative Free Cash Flow	Negative Free Cash Flow	Negative Free Cash Flow	-$0.49	-10%	-1%	-10%	0.00%
Synutra International, Inc.	SYUT	Consumer Goods	$3.83	$7.65	$11.48	$22.95	$0.51	19%	39%	19%	0.00%
Sypris Solutions, Inc.	SYPR	Computers	Negative Free Cash Flow	Negative Free Cash Flow	Negative Free Cash Flow	Negative Free Cash Flow	-$0.35	-10%	-594%	-10%	2.56%
Sysco Corporation	SYY	Retail	$13.73	$27.45	$41.18	$82.35	$1.83	13%	34%	8%	3.45%
Systemax, Inc.	SYX	Retail	$1.28	$2.55	$3.83	$7.65	$0.17	1%	67%	1%	0.00%
Tableau Software Inc Class A	DATA	Software	$0.75	$1.50	$2.25	$4.50	$0.10	3%	64%	3%	0.00%
Tahoe Resources, Inc.	TAHO	Commodities	Negative Free Cash Flow	Negative Free Cash Flow	Negative Free Cash Flow	Negative Free Cash Flow	-$1.53	-28%	-141%	-28%	0.00%
Take-Two Interactive Software, Inc.	TTWO	Software	$2.85	$5.70	$8.55	$17.10	$0.38	4%	39%	4%	0.00%
TAL International Group, Inc.	TAL	Rentals	Negative Free Cash Flow	Negative Free Cash Flow	Negative Free Cash Flow	Negative Free Cash Flow	-$14.96	-17%	268%	-14%	5.70%

NAME	TICKER	INDUSTRY	2014 BUY PRICE OPINION	2014 HOLD PRICE OPINION	2014 SELL PRICE OPINION	2014 SHORT PRICE OPINION	2014 MYCROFT FREE CASH FLOW PER SHARE ESTIMATE	2014 MYCROFT FREE CASH FLOW RETURN ON TOTAL CAPITAL ESTIMATE (FROIC) >15% = Great	2014 MYCROFT CAPFLOW ESTIMATE <33% = Great BUT NO NEGATIVE RESULTS	2014 MYCROFT MICHAELIS GROWTH RATE ESTIMATE >15% = Great	DIVIDEND YIELD
Step #1 = Look up the company's current stock market price on the day of analysis and compare it to our 2014 Buy, Hold, Sell & Short Price.												
Step #2 =Take the company's current market price; divide it by the "2014 Mycroft Free Cash Flow Per Share estimate." This gives the "Price to Free Cash Flow."												
All results below are based on the 2014 year end estimates using the "2014 Mycroft Michaelis Growth Rate" and are good until December 31, 2014.												
Taminco Corp	TAM	Chemicals	$6.08	$12.15	$18.23	$36.45	$0.81	3%	56%	3%	0.00%
Tandy Leather Factory, Inc.	TLF	Apparel & Furniture	$3.38	$6.75	$10.13	$20.25	$0.45	10%	51%	10%	0.00%
Tangoe Inc	TNGO	Software	$3.98	$7.95	$11.93	$23.85	$0.53	12%	10%	12%	0.00%
Targa Resources Corp	TRGP	Oil & Gas	Negative Free Cash Flow	Negative Free Cash Flow	Negative Free Cash Flow	Negative Free Cash Flow	-$9.50	-23%	204%	-25%	2.99%
Targacept, Inc.	TRGT	Biotech	Negative Free Cash Flow	Negative Free Cash Flow	Negative Free Cash Flow	Negative Free Cash Flow	-$1.25	-26%	-1%	-26%	0.00%
Target Corp	TGT	Retail	$44.03	$88.05	$132.08	$264.15	$5.87	11%	52%	10%	2.65%
Taser International, Inc.	TASR	Aerospace & Defense	$4.43	$8.85	$13.28	$26.55	$0.59	29%	8%	29%	0.00%
Taylor Morrison Home Corp	TMHC	Homebuilding	Negative Free Cash Flow	Negative Free Cash Flow	Negative Free Cash Flow	Negative Free Cash Flow	-$3.49	-25%	-1%	-25%	0.00%
Team Health Holdings Inc	TMH	Services	$11.25	$22.50	$33.75	$67.50	$1.50	16%	18%	16%	0.00%
Team, Inc.	TISI	Business Services	$12.90	$25.80	$38.70	$77.40	$1.72	9%	44%	9%	0.00%
TearLab Corpoartion	TEAR	Medical	Negative Free Cash Flow	Negative Free Cash Flow	Negative Free Cash Flow	Negative Free Cash Flow	-$0.38	-172%	0%	-172%	0.00%

NAME	TICKER	INDUSTRY	2014 BUY PRICE OPINION	2014 HOLD PRICE OPINION	2014 SELL PRICE OPINION	2014 SHORT PRICE OPINION	2014 MYCROFT FREE CASH FLOW PER SHARE ESTIMATE	2014 MYCROFT FREE CASH FLOW RETURN ON TOTAL CAPITAL ESTIMATE (FROIC) >15% = Great	2014 MYCROFT CAPFLOW ESTIMATE <33% = Great BUT NO NEGATIVE RESULTS	2014 MYCROFT MICHAELIS GROWTH RATE ESTIMATE >15% = Great	DIVIDEND YIELD
Step #1 = Look up the company's current stock market price on the day of analysis and compare it to our 2014 Buy, Hold, Sell & Short Price.										
Step #2 =Take the company's current market price; divide it by the "2014 Mycroft Free Cash Flow Per Share estimate." This gives the "Price to Free Cash Flow."										
All results below are based on the 2014 year end estimates using the "2014 Mycroft Michaelis Growth Rate" and are good until December 31, 2014.										
Tech Data Corporation	TECD	Computers	$28.80	$57.60	$86.40	$172.80	$3.84	7%	7%	7%	0.00%
Techne Corporation	TECH	Biotech	$22.50	$45.00	$67.50	$135.00	$3.00	14%	18%	9%	1.55%
Technical Communications Corp	TCCO	Communication	Negative Free Cash Flow	Negative Free Cash Flow	Negative Free Cash Flow	Negative Free Cash Flow	-$1.64	-28%	-4%	-28%	5.90%
TECO Energy Inc	TE	Utilities	$8.25	$16.50	$24.75	$49.50	$1.10	4%	70%	6%	5.30%
Tecumseh Products Company	TECUA	Industrial	Negative Free Cash Flow	Negative Free Cash Flow	Negative Free Cash Flow	Negative Free Cash Flow	-$0.69	-6%	-540%	-6%	0.00%
Teekay Corporation	TK	Transportation	Negative Free Cash Flow	Negative Free Cash Flow	Negative Free Cash Flow	Negative Free Cash Flow	-$6.01	-7%	295%	-5%	3.09%
Teekay Tankers, Ltd.	TNK	Transportation	$3.38	$6.75	$10.13	$20.25	$0.45	4%	6%	7%	4.46%
Tejon Ranch Co	TRC	Real Estate	Negative Free Cash Flow	Negative Free Cash Flow	Negative Free Cash Flow	Negative Free Cash Flow	-$0.50	-4%	184%	-4%	0.00%
TeleCommunication Systems, Inc.	TSYS	Software	$2.85	$5.70	$8.55	$17.10	$0.38	12%	42%	12%	0.00%
Teledyne Technologies Inc	TDY	Aerospace & Defense	$27.00	$54.00	$81.00	$162.00	$3.60	10%	38%	10%	0.00%
Teleflex Inc.	TFX	Medical	$15.90	$31.80	$47.70	$95.40	$2.12	3%	46%	3%	1.73%

NAME	TICKER	INDUSTRY	2014 BUY PRICE OPINION	2014 HOLD PRICE OPINION	2014 SELL PRICE OPINION	2014 SHORT PRICE OPINION	2014 MYCROFT FREE CASH FLOW PER SHARE ESTIMATE	2014 MYCROFT FREE CASH FLOW RETURN ON TOTAL CAPITAL ESTIMATE (FROIC) >15% = Great	2014 MYCROFT CAPFLOW ESTIMATE <33% = Great BUT NO NEGATIVE RESULTS	2014 MYCROFT MICHAELIS GROWTH RATE ESTIMATE >15% = Great	DIVIDEND YIELD
Step #1 = Look up the company's current stock market price on the day of analysis and compare it to our 2014 Buy, Hold, Sell & Short Price.											
Step #2 =Take the company's current market price; divide it by the "2014 Mycroft Free Cash Flow Per Share estimate." This gives the "Price to Free Cash Flow."											
All results below are based on the 2014 year end estimates using the "2014 Mycroft Michaelis Growth Rate" and are good until December 31, 2014.											
Telenav, Inc.	TNAV	Computers	$9.00	$18.00	$27.00	$54.00	$1.20	19%	7%	19%	0.00%
Telephone and Data Systems, Inc.	TDS	Communication	$17.55	$35.10	$52.65	$105.30	$2.34	4%	78%	5%	1.76%
TeleTech Holdings, Inc.	TTEC	Business Services	$10.13	$20.25	$30.38	$60.75	$1.35	11%	37%	11%	0.00%
Telik, Inc.	TELK	Drugs	Negative Free Cash Flow	Negative Free Cash Flow	Negative Free Cash Flow	Negative Free Cash Flow	-$1.75	-227%	0%	-227%	0.00%
Tellabs, Inc.	TLAB	Communication	Negative Free Cash Flow	Negative Free Cash Flow	Negative Free Cash Flow	Negative Free Cash Flow	$0.00	0%	103%	0%	3.39%
Tempur Sealy International Inc	TPX	Apparel & Furniture	$5.55	$11.10	$16.65	$33.30	$0.74	6%	54%	6%	0.00%
Tenet Healthcare Corp	THC	Health Care	$1.28	$2.55	$3.83	$7.65	$0.17	0%	97%	0%	0.00%
Tennant Company	TNC	Industrial	$15.53	$31.05	$46.58	$93.15	$2.07	13%	31%	9%	1.30%
Tenneco Inc	TEN	Autos	$17.55	$35.10	$52.65	$105.30	$2.34	8%	67%	8%	0.00%
Teradata Corporation	TDC	Computers	$26.48	$52.95	$79.43	$158.85	$3.53	23%	23%	23%	0.00%
Teradyne Inc	TER	Semiconductors	$10.88	$21.75	$32.63	$65.25	$1.45	12%	31%	12%	0.00%

NAME	TICKER	INDUSTRY	2014 BUY PRICE OPINION	2014 HOLD PRICE OPINION	2014 SELL PRICE OPINION	2014 SHORT PRICE OPINION	2014 MYCROFT FREE CASH FLOW PER SHARE ESTIMATE	2014 MYCROFT FREE CASH FLOW RETURN ON TOTAL CAPITAL ESTIMATE (FROIC) >15% = Great	2014 MYCROFT CAPFLOW ESTIMATE <33% = Great BUT NO NEGATIVE RESULTS	2014 MYCROFT MICHAELIS GROWTH RATE ESTIMATE >15% = Great	DIVIDEND YIELD
Step #1 = Look up the company's current stock market price on the day of analysis and compare it to our 2014 Buy, Hold, Sell & Short Price.											
Step #2 =Take the company's current market price; divide it by the "2014 Mycroft Free Cash Flow Per Share estimate." This gives the "Price to Free Cash Flow."											
All results below are based on the 2014 year end estimates using the "2014 Mycroft Michaelis Growth Rate" and are good until December 31, 2014.											
Terex Corp	TEX	Agriculture	$22.88	$45.75	$68.63	$137.25	$3.05	7%	22%	7%	0.00%
Tesaro Inc	TSRO	Biotech	Negative Free Cash Flow	Negative Free Cash Flow	Negative Free Cash Flow	Negative Free Cash Flow	-$1.90	-37%	-2%	-37%	0.00%
Tesco Corporation	TESO	Oil & Gas	Negative Free Cash Flow	Negative Free Cash Flow	Negative Free Cash Flow	Negative Free Cash Flow	-$0.04	0%	103%	0%	0.00%
Tesla Motors, Inc.	TSLA	Autos	Negative Free Cash Flow	Negative Free Cash Flow	Negative Free Cash Flow	Negative Free Cash Flow	-$2.78	-33%	-199%	-33%	0.00%
Tesoro Corporation	TSO	Oil & Gas	$6.83	$13.65	$20.48	$40.95	$0.91	2%	83%	2%	2.17%
Tessco Technologies	TESS	Computers	Negative Free Cash Flow	Negative Free Cash Flow	Negative Free Cash Flow	Negative Free Cash Flow	-$1.28	-10%	-122%	-13%	2.24%
Tessera Technologies, Inc.	TSRA	Semiconductors	Negative Free Cash Flow	Negative Free Cash Flow	Negative Free Cash Flow	Negative Free Cash Flow	-$1.56	-14%	-114%	-16%	2.02%
Tetra Tech, Inc.	TTEK	Engineering	$14.63	$29.25	$43.88	$87.75	$1.95	10%	21%	10%	0.00%
Tetra Technologies, Inc.	TTI	Oil & Gas	Negative Free Cash Flow	Negative Free Cash Flow	Negative Free Cash Flow	Negative Free Cash Flow	-$0.60	-6%	184%	-6%	0.00%
Tetraphase Pharmaceuticals Inc	TTPH	Drugs	Negative Free Cash Flow	Negative Free Cash Flow	Negative Free Cash Flow	Negative Free Cash Flow	-$0.62	-18%	-1%	-18%	0.00%
Texas Industries Inc	TXI	Building Supplies	Negative Free Cash Flow	Negative Free Cash Flow	Negative Free Cash Flow	Negative Free Cash Flow	-$2.08	-4%	279%	-4%	0.00%

NAME	TICKER	INDUSTRY	2014 BUY PRICE OPINION	2014 HOLD PRICE OPINION	2014 SELL PRICE OPINION	2014 SHORT PRICE OPINION	2014 MYCROFT FREE CASH FLOW PER SHARE ESTIMATE	2014 MYCROFT FREE CASH FLOW RETURN ON TOTAL CAPITAL ESTIMATE (FROIC) >15% = Great	2014 MYCROFT CAPFLOW ESTIMATE <33% = Great BUT NO NEGATIVE RESULTS	2014 MYCROFT MICHAELIS GROWTH RATE ESTIMATE >15% = Great	DIVIDEND YIELD
Texas Instruments, Inc.	TXN	Semiconductors	$22.65	$45.30	$67.95	$135.90	$3.02	21%	13%	15%	2.80%
Texas Roadhouse, Inc.	TXRH	Restaurants	$9.08	$18.15	$27.23	$54.45	$1.21	14%	50%	10%	1.91%
Textainer Group Holdings, Ltd.	TGH	Rentals	Negative Free Cash Flow	Negative Free Cash Flow	Negative Free Cash Flow	Negative Free Cash Flow	-$15.14	-34%	389%	-33%	5.00%
Textron Inc	TXT	Aerospace & Defense	Negative Free Cash Flow	Negative Free Cash Flow	Negative Free Cash Flow	Negative Free Cash Flow	-$0.28	-1%	118%	-1%	0.27%
Textura Corp	TXTR	Software	Negative Free Cash Flow	Negative Free Cash Flow	Negative Free Cash Flow	Negative Free Cash Flow	-$0.54	-12%	-7%	-12%	0.00%
TG Therapeutics Inc	TGTX	Biotech	Negative Free Cash Flow	Negative Free Cash Flow	Negative Free Cash Flow	Negative Free Cash Flow	-$0.26	-59%	0%	-59%	0.00%
Theragenics Corporation	TGX	Medical	$2.63	$5.25	$7.88	$15.75	$0.35	12%	20%	12%	0.00%
TherapeuticsMD Inc	TXMD	Drugs	Negative Free Cash Flow	Negative Free Cash Flow	Negative Free Cash Flow	Negative Free Cash Flow	-$0.14	-43%	-2%	-43%	0.00%
Theravance, Inc.	THRX	Biotech	Negative Free Cash Flow	Negative Free Cash Flow	Negative Free Cash Flow	Negative Free Cash Flow	-$1.24	-51%	-32%	-51%	0.00%
Thermo Fisher Scientific Inc	TMO	Medical	$35.78	$71.55	$107.33	$214.65	$4.77	7%	16%	7%	0.66%
Thermon Group Holdings Inc	THR	Industrial	$11.18	$22.35	$33.53	$67.05	$1.49	12%	12%	12%	0.00%

Step #1 = Look up the company's current stock market price on the day of analysis and compare it to our 2014 Buy, Hold, Sell & Short Price.

Step #2 = Take the company's current market price; divide it by the "2014 Mycroft Free Cash Flow Per Share estimate." This gives the "Price to Free Cash Flow."

All results below are based on the 2014 year end estimates using the "2014 Mycroft Michaelis Growth Rate" and are good until December 31, 2014.

NAME	TICKER	INDUSTRY	2014 BUY PRICE OPINION	2014 HOLD PRICE OPINION	2014 SELL PRICE OPINION	2014 SHORT PRICE OPINION	2014 MYCROFT FREE CASH FLOW PER SHARE ESTIMATE	2014 MYCROFT FREE CASH FLOW RETURN ON TOTAL CAPITAL ESTIMATE (FROIC) >15% = Great	2014 MYCROFT CAPFLOW ESTIMATE <33% = Great BUT NO NEGATIVE RESULTS	2014 MYCROFT MICHAELIS GROWTH RATE ESTIMATE >15% = Great	DIVIDEND YIELD

Step #1 = Look up the company's current stock market price on the day of analysis and compare it to our 2014 Buy, Hold, Sell & Short Price.

Step #2 =Take the company's current market price; divide it by the "2014 Mycroft Free Cash Flow Per Share estimate." This gives the "Price to Free Cash Flow."

All results below are based on the 2014 year end estimates using the "2014 Mycroft Michaelis Growth Rate" and are good until December 31, 2014.

NAME	TICKER	INDUSTRY	BUY	HOLD	SELL	SHORT	FCF/SHARE	FROIC	CAPFLOW	GROWTH	DIV YIELD
TheStreet, Inc.	TST	Internet	Negative Free Cash Flow	Negative Free Cash Flow	Negative Free Cash Flow	Negative Free Cash Flow	-$0.08	-4%	-72%	-4%	0.00%
Thomas Properties Group, Inc.	TPGI	Real Estate	Negative Free Cash Flow	Negative Free Cash Flow	Negative Free Cash Flow	Negative Free Cash Flow	-$0.47	-6%	-267%	-6%	1.32%
Thomson Reuters Corporation	TRI	Publishing	$15.08	$30.15	$45.23	$90.45	$2.01	7%	40%	6%	3.74%
Thor Industries, Inc.	THO	Autos	$16.73	$33.45	$50.18	$100.35	$2.23	13%	15%	10%	1.38%
Thoratec Corporation	THOR	Medical	$13.13	$26.25	$39.38	$78.75	$1.75	14%	12%	14%	0.00%
Threshold Pharmaceuticals, Inc.	THLD	Biotech	Negative Free Cash Flow	Negative Free Cash Flow	Negative Free Cash Flow	Negative Free Cash Flow	$0.50	-117%	1%	-117%	0.00%
TIBCO Software, Inc.	TIBX	Software	$9.98	$19.95	$29.93	$59.85	$1.33	13%	9%	13%	0.00%
Tidewater, Inc.	TDW	Oil & Gas	Negative Free Cash Flow	Negative Free Cash Flow	Negative Free Cash Flow	Negative Free Cash Flow	-$7.49	-11%	350%	-10%	1.72%
Tiffany & Co.	TIF	Retail	$12.98	$25.95	$38.93	$77.85	$1.73	6%	58%	3%	1.72%
TigerLogic Corporation	TIGR	Software	Negative Free Cash Flow	Negative Free Cash Flow	Negative Free Cash Flow	Negative Free Cash Flow	-$0.08	-7%	-4%	-7%	0.00%
Tile Shop Holdings Inc	TTS	Building Supplies	Negative Free Cash Flow	Negative Free Cash Flow	Negative Free Cash Flow	Negative Free Cash Flow	-$0.19	-13%	133%	-13%	0.00%

NAME	TICKER	INDUSTRY	2014 BUY PRICE OPINION	2014 HOLD PRICE OPINION	2014 SELL PRICE OPINION	2014 SHORT PRICE OPINION	2014 MYCROFT FREE CASH FLOW PER SHARE ESTIMATE	2014 MYCROFT FREE CASH FLOW RETURN ON TOTAL CAPITAL ESTIMATE (FROIC) >15% = Great	2014 MYCROFT CAPFLOW ESTIMATE <33% = Great BUT NO NEGATIVE RESULTS	2014 MYCROFT MICHAELIS GROWTH RATE ESTIMATE >15% = Great	DIVIDEND YIELD
Step #1 = Look up the company's current stock market price on the day of analysis and compare it to our 2014 Buy, Hold, Sell & Short Price.											
Step #2 =Take the company's current market price; divide it by the "2014 Mycroft Free Cash Flow Per Share estimate." This gives the "Price to Free Cash Flow."											
All results below are based on the 2014 year end estimates using the "2014 Mycroft Michaelis Growth Rate" and are good until December 31, 2014.											
Tilly's Inc	TLYS	Retail	$0.98	$1.95	$2.93	$5.85	$0.13	3%	91%	3%	0.00%
Time Warner Cable Inc	TWC	Communication	$63.90	$127.80	$191.70	$383.40	$8.52	7%	59%	7%	2.35%
Time Warner Inc	TWX	Entertainment	$33.15	$66.30	$99.45	$198.90	$4.42	8%	13%	7%	1.82%
Timken Company	TKR	Industrial	$16.80	$33.60	$50.40	$100.80	$2.24	7%	62%	6%	1.48%
Titan International, Inc.	TWI	Autos	$12.98	$25.95	$38.93	$77.85	$1.73	9%	49%	9%	0.12%
Titan Machinery, Inc.	TITN	Retail	Negative Free Cash Flow	Negative Free Cash Flow	Negative Free Cash Flow	Negative Free Cash Flow	-$5.63	-20%	-70%	-20%	0.00%
Tivo, Inc.	TIVO	Communication	$65.10	$130.20	$195.30	$390.60	$8.68	82%	1%	82%	0.00%
TJX Companies	TJX	Retail	$19.80	$39.60	$59.40	$118.80	$2.64	33%	41%	25%	1.06%
T-Mobile US Inc	TMUS	Communication	Negative Free Cash Flow	Negative Free Cash Flow	Negative Free Cash Flow	Negative Free Cash Flow	-$1.01	-4%	174%	-4%	0.00%
TMS International Corp	TMS	Industrial	$1.13	$2.25	$3.38	$6.75	$0.15	1%	94%	1%	2.30%
Toll Brothers Inc	TOL	Homebuilding	Negative Free Cash Flow	Negative Free Cash Flow	Negative Free Cash Flow	Negative Free Cash Flow	-$2.50	-8%	-7%	-8%	0.00%

NAME	TICKER	INDUSTRY	2014 BUY PRICE OPINION	2014 HOLD PRICE OPINION	2014 SELL PRICE OPINION	2014 SHORT PRICE OPINION	2014 MYCROFT FREE CASH FLOW PER SHARE ESTIMATE	2014 MYCROFT FREE CASH FLOW RETURN ON TOTAL CAPITAL ESTIMATE (FROIC) >15% = Great	2014 MYCROFT CAPFLOW ESTIMATE <33% = Great BUT NO NEGATIVE RESULTS	2014 MYCROFT MICHAELIS GROWTH RATE ESTIMATE >15% = Great	DIVIDEND YIELD
Step #1 = Look up the company's current stock market price on the day of analysis and compare it to our 2014 Buy, Hold, Sell & Short Price.										
Step #2 =Take the company's current market price; divide it by the "2014 Mycroft Free Cash Flow Per Share estimate." This gives the "Price to Free Cash Flow."										
All results below are based on the 2014 year end estimates using the "2014 Mycroft Michaelis Growth Rate" and are good until December 31, 2014.										
Tootsie Roll Industries	TR	Consumer Goods	$14.33	$28.65	$42.98	$85.95	$1.91	15%	9%	14%	1.05%
Tornier N.V.	TRNX	Medical	Negative Free Cash Flow	Negative Free Cash Flow	Negative Free Cash Flow	Negative Free Cash Flow	-$0.21	-2%	154%	-2%	0.00%
Toro Company	TTC	Industrial	$19.80	$39.60	$59.40	$118.80	$2.64	21%	28%	17%	1.02%
Total System Services, Inc.	TSS	Software	$12.23	$24.45	$36.68	$73.35	$1.63	17%	34%	14%	1.37%
Tower International Inc	TOWR	Industrial	$33.68	$67.35	$101.03	$202.05	$4.49	15%	0%	15%	0.00%
Towers Watson & Co. Class A	TW	Business Services	$48.00	$96.00	$144.00	$288.00	$6.40	13%	24%	12%	0.51%
Towerstream Corporation	TWER	Communication	Negative Free Cash Flow	Negative Free Cash Flow	Negative Free Cash Flow	Negative Free Cash Flow	-$0.37	-32%	-112%	-32%	0.00%
Town Sports International Holdings, Inc.	CLUB	Travel & Leisure	$15.60	$31.20	$46.80	$93.60	$2.08	20%	40%	20%	0.00%
Tractor Supply	TSCO	Retail	$11.48	$22.95	$34.43	$68.85	$1.53	9%	64%	3%	0.79%
Transact Technologies, Inc.	TACT	Computers	$4.13	$8.25	$12.38	$24.75	$0.55	13%	22%	8%	2.61%
Transcept Pharmaceuticals, Inc.	TSPT	Biotech	Negative Free Cash Flow	Negative Free Cash Flow	Negative Free Cash Flow	Negative Free Cash Flow	-$0.80	-19%	0%	-19%	0.00%

NAME	TICKER	INDUSTRY	2014 BUY PRICE OPINION	2014 HOLD PRICE OPINION	2014 SELL PRICE OPINION	2014 SHORT PRICE OPINION	2014 MYCROFT FREE CASH FLOW PER SHARE ESTIMATE	2014 MYCROFT FREE CASH FLOW RETURN ON TOTAL CAPITAL ESTIMATE (FROIC) >15% = Great	2014 MYCROFT CAPFLOW ESTIMATE <33% = Great BUT NO NEGATIVE RESULTS	2014 MYCROFT MICHAELIS GROWTH RATE ESTIMATE >15% = Great	DIVIDEND YIELD
\multicolumn{12}{l}{Step #1 = Look up the company's current stock market price on the day of analysis and compare it to our 2014 Buy, Hold, Sell & Short Price.}
\multicolumn{12}{l}{Step #2 =Take the company's current market price; divide it by the "2014 Mycroft Free Cash Flow Per Share estimate." This gives the "Price to Free Cash Flow."}
\multicolumn{12}{l}{All results below are based on the 2014 year end estimates using the "2014 Mycroft Michaelis Growth Rate" and are good until December 31, 2014.}
TransDigm Group Inc	TDG	Aerospace & Defense	$60.68	$121.35	$182.03	$364.05	$8.09	9%	8%	9%	0.00%
Travelzoo, Inc.	TZOO	Internet	$25.05	$50.10	$75.15	$150.30	$3.34	60%	12%	60%	0.00%
TRC Companies, Inc.	TRR	Waste Management	$2.48	$4.95	$7.43	$14.85	$0.33	10%	28%	10%	0.00%
Tredegar Corporation	TG	Autos	$3.98	$7.95	$11.93	$23.85	$0.53	4%	78%	3%	1.12%
Treehouse Foods, Inc.	THS	Consumer Goods	$20.63	$41.25	$61.88	$123.75	$2.75	4%	47%	4%	0.00%
Trex Company, Inc.	TREX	Building Supplies	$21.23	$42.45	$63.68	$127.35	$2.83	29%	21%	29%	0.00%
TRI Pointe Homes Inc	TPH	Homebuilding	Negative Free Cash Flow	Negative Free Cash Flow	Negative Free Cash Flow	Negative Free Cash Flow	-$5.00	-51%	0%	-51%	0.00%
Triangle Petroleum Corp	TPLM	Oil & Gas	Negative Free Cash Flow	Negative Free Cash Flow	Negative Free Cash Flow	Negative Free Cash Flow	-$2.52	-53%	794%	-53%	0.00%
TriMas Corporation	TRS	Industrial	$9.23	$18.45	$27.68	$55.35	$1.23	6%	50%	6%	0.00%
Trimble Navigation Ltd.	TRMB	Computers	$9.23	$18.45	$27.68	$55.35	$1.23	11%	21%	11%	0.00%
Trinity Industries, Inc.	TRN	Transportation	Negative Free Cash Flow	Negative Free Cash Flow	Negative Free Cash Flow	Negative Free Cash Flow	-$0.33	-1%	104%	0%	1.33%

NAME	TICKER	INDUSTRY	2014 BUY PRICE OPINION	2014 HOLD PRICE OPINION	2014 SELL PRICE OPINION	2014 SHORT PRICE OPINION	2014 MYCROFT FREE CASH FLOW PER SHARE ESTIMATE	2014 MYCROFT FREE CASH FLOW RETURN ON TOTAL CAPITAL ESTIMATE (FROIC) >15% = Great	2014 MYCROFT CAPFLOW ESTIMATE <33% = Great BUT NO NEGATIVE RESULTS	2014 MYCROFT MICHAELIS GROWTH RATE ESTIMATE >15% = Great	DIVIDEND YIELD
Step #1 = Look up the company's current stock market price on the day of analysis and compare it to our 2014 Buy, Hold, Sell & Short Price.											
Step #2 =Take the company's current market price; divide it by the "2014 Mycroft Free Cash Flow Per Share estimate." This gives the "Price to Free Cash Flow."											
All results below are based on the 2014 year end estimates using the "2014 Mycroft Michaelis Growth Rate" and are good until December 31, 2014.											
TripAdvisor Inc	TRIP	Internet	$15.15	$30.30	$45.45	$90.90	$2.02	20%	14%	20%	0.00%
Triquint Semiconductor	TQNT	Semiconductors	Negative Free Cash Flow	Negative Free Cash Flow	Negative Free Cash Flow	Negative Free Cash Flow	-$0.22	-4%	149%	-4%	0.00%
Triumph Group, Inc.	TGI	Aerospace & Defense	$13.73	$27.45	$41.18	$82.35	$1.83	3%	60%	3%	0.21%
Trius Therapeutics, Inc.	TSRX	Medical	Negative Free Cash Flow	Negative Free Cash Flow	Negative Free Cash Flow	Negative Free Cash Flow	-$1.14	-101%	-1%	-101%	0.00%
Trueblue, Inc.	TBI	Services	$6.68	$13.35	$20.03	$40.05	$0.89	9%	32%	9%	0.00%
Trulia Inc	TRLA	Internet	$0.15	$0.30	$0.45	$0.90	$0.02	0%	93%	0%	0.00%
TRW Automotive Holdings Corp	TRW	Autos	$17.93	$35.85	$53.78	$107.55	$2.39	5%	72%	5%	0.00%
TTM Technologies, Inc.	TTMI	Computers	$5.03	$10.05	$15.08	$30.15	$0.67	5%	71%	5%	0.00%
Tuesday Morning Corporation	TUES	Retail	Negative Free Cash Flow	Negative Free Cash Flow	Negative Free Cash Flow	Negative Free Cash Flow	-$0.30	-6%	-301%	-6%	0.00%
Tumi Holdings Inc	TUMI	Retail	$5.33	$10.65	$15.98	$31.95	$0.71	13%	34%	13%	0.00%
Tupperware Brands Corporation	TUP	Consumer Goods	$51.68	$103.35	$155.03	$310.05	$6.89	76%	21%	40%	2.94%

NAME	TICKER	INDUSTRY	2014 BUY PRICE OPINION	2014 HOLD PRICE OPINION	2014 SELL PRICE OPINION	2014 SHORT PRICE OPINION	2014 MYCROFT FREE CASH FLOW PER SHARE ESTIMATE	2014 MYCROFT FREE CASH FLOW RETURN ON TOTAL CAPITAL ESTIMATE (FROIC) >15% = Great	2014 MYCROFT CAPFLOW ESTIMATE <33% = Great BUT NO NEGATIVE RESULTS	2014 MYCROFT MICHAELIS GROWTH RATE ESTIMATE >15% = Great	DIVIDEND YIELD
Tutor Perini Corp	TPC	Engineering	Negative Free Cash Flow	Negative Free Cash Flow	Negative Free Cash Flow	Negative Free Cash Flow	-$2.55	-7%	-64%	-7%	0.00%
tw telecom inc	TWTC	Communication	$5.33	$10.65	$15.98	$31.95	$0.71	10%	80%	10%	0.00%
Twenty-First Century Fox Inc Class A	FOXA	Entertainment	$8.18	$16.35	$24.53	$49.05	$1.09	7%	21%	6%	0.77%
Twin Disc, Inc.	TWIN	Industrial	$15.45	$30.90	$46.35	$92.70	$2.06	12%	29%	11%	1.39%
Tyler Technologies, Inc.	TYL	Software	$13.58	$27.15	$40.73	$81.45	$1.81	20%	28%	20%	0.00%
Tyson Foods, Inc. Class A	TSN	Consumer Goods	$15.00	$30.00	$45.00	$90.00	$2.00	8%	47%	7%	0.66%
U.S. Auto Parts Network, Inc.	PRTS	Retail	Negative Free Cash Flow	Negative Free Cash Flow	Negative Free Cash Flow	Negative Free Cash Flow	-$0.22	-32%	437%	-32%	0.00%
U.S. Energy Corp.	USEG	Oil & Gas	Negative Free Cash Flow	Negative Free Cash Flow	Negative Free Cash Flow	Negative Free Cash Flow	-$0.25	-6%	156%	-6%	0.00%
U.S. Physical Therapy	USPH	Health Care	$27.68	$55.35	$83.03	$166.05	$3.69	25%	11%	23%	1.43%
Ubiquiti Networks Inc	UBNT	Communication	$16.95	$33.90	$50.85	$101.70	$2.26	80%	5%	80%	0.00%
UFP Technologies, Inc.	UFPT	Containers	$5.63	$11.25	$16.88	$33.75	$0.75	6%	69%	6%	0.00%

Step #1 = Look up the company's current stock market price on the day of analysis and compare it to our 2014 Buy, Hold, Sell & Short Price.

Step #2 =Take the company's current market price; divide it by the "2014 Mycroft Free Cash Flow Per Share estimate." This gives the "Price to Free Cash Flow."

All results below are based on the 2014 year end estimates using the "2014 Mycroft Michaelis Growth Rate" and are good until December 31, 2014.

NAME	TICKER	INDUSTRY	2014 BUY PRICE OPINION	2014 HOLD PRICE OPINION	2014 SELL PRICE OPINION	2014 SHORT PRICE OPINION	2014 MYCROFT FREE CASH FLOW PER SHARE ESTIMATE	2014 MYCROFT FREE CASH FLOW RETURN ON TOTAL CAPITAL ESTIMATE (FROIC) >15% = Great	2014 MYCROFT CAPFLOW ESTIMATE <33% = Great BUT NO NEGATIVE RESULTS	2014 MYCROFT MICHAELIS GROWTH RATE ESTIMATE >15% = Great	DIVIDEND YIELD
Step #1 = Look up the company's current stock market price on the day of analysis and compare it to our 2014 Buy, Hold, Sell & Short Price.											
Step #2 =Take the company's current market price; divide it by the "2014 Mycroft Free Cash Flow Per Share estimate." This gives the "Price to Free Cash Flow."											
All results below are based on the 2014 year end estimates using the "2014 Mycroft Michaelis Growth Rate" and are good until December 31, 2014.											
UGI Corporation	UGI	Utilities	$30.75	$61.50	$92.25	$184.50	$4.10	7%	48%	8%	2.92%
UIL Holdings Corporation	UIL	Utilities	$11.70	$23.40	$35.10	$70.20	$1.56	3%	79%	4%	4.70%
Ulta Salon Cosmetics & Fragrances, Inc.	ULTA	Retail	$8.03	$16.05	$24.08	$48.15	$1.07	8%	76%	8%	0.00%
Ultimate Software Group, Inc.	ULTI	Software	$8.78	$17.55	$26.33	$52.65	$1.17	19%	47%	19%	0.00%
Ultra Clean Holdings, Inc.	UCTT	Semiconductors	$9.90	$19.80	$29.70	$59.40	$1.32	20%	3%	20%	0.00%
Ultra Petroleum Corporation	UPL	Oil & Gas	$3.08	$6.15	$9.23	$18.45	$0.41	4%	89%	4%	0.00%
Ultralife Batteries, Inc.	ULBI	Industrial	$2.55	$5.10	$7.65	$15.30	$0.34	8%	22%	8%	0.00%
Ultratech, Inc.	UTEK	Semiconductors	$7.13	$14.25	$21.38	$42.75	$0.95	6%	46%	6%	0.00%
Under Armour, Inc. Class A	UA	Apparel & Furniture	$5.33	$10.65	$15.98	$31.95	$0.71	8%	49%	8%	0.00%
Unifi, Inc.	UFI	Homebuilding	$23.93	$47.85	$71.78	$143.55	$3.19	14%	9%	14%	0.00%
UniFirst Corporation	UNF	Apparel & Furniture	$40.05	$80.10	$120.15	$240.30	$5.34	9%	50%	9%	0.15%

NAME	TICKER	INDUSTRY	2014 BUY PRICE OPINION	2014 HOLD PRICE OPINION	2014 SELL PRICE OPINION	2014 SHORT PRICE OPINION	2014 MYCROFT FREE CASH FLOW PER SHARE ESTIMATE	2014 MYCROFT FREE CASH FLOW RETURN ON TOTAL CAPITAL ESTIMATE (FROIC) >15% = Great	2014 MYCROFT CAPFLOW ESTIMATE <33% = Great BUT NO NEGATIVE RESULTS	2014 MYCROFT MICHAELIS GROWTH RATE ESTIMATE >15% = Great	DIVIDEND YIELD
Step #1 = Look up the company's current stock market price on the day of analysis and compare it to our 2014 Buy, Hold, Sell & Short Price.										
Step #2 =Take the company's current market price; divide it by the "2014 Mycroft Free Cash Flow Per Share estimate." This gives the "Price to Free Cash Flow."										
All results below are based on the 2014 year end estimates using the "2014 Mycroft Michaelis Growth Rate" and are good until December 31, 2014.										
Unilife Corporation	UNIS	Medical	Negative Free Cash Flow	Negative Free Cash Flow	Negative Free Cash Flow	Negative Free Cash Flow	-$0.47	-73%	-6%	-73%	0.00%
Union Pacific Corp	UNP	Transportation	$45.98	$91.95	$137.93	$275.85	$6.13	9%	59%	6%	2.01%
Uni-pixel, Inc.	UNXL	Computers	Negative Free Cash Flow	Negative Free Cash Flow	Negative Free Cash Flow	Negative Free Cash Flow	-$0.62	-13%	422%	-13%	0.00%
Unisys Corporation	UIS	Software	$13.13	$26.25	$39.38	$78.75	$1.75	-6%	65%	-6%	0.00%
Unit Corporation	UNT	Oil & Gas	Negative Free Cash Flow	Negative Free Cash Flow	Negative Free Cash Flow	Negative Free Cash Flow	-$12.88	-26%	191%	-26%	0.00%
United Continental Holdings Inc	UAL	Airlines	Negative Free Cash Flow	Negative Free Cash Flow	Negative Free Cash Flow	Negative Free Cash Flow	-$2.32	-7%	159%	-7%	0.00%
United Natural Foods, Inc.	UNFI	Retail	$2.93	$5.85	$8.78	$17.55	$0.39	2%	71%	2%	0.00%
United Online, Inc.	UNTD	Internet	$5.33	$10.65	$15.98	$31.95	$0.71	9%	26%	8%	5.00%
United Parcel Service Inc (UPS) Class B	UPS	Transportation	$43.43	$86.85	$130.28	$260.55	$5.79	31%	32%	18%	2.79%
United Rentals Inc	URI	Rentals	Negative Free Cash Flow	Negative Free Cash Flow	Negative Free Cash Flow	Negative Free Cash Flow	-$3.00	-3%	122%	-3%	0.00%
United States Antimony Corporation	UAMY	Commodities	Negative Free Cash Flow	Negative Free Cash Flow	Negative Free Cash Flow	Negative Free Cash Flow	-$0.05	-28%	5250%	-28%	0.00%

NAME	TICKER	INDUSTRY	2014 BUY PRICE OPINION	2014 HOLD PRICE OPINION	2014 SELL PRICE OPINION	2014 SHORT PRICE OPINION	2014 MYCROFT FREE CASH FLOW PER SHARE ESTIMATE	2014 MYCROFT FREE CASH FLOW RETURN ON TOTAL CAPITAL ESTIMATE (FROIC) >15% = Great	2014 MYCROFT CAPFLOW ESTIMATE <33% = Great BUT NO NEGATIVE RESULTS	2014 MYCROFT MICHAELIS GROWTH RATE ESTIMATE >15% = Great	DIVIDEND YIELD
Step #1 = Look up the company's current stock market price on the day of analysis and compare it to our 2014 Buy, Hold, Sell & Short Price.											
Step #2 =Take the company's current market price; divide it by the "2014 Mycroft Free Cash Flow Per Share estimate." This gives the "Price to Free Cash Flow."											
All results below are based on the 2014 year end estimates using the "2014 Mycroft Michaelis Growth Rate" and are good until December 31, 2014.											
United States Cellular Corporation	USM	Communication	$8.40	$16.80	$25.20	$50.40	$1.12	2%	90%	2%	0.00%
United States Lime & Minerals, Inc.	USLM	Building Supplies	$31.88	$63.75	$95.63	$191.25	$4.25	14%	27%	14%	0.00%
United States Steel Corporation	X	Steel	$5.25	$10.50	$15.75	$31.50	$0.70	1%	85%	2%	0.98%
United Stationers Inc.	USTR	Industrial	$30.90	$61.80	$92.70	$185.40	$4.12	12%	21%	11%	1.37%
United Technologies Corp	UTX	Industrial	$35.25	$70.50	$105.75	$211.50	$4.70	9%	35%	6%	1.98%
United Therapeutics Corporation	UTHR	Biotech	$63.83	$127.65	$191.48	$382.95	$8.51	24%	10%	24%	0.00%
United-Guardian, Inc.	UG	Consumer Goods	$11.25	$22.50	$33.75	$67.50	$1.50	44%	4%	16%	3.67%
UnitedHealth Group Inc	UNH	Health Care	$20.78	$41.55	$62.33	$124.65	$2.77	6%	31%	5%	1.49%
UniTek Global Services, Inc.	UNTK	Engineering	$1.35	$2.70	$4.05	$8.10	$0.18	2%	63%	2%	0.00%
Unitil Corporation	UTL	Utilities	$1.35	$2.70	$4.05	$8.10	$0.18	0%	97%	2%	4.70%
Universal Corporation	UVV	Tobacco	$7.43	$14.85	$22.28	$44.55	$0.99	2%	55%	2%	3.90%

NAME	TICKER	INDUSTRY	2014 BUY PRICE OPINION	2014 HOLD PRICE OPINION	2014 SELL PRICE OPINION	2014 SHORT PRICE OPINION	2014 MYCROFT FREE CASH FLOW PER SHARE ESTIMATE	2014 MYCROFT FREE CASH FLOW RETURN ON TOTAL CAPITAL ESTIMATE (FROIC) >15% = Great	2014 MYCROFT CAPFLOW ESTIMATE <33% = Great BUT NO NEGATIVE RESULTS	2014 MYCROFT MICHAELIS GROWTH RATE ESTIMATE >15% = Great	DIVIDEND YIELD
Step #1 = Look up the company's current stock market price on the day of analysis and compare it to our 2014 Buy, Hold, Sell & Short Price.											
Step #2 =Take the company's current market price; divide it by the "2014 Mycroft Free Cash Flow Per Share estimate." This gives the "Price to Free Cash Flow."											
All results below are based on the 2014 year end estimates using the "2014 Mycroft Michaelis Growth Rate" and are good until December 31, 2014.											
Universal Display Corporation	OLED	Computers	Negative Free Cash Flow	Negative Free Cash Flow	Negative Free Cash Flow	Negative Free Cash Flow	-$1.91	-25%	466%	-25%	0.00%
Universal Electronics Inc.	UEIC	Computers	$16.80	$33.60	$50.40	$100.80	$2.24	12%	28%	12%	0.00%
Universal Forest Products Inc.	UFPI	Building Supplies	Negative Free Cash Flow	Negative Free Cash Flow	Negative Free Cash Flow	Negative Free Cash Flow	-$2.57	-8%	-241%	-9%	0.97%
Universal Health Services, Inc. Class B	UHS	Health Care	$35.18	$70.35	$105.53	$211.05	$4.69	7%	49%	7%	0.28%
Universal Power Group, Inc.	UPG	Computers	$10.58	$21.15	$31.73	$63.45	$1.41	24%	7%	24%	0.00%
Universal Security Instruments, Inc.	UUU	Computers	Negative Free Cash Flow	Negative Free Cash Flow	Negative Free Cash Flow	Negative Free Cash Flow	-$0.44	-4%	0%	-4%	0.00%
Universal Stainless & Alloy Products	USAP	Steel	$11.78	$23.55	$35.33	$70.65	$1.57	3%	69%	3%	0.00%
Universal Technical Institute, Inc.	UTI	Education	$1.13	$2.25	$3.38	$6.75	$0.15	3%	75%	-1%	3.64%
Universal Truckload Services, Inc.	UACL	Transportation	$12.08	$24.15	$36.23	$72.45	$1.61	43%	39%	34%	0.99%
UNS Energy Corp	UNS	Utilities	$14.33	$28.65	$42.98	$85.95	$1.91	3%	80%	4%	3.80%
Unwired Planet Inc	UPIP	Software	Negative Free Cash Flow	Negative Free Cash Flow	Negative Free Cash Flow	Negative Free Cash Flow	-$0.70	-160%	0%	-160%	0.00%

NAME	TICKER	INDUSTRY	2014 BUY PRICE OPINION	2014 HOLD PRICE OPINION	2014 SELL PRICE OPINION	2014 SHORT PRICE OPINION	2014 MYCROFT FREE CASH FLOW PER SHARE ESTIMATE	2014 MYCROFT FREE CASH FLOW RETURN ON TOTAL CAPITAL ESTIMATE (FROIC) >15% = Great	2014 MYCROFT CAPFLOW ESTIMATE <33% = Great BUT NO NEGATIVE RESULTS	2014 MYCROFT MICHAELIS GROWTH RATE ESTIMATE >15% = Great	DIVIDEND YIELD
Step #1 = Look up the company's current stock market price on the day of analysis and compare it to our 2014 Buy, Hold, Sell & Short Price.											
Step #2 =Take the company's current market price; divide it by the "2014 Mycroft Free Cash Flow Per Share estimate." This gives the "Price to Free Cash Flow."											
All results below are based on the 2014 year end estimates using the "2014 Mycroft Michaelis Growth Rate" and are good until December 31, 2014.											
UQM Technologies, Inc.	UQM	Industrial	Negative Free Cash Flow	Negative Free Cash Flow	Negative Free Cash Flow	Negative Free Cash Flow	-$0.14	-22%	-13%	-22%	0.00%
Uranerz Energy Corporation	URZ	Commodities	Negative Free Cash Flow	Negative Free Cash Flow	Negative Free Cash Flow	Negative Free Cash Flow	-$0.20	-999%	-276%	-999%	0.00%
Uranium Energy Corporation	UEC	Commodities	Negative Free Cash Flow	Negative Free Cash Flow	Negative Free Cash Flow	Negative Free Cash Flow	-$0.19	-28%	-5%	-28%	0.00%
Uranium Resources, Inc.	URRE	Commodities	Negative Free Cash Flow	Negative Free Cash Flow	Negative Free Cash Flow	Negative Free Cash Flow	-$0.99	-42%	-15%	-42%	0.00%
Urban Outfitters Inc.	URBN	Retail	$19.65	$39.30	$58.95	$117.90	$2.62	21%	31%	21%	0.00%
Uroplasty, Inc.	UPI	Medical	Negative Free Cash Flow	Negative Free Cash Flow	Negative Free Cash Flow	Negative Free Cash Flow	-$0.07	-10%	-26%	-10%	0.00%
URS Corporation	URS	Engineering	$40.50	$81.00	$121.50	$243.00	$5.40	6%	24%	7%	1.66%
US Airways Group Inc	LCC	Airlines	Negative Free Cash Flow	Negative Free Cash Flow	Negative Free Cash Flow	Negative Free Cash Flow	-$1.08	-17%	119%	-17%	0.00%
US Concrete Inc	USCR	Building Supplies	$6.98	$13.95	$20.93	$41.85	$0.93	8%	53%	8%	0.00%
US Ecology, Inc.	ECOL	Waste Management	$6.15	$12.30	$18.45	$36.90	$0.82	8%	61%	3%	2.57%
US Silica Holdings Inc	SLCA	Commodities	Negative Free Cash Flow	Negative Free Cash Flow	Negative Free Cash Flow	Negative Free Cash Flow	-$0.60	-6%	148%	-9%	1.99%

NAME	TICKER	INDUSTRY	2014 BUY PRICE OPINION	2014 HOLD PRICE OPINION	2014 SELL PRICE OPINION	2014 SHORT PRICE OPINION	2014 MYCROFT FREE CASH FLOW PER SHARE ESTIMATE	2014 MYCROFT FREE CASH FLOW RETURN ON TOTAL CAPITAL ESTIMATE (FROIC) >15% = Great	2014 MYCROFT CAPFLOW ESTIMATE <33% = Great BUT NO NEGATIVE RESULTS	2014 MYCROFT MICHAELIS GROWTH RATE ESTIMATE >15% = Great	DIVIDEND YIELD
Step #1 = Look up the company's current stock market price on the day of analysis and compare it to our 2014 Buy, Hold, Sell & Short Price.											
Step #2 =Take the company's current market price; divide it by the "2014 Mycroft Free Cash Flow Per Share estimate." This gives the "Price to Free Cash Flow."											
All results below are based on the 2014 year end estimates using the "2014 Mycroft Michaelis Growth Rate" and are good until December 31, 2014.											
USA Mobility, Inc.	USMO	Communication	$21.30	$42.60	$63.90	$127.80	$2.84	20%	17%	19%	3.67%
USA Technologies, Inc.	USAT	Business Services	Negative Free Cash Flow	Negative Free Cash Flow	Negative Free Cash Flow	Negative Free Cash Flow	-$0.10	-17%	170%	-17%	0.00%
USA Truck	USAK	Transportation	$3.00	$6.00	$9.00	$18.00	$0.40	4%	84%	4%	0.00%
Usana Health Sciences, Inc.	USNA	Consumer Goods	$67.73	$135.45	$203.18	$406.35	$9.03	41%	8%	41%	0.00%
USEC Inc.	USU	Commodities	Negative Free Cash Flow	Negative Free Cash Flow	Negative Free Cash Flow	Negative Free Cash Flow	-$12.53	-56%	9%	-56%	0.00%
USG Corp	USG	Building Supplies	Negative Free Cash Flow	Negative Free Cash Flow	Negative Free Cash Flow	Negative Free Cash Flow	-$0.51	-2%	210%	-2%	0.00%
Utah Medical Products	UTMD	Medical	$27.23	$54.45	$81.68	$163.35	$3.63	19%	2%	15%	1.95%
UTi Worldwide, Inc.	UTIW	Transportation	Negative Free Cash Flow	Negative Free Cash Flow	Negative Free Cash Flow	Negative Free Cash Flow	-$0.84	-9%	1132%	-9%	0.40%
VAALCO Energy, Inc.	EGY	Oil & Gas	Negative Free Cash Flow	Negative Free Cash Flow	Negative Free Cash Flow	Negative Free Cash Flow	-$0.51	-13%	152%	-13%	0.00%
Vail Resorts, Inc.	MTN	Travel & Leisure	$35.10	$70.20	$105.30	$210.60	$4.68	11%	37%	10%	1.20%
Valassis Communications Inc	VCI	Advertising	$36.08	$72.15	$108.23	$216.45	$4.81	15%	1%	15%	4.30%

NAME	TICKER	INDUSTRY	2014 BUY PRICE OPINION	2014 HOLD PRICE OPINION	2014 SELL PRICE OPINION	2014 SHORT PRICE OPINION	2014 MYCROFT FREE CASH FLOW PER SHARE ESTIMATE	2014 MYCROFT FREE CASH FLOW RETURN ON TOTAL CAPITAL ESTIMATE (FROIC) >15% = Great	2014 MYCROFT CAPFLOW ESTIMATE <33% = Great BUT NO NEGATIVE RESULTS	2014 MYCROFT MICHAELIS GROWTH RATE ESTIMATE >15% = Great	DIVIDEND YIELD
Step #1 = Look up the company's current stock market price on the day of analysis and compare it to our 2014 Buy, Hold, Sell & Short Price.											
Step #2 =Take the company's current market price; divide it by the "2014 Mycroft Free Cash Flow Per Share estimate." This gives the "Price to Free Cash Flow."											
All results below are based on the 2014 year end estimates using the "2014 Mycroft Michaelis Growth Rate" and are good until December 31, 2014.											
Valero Energy Corporation	VLO	Oil & Gas	$39.83	$79.65	$119.48	$238.95	$5.31	14%	52%	14%	2.50%
Valmont Industries, Inc.	VMI	Industrial	$83.70	$167.40	$251.10	$502.20	$11.16	14%	30%	13%	0.71%
Valspar Corporation	VAL	Chemicals	$28.65	$57.30	$85.95	$171.90	$3.82	14%	24%	11%	1.42%
ValueClick, Inc.	VCLK	Internet	$18.45	$36.90	$55.35	$110.70	$2.46	20%	7%	20%	0.00%
ValueVision Media, Inc.	VVTV	Retail	Negative Free Cash Flow	Negative Free Cash Flow	Negative Free Cash Flow	Negative Free Cash Flow	-$0.12	-5%	245%	-5%	0.00%
Vanda Pharmaceuticals, Inc.	VNDA	Biotech	Negative Free Cash Flow	Negative Free Cash Flow	Negative Free Cash Flow	Negative Free Cash Flow	-$1.48	-821%	0%	-821%	0.00%
Vanguard Health Systems Inc	VHS	Health Care	Negative Free Cash Flow	Negative Free Cash Flow	Negative Free Cash Flow	Negative Free Cash Flow	-$1.54	-4%	140%	-4%	0.00%
Vantage Drilling Co	VTG	Oil & Gas	Negative Free Cash Flow	Negative Free Cash Flow	Negative Free Cash Flow	Negative Free Cash Flow	-$1.26	-15%	-37%	-15%	0.00%
Vantiv Inc	VNTV	Business Services	$17.78	$35.55	$53.33	$106.65	$2.37	22%	15%	22%	0.00%
Varian Medical Systems, Inc.	VAR	Medical	$35.93	$71.85	$107.78	$215.55	$4.79	25%	16%	25%	0.00%
Vasco Data Security International, Inc.	VDSI	Software	$4.20	$8.40	$12.60	$25.20	$0.56	12%	7%	12%	0.00%

NAME	TICKER	INDUSTRY	2014 BUY PRICE OPINION	2014 HOLD PRICE OPINION	2014 SELL PRICE OPINION	2014 SHORT PRICE OPINION	2014 MYCROFT FREE CASH FLOW PER SHARE ESTIMATE	2014 MYCROFT FREE CASH FLOW RETURN ON TOTAL CAPITAL ESTIMATE (FROIC) >15% = Great	2014 MYCROFT CAPFLOW ESTIMATE <33% = Great BUT NO NEGATIVE RESULTS	2014 MYCROFT MICHAELIS GROWTH RATE ESTIMATE >15% = Great	DIVIDEND YIELD
Step #1 = Look up the company's current stock market price on the day of analysis and compare it to our 2014 Buy, Hold, Sell & Short Price.											
Step #2 =Take the company's current market price; divide it by the "2014 Mycroft Free Cash Flow Per Share estimate." This gives the "Price to Free Cash Flow."											
All results below are based on the 2014 year end estimates using the "2014 Mycroft Michaelis Growth Rate" and are good until December 31, 2014.											
Vascular Solutions, Inc.	VASC	Medical	$3.75	$7.50	$11.25	$22.50	$0.50	9%	61%	9%	0.00%
VCA Antech, Inc.	WOOF	Health Care	$17.10	$34.20	$51.30	$102.60	$2.28	10%	28%	10%	0.00%
Vector Group, Ltd.	VGR	Tobacco	$3.68	$7.35	$11.03	$22.05	$0.49	-17%	31%	115%	10.10%
Vectren Corp	VVC	Utilities	$5.48	$10.95	$16.43	$32.85	$0.73	2%	86%	2%	4.30%
Veeco Instruments Inc	VECO	Semiconductors	$11.25	$22.50	$33.75	$67.50	$1.50	7%	45%	7%	0.00%
Venaxis Inc	APPY	Medical	Negative Free Cash Flow	Negative Free Cash Flow	Negative Free Cash Flow	Negative Free Cash Flow	-$0.33	-37%	-3%	-37%	0.00%
Ventrus Biosciences, Inc.	VTUS	Drugs	Negative Free Cash Flow	Negative Free Cash Flow	Negative Free Cash Flow	Negative Free Cash Flow	-$0.82	-52%	0%	-52%	0.00%
Vera Bradley, Inc.	VRA	Apparel & Furniture	$1.05	$2.10	$3.15	$6.30	$0.14	2%	85%	2%	0.00%
Verastem Inc	VSTM	Biotech	Negative Free Cash Flow	Negative Free Cash Flow	Negative Free Cash Flow	Negative Free Cash Flow	-$1.00	-34%	-1%	-34%	0.00%
Verenium Corporation	VRNM	Biotech	Negative Free Cash Flow	Negative Free Cash Flow	Negative Free Cash Flow	Negative Free Cash Flow	-$1.51	-94%	-19%	-94%	0.00%
VeriFone Systems, Inc.	PAY	Industrial	$12.83	$25.65	$38.48	$76.95	$1.71	7%	31%	7%	0.00%

NAME	TICKER	INDUSTRY	2014 BUY PRICE OPINION	2014 HOLD PRICE OPINION	2014 SELL PRICE OPINION	2014 SHORT PRICE OPINION	2014 MYCROFT FREE CASH FLOW PER SHARE ESTIMATE	2014 MYCROFT FREE CASH FLOW RETURN ON TOTAL CAPITAL ESTIMATE (FROIC) >15% = Great	2014 MYCROFT CAPFLOW ESTIMATE <33% = Great BUT NO NEGATIVE RESULTS	2014 MYCROFT MICHAELIS GROWTH RATE ESTIMATE >15% = Great	DIVIDEND YIELD
Step #1 = Look up the company's current stock market price on the day of analysis and compare it to our 2014 Buy, Hold, Sell & Short Price.										
Step #2 =Take the company's current market price; divide it by the "2014 Mycroft Free Cash Flow Per Share estimate." This gives the "Price to Free Cash Flow."										
All results below are based on the 2014 year end estimates using the "2014 Mycroft Michaelis Growth Rate" and are good until December 31, 2014.										
Verint Systems, Inc.	VRNT	Software	$21.83	$43.65	$65.48	$130.95	$2.91	12%	12%	12%	0.00%
VeriSign, Inc.	VRSN	Software	$61.58	$123.15	$184.73	$369.45	$8.21	124%	11%	124%	0.00%
Verisk Analytics, Inc.	VRSK	Business Services	$24.75	$49.50	$74.25	$148.50	$3.30	30%	19%	30%	0.00%
Verizon Communications Inc	VZ	Communication	$38.03	$76.05	$114.08	$228.15	$5.07	16%	62%	13%	4.50%
Vermillion, Inc.	VRML	Medical	Negative Free Cash Flow	Negative Free Cash Flow	Negative Free Cash Flow	Negative Free Cash Flow	-$0.34	-64%	0%	-64%	0.00%
Versar, Inc.	VSR	Engineering	$4.20	$8.40	$12.60	$25.20	$0.56	12%	5%	12%	0.00%
Vertex Pharmaceuticals	VRTX	Biotech	$0.38	$0.75	$1.13	$2.25	$0.05	1%	85%	1%	0.00%
VF Corporation	VFC	Apparel & Furniture	$88.73	$177.45	$266.18	$532.35	$11.83	16%	23%	13%	1.80%
Viacom, Inc.	VIAB	Entertainment	$48.15	$96.30	$144.45	$288.90	$6.42	18%	5%	15%	1.46%
Viad Corporation	VVI	Business Services	$5.78	$11.55	$17.33	$34.65	$0.77	4%	66%	3%	1.64%
Viasat Inc	VSAT	Communication	Negative Free Cash Flow	Negative Free Cash Flow	Negative Free Cash Flow	Negative Free Cash Flow	-$2.16	-7%	168%	-7%	0.00%

NAME	TICKER	INDUSTRY	2014 BUY PRICE OPINION	2014 HOLD PRICE OPINION	2014 SELL PRICE OPINION	2014 SHORT PRICE OPINION	2014 MYCROFT FREE CASH FLOW PER SHARE ESTIMATE	2014 MYCROFT FREE CASH FLOW RETURN ON TOTAL CAPITAL ESTIMATE (FROIC) >15% = Great	2014 MYCROFT CAPFLOW ESTIMATE <33% = Great BUT NO NEGATIVE RESULTS	2014 MYCROFT MICHAELIS GROWTH RATE ESTIMATE >15% = Great	DIVIDEND YIELD
Step #1 = Look up the company's current stock market price on the day of analysis and compare it to our 2014 Buy, Hold, Sell & Short Price.											
Step #2 =Take the company's current market price; divide it by the "2014 Mycroft Free Cash Flow Per Share estimate." This gives the "Price to Free Cash Flow."											
All results below are based on the 2014 year end estimates using the "2014 Mycroft Michaelis Growth Rate" and are good until December 31, 2014.											
Vical Incorporated	VICL	Biotech	Negative Free Cash Flow	Negative Free Cash Flow	Negative Free Cash Flow	Negative Free Cash Flow	-$0.32	-38%	-3%	-38%	0.00%
Vicor Corporation	VICR	Computers	Negative Free Cash Flow	Negative Free Cash Flow	Negative Free Cash Flow	Negative Free Cash Flow	-$0.18	-5%	5500%	-5%	0.00%
Video Display Corporation	VIDE	Computers	$2.18	$4.35	$6.53	$13.05	$0.29	5%	12%	5%	0.00%
Village Super Market, Inc. Class A	VLGEA	Retail	$21.15	$42.30	$63.45	$126.90	$2.82	15%	34%	12%	2.71%
Virco Manufacturing Corporation	VIRC	Industrial	Negative Free Cash Flow	Negative Free Cash Flow	Negative Free Cash Flow	Negative Free Cash Flow	-$0.12	-6%	320%	-6%	0.00%
VirnetX Holding Corp	VHC	Software	Negative Free Cash Flow	Negative Free Cash Flow	Negative Free Cash Flow	Negative Free Cash Flow	-$0.35	-43%	0%	-43%	0.00%
ViroPharma, Inc.	VPHM	Biotech	Negative Free Cash Flow	Negative Free Cash Flow	Negative Free Cash Flow	Negative Free Cash Flow	-$0.37	-3%	-9%	-3%	0.00%
Virtusa Corporation	VRTU	Software	$2.18	$4.35	$6.53	$13.05	$0.29	3%	60%	3%	0.00%
Vishay Intertechnology, Inc.	VSH	Semiconductors	$7.65	$15.30	$22.95	$45.90	$1.02	6%	52%	6%	0.00%
Vishay Precision Group, Inc.	VPG	Computers	$7.65	$15.30	$22.95	$45.90	$1.02	6%	31%	6%	0.00%
VistaPrint, Ltd.	VPRT	Advertising	$13.50	$27.00	$40.50	$81.00	$1.80	13%	62%	13%	0.00%

NAME	TICKER	INDUSTRY	2014 BUY PRICE OPINION	2014 HOLD PRICE OPINION	2014 SELL PRICE OPINION	2014 SHORT PRICE OPINION	2014 MYCROFT FREE CASH FLOW PER SHARE ESTIMATE	2014 MYCROFT FREE CASH FLOW RETURN ON TOTAL CAPITAL ESTIMATE (FROIC) >15% = Great	2014 MYCROFT CAPFLOW ESTIMATE <33% = Great BUT NO NEGATIVE RESULTS	2014 MYCROFT MICHAELIS GROWTH RATE ESTIMATE >15% = Great	DIVIDEND YIELD
Step #1 = Look up the company's current stock market price on the day of analysis and compare it to our 2014 Buy, Hold, Sell & Short Price.											
Step #2 =Take the company's current market price; divide it by the "2014 Mycroft Free Cash Flow Per Share estimate." This gives the "Price to Free Cash Flow."											
All results below are based on the 2014 year end estimates using the "2014 Mycroft Michaelis Growth Rate" and are good until December 31, 2014.											
Visteon Corp.	VC	Autos	$24.15	$48.30	$72.45	$144.90	$3.22	8%	62%	8%	0.00%
Vitacost.com, Inc.	VITC	Retail	Negative Free Cash Flow	Negative Free Cash Flow	Negative Free Cash Flow	Negative Free Cash Flow	-$0.12	-7%	326%	-7%	0.00%
Vitamin Shoppe, Inc.	VSI	Retail	$10.50	$21.00	$31.50	$63.00	$1.40	8%	53%	8%	0.00%
Vitesse Semiconductor Corp	VTSS	Semiconductors	Negative Free Cash Flow	Negative Free Cash Flow	Negative Free Cash Flow	Negative Free Cash Flow	-$0.05	-3%	-18%	-3%	0.00%
Vivus	VVUS	Biotech	Negative Free Cash Flow	Negative Free Cash Flow	Negative Free Cash Flow	Negative Free Cash Flow	-$2.08	-113%	-2%	-113%	0.00%
VMware, Inc.	VMW	Software	$40.80	$81.60	$122.40	$244.80	$5.44	28%	15%	28%	0.00%
Vocera Communications Inc	VCRA	Communication	$1.13	$2.25	$3.38	$6.75	$0.15	3%	54%	3%	0.00%
Vocus, Inc.	VOCS	Software	$4.80	$9.60	$14.40	$28.80	$0.64	13%	39%	13%	0.00%
Volcano Corporation	VOLC	Medical	Negative Free Cash Flow	Negative Free Cash Flow	Negative Free Cash Flow	Negative Free Cash Flow	-$0.31	-3%	173%	-3%	0.00%
Voltari Corp	VLTC	Communication	$16.95	$33.90	$50.85	$101.70	$2.26	21%	14%	21%	0.00%
Volterra Semiconductor Corporation	VLTR	Semiconductors	$8.55	$17.10	$25.65	$51.30	$1.14	13%	21%	13%	0.00%

NAME	TICKER	INDUSTRY	2014 BUY PRICE OPINION	2014 HOLD PRICE OPINION	2014 SELL PRICE OPINION	2014 SHORT PRICE OPINION	2014 MYCROFT FREE CASH FLOW PER SHARE ESTIMATE	2014 MYCROFT FREE CASH FLOW RETURN ON TOTAL CAPITAL ESTIMATE (FROIC) >15% = Great	2014 MYCROFT CAPFLOW ESTIMATE <33% = Great BUT NO NEGATIVE RESULTS	2014 MYCROFT MICHAELIS GROWTH RATE ESTIMATE >15% = Great	DIVIDEND YIELD
Step #1 = Look up the company's current stock market price on the day of analysis and compare it to our 2014 Buy, Hold, Sell & Short Price.											
Step #2 =Take the company's current market price; divide it by the "2014 Mycroft Free Cash Flow Per Share estimate." This gives the "Price to Free Cash Flow."											
All results below are based on the 2014 year end estimates using the "2014 Mycroft Michaelis Growth Rate" and are good until December 31, 2014.											
Vonage Holdings Corporation	VG	Communication	$3.60	$7.20	$10.80	$21.60	$0.48	24%	24%	24%	0.00%
VOXX International Corp Class A	VOXX	Computers	$7.88	$15.75	$23.63	$47.25	$1.05	4%	38%	4%	0.00%
Vringo, Inc.	VRNG	Software	Negative Free Cash Flow	Negative Free Cash Flow	Negative Free Cash Flow	Negative Free Cash Flow	-$0.55	-34%	-100%	-34%	0.00%
VSE Corporation	VSEC	Engineering	$80.25	$160.50	$240.75	$481.50	$10.70	16%	20%	16%	0.82%
Vulcan Materials Company	VMC	Building Supplies	$4.43	$8.85	$13.28	$26.55	$0.59	1%	61%	1%	0.08%
W&T Offshore Inc	WTI	Oil & Gas	Negative Free Cash Flow	Negative Free Cash Flow	Negative Free Cash Flow	Negative Free Cash Flow	-$4.77	-28%	181%	-28%	2.12%
W. R. Grace & Co.	GRA	Chemicals	$43.43	$86.85	$130.28	$260.55	$5.79	24%	29%	24%	0.00%
W.W. Grainger, Inc.	GWW	Industrial	$89.78	$179.55	$269.33	$538.65	$11.97	20%	25%	14%	1.38%
Wabash National Corporation	WNC	Truck Manufacturing	$9.23	$18.45	$27.68	$55.35	$1.23	10%	19%	10%	0.00%
Wabco Holdings Incorporated	WBC	Autos	$40.20	$80.40	$120.60	$241.20	$5.36	31%	26%	31%	0.00%
WageWorks Inc	WAGE	Business Services	$13.80	$27.60	$41.40	$82.80	$1.84	26%	29%	26%	0.00%

NAME	TICKER	INDUSTRY	2014 BUY PRICE OPINION	2014 HOLD PRICE OPINION	2014 SELL PRICE OPINION	2014 SHORT PRICE OPINION	2014 MYCROFT FREE CASH FLOW PER SHARE ESTIMATE	2014 MYCROFT FREE CASH FLOW RETURN ON TOTAL CAPITAL ESTIMATE (FROIC) >15% = Great	2014 MYCROFT CAPFLOW ESTIMATE <33% = Great BUT NO NEGATIVE RESULTS	2014 MYCROFT MICHAELIS GROWTH RATE ESTIMATE >15% = Great	DIVIDEND YIELD
Walgreen Company	WAG	Retail	$22.73	$45.45	$68.18	$136.35	$3.03	12%	34%	9%	2.48%
Walker & Dunlop, Inc.	WD	Real Estate	Negative Free Cash Flow	Negative Free Cash Flow	Negative Free Cash Flow	Negative Free Cash Flow	-$1.65	-7%	-5%	-7%	0.00%
Wal-Mart Stores Inc	WMT	Retail	$29.25	$58.50	$87.75	$175.50	$3.90	10%	53%	8%	2.54%
Walt Disney Co	DIS	Entertainment	$25.13	$50.25	$75.38	$150.75	$3.35	10%	33%	9%	1.17%
Walter Energy Inc	WLT	Coal	Negative Free Cash Flow	Negative Free Cash Flow	Negative Free Cash Flow	Negative Free Cash Flow	-$3.80	-8%	-1843%	-7%	0.26%
Warner Chilcott PLC Class A	WCRX	Drugs	$28.35	$56.70	$85.05	$170.10	$3.78	26%	7%	24%	2.33%
Warren Resources, Inc.	WRES	Oil & Gas	$8.78	$17.55	$26.33	$52.65	$1.17	23%	3%	23%	0.00%
Washington Post Company	WPO	Publishing	$326.85	$653.70	$980.55	$1,961.10	$43.58	9%	41%	9%	1.68%
Waste Connections, Inc.	WCN	Waste Management	$19.50	$39.00	$58.50	$117.00	$2.60	10%	37%	9%	0.92%
Waste Management Inc	WM	Waste Management	$16.73	$33.45	$50.18	$100.35	$2.23	6%	56%	6%	3.57%
Waters Corporation	WAT	Medical	$35.78	$71.55	$107.33	$214.65	$4.77	16%	25%	16%	0.00%

Step #1 = Look up the company's current stock market price on the day of analysis and compare it to our 2014 Buy, Hold, Sell & Short Price.

Step #2 =Take the company's current market price; divide it by the "2014 Mycroft Free Cash Flow Per Share estimate." This gives the "Price to Free Cash Flow."

All results below are based on the 2014 year end estimates using the "2014 Mycroft Michaelis Growth Rate" and are good until December 31, 2014.

NAME	TICKER	INDUSTRY	2014 BUY PRICE OPINION	2014 HOLD PRICE OPINION	2014 SELL PRICE OPINION	2014 SHORT PRICE OPINION	2014 MYCROFT FREE CASH FLOW PER SHARE ESTIMATE	2014 MYCROFT FREE CASH FLOW RETURN ON TOTAL CAPITAL ESTIMATE (FROIC) >15% = Great	2014 MYCROFT CAPFLOW ESTIMATE <33% = Great BUT NO NEGATIVE RESULTS	2014 MYCROFT MICHAELIS GROWTH RATE ESTIMATE >15% = Great	DIVIDEND YIELD

Step #1 = Look up the company's current stock market price on the day of analysis and compare it to our 2014 Buy, Hold, Sell & Short Price.

Step #2 =Take the company's current market price; divide it by the "2014 Mycroft Free Cash Flow Per Share estimate." This gives the "Price to Free Cash Flow."

All results below are based on the 2014 year end estimates using the "2014 Mycroft Michaelis Growth Rate" and are good until December 31, 2014.

NAME	TICKER	INDUSTRY	BUY	HOLD	SELL	SHORT	FCF/SHARE	FROIC	CAPFLOW	MICHAELIS	DIV YIELD
Watsco, Inc.	WSO	Computers	$34.73	$69.45	$104.18	$208.35	$4.63	14%	8%	12%	1.09%
Watts Water Technologies, Inc.	WTS	Industrial	$21.08	$42.15	$63.23	$126.45	$2.81	7%	30%	7%	0.94%
Wausau Paper Corporation	WPP	Forest Products	Negative Free Cash Flow	Negative Free Cash Flow	Negative Free Cash Flow	Negative Free Cash Flow	-$1.91	-32%	14402%	-33%	0.99%
Wayside Technology Group, Inc.	WSTG	Computers	$7.35	$14.70	$22.05	$44.10	$0.98	13%	6%	9%	4.90%
WD-40 Company	WDFC	Chemicals	$23.10	$46.20	$69.30	$138.60	$3.08	23%	6%	14%	1.98%
Web.com Group, Inc.	WWWW	Internet	$11.03	$22.05	$33.08	$66.15	$1.47	9%	25%	9%	0.00%
WebMD Health Corporation	WBMD	Software	$9.00	$18.00	$27.00	$54.00	$1.20	4%	31%	4%	0.00%
Weight Watchers International, Inc.	WTW	Services	$46.28	$92.55	$138.83	$277.65	$6.17	34%	24%	31%	1.86%
Weis Markets, Inc.	WMK	Retail	$3.00	$6.00	$9.00	$18.00	$0.40	1%	92%	0%	2.47%
WellCare Health Plans, Inc.	WCG	Health Care	$10.13	$20.25	$30.38	$60.75	$1.35	4%	50%	4%	0.00%
WellPoint Inc	WLP	Health Care	-$7.50	-$15.00	-$22.50	-$45.00	-$1.00	-1%	212%	0%	1.68%

NAME	TICKER	INDUSTRY	2014 BUY PRICE OPINION	2014 HOLD PRICE OPINION	2014 SELL PRICE OPINION	2014 SHORT PRICE OPINION	2014 MYCROFT FREE CASH FLOW PER SHARE ESTIMATE	2014 MYCROFT FREE CASH FLOW RETURN ON TOTAL CAPITAL ESTIMATE (FROIC) >15% = Great	2014 MYCROFT CAPFLOW ESTIMATE <33% = Great BUT NO NEGATIVE RESULTS	2014 MYCROFT MICHAELIS GROWTH RATE ESTIMATE >15% = Great	DIVIDEND YIELD
Step #1 = Look up the company's current stock market price on the day of analysis and compare it to our 2014 Buy, Hold, Sell & Short Price.											
Step #2 =Take the company's current market price; divide it by the "2014 Mycroft Free Cash Flow Per Share estimate." This gives the "Price to Free Cash Flow."											
All results below are based on the 2014 year end estimates using the "2014 Mycroft Michaelis Growth Rate" and are good until December 31, 2014.											
Wells-Gardner Electronic	WGA	Computers	$0.98	$1.95	$2.93	$5.85	$0.13	7%	6%	7%	0.00%
Wendy's Co	WEN	Restaurants	$1.35	$2.70	$4.05	$8.10	$0.18	2%	74%	2%	2.42%
Werner Enterprises, Inc.	WERN	Transportation	$3.15	$6.30	$9.45	$18.90	$0.42	4%	87%	3%	0.82%
Wesco Aircraft Holdings Inc	WAIR	Industrial	$5.40	$10.80	$16.20	$32.40	$0.72	4%	0%	4%	0.00%
Wesco International, Inc.	WCC	Industrial	$46.88	$93.75	$140.63	$281.25	$6.25	12%	8%	12%	0.00%
West Corp	WSTC	Business Services	$18.60	$37.20	$55.80	$111.60	$2.48	-31%	34%	-17%	4.10%
West Marine Inc.	WMAR	Retail	Negative Free Cash Flow	Negative Free Cash Flow	Negative Free Cash Flow	Negative Free Cash Flow	-$0.08	-1%	108%	-1%	0.00%
West Pharmaceutical Services, Inc.	WST	Medical	$16.73	$33.45	$50.18	$100.35	$2.23	7%	67%	6%	0.50%
Westar Energy, Inc.	WR	Utilities	Negative Free Cash Flow	Negative Free Cash Flow	Negative Free Cash Flow	Negative Free Cash Flow	-$0.51	-1%	109%	1%	4.50%
Westell Technologies, Inc.	WSTL	Communication	Negative Free Cash Flow	Negative Free Cash Flow	Negative Free Cash Flow	Negative Free Cash Flow	-$0.21	-10%	-3%	-10%	0.00%
Western Digital Corporation	WDC	Computers	$83.03	$166.05	$249.08	$498.15	$11.07	22%	31%	21%	1.52%

NAME	TICKER	INDUSTRY	2014 BUY PRICE OPINION	2014 HOLD PRICE OPINION	2014 SELL PRICE OPINION	2014 SHORT PRICE OPINION	2014 MYCROFT FREE CASH FLOW PER SHARE ESTIMATE	2014 MYCROFT FREE CASH FLOW RETURN ON TOTAL CAPITAL ESTIMATE (FROIC) >15% = Great	2014 MYCROFT CAPFLOW ESTIMATE <33% = Great BUT NO NEGATIVE RESULTS	2014 MYCROFT MICHAELIS GROWTH RATE ESTIMATE >15% = Great	DIVIDEND YIELD
Step #1 = Look up the company's current stock market price on the day of analysis and compare it to our 2014 Buy, Hold, Sell & Short Price.											
Step #2 =Take the company's current market price; divide it by the "2014 Mycroft Free Cash Flow Per Share estimate." This gives the "Price to Free Cash Flow."											
All results below are based on the 2014 year end estimates using the "2014 Mycroft Michaelis Growth Rate" and are good until December 31, 2014.											
Western Refining Inc	WNR	Oil & Gas	$76.13	$152.25	$228.38	$456.75	$10.15	42%	30%	40%	2.54%
Westinghouse Air Brake Technologies	WAB	Transportation	$18.90	$37.80	$56.70	$113.40	$2.52	12%	14%	11%	0.26%
Westlake Chemical Corporation	WLK	Chemicals	$2.10	$4.20	$6.30	$12.60	$0.28	1%	97%	-1%	0.87%
Westmoreland Coal Co	WLB	Coal	$33.08	$66.15	$99.23	$198.45	$4.41	44%	34%	44%	0.00%
Wet Seal, Inc.	WTSL	Retail	Negative Free Cash Flow	Negative Free Cash Flow	Negative Free Cash Flow	Negative Free Cash Flow	-$0.49	-38%	-74%	-38%	0.00%
WEX Inc	WEX	Business Services	$28.58	$57.15	$85.73	$171.45	$3.81	14%	16%	14%	0.00%
Weyco Group, Inc.	WEYS	Apparel & Furniture	$14.03	$28.05	$42.08	$84.15	$1.87	11%	32%	9%	2.91%
Weyerhaeuser Co	WY	Forest Products	$5.85	$11.70	$17.55	$35.10	$0.78	4%	36%	2%	3.10%
WGL Holdings, Inc.	WGL	Utilities	Negative Free Cash Flow	Negative Free Cash Flow	Negative Free Cash Flow	Negative Free Cash Flow	-$0.19	-1%	104%	-1%	4.00%
Whirlpool Corporation	WHR	Computers	$38.25	$76.50	$114.75	$229.50	$5.10	6%	55%	5%	1.84%
WhiteWave Foods Co	WWAV	Consumer Goods	$3.45	$6.90	$10.35	$20.70	$0.46	6%	60%	6%	0.00%

NAME	TICKER	INDUSTRY	2014 BUY PRICE OPINION	2014 HOLD PRICE OPINION	2014 SELL PRICE OPINION	2014 SHORT PRICE OPINION	2014 MYCROFT FREE CASH FLOW PER SHARE ESTIMATE	2014 MYCROFT FREE CASH FLOW RETURN ON TOTAL CAPITAL ESTIMATE (FROIC) >15% = Great	2014 MYCROFT CAPFLOW ESTIMATE <33% = Great BUT NO NEGATIVE RESULTS	2014 MYCROFT MICHAELIS GROWTH RATE ESTIMATE >15% = Great	DIVIDEND YIELD

Step #1 = Look up the company's current stock market price on the day of analysis and compare it to our 2014 Buy, Hold, Sell & Short Price.

Step #2 =Take the company's current market price; divide it by the "2014 Mycroft Free Cash Flow Per Share estimate." This gives the "Price to Free Cash Flow."

All results below are based on the 2014 year end estimates using the "2014 Mycroft Michaelis Growth Rate" and are good until December 31, 2014.

NAME	TICKER	INDUSTRY	BUY	HOLD	SELL	SHORT	FCF/SHARE	FROIC	CAPFLOW	GROWTH	DIV YIELD
Whiting Petroleum Corporation	WLL	Oil & Gas	Negative Free Cash Flow	Negative Free Cash Flow	Negative Free Cash Flow	Negative Free Cash Flow	-$7.04	-16%	155%	-16%	0.00%
Whole Foods Market, Inc.	WFM	Retail	$17.93	$35.85	$53.78	$107.55	$2.39	20%	24%	17%	0.71%
Willamette Valley Vineyards	WVVI	Beverages	Negative Free Cash Flow	Negative Free Cash Flow	Negative Free Cash Flow	Negative Free Cash Flow	-$0.02	0%	105%	0%	0.00%
Willbros Group, Inc.	WG	Oil & Gas	Negative Free Cash Flow	Negative Free Cash Flow	Negative Free Cash Flow	Negative Free Cash Flow	-$1.13	-17%	-22%	-17%	0.00%
William Lyon Homes	WLH	Homebuilding	Negative Free Cash Flow	Negative Free Cash Flow	Negative Free Cash Flow	Negative Free Cash Flow	-$1.20	-12%	0%	-12%	0.00%
Williams Companies Inc	WMB	Oil & Gas	Negative Free Cash Flow	Negative Free Cash Flow	Negative Free Cash Flow	Negative Free Cash Flow	-$1.46	-7%	147%	-10%	4.10%
Williams-Sonoma, Inc.	WSM	Retail	$7.80	$15.60	$23.40	$46.80	$1.04	7%	69%	1%	2.20%
Willis Lease Finance Corporation	WLFC	Rentals	Negative Free Cash Flow	Negative Free Cash Flow	Negative Free Cash Flow	Negative Free Cash Flow	-$6.46	-6%	179%	-6%	0.00%
Windstream Holdings, Inc.	WIN	Communication	$8.25	$16.50	$24.75	$49.50	$1.10	6%	65%	12%	12.50%
Winmark Corporation	WINA	Retail	Negative Free Cash Flow	Negative Free Cash Flow	Negative Free Cash Flow	Negative Free Cash Flow	-$0.75	-14%	119%	-17%	0.27%
Winnebago Industries	WGO	Autos	Negative Free Cash Flow	Negative Free Cash Flow	Negative Free Cash Flow	Negative Free Cash Flow	-$0.81	-14%	-22%	-14%	0.00%

NAME	TICKER	INDUSTRY	2014 BUY PRICE OPINION	2014 HOLD PRICE OPINION	2014 SELL PRICE OPINION	2014 SHORT PRICE OPINION	2014 MYCROFT FREE CASH FLOW PER SHARE ESTIMATE	2014 MYCROFT FREE CASH FLOW RETURN ON TOTAL CAPITAL ESTIMATE (FROIC) >15% = Great	2014 MYCROFT CAPFLOW ESTIMATE <33% = Great BUT NO NEGATIVE RESULTS	2014 MYCROFT MICHAELIS GROWTH RATE ESTIMATE >15% = Great	DIVIDEND YIELD
Step #1 = Look up the company's current stock market price on the day of analysis and compare it to our 2014 Buy, Hold, Sell & Short Price.											
Step #2 =Take the company's current market price; divide it by the "2014 Mycroft Free Cash Flow Per Share estimate." This gives the "Price to Free Cash Flow."											
All results below are based on the 2014 year end estimates using the "2014 Mycroft Michaelis Growth Rate" and are good until December 31, 2014.											
Wisconsin Energy Corporation	WEC	Utilities	$19.13	$38.25	$57.38	$114.75	$2.55	6%	56%	6%	3.84%
WMS Industries, Inc.	WMS	Travel & Leisure	Negative Free Cash Flow	Negative Free Cash Flow	Negative Free Cash Flow	Negative Free Cash Flow	-$0.38	-2%	114%	-2%	0.00%
Wolverine World Wide	WWW	Apparel & Furniture	$24.53	$49.05	$73.58	$147.15	$3.27	20%	15%	18%	0.42%
Woodward, Inc.	WWD	Industrial	$13.50	$27.00	$40.50	$81.00	$1.80	8%	46%	7%	0.78%
Workday Inc Class A	WDAY	Software	Negative Free Cash Flow	Negative Free Cash Flow	Negative Free Cash Flow	Negative Free Cash Flow	-$0.23	-6%	4280%	-6%	0.00%
World Fuel Services Corporation	INT	Oil & Gas	$34.88	$69.75	$104.63	$209.25	$4.65	15%	13%	15%	0.40%
World Wrestling Entertainment, Inc.	WWE	Entertainment	Negative Free Cash Flow	Negative Free Cash Flow	Negative Free Cash Flow	Negative Free Cash Flow	-$0.07	-2%	122%	-10%	4.40%
Worthington Industries	WOR	Industrial	$28.88	$57.75	$86.63	$173.25	$3.85	21%	16%	19%	1.75%
WPX Energy Inc Class A	WPX	Oil & Gas	Negative Free Cash Flow	Negative Free Cash Flow	Negative Free Cash Flow	Negative Free Cash Flow	-$3.00	-9%	194%	-9%	0.00%
Wright Medical Group, Inc.	WMGI	Medical	$1.20	$2.40	$3.60	$7.20	$0.16	1%	77%	1%	0.00%
WSI Industries, Inc.	WSCI	Industrial	$0.23	$0.45	$0.68	$1.35	$0.03	0%	98%	0%	2.43%

NAME	TICKER	INDUSTRY	2014 BUY PRICE OPINION	2014 HOLD PRICE OPINION	2014 SELL PRICE OPINION	2014 SHORT PRICE OPINION	2014 MYCROFT FREE CASH FLOW PER SHARE ESTIMATE	2014 MYCROFT FREE CASH FLOW RETURN ON TOTAL CAPITAL ESTIMATE (FROIC) >15% = Great	2014 MYCROFT CAPFLOW ESTIMATE <33% = Great BUT NO NEGATIVE RESULTS	2014 MYCROFT MICHAELIS GROWTH RATE ESTIMATE >15% = Great	DIVIDEND YIELD
Step #1 = Look up the company's current stock market price on the day of analysis and compare it to our 2014 Buy, Hold, Sell & Short Price.											
Step #2 =Take the company's current market price; divide it by the "2014 Mycroft Free Cash Flow Per Share estimate." This gives the "Price to Free Cash Flow."											
All results below are based on the 2014 year end estimates using the "2014 Mycroft Michaelis Growth Rate" and are good until December 31, 2014.											
Wyndham Worldwide Corporation	WYN	Travel & Leisure	$57.08	$114.15	$171.23	$342.45	$7.61	16%	21%	15%	1.87%
Wynn Resorts Ltd	WYNN	Travel & Leisure	$96.68	$193.35	$290.03	$580.05	$12.89	22%	22%	16%	2.65%
Xcel Energy Inc	XEL	Utilities	Negative Free Cash Flow	Negative Free Cash Flow	Negative Free Cash Flow	Negative Free Cash Flow	-$1.71	-5%	138%	-4%	4.10%
XenoPort, Inc.	XNPT	Biotech	Negative Free Cash Flow	Negative Free Cash Flow	Negative Free Cash Flow	Negative Free Cash Flow	-$1.24	-68%	-1%	-68%	0.00%
Xerium Technologies, Inc.	XRM	Forest Products	$7.58	$15.15	$22.73	$45.45	$1.01	4%	60%	4%	0.00%
Xerox Corporation	XRX	Software	$15.45	$30.90	$46.35	$92.70	$2.06	12%	17%	13%	2.24%
Xilinx Inc	XLNX	Semiconductors	$18.98	$37.95	$56.93	$113.85	$2.53	17%	5%	11%	2.13%
XO Group Inc	XOXO	Retail	$5.03	$10.05	$15.08	$30.15	$0.67	11%	22%	11%	0.00%
XOMA Corp	XOMA	Biotech	Negative Free Cash Flow	Negative Free Cash Flow	Negative Free Cash Flow	Negative Free Cash Flow	-$0.54	-319%	-5%	-319%	0.00%
XPO Logistics Inc	XPO	Transportation	Negative Free Cash Flow	Negative Free Cash Flow	Negative Free Cash Flow	Negative Free Cash Flow	-$2.06	-33%	-13%	-33%	0.00%
XRS Corp	XRSC	Software	$1.20	$2.40	$3.60	$7.20	$0.16	9%	47%	9%	0.00%

NAME	TICKER	INDUSTRY	2014 BUY PRICE OPINION	2014 HOLD PRICE OPINION	2014 SELL PRICE OPINION	2014 SHORT PRICE OPINION	2014 MYCROFT FREE CASH FLOW PER SHARE ESTIMATE	2014 MYCROFT FREE CASH FLOW RETURN ON TOTAL CAPITAL ESTIMATE (FROIC) >15% = Great	2014 MYCROFT CAPFLOW ESTIMATE <33% = Great BUT NO NEGATIVE RESULTS	2014 MYCROFT MICHAELIS GROWTH RATE ESTIMATE >15% = Great	DIVIDEND YIELD
Step #1 = Look up the company's current stock market price on the day of analysis and compare it to our 2014 Buy, Hold, Sell & Short Price.											
Step #2 =Take the company's current market price; divide it by the "2014 Mycroft Free Cash Flow Per Share estimate." This gives the "Price to Free Cash Flow."											
All results below are based on the 2014 year end estimates using the "2014 Mycroft Michaelis Growth Rate" and are good until December 31, 2014.											
Xylem Inc	XYL	Industrial	$9.30	$18.60	$27.90	$55.80	$1.24	7%	35%	6%	1.72%
Yahoo! Inc	YHOO	Internet	Negative Free Cash Flow	Negative Free Cash Flow	Negative Free Cash Flow	Negative Free Cash Flow	-$0.73	-5%	-146%	-5%	0.00%
Yelp Inc Class A	YELP	Internet	Negative Free Cash Flow	Negative Free Cash Flow	Negative Free Cash Flow	Negative Free Cash Flow	-$0.10	-4%	188%	-4%	0.00%
York Water Company	YORW	Utilities	$4.20	$8.40	$12.60	$25.20	$0.56	4%	59%	3%	2.78%
YRC Worldwide, Inc.	YRCW	Transportation	Negative Free Cash Flow	Negative Free Cash Flow	Negative Free Cash Flow	Negative Free Cash Flow	-$9.46	-14%	-272%	-14%	0.00%
Yum Brands Inc	YUM	Restaurants	$17.03	$34.05	$51.08	$102.15	$2.27	18%	56%	8%	1.86%
Zagg, Inc.	ZAGG	Retail	$6.53	$13.05	$19.58	$39.15	$0.87	14%	8%	14%	0.00%
Zale Corporation	ZLC	Retail	Negative Free Cash Flow	Negative Free Cash Flow	Negative Free Cash Flow	Negative Free Cash Flow	-$0.78	-4%	-679%	-4%	0.00%
Zebra Technologies Corporation	ZBRA	Industrial	$28.95	$57.90	$86.85	$173.70	$3.86	18%	13%	18%	0.00%
ZELTIQ Aesthetics Inc	ZLTQ	Medical	Negative Free Cash Flow	Negative Free Cash Flow	Negative Free Cash Flow	Negative Free Cash Flow	-$0.59	-33%	-6%	-33%	0.00%
Zep, Inc.	ZEP	Chemicals	$3.83	$7.65	$11.48	$22.95	$0.51	4%	56%	3%	1.02%

NAME	TICKER	INDUSTRY	2014 BUY PRICE OPINION	2014 HOLD PRICE OPINION	2014 SELL PRICE OPINION	2014 SHORT PRICE OPINION	2014 MYCROFT FREE CASH FLOW PER SHARE ESTIMATE	2014 MYCROFT FREE CASH FLOW RETURN ON TOTAL CAPITAL ESTIMATE (FROIC) >15% = Great	2014 MYCROFT CAPFLOW ESTIMATE <33% = Great BUT NO NEGATIVE RESULTS	2014 MYCROFT MICHAELIS GROWTH RATE ESTIMATE >15% = Great	DIVIDEND YIELD
Step #1 = Look up the company's current stock market price on the day of analysis and compare it to our 2014 Buy, Hold, Sell & Short Price.										
Step #2 =Take the company's current market price; divide it by the "2014 Mycroft Free Cash Flow Per Share estimate." This gives the "Price to Free Cash Flow."										
All results below are based on the 2014 year end estimates using the "2014 Mycroft Michaelis Growth Rate" and are good until December 31, 2014.										
Zhone Technologies, Inc.	ZHNE	Communication	Negative Free Cash Flow	Negative Free Cash Flow	Negative Free Cash Flow	Negative Free Cash Flow	-$0.01	-1%	950%	-1%	0.00%
Zillow Inc	Z	Internet	$0.38	$0.75	$1.13	$2.25	$0.05	1%	92%	1%	0.00%
Zimmer Holdings Inc	ZMH	Medical	$37.50	$75.00	$112.50	$225.00	$5.00	10%	28%	9%	0.99%
Zion Oil & Gas, Inc.	ZN	Oil & Gas	Negative Free Cash Flow	Negative Free Cash Flow	Negative Free Cash Flow	Negative Free Cash Flow	-$0.26	-58%	-48%	-58%	0.00%
ZIOPHARM Oncology, Inc.	ZIOP	Biotech	Negative Free Cash Flow	Negative Free Cash Flow	Negative Free Cash Flow	Negative Free Cash Flow	-$0.85	-371%	-1%	-371%	0.00%
ZipRealty, Inc.	ZIPR	Real Estate	Negative Free Cash Flow	Negative Free Cash Flow	Negative Free Cash Flow	Negative Free Cash Flow	-$0.33	-53%	-53%	-53%	0.00%
Zix Corporation	ZIXI	Software	$0.90	$1.80	$2.70	$5.40	$0.12	10%	22%	10%	0.00%
Zoetis Inc	ZTS	Drugs	$9.60	$19.20	$28.80	$57.60	$1.28	36%	23%	28%	0.83%
Zogenix, Inc.	ZGNX	Drugs	Negative Free Cash Flow	Negative Free Cash Flow	Negative Free Cash Flow	Negative Free Cash Flow	-$0.48	-240%	-2%	-240%	0.00%
Zoltek Companies, Inc.	ZOLT	Industrial	$0.60	$1.20	$1.80	$3.60	$0.08	1%	84%	1%	0.00%
Zumiez, Inc.	ZUMZ	Retail	$6.98	$13.95	$20.93	$41.85	$0.93	9%	60%	9%	0.00%

NAME	TICKER	INDUSTRY	2014 BUY PRICE OPINION	2014 HOLD PRICE OPINION	2014 SELL PRICE OPINION	2014 SHORT PRICE OPINION	2014 MYCROFT FREE CASH FLOW PER SHARE ESTIMATE	2014 MYCROFT FREE CASH FLOW RETURN ON TOTAL CAPITAL ESTIMATE (FROIC) >15% = Great	2014 MYCROFT CAPFLOW ESTIMATE <33% = Great BUT NO NEGATIVE RESULTS	2014 MYCROFT MICHAELIS GROWTH RATE ESTIMATE >15% = Great	DIVIDEND YIELD
Step #1 = Look up the company's current stock market price on the day of analysis and compare it to our 2014 Buy, Hold, Sell & Short Price.											
Step #2 =Take the company's current market price; divide it by the "2014 Mycroft Free Cash Flow Per Share estimate." This gives the "Price to Free Cash Flow."											
All results below are based on the 2014 year end estimates using the "2014 Mycroft Michaelis Growth Rate" and are good until December 31, 2014.											
Zygo Corporation	ZIGO	Computers	Negative Free Cash Flow	Negative Free Cash Flow	Negative Free Cash Flow	Negative Free Cash Flow	-$0.23	-2%	165%	-2%	0.00%
Zynga Inc Class A	ZNGA	Software	$0.45	$0.90	$1.35	$2.70	$0.06	3%	35%	3%	0.00%

APPENDIX

Backtest showing the power of Price to Free Cash Flow in the Investment Process

1950-2009

Mycroft Psaras
Mycroft Research LLC.

The following backtest was performed to validate the importance of price to free cash flow in the investment process. The key formula used in this backtest is "price to free cash flow per share," which we calculate as follows;

$$P/FCF = (Market\ Price\ per\ share)/((cash\ flow\text{-}capital\ spending)/\ (diluted\ shares\ outstanding))).$$

The backtest of price to free cash flow per share was performed over a multi-year time frame, (1950 to 2009), using the thirty stocks that make up the Dow Jones Industrial Average (DJIA).

Starting on January 1st of each year from 1950 to 2009 inclusive, I determined which companies in the Dow Jones Industrial Average would have been purchased using the criteria of those whose price to free cash flow per share was 15 or less. I then purchased these companies and held them for exactly one year, selling them on December 31st of the same year (named the Price to Free Cash Flow, or PFCF portfolio). I repeated this process for all subsequent years, for a total of sixty years. I repeated the same strategy, but purchased all 30 companies in the DJIA, with no other basis for selection (named the DJIA portfolio). The results, outlined below, confirm the validity of our methods and show that a Price to Free Cash Flow based strategy not only works, but works very well.

Specifically, in terms of relative performance, the PFCF picks beat the DJIA in fifty-five of sixty years tested. Moreover, the average annualized gain for the PFCF Portfolio was +21.08% per year over sixty years, compared to an average annualized gain of the DJIA Portfolio of just +6.77%, over sixty years. Thus, if I started with $10,000 in each of the two portfolios (PFCF vs. DJIA), on January 1st, 1950, then at the end of sixty years, the DJIA would be worth $511,469.76 and the PFCF would be worth $965,001,511.

The results do not include taxes being paid in each of those years but was run as a side-by-side comparison to the Dow Jones 30 Index. The back-test results of the PFCF portfolio came very close to Warren Buffett's actual annualized average return as shown in Berkshire Hathaway's 2009 Annual Report (Page 2):
Compounded Annual Gain – 1965-2009 . . . .20.3%

On introducing the actual data, I have broken it down into four parts, as follows:

<u>Part 1: The components of the DJIA for each year.</u> Since the components were similar for many consecutive years, we decided to post the updated DJIA list only in those years where changes were made to the index.

<u>Part 2: The side-by-side comparison of yearly percentage gain for the PFCF Portfolio vs. that of the DJIA Index performance.</u>

<u>Part 3: Purchases made using "Price to Free Cash Flow" for the years 1950-2009, which enable the performance of each purchase to be evaluated retrospectively.</u>

<u>Part 4: Yearly side-by-side cumulative performance of "Price to Free Cash Flow" vs. that of the DJIA, in actual dollars, starting with $10,000 in each portfolio on January 1, 1950, and ending December 31, 2009.</u>

PART 1

The Components of the Dow Jones Industrial Average 1950-2009

1950-1955

Allied Chemical
Allied Can
American Smelting
American Telephone & Telegraph
American Tobacco
Bethlehem Steel
Chrysler
Corn Products Refining
Du Pont
Eastman Kodak
General Electric
General Foods
General Motors
Goodyear
International Harvester
International Nickel
Johns-Manville
Loew's
National Distillers
National Steel
Procter & Gamble
Sears Roebuck & Co
Standard Oil of California
Standard Oil (N.J.)
Texas Corporation
Union Carbide
United Aircraft
U.S. Steel
Westinghouse Electric
Woolworth

1956-1958

Allied Chemical
Allied Can
American Smelting
American Telephone & Telegraph
American Tobacco
Bethlehem Steel
Chrysler
Corn Products Refining
Du Pont
Eastman Kodak
General Electric
General Foods
General Motors
Goodyear
International Harvester
International Nickel
International Paper
Johns-Manville
National Distillers
National Steel
Procter & Gamble
Sears Roebuck & Co
Standard Oil of California
Standard Oil (N.J.)
Texas Corporation
Union Carbide
United Aircraft
U.S. Steel
Westinghouse Electric
Woolworth

1959-1975

Allied Chemical
Aluminum Company of America
American Can
American Telephone & Telegraph
American Tobacco
Anaconda
Bethlehem Steel
Chrysler
Du Pont
Eastman Kodak
General Electric
General Foods
General Motors
Goodyear
International Harvester
International Nickel (name changed to Inco on April 21, 1976)
International Paper
Johns-Manville
Owen's-Illinois Glass
Procter & Gamble
Sears Roebuck & Co
Standard Oil of California
Standard Oil (N.J.) (name changed to Exxon on November 1, 1972)
Swift & Co. (name changed to Esmark on May 30, 1973)
Texas Corporation
Union Carbide
United Aircraft (name changed to United Technologies on May 1, 1975)
U.S. Steel
Westinghouse Electric
Woolworth

1976-1978

Allied Chemical
Aluminum Company of America
American Can
American Telephone & Telegraph
American Tobacco
Bethlehem Steel
Chrysler
Du Pont
Eastman Kodak
Esmark
Exxon
General Electric
General Foods
General Motors
Goodyear
International Harvester
Inco
International Paper
Johns-Manville
Minnesota Mining & Manufacturing
Owen's-Illinois Glass
Procter & Gamble
Sears Roebuck & Co
Standard Oil of California
Texas Corporation
Union Carbide
United Technologies
U.S. Steel
Westinghouse Electric
Woolworth

1979-1981

Allied Chemical
Aluminum Company of America
American Can
American Telephone & Telegraph
American Tobacco
Bethlehem Steel
Du Pont
Eastman Kodak
Exxon
General Electric
General Foods
General Motors
Goodyear
International Business Machines
International Harvester
Inco
International Paper
Johns-Manville
Merck
Minnesota Mining & Manufacturing
Owen's-Illinois Glass
Procter & Gamble
Sears Roebuck & Co
Standard Oil of California
Texas Corporation
Union Carbide
United Aircraft
U.S. Steel
Westinghouse Electric
Woolworth

1982-84

Allied Chemical (renamed Allied-Signal Inc. in 1985)
Aluminum Company of America
American Can
American Express Co.
American Telephone & Telegraph
American Tobacco
Bethlehem Steel
Du Pont
Eastman Kodak
Exxon
General Electric
General Foods
General Motors
Goodyear
International Business Machines
International Harvester
Inco
International Paper
Merck
Minnesota Mining & Manufacturing
Owen's-Illinois Glass
Procter & Gamble
Sears Roebuck & Co
Standard Oil of California (renamed Chevron in 1984)
Texas Corporation
Union Carbide
United Aircraft
U.S. Steel
Westinghouse Electric
Woolworth

1985-1986

Allied-Signal Inc. (renamed Allied-Signal Inc. in 1985)
Aluminum Company of America
American Can
American Express
American Telephone & Telegraph
Bethlehem Steel
Chevron Corporation
Du Pont
Eastman Kodak
Exxon
General Electric
General Motors
Goodyear
Inco
International Business Machines
International Harvester (renamed Navistar International Corp. in 1986)
International Paper
McDonald's Corporation
Merck & Company
Minnesota Mining & Manufacturing
Owen's-Illinois
Philip Morris Companies
Procter & Gamble
Sears Roebuck & Co
Texaco
Union Carbide
United Technologies
U.S. Steel (renamed USX Corp. in 1986)
Westinghouse Electric
Woolworth

1987-1990

Allied-Signal Inc.
Aluminum Company of America
American Can (name changed to Primerica Corp. in 1987)
American Express
American Telephone & Telegraph
Bethlehem Steel
Boeing Co.
Chevron Corporation
Coca-Cola Co.
Du Pont
Eastman Kodak
Exxon
General Electric
General Motors
Goodyear
International Business Machines
International Paper
McDonald's Corporation
Merck & Company
Minnesota Mining & Manufacturing
Navistar International Corp.
Philip Morris Companies
Procter & Gamble
Sears Roebuck & Co
Texaco
Union Carbide
United Technologies
USX Corporation
Westinghouse Electric
Woolworth

1991-1996

American Telephone and Telegraph (renamed AT&T Corp. in 1994)
Allied-Signal
Alcoa
American Express
Bethlehem Steel
Boeing
Caterpillar Inc.
Chevron Corporation
Coca Cola
Walt Disney Co.
Du Pont
Eastman Kodak
Exxon
General Electric
General Motors
Goodyear
International Business Machines
International Paper
McDonald's Corporation
Merck & Company
Minnesota Mining & Manufacturing
Morgan J. P.
Philip Morris Companies
Procter & Gamble
Sears Roebuck & Co
Texaco
Union Carbide
United Technologies
Westinghouse Electric
Woolworth

1997-1998

Allied-Signal

Aluminum Company of America (name changed to Alcoa, Inc. in 1999)

American Express

Boeing

Caterpillar

Chevron Corporation

Coca Cola

Disney

Du Pont

Eastman Kodak

Exxon

General Electric

General Motors

Goodyear

Hewlett Packard

International Business Machines

International Paper

Johnson & Johnson

McDonald's Corporation

Merck & Company

Minnesota Mining & Manufacturing

Morgan J. P.

Philip Morris Companies

Procter & Gamble

Sears Roebuck & Co

Travelers Group (name changed to Citigroup Inc. in 1998)

Union Carbide

United Technologies

Wal-Mart Stores

1999-2006

AT&T
Alcoa
American Express
Boeing
Caterpillar
Citigroup
Coca Cola
Disney
Du Pont
Eastman Kodak
Exxon (name changed to Exxon Mobil Corp. in 1999)
General Electric
General Motors
Hewlett Packard
Home Depot
Honeywell International Inc.
Intel Corporation
International Business Machines
International Paper
Johnson & Johnson
McDonald's Corporation
Merck & Company
Microsoft Corporation
Minnesota Mining & Manufacturing
Morgan J. P. (name changed J. P. Morgan Chase and Co. in 2001 after merging with Chase Manhattan Corp.)
Philip Morris Companies
Procter & Gamble
SBC Communications
United Technologies
Wal-Mart Stores

2007-2008

AT&T
Alcoa
Altria Group
American Express
Boeing
Caterpillar
Citigroup
Coca Cola
Disney
Du Pont
Exxon Mobil Corp.
General Electric
General Motors
Hewlett Packard
Home Depot
Honeywell International Inc.
Intel Corporation
International Business Machines
Johnson & Johnson
McDonald's Corporation
Merck & Company
Microsoft Corporation
Minnesota Mining & Manufacturing
J. P. Morgan Chase
Pfizer
Procter & Gamble
United Technologies
Verizon
Wal-Mart Stores

2009

AT&T
Alcoa
American Express
Bank of America
Boeing
Caterpillar
Chevron
Citigroup
Coca Cola
Disney
Du Pont
Exxon Mobil Corp.
General Electric
General Motors
Hewlett Packard
Home Depot
Intel Corporation
International Business Machines
Johnson & Johnson
J.P. Morgan Chase
Kraft Foods
McDonald's Corporation
Merck & Company
Microsoft Corporation
Minnesota Mining & Manufacturing
Pfizer
Procter & Gamble
United Technologies
Verizon
Wal-Mart Stores

PART 2

YEAR TO YEAR PERFORMANCE COMPARISON OF PFCF VS. DJIA

YEAR	PRICE TO FREE CASH FLOW	DJIA
1950	+ 31.13%	+17.62%
1951	+ 28.05%	+14.36%
1952	+ 16.88%	+ 0.51%
1953	+ 4.77%	+ 3.80%
1954	+ 64.80%	+ 43.96%
1955	+ 29.42%	+ 20.77%
1956	+ 13.86%	+ 2.27%
1957	+ 11.52%	- 12.77%
1958	+ 52.66%	+ 33.96%
1959	+ 26.94%	+ 16.39%
1960	- 15.20%	- 9.34%
1961	+ 33.23%	+ 18.72%
1962	+ 12.12%	- 10.81%
1963	+ 43.86%	+ 17.00%
1964	+ 18.81%	+ 14.57%
1965	+ 22.34%	+ 10.88%
1966	- 9.40%	- 18.94%
1967	+ 34.65%	+ 15.20%
1968	+ 6.99%	+ 4.26%
1969	- 0.33%	- 15.19%
1970	+ 31.82%	+ 4.82%
1971	+ 1.57%	+ 6.11%
1972	+ 27.32%	+ 14.58%
1973	- 14.54%	- 19.38%
1974	+ 19.51%	- 25.05%
1975	+ 52.85%	+ 38.32%

YEAR	PRICE TO FREE CASH FLOW	DJIA
1976	+ 46.48%	+ 17.86%
1977	- 1.77%	- 17.26%
1978	+ 12.45%	- 3.15%
1979	+ 18.57%	+ 4.19%
1980	+ 33.57%	+ 14.93%
1981	+ 10.62%	- 9.23%
1982	+ 55.82%	+ 19.60%
1983	+ 35.23%	+ 20.26%
1984	+ 6.49%	- 3.73%
1985	+ 35.77%	+ 27.66%
1986	+ 35.17%	+ 22.58%
1987	+ 34.19%	+ 2.26%
1988	+ 23.44%	+ 11.85%
1989	+ 35.96%	+ 26.96%
1990	+ 27.16%	- 4.36%
1991	+ 99.09%	+ 20.32%
1992	+ 23.17%	+ 4.17%
1993	+ 34.21%	+ 13.72%
1994	+ 14.20%	+ 2.14%
1995	+ 32.84%	+ 33.45%
1996	+ 21.72%	+ 26.01%
1997	+ 36.30%	+ 22.64%
1998	+ 37.71%	+ 16.10%
1999	+ 16.50%	+ 25.22%
2000	+ 19.96%	- 6.17%
2001	- 3.91%	- 7.10%
2002	- 3.58%	- 15.87%
2003	+ 28.96%	+ 23.98%
2004	+ 8.94%	+ 3.14%
2005	+ 3.41%	- 0.11%
2006	+ 31.10%	+ 16.29%
2007	+ 16.72%	+ 6.34%
2008	- 22.39%	- 32.71%
2009	+ 22.95%	+ 15.43%

Purchases made using "Price to Free Cash Flow" for the years 1950-2007

1950

American Smelting	+ 40.60%
American Tobacco	- 8.85%
Bethlehem Steel	+ 55.81%
Chrysler	+ 21.63%
Corn Products Refining	+ 1.35%
Dupont	+ 43.53%
General Electric	+ 27.14%
General Foods	- .90%
General Motors	+ 37.50%
Goodyear Tire & Rubber	+ 59.00%
International Harvester	+ 24.14%
Johns Manville	+ 2.27%
National Distillers	+ 29.50%
National Steel	+ 73.02%
Standard Oil of New Jersey	+ 41.69%
Union Carbide	+ 29.72%
U.S. Steel	+ 71.23%
Westinghouse Electric	+ 11.89%

1951

American Smelting	+ 38.23%
American Tobacco	+ 2.92%
Bethlehem Steel	+ 14.59%
Corn Products Refining	+ 8.42%
General Motors	+ 25.36%
Goodyear Tire & Rubber	+ 40.85%
International Harvester	+ 13.69%
Johns Manville	+ 49.71%
Standard Oil of California	+ 16.15%
Standard Oil of New Jersey	+ 70.57%

1952

American Smelting	- 2.64%
American Tobacco	+ 6.58%
Chrysler	+ 47.86%
Corn Products Refining	+ 9.72%
General Motors	+ 40.10%
International Harvester	- 0.14%

1953

American Tobacco	+ 0.38%
Bethlehem Steel	- 2.26%
Corn Products Refining	+11.14%
Goodyear Tire & Rubber	+ 2.97%
International Harvester	- 11.45%
United Aircraft	+27.84%

1954

American Smelting	+ 70.07%
American Tobacco	+ 12.60%
Bethlehem Steel	+126.24%
Corn Products Refining	+ 20.01%
Dupont	+ 59.53%
General Foods	+ 33.42%
Goodyear	+112.26%
International Nickel	+ 74.97%
Standard Oil of California	+ 51.30%
Standard Oil of New Jersey	+ 59.92%
United Aircraft	+ 77.48%
U.S. Steel	+ 93.99%
Westinghouse Electric	+ 50.60%

1955

American Smelting	+ 15.53%
American Tobacco	+ 31.16%
Bethlehem Steel	+ 55.22%
Corn Products Refining	+ 4.97%
Dupont	+ 40.60%
General Foods	+ 26.92%
General Motors	+ 46.88%
Goodyear Tire & Rubber	+ 26.11%
International Harvester	+ 1.99%
International Nickel	+ 44.83%

1956

American Smelting	+ 25.06%
American Tobacco	- 3.99%
Corn Products Refining	+ 9.07%
International Harvester	+ 10.96%
International Nickel	+ 32.93%

1957

American Tobacco	+ 11.20%
Chrysler	- 20.36%
Corn Products Refining	+ 20.68%

1958

American Tobacco	+ 30.92%
Bethlehem Steel	+ 50.58%
Corn Products Refining	+ 63.50%
General Foods	+ 52.89%
General Motors	+ 53.73%
International Harvester	+ 64.35%

1959

Allied Chemical	+ 27.44%
Anaconda	+ 8.87%
American Tobacco	+ 16.73%
Swift	+ 35.52%
International Harvester	+ 18.26%
Westinghouse Electric	+ 54.81%

1960

Anaconda	- 28.13%
American Tobacco	+ 24.74%
Chrysler	- 42.22%

1961

Anaconda	+ 17.53%
American Tobacco	+ 58.19%
Chrysler	+ 30.34%
General Motors	+ 45.23%
International Harvester	+ 14.87%

1962

Anaconda	– 11.57%
Chrysler	+ 53.32%
General Motors	+ 6.58%
International Harvester	+ .16%

1963

American Tobacco	+ 2.13%
Chrysler	+130.37%
General Motors	+ 40.43%
Johns Manville	+ 18.02%
U.S. Steel	+ 28.37%

1964

Anaconda	+ 17.11%
American Tobacco	+ 21.49%
Swift	+ 36.05%
International Harvester	+ 30.03%
Union Carbide	+ 8.38%
U.S. Steel	– .23%

1965

Anaconda	+ 54.30%
American Tobacco	+ 21.43%
Johns Manville	+ 7.24%
U.S. Steel	+ 6.37%

1966

Johns Manville	– 9.40%

1967

American Tobacco	+ 9.88%
Chrysler	+ 89.43%
General Motors	+ 31.39%
International Harvester	+ 7.90%

1968

Allied Chemical	– 5.25%
American Tobacco	+ 23.11%
Chrysler	+ 3.11%

1969

American Tobacco	- 0.33%

1970

American Brands	+ 31.82%

1971

American Can	- 10.50%
American Brands	- 2.77%
Chrysler	+ 4.38%
International Harvester	+15.18%

1972

American Can	+ .60%
American Brands	+ 5.97%
Chrysler	+ 45.33%
General Motors	+ 5.00%
International Harvester	+ 33.81%
Alcoa	+ 25.90%
Standard Oil of California	+ 48.54%
Union Carbide	+ 23.08%
United Aircraft	+ 57.62%

1973

American Can	- 10.04%
American Brands	- 18.01%
Bethlehem Steel	+16.43%
General Motors	- 37.66%
International Harvester	- 29.25%
Standard Oil of California	- 8.45%
Union Carbide	- 27.75%
United Aircraft	- 42.58%
U.S. Steel	+26.25%

1974

American Can	+ 18.86%
American Brands	+ 1.18%
Union Carbide	+ 27.33%
United Aircraft	+ 44.95%
U.S Steel	+ 5.25%

1975

American Can	+ 15.78%
American Brands	+ 24.99%
General Foods	+ 62.38%
General Motors	+ 98.46%
Goodyear Tire and Rubber	+ 76.85%
United Technologies	+ 48.05%
Westinghouse Electric	+ 43.77%

1976

American Can	+ 29.88%
American Brands	+ 25.07%
United Technologies	+ 71.51%
General Foods	+ 14.57%
Chrysler	+ 94.05%
General Motors	+ 41.00%
Westinghouse Electric	+ 39.04%
International Harvester	+ 56.84%
Standard Oil of California	+ 46.38%

1977

American Can	+ 5.13%
American Brands	+ .11%
Du Pont	- 7.11%
General Motors	- 12.90%
International Harvester	- 3.18%
Standard Oil of California	+ .06%
United Technologies	- 4.66%
Westinghouse Electric	+ 8.37%

1978

MMM	+ 33.66%
American Brands	+ 24.08%
Bethlehem Steel	+ 0.00%
Du Pont	+ 9.45%
Eastman Kodak	+ 18.78%
General Motors	- 3.69%
Alcoa	+ 6.06%
Standard Oil of California	+ 28.62%
Westinghouse Electric	- 2.91%

1979

American Brands	+ 41.94%
Bethlehem Steel	+ 12.74%
Du Pont	+ 1.88%
Eastman Kodak	- 14.11%
General Foods	+ 9.90%
International Harvester	+ 13.72%
INCO	+ 55.24%
Alcoa	+ 20.16%
Standard Oil of California	+ 25.70%

1980

MMM	+ 22.19%
American Brands	+ 27.82%
Eastman Kodak	+ 50.75%
General Foods	- 3.67%
Goodyear Tire and Rubber	+ 34.37%
INCO	- 12.11%
Standard Oil of California	+ 81.64%
U.S. Steel	+ 50.57%
Owens Illinois	+ 32.15%
Westinghouse Electric	+ 52.03%

1981

American Brands	+ 2.45%
Bethlehem Steel	- 5.78%
Goodyear Tire and Rubber	+ 26.88%
Alcoa	- 8.67%
U.S. Steel	+ 27.17%
Owens Illinois	+ 21.67%

1982

Goodyear Tire and Rubber	+ 91.05%
American Brands	+ 33.57%
General Foods	+ 31.73%
General Electric	+ 70.76%
Procter and Gamble	+ 51.98%

1983

American Can	+ 59.60%
American Brands	+ 35.97%
IBM	+ 30.33%
General Motors	+ 23.09%
General Electric	+ 27.06%
General Foods	+ 35.33%

1984

General Foods	+ 13.43%
U.S. Steel	- 10.70%
General Motors	+ 9.14%
American Can	+ 13.92%
American Brands	+ 14.43%
Westinghouse Electric	- 1.27%

1985

Westinghouse Electric	+ 74.07%
American Can	+ 24.55%
AT & T	+ 32.82%
Phillip Morris	+ 13.67%
General Motors	- 4.15%
Inco	+ 8.68%
Union Carbide	+100.75%

1986

American Can	+ 45.04%
AT & T	+ 4.80%
Philip Morris	+ 73.13%
Chevron	+ 25.31%
Westinghouse Electric	+ 27.58%

1987

Bethlehem Steel	+168.00%
IBM	- 0.29%
Philip Morris	+ 21.87%
Texaco	+ 12.20%
Union Carbide	+ 1.70%
USX Corp.	+ 43.95%
Westinghouse Electric	- 8.34%

1988

Alcoa	+ 22.35%
AT&T Corp.	+ 10.93%
Bethlehem Steel	+ 38.81%
Boeing	+ 67.64%
Chevron	+ 21.51%
Texaco	+ 39.26%
General Motors	+ 44.20%
General Electric	+ 4.34%
Westinghouse Electric	+ 9.07%
United Technologies	+ 25.53%
USX Corp.	+ 2.35%
Union Carbide	+ 24.71%
Proctor and Gamble	+ 5.07%
Philip Morris	+ 23.44%
International Paper	+ 13.24%

1989

Allied Signal	+ 12.85%
Alcoa	+ 36.25%
AT&T Corp.	+ 64.76%
Bethlehem Steel	- 20.43%
Coca Cola	+ 75.80%
Union Carbide	- 4.78%
General Motors	+ 7.96%
Philip Morris	+ 67.18%
General Electric	+ 47.26%
Westinghouse Electric	+ 44.29%
Proctor & Gamble	+ 75.83%
International Paper	+ 24.58%

1990

Philip Morris	+ 27.16%

1991

Goodyear Tire & Rubber	+ 202.76%
General Electric	+ 36.61%
Philip Morris	+ 57.90%

1992

General Electric	+ 17.09%
Goodyear Tire & Rubber	+ 29.25%

1993

Boeing	+ 9.94%
Caterpillar	+ 67.09%
General Electric	+ 25.28%
General Motors	+ 71.18%
Goodyear Tire & Rubber	+ 34.62%
IBM	+ 21.77%
United Technologies	+ 32.78%
Westinghouse Electric	+ 10.99%

1994

Boeing	+ 10.98%
Caterpillar	+ 24.55%
Du Pont	+ 19.97%
General Motors	- 21.78%
IBM	+ 32.88%
Philip Morris	+ 8.04%
Union Carbide	+ 34.64%
United Technology	+ 4.31%

1995

United Technologies	+ 53.92%
Allied Signal	+ 41.68%
Caterpillar	+ 7.39%
Union Carbide	+ 30.21%
Alcoa	+ 23.75%
General Motors	+ 26.29%
Goodyear Tire & Rubber	+ 37.17%
Eastman Kodak	+ 43.87%
Du Pont	+ 27.74%
General Electric	+ 44.00%
IBM	+ 25.68%
International Paper	+ 3.24%
Philip Morris	+ 61.92%

1996

Philip Morris	+ 29.06%
Allied Signal	+ 42.69%
United Technologies	+ 41.81%
Alcoa	+ 22.27%
Bethlehem Steel	- 36.04%
Caterpillar	+ 30.64%
General Motors	+ 3.74%
Goodyear Tire & Rubber	+ 15.31%
IBM	+ 66.89%
International Paper	+ 11.56%
Union Carbide	+ 11.00%

1997

Caterpillar	+ 58.25%
IBM	+ 38.64%
General Motors	+ 12.00%

1998

General Motors	+ 21.82%
United Technologies	+ 53.60%

1999

Boeing	+ 28.72%
General Motors	+ 4.28%

2000

Boeing	+ 61.43%
Caterpillar	+ 3.39%
Eastman Kodak	- 37.95%
General Motors	- 27.17%
Philip Morris	+100.09%

2001

Eastman Kodak	- 20.31%
General Motors	- 0.66%
Philip Morris	+ 9.25%

2002

Boeing	- 13.17%
Eastman Kodak	+ 25.17%
General Motors	- 20.04%
Philip Morris	- 6.28%

2003

AT&T Corp.	- 19.19%
Alcoa	+ 69.44%
Eastman Kodak	- 23.46%
General Motors	+ 50.29%
Hewlett Packard	+ 33.54%
International Paper	+ 26.14%
McDonalds	+ 55.54%
Altria Group	+ 40.78%
SBC Communication	+ 1.22%
United Technologies	+ 55.33%

2004

AT&T Corp.	- 1.43%
Eastman Kodak	+ 27.58%
Exxon Mobil	+ 27.61%
General Motors	- 21.23%
Altria Group	+ 17.46%
SBC Communications	+ 3.64

2005

Altria	+ 23.23%
AT&T	- 4.69%
Exxon Mobil	+ 9.98%
General Motors	- 53.38%
Hewlett Packard	+ 35.56%
Merck	- 0.56%
Pfizer	- 14.61%

2006

Altria	+ 14.47%
AT&T	+ 45.98%
Boeing	+ 26.19%
Caterpillar	+ 5.62%
Exxon Mobil	+ 25.82%
General Motors	+ 60.67%
Hewlett Packard	+ 40.68%
Honeywell	+ 21.55%
IBM	+ 17.83%
Merck	+ 34.07%
Pfizer	+ 9.51%
United Technologies	+ 10.75%
Walt Disney	+ 42.32%

2007

AT&T	+ 23.35%
Caterpillar	+ 20.83%
Exxon Mobil	+ 28.51%
General Motors	- 15.48%
IBM	+ 11.13%
Merck	+ 32.00%
Pfizer	- 13.54%
United Technologies	+ 21.86%

2008

Dupont	- 39.16%
Exxon Mobil	-13.46%
International Business Machines	- 18.34%
Pfizer	- 18.59%

2009

AT&T	+ 4.22%
Boeing	+ 20.75%
Chevron	+ 3.73%
Dupont	+ 34.10%
Exxon Mobil	- 14.56%
General Electric	- 1.56%
Hewlett Packard	+ 42.66%
Home Depot	+ 20.72%
International Business Machines	+ 52.96%
Johnson & Johnson	+ 10.26%
Merck	+ 24.66%
Microsoft	+ 50.68%
MMM	+ 44.74%
Pfizer	+ 4.57%
United Technologies	+ 30.66%
Walt Disney	+ 38.72%

PART 4

Compounded return of $10,000 invested in 1950 in each would be worth

YEAR	PRICE TO FREE CASH FLOW	DJIA
1950	$ 13,113	$ 11,762
1951	$ 16,791	$ 13,451
1952	$ 19,625	$ 13,519
1953	$ 20,561	$ 14,032
1954	$ 33,884	$ 20,201
1955	$ 43,852	$ 24,397
1956	$ 49,930	$ 24,951
1957	$ 51,847	$ 21,765
1958	$ 79,150	$ 29,156
1959	$ 100,473	$ 33,935
1960	$ 85,201	$ 30,766
1961	$ 113,513	$ 36,525
1962	$ 127,270	$ 32,577
1963	$ 183,090	$ 38,115
1964	$ 217,529	$ 43,668
1965	$ 266,125	$ 48,420
1966	$ 241,109	$ 39,249
1967	$ 324,654	$ 45,215
1968	$ 347,347	$ 47,141
1969	$ 346,201	$ 39,981
1970	$ 456,362	$ 41,907
1971	$ 463,527	$ 44,468
1972	$ 590,163	$ 50,952
1973	$ 504,353	$ 41,077
1974	$ 602,752	$ 30,787
1975	$ 921,307	$ 42,585

YEAR	PRICE TO FREE CASH FLOW	DJIA
1976	$ 1,349,530	$ 50,191
1977	$ 1,325,644	$ 41,527
1978	$ 1,490,687	$ 40,220
1979	$ 1,767,507	$ 41,904
1980	$ 2,360,859	$ 48,161
1981	$ 2,611,582	$ 43,716
1982	$ 4,069,367	$ 52,284
1983	$ 5,503,006	$ 62,877
1984	$ 5,860,151	$ 60,531
1985	$ 7,956,327	$ 77,274
1986	$ 10,754,726	$ 94,723
1987	$ 14,431,767	$ 96,864
1988	$ 17,814,573	$ 108,343
1989	$ 24,220,693	$ 137,552
1990	$ 30,799,033	$ 131,554
1991	$ 61,317,795	$ 158.287
1992	$ 75,525,128	$ 164,886
1993	$ 101,362,274	$ 187,510
1994	$ 115,756,717	$ 191,522
1995	$ 153,769,894	$ 255,586
1996	$ 187,168,715	$ 322,064
1997	$ 255,110,959	$ 394,980
1998	$ 351,313,302	$ 458,571
1999	$ 409,279,996	$ 574,233
2000	$ 490,972,284	$ 538,802
2001	$ 471,775,267	$ 500,548
2002	$ 454,885,713	$ 421,111
2003	$ 586,620,615	$ 522,093
2004	$ 639,064,498	$ 538,487
2005	$ 660,869,431	$ 532,500
2006	$ 866,433,448	$ 619,233
2007	$1,011,301,128	$ 658,492
2008	$ 784,873,128	$ 443,100
2009	$ 965,001,511	$ 511,470

©2014 Mycroft Psaras

13415170R00157

Made in the USA
San Bernardino, CA
13 December 2018